With Death Before Us

A Memoir

MARY LOU MIRANTE

authorHOUSE®

AuthorHouse™
1663 Liberty Drive
Bloomington, IN 47403
www.authorhouse.com
Phone: 1-800-839-8640

Published by AuthorHouse 11/30/2012

ISBN: 978-1-4772-8427-8 (e)
ISBN: 978-1-4772-8428-5 (hc)
ISBN: 978-1-4772-8429-2 (sc)

Library of Congress Control Number: 2012920233

Dedication

In memory of my "Beloved Husband Tony"
If it weren't for my entire family, the book would have never come to pass...
I want to thank our children Anthony, Tammy, Michael, Mario, and Joey
for all their endless support, along with their spouses, Paul and Michael.
Last but, by far the least the loves of my life, Adriana and Carissa. They
were all my back bone in what ever way they could offer to help, which
gave me the strength to continue on the journey.

If I wrote a zillion words that would not be enough to express my gratitude
for all you've each done in your own way. Except to express from the
bottom of my heart a big, "Thank YOU." I LOVE YOU ALL!

Acknowledgements

With loving gratitude to; Patti O'Brien for her thoughtful feedback and guidance, in pushing me to go back to the book, may she rest in peace.

Best friend, Arlene Calcagno; for her endless support and hours of proof reading.

The Schaumburg writer's group, who were all fantastic, guiding me and who gave me the strength and support to reach this goal!

As for Mario Mirante, Tammy Saia and Paul VanDeZande, the book would have never come to completion if it weren't for your twenty-four hour; support, guidance, and encouragement to this final stage.

A special thank you to Adriana and Carissa Saia my granddaughters' who designed the cover of the book; and for taking the time during their busy last year of college. Making their Papa number one and a very important person in their lives!

Last but, far from the least; Thank you to ALL of my friends who helped in ways; they may not even be aware of how important their support was! May God bless each and every one of you for believing in me—!

With Death Before Us

*D*r. Bane's face looked saddened as she entered the exam room where Tony and I waited. I fought to hold back the tears but lost, when Dr. Bane told us the bad news. As we sat in the exam room, tears filled my eyes as I looked at Tony. Tony had a blank look on his face as he stared at me. To endure another cancer scare so soon after the last was unthinkable, especially since all three cancer scares occurred at a time—Christmas—when we were supposed to be joyous? I didn't think we could bear another episode of cancer. I saw by the numbed look on Tony's face he felt the same.

Tony had gone for his routine check-up back in December of 1999 so he would have a clean bill of health before we left for Maui. However, the doctor wanted him to have a stress test for his heart, and a chest X-ray, to make sure the cancer hadn't returned. Dr. Bane called with the results the week before Christmas. Tony's heart was okay, but a "new nodule" showed up on his lung. "Tony you'll need another X-ray in three weeks, to keep a close eye on the spot," the doctor said. It was Christmastime, and not quite a year since his last lung surgery. Tony already had two lobectomies for lung cancer. Two years earlier he had had a lobectomy and again last year. To say we were both extremely upset about the "new nodule" was unexaggerated. Neither one of us knew what to say to the other—leaving us speechless.

Throughout the holidays, the specter of cancer distracted our minds, all seven of us: Tony, me, and our five children. Anthony the oldest, was a successful hairdresser working on movies and plays as well as working at a salon. He had an interesting, exciting career and sometimes even traveled. Paul is Anthony's partner; they've been together for forever since they were very young he's been just like a son to us, also with a great position at Sears. Tammy was our only daughter and the apple of her father's eye. We called her "Princess." She's married to Mike, and they have beautiful twin daughters, Adriana and Carissa, born on Tammy's birthday. The twins called us Nane and Papa, and they were our joy in life. Tammy was also my partner in a busy, successful party store. Our middle child Michael was handy as hell. There wasn't a thing that kid couldn't do once he set his mind to it. He had just started his own mold-making shop. Mario, had suffered bouts of severe depression, an illness he had battles for years.

In spite of his problems, he was a perseverant fighter. He managed the party store. He was a creative, diligent worker and took pride in designing specialty balloon sculptures for both corporate and personal customers. Joey, the "baby" of the family, had a job working for a gasket company. He'd worked his way up the ranks, starting at the bottom in the warehouse, to sales manager. He had just married that past November. Tony and I were proud of their achievements that included owning their own homes. We were proud to have raised independent people.

We were a close-knit family and helped each other in times of need. If one needed money, help around the house, a ride somewhere, anything at all, one of us was there to help. I always told them as young children how important that was. "That's what family was all about," "I'd tell them." "It's important." When teaching our children that lesson, never in my dreams, did I think that someday, Tony and I would be the ones in need!

Tony had worked for a large food warehouse for thirty years, and we had invested through the company's profit sharing, which helped us become financially set, and mortgage free. We weren't rich by any means, but we weren't hurting either. We had just started to enjoy our lives, after raising our children. We traveled, went on cruises, visited different states, and visited friends who had moved out of town. It was a joyous, wonderful time in our lives, 'Only to find ourselves once again facing a cancer scare!'

Five years earlier, at age fifty-seven, Tony went on disability after the second open-heart surgery. Tony had had medical problems all his life, with everything from hemorrhoids to back surgery and everything in between. Despite all his illnesses, he had worked hard to give us his very best, and had often worked two jobs so we could make ends meet. He took and did all the fun things with us; fished, camped, flew kites, sledding down big hills with the hot chocolate waiting in the thermos, outdoor movies.... If Tony and I watched a late movie together, during intermission, he'd disappear, reappearing with either candy bars or fresh donuts for a treat, he was thoughtful that way.

Tony went for another chest X-ray, per doctor's orders back in December. Three weeks had already passed since the last chest X-ray, and it was a few days before we were scheduled to leave for Maui. We became more excited, the closer it came to our departure.

Two days before we were to leave, I was finishing the packing when the telephone rang. Dr. Bane was on the other end. When she called instead of her nurse, it was never good news—I immediately knew there was a "bomb" about to be dropped. I started trembling before she spoke a word. She asked for Tony. I hollered to him to pick up the phone, I stayed on the extension—wanting to hear what she said.

"This saddens me to have to tell you this, but the spot on your lung has grown, and you need a bronchoscopy right away," she said. Both of our hearts fell straight down to our toes.

I asked, "Could we postpone the bronchoscopy, were supposed to leave for Maui in two days."

She said, "I'll have Dr. Lucas, the lung specialists call you."

Dr. Lucas called us back immediately, and said, "Go on your trip. We can do the bronchoscopy when you get back." Tony and I were relieved, thinking if the nodule were that serious the doctor wouldn't have allowed us to go. Anthony and Paul were going too; we had been traveling together the past few years.

After getting off the phone with the specialist, Tony left right away to pick up the twins from school, which he did quite often. That day he was picking them up from Score, an extended schooling like tutoring. The twins had started school earlier, at age five because of their birthdays, and Tammy didn't want them to get behind which was why they attended Score. Mike worked nights and Tammy ran the party store we'd opened fifteen years earlier, so we helped with the twins as often as possible.

The same year—1987—that we opened the party store, Tony had the first open-heart surgery; the second one was seven years later. I still worked from home doing the paperwork for the store. Our life was at its best, and everything, seemed to be on an upswing, we thought!

About the time Tony should have been back with the twins, the doorbell rang, Ding-dong, Ding-dong. I ran to the door, Ding-dong, Ding-dong! Ringing the doorbell like that was something the twins enjoyed; it tickled them down to their toes. It was the twins at the door, but much to my surprise they weren't tickled at all; they were in a dither.

I could hear the concern in their voices, they said, "Nane, Papa's in the car; he told us to come and get you; he doesn't feel well; he's very sick. He even pulled over to the side of the highway, and told us he was really sick." My thoughts fled—I was frightened.

Just as I rushed to go to the car, Tony fell through the door, lethargic, weak, and barely able to stand. I grabbed him and tried to hold him up long enough to help him into the powder room. I sat him on the toilet seat. Asking, "Does your chest or arm hurt?" Tony wasn't able to speak, he kept losing consciousness; I called the twins and told them, "Hold Papa up." I ran to the refrigerator to grab a nitro to put under his tongue right away. The nitro didn't seem to help; he kept losing consciousness. I couldn't get Tony to stay coherent, I kept giving him juice and water to help hydrate him, but that didn't help. I immediately called 911 for an ambulance; the twins stayed out of the way, speechless, we were all terrified that Tony would die. I didn't know what was happening to him. I kept thinking, *is it his heart? Nerves?* I was confused because he'd just had his heart checked the month before, and it was fine.

Our neighbor saw the ambulance arrive, and ran over. She said, "Go to the hospital with Tony; I'll stay with the twins." The paramedics worked feverishly on Tony to stabilize him enough to transport him to the hospital. As they were starting an IV and giving him oxygen I hollered to Tony, almost screaming, "Breathe."

"Why are you screaming?" The female paramedic said.

I explained, "I'm screaming so he hears me." In my hysteria, I called Tammy and told her, "I'm losing him." Tammy assumed I was referring to her dad, and was shocked, by what I said. "I'm on my way, I'll meet you at the house," she said. Then I called our sons crying.

I thought we were going to lose Tony right then and there. I thought *after all, how lucky could one person be, with already surviving—two lung surgeries and two open-heart surgeries.* I kept praying, *"Please Dear God, keep him safe."*

I wasn't a regular at church but I am a believer. God has helped me through a lot in my lifetime. Getting through the loss of our first son was difficult.

Just as we were leaving in the ambulance, our children arrived at the house one by one. We all went to the hospital: I in the ambulance with Tony, our sons and daughter in their cars. As soon as we arrived, the emergency room nurse called Tony's cardiologist. "Dr. Wilton will be right over," she said.

The ER nurse was sweet as she could be, and went overboard trying to put Tony at ease. She comforted him by talking softly, and reassuring him, saying he was doing fine as she checked his pulse and blood pressure every few minutes. She stayed right at Tony's side the entire time.

When Dr. Wilton arrived; he let me stay in the room, as he proceeded to have all kinds of drugs pumped into him. I watched the monitors, and I could see the results of Tony's heartbeats on the screen. At that point, ignorance would have been a blessing; I hoped my thoughts of another heart surgery were wrong. Dr. Wilton told the nurse, "Get things set up for an emergency angiogram right away!"

I asked Dr. Wilton, "It's his heart, isn't it?" He put his finger up to his lips in a shush motion, as he nodded his head, "Yes." I was beside myself, wondering how much more Tony could endure, as I prayed even harder: *Please—please—please—Dear God, hear my prayers, please! Don't take Tony from me.*

They took Tony immediately to the catheterization laboratory at the other end of the hospital. Our children and I followed him like puppies. I was terrified out of my mind, as I waited for the test to be over, I paced like a rabid dog. It was near twelve midnight by then; outside it was dark and gloomy. At night that part of the hospital was only used for emergencies; it was desolate, and spooky. Without a soul in sight, we were all alone to face our fear. It felt like Tony was in the laboratory of Frankenstein.

After Dr. Wilton finished the angiogram, he came out to speak to us, but he didn't give us much hope. He said, "Tony needs three new bypasses immediately." Another open-heart surgery—on top of the two previous lung surgeries, it didn't look good. Dr. Wilton continued, "This will be a very hard recovery for him, if he even makes it!"

Beside Tony's heart, the doctors were concerned about the veins in the calves of his legs. They weren't the best veins to use because they were much smaller than the hearts. Tony's larger veins had already been used for the last two heart surgeries.

Dr. Wilton said, "If the veins in his calves can be used at all, it will be a miracle."

By then it was after midnight, and we were scared and fatigued with stress that Tony wouldn't pull through the surgery.

While the heart surgeon and the anesthesiologist were called for the emergency surgery, Tony was moved to the intensive care unit, so he could be watched more closely. When all the doctors arrived, we stood around Tony's bed. Dr.Vital the heart surgeon, Dr. Wilton the cardiologist, Dr. Bane our family doctor, the anesthesiologist and us. We listened intently as the doctors explained and discussed what had to be done. Not one of them said anything positive, repeating what had been said earlier about the veins. Considering all Tony's problems and all the previous surgeries, cancer plus heart disease, high blood pressure, hardening of the arteries, high cholesterol, and the nodule on his lung, the prognosis was negative. Having his chest cracked open for a fifth time was unheard of.

I was speechless over what had happened. By then, our children, the twins, our son-in-law Mike, Paul, Tony's sister Aida and I stood there, horrified by what lay ahead.

Dr. Vital said, "We need to get Tony prepped for surgery." They needed to shave and sedate him before they started. The doctors told us we could see him before they took him into the operating room. We were all wringing our hands and fidgeting as we waited to see him again. No one said anything—we were lost in our own thoughts and fears. I thought *is he going to make it through the surgery? He's had so many already, are they going to be able to use his veins to save him will they hold up?* Question after question ran through my mind, the thoughts wouldn't stop!

When we saw Tony again he was heavily sedated; he didn't know what was going on.

I told him, "I love you very much, and may God be with you." We each gave him lots of hugs, and kisses. As they wheeled Tony away, the tears rolled down my cheeks silently. Just before the doors closed behind him I told him, "Fight like hell; I'll be right outside the door waiting for you."

As he faded away down the hall, I wondered if it would be my last time to see him alive. I couldn't stand the thought of that possibility, so I immediately switched to a positive attitude and continued praying. Everything had to be all right, I could never go on without him.

I sent him off with my heart torn to pieces and my mind filled with worry and anguish.

After the Surgery

Dr. Vital had told us Tony would be in surgery about six to seven hours. We all stayed, except for the twins and our son-in-law Mike. We agreed it was best that the twins went home to sleep. They weren't happy about that. Their Papa was one of the most important people in their lives; they didn't want to leave him.

Our children, Aida, and I lay all over the waiting room, sprawled on the floor, chairs and couches. Our children used their jackets either as pillows or blankets. The tiny waiting room with pale blue walls—supposed to be comforting and soothing—was a torture chamber for us. Mario and I stayed up the entire night while the others slept. There was no way I could sleep. I kept pacing, and going in and out of the hospital to smoke and calm my nerves with Mario. In between our cigarettes we'd visit the chapel, praying— praying— like I had done many times before. *Please, Dear God, don't let anything happen to Tony. Give the doctors the knowledge, confidence, and strength to do the job that needs to be done to save Tony's life.*

That night was long, grueling, and dreadful. Our children tried to get some sleep, since they had to work the next day, providing everything went well with their dad.

After; an awful, fatiguing, six-and-a-half hours, Dr. Vital finally came out of the operating room. He looked exhausted and drained. He said, "The surgery is over, Tony's in recovery; and the next twenty-four hours will tell if he'll make it. It was tough!" Tony's veins were very small, but Dr. Vital had accomplished all the bypasses. We'd be able to see Tony in a few minutes, but he would still be heavily sedated. By that time our children were bright eyed as they listened to what the doctor said. I was relieved and pleased that Tony had made it that far.

Prayers continued! Praying together and separate; we went to the chapel as we felt the need to pray.

We took turns going in to see Tony. After the children saw him they left for work, knowing that their dad was doing as well as could be expected. Tony would be sedated the rest of the day—no need for them to be there. They said, "We'll call you later to see how dad's doing."

I assured them that if anything changed I'd call them immediately. Aida, however, stayed with me until later that day, making sure that Tony and I were doing okay.

Later that night, all our children returned bringing dinner. After they each saw their dad, we ate, and then they left. Tony wasn't even aware we visited him; he was still under heavy sedation.

I stayed at the hospital again that night. Twenty-four hours after the surgery, the open-heart unit nurse, Patty started removing all the exterior life support. She had a difficult time removing the breathing machine because Tony was having difficulty breathing. She said, "I laid my body across his to hold him down so he didn't pull any tubes out. Assuring him that he was okay and everything was all right. I was then able to remove the tube successfully." She had been an absolute angel in disguise the way she handled Tony, very patiently and kind. I believe that's why Tony did so well: our prayers were being answered. And my prayers continued.

I still hadn't left the hospital grounds; I slept in the waiting room. I only went as far as the smoking shed outside. And I kept going in and out all night, checking on Tony's progress. I was petrified to be more than a few feet away from him.

Tony finally started to come around the next afternoon. Thank God! Day two after the surgery Tony finally woke up. It was a good sign that Tony hadn't lost his appetite; he was stating that he was hungry. I couldn't have been more relieved. Eating was very important for his recovery, in order to regain strength. Happy, wasn't the word, I was delighted, I couldn't Thank God enough for answering my prayers.

Forty-eight hours later Tony went off all life support, but recovering a little slower than he had in the past, just as the doctors had predicted. Tony had been called the Bionic Man after his second heart surgery. Then, after his second lung surgery, they called him the Steel Man because he was such a fighter. Now, they were calling him the Miracle Man.

Day by day Tony got a tiny bit better and stronger. Although I saw that he wasn't bouncing back as quickly as he had in the past, he was improving. It was evident that the latest surgery really had taken a toll on him. It took him longer to become mobile, and he was kept in intensive care longer.

We still had that spot on Tony's lung hanging over our heads like a black haunting cloud. The doctors kept a close eye on it by taking many tests and X-rays daily. Seven days had passed and Tony was still in intensive care. The doctors weren't taking any chances; they were watching him very closely.

Aborted Trip

We never got to Maui. Right after the heart surgery was over, and we saw that Tony was holding his own; I told Anthony and Paul to go ahead to Maui, without us. Anthony couldn't do anything for his dad so there was no reason to cancel his trip. It was bad enough that Tony and I couldn't go, but felt they should still go try to enjoy themselves knowing that we'd be with them in our minds. Against their better judgment, they went.

I'm not so sure how much they enjoyed themselves. Anthony was distressed about his dad, calling us daily from Maui. The nurse in intensive care was kind enough to bring a phone in so that he could talk to his dad, even though phones weren't allowed. Tony loved hearing all about Maui: where they went, what they were doing, and what had changed from the previous year. It was fun and sad at the same time hearing about Maui— Tony and I had been excited and so looking forward to going on that trip. It would have been a milestone for me, because a year prior we were there right after Tony's second lung surgery. At that time, I thought Tony might never see Maui again. It seemed as though we were going to make it back after all, but didn't—.

Ten days later—eight of which were in intensive care—Tony went home. He was anxious to get home; I thought it was too soon and he was far too weak. But Tony insisted he wanted to go home thinking he would recuperate faster there. But he could hardly walk.

With this surgery, Tony was exceptionally weak. Both calves of his legs had been cut to use part of the veins, which was more painful than when they used the thigh veins. I was a total bundle of nerves. I didn't feel he was strong enough, and I was afraid he wouldn't have the strength to go up the stairs to the bedroom, or that he might fall and get hurt.

On the way home, as we were just about to pass Burger King, Tony said, "I want to stop and eat; I have a taste for Burger King." There we were with Tony's feet swollen and bulging out of his slippers, and his legs so sore he could hardly walk, we went in. I had parked as close to the doors as I could, so he didn't have too far to walk. Tony wanted to eat his hamburger there, while it was still hot and fresh. He sat in the booth facing the windows, while I went to get the food. I brought the food back, and we started to eat.

I said, "Tony, this is a treat; you need to start watching your diet more closely. You can't have a fourth open-heart surgery; you have no veins left."

"I know I'm lucky, turn around and look at what I'm looking at out the window." I turned around to look "Or I'll be visiting there," he said. He was looking directly at the funeral home across the street. We both chuckled.

After being home a couple of days and resting, Tony was still extremely weak, and I felt a sense of uneasiness. However, we had a doctor's appointment that day. Tony seemed to be retaining water, and was taking a lot of pills. I planned to relay my concerns to Dr. Bane.

Once we got to her office, Dr. Bane took one look at Tony and put him right back in the hospital. Tony had congestive heart failure his feet and

9

abdomen were swollen like balloons. He was puffed up like someone had pumped him up with air and he was ready to explode. At the hospital, Tony was immediately given Lasix and lost eight pounds of water that first night. Dr. Bane kept Tony on Lasix, and put him on a strict diet, with no, salt and limited, measured liquids. I remembered the Big Whopper and wished I had forbid Tony from eating it. Again, I stayed at the hospital, never farther then a few feet from him, sleeping in a chair right next to his bed. So that if he had a problem, I was right at his side, terrified something was going to happen to him.

Hospitalized three days that time and released. Home again! He was doing a little better, and I watched him closely. I weighed him daily, watched his diet, and limited his fluids just like I was told. I had to shower and dress him; he was so weak from the surgery and sore from the cuts in his legs and chest. When I showered him, I sat him on a plastic patio chair in the shower, afterward sat him on the toilet seat to dress him. He didn't have the strength to stand for any length of time.

A couple of days later just as Tony awoke, he complained about having chest pains. I became frantic, but he didn't want me to call an ambulance. I didn't want to take any chances, but he refused to go to the hospital. I couldn't blame him, but chest pains were nothing to fool around with. I said, "I won't call an ambulance—. I'll take you to the hospital myself."

"I'll be all right; just wait awhile." I called Tammy to help me convince her dad that he had no choice; he'd come too far to blow it now. Together, we finally convinced him to just go to the hospital to have his heart checked. If nothing was wrong, we'd come right back home.

We struggled to get Tony out of the bed, down thirteen stairs, and to the car. Because he was so weak, he felt like dead weight. He was still in his pajamas, robe, and slippers. I just threw his coat over his shoulders, got him into the car and off we went. Thank God, the hospital was only ten minutes away. I was terrified because I hadn't called an ambulance like I wanted to and was afraid something would happen to Tony while I drove. What would I do then? I drove as fast as I could without causing an accident or getting a ticket. If a policeman had stopped me, I would have asked him to escort us to the hospital.

While I drove, I grabbed my cell punched in the memorized phone number and called the hospital emergency room to let them know we were on our way. I explained to the nurse that he was an open-heart patient and he was having chest pain, so they could be prepared and waiting with a wheelchair. What seemed like hours were in fact only minutes before we arrived. A nurse was waiting for us at the emergency room door—with the wheelchair.

The nurse immediately took Tony into the emergency room, while I parked the car. I'm not quite sure why, but the emergency room staff all had gotten a kick out of me calling. I guess they found it unusual. They even went so far as to tell our doctor, Dr. Bane told me later that day. But calling the ER was a safety net for me in case anything happened to Tony in the car, they could tell me what to do. Tony was admitted to the hospital.

The next morning, Dr Wilton scheduled him for another angiogram. Something was definitely wrong with his heart. Then the trauma, nervousness and worry started, once again. What was going on now? I couldn't imagine, I could only wonder. Dr. Wilton really didn't want to do another angiogram, but told me, "Tony's between a life and death situation." The angiogram will be intrusive to the heart," he said, "It's a very dangerous procedure, but it's he only way to know exactly what is going on." The doctor decided to go ahead with the angiogram. I was crazed with worry wringing my hands I prayed like I'd done before. I was so nervous I could have bitten my nails to the quick.

Once more they put Tony into intensive care. Although the angiogram was scheduled for ten the next morning, Tony was bumped to a later time because of someone else's emergency angiogram. Finally, five hours later they took him down to the catheterization laboratory. Our children and I had been there all day. The tension was excruciating. Having been through that experience many times, I knew angiograms could be very dangerous even under normal circumstances. Tony's situation was life threatening and the doctors didn't want to do it so soon after the last surgery. Tony's heart had already been traumatized, and to put him through further trauma could be seriously dangerous. But, we had no choice. It was the only way to know what was causing his chest pain. "If we do nothing Tony could die," Dr. Wilton explained, "To save his life this has to be done." The intensity of the situation was beyond belief with all Tony had gone through up to that moment.

At last, about one o'clock that afternoon they came to get Tony. It had been a long day for all of us, including Dr. Wilton. Once again there were hugs, kisses, well wishes and many prayers. My heart ached as they took Tony away. Again!

Dr. Wilton told me, "It will take twenty to thirty minutes." And he let me stay with Tony until they took him into the catherization laboratories. Immediately I started counting the minutes. Twenty minutes. Thirty minutes. It seemed like days, weeks, forever. Tony's sister Aida had arrived. She and our children waited in the room outside of the catherization laboratories doors. It was the same waiting room we were in the last time, not that long ago. That time it was daylight so the room wasn't as spooky. But the stress was the same as it had been that night, if not worse, because Tony had already escaped deaths door many times. Once again, I was petrified that he wouldn't pull through.

Twenty minutes passed, and I knew the test should almost be over. Dr. Wilton should be walking out the door any minute with the results.

Suddenly we heard a loud and clear "CODE BLUE, CODE BLUE" my heart leaped. I thought *"Oh God help us"*. Someone's heart stopped; it needs to be resuscitated, and hopefully revived.

I grabbed my chest and jumped to my feet as I saw the "CODE BLUE" staff running towards the catherization laboratory where Tony was. I feared the worst; went numb, scared, I trembled, not knowing if it was Tony or another patient. I wanted to run through the door with them to see if Tony was okay. My gut told me it was Tony. I just knew it. I couldn't stand the anticipation. In the background I could barely hear our children's voices telling me to clam down, as I paced back and forth never taking my eyes off those doors. I felt like I was in another orbit. Things were happening around me, but I couldn't comprehend them, my mind was reeling out of control.

As I sat back down, a nicely dressed woman with short dark hair appeared at my side from nowhere. She sat down next to me attempting to comfort and console me. She talked softly and held my hands in hers gently rubbing them. She must have seen the fear on my white pasty face, as tears from terror rolled down my cheeks.

At last, the liaison cardiac nurse came out the door. As she did, I ran up to her and asked her if Tony was okay. I knew her from Tony's past heart surgeries.

She said, "Dr. Wilton is just finishing up and he'll be out in a minute." In my hysteria I pleaded with her *please* go back in to make sure Tony was okay.

With that, Dr. Wilton bolted through the swinging doors. His face was pale and he looked like someone had just died. Someone had—Tony died—but had been successfully resuscitated. Thank God. Dr Wilton was frustrated and livid about what had just happened to Tony. He was upset that Tony hadn't followed his diet; exercised, or done the things he was supposed to do over the years. As a result, Tony had hardening of the arteries, a bad heart, high blood pressure, high cholesterol and now he had just "coded" on him. Dr. Wilton wasn't happy about it, he had been challenged. In that instant, I remembered all the arguments Tony and I had over his diet, for many years. In addition, the nagging I had done every time he put something in his mouth that he shouldn't have been eating. Tony said, "If I can't eat what I want. I might as well be dead." I wished he had listened to me; maybe he wouldn't have been in that situation now.

Dr. Wilton said, "Doctors can only do so much. We're not Gods." He told us that one of Tony's new bypasses had closed. It was a small artery in the lower part of the heart.

Dr. Wilton said, "This may sound terrible, but if he had a heart attack in that area of the heart, it would be a blessing. That part of the heart would die and the rest of the heart would heal itself. If that part of the heart didn't die Tony would continue to have chest pain, which could weaken the rest of the heart. The prognosis once again was one of gloom and doom.

Dr. Wilton continued, "Even though we resuscitated Tony he's still critical, and with everything against him it doesn't look good."

Hearing those words, "It doesn't look good" echoed in my ears. I was irritated and angry at the doctor's honesty and the results of the angiogram. I became hysterical— shaking and crying uncontrollably. It had just been too much to handle. The stress, worry, and anxiety had finally got the best of me. The shock of what I had heard ignited sparks in every nerve in my body. I fell apart and started ranting out loud, "Oh my God. Oh my God. Please don't let anything happen to Tony, keep him safe." I kept ranting like a crazy person.

There were nurses all around me, one of Tony's male nurses tried to calm me down and help me gain control of myself. They gave me water, and juice, and kept talking to me. The nurses explained that Tony couldn't see me the way I was. If I wanted to see him, I had to compose myself. That would upset him and it wouldn't be good for him to see me upset.

I quickly gained control of myself so that I could go see him. I had been so upset I couldn't even console our children. I had totally flipped. Again, I started praying; I closed my hands tightly and shook them up and down in my nervousness. I prayed and prayed and prayed. *Please dear God he's gone through so much, please spare him*. It gave me peace to pray and put the situation in Gods hands. My prayers had been answered before and I counted on them to be answered once more.

Later that evening I asked our children, "Who was the lady that comforted me?" They told me they didn't know who she was either. We never did find out whom that kind, loving woman was, or where she came from. She must have been an angel sent from heaven.

Another series of tests were taken, electro cardiograms, and more X-rays. The doctors watched Tony carefully with eagle eyes.

Anthony continued to call us daily from Maui, and I kept him abreast of what was going on. Our poor son was in absolute horror. He'd be returning in a couple of days, but with his father facing death's door he wanted to come home right away. With travel time being eight to nine hours it made no sense to leave, because he would only be home one day sooner.

We had just received the news; that part of Tony's heart had died, everything seemed to be okay again. In my eyes, it was a miracle because Tony could have died four times; from congestive heart failure, heart surgery; angiogram when he coded, from the death of that part of the heart; even so, the danger remained that something else could happen to his heart. Tony was still in bad shape, but the prognosis had improved. Dr. Bane and I convinced Anthony to stay in Maui and come home as scheduled. He reluctantly agreed even though he found himself unable to enjoy his vacation due to fears about his father and guilt from not being with us during the crisis.

Whenever Tony was in the hospital I would stay with him day and night. Although being in the hospital proved to be quite fatiguing and stressful, I preferred to be there with him over worrying at home alone. Part of my fear stemmed from the experience I had with my mother, whom I lost twenty-two years earlier. She had been hospitalized with a massive heart attack. At first the doctors told me that she would be all right and that I should go home. After all, we both needed our rest. Then, during the night, I received a call that she'd had another heart attack. I needed to get to the hospital right away. When I arrived there, the priest was giving my mother last rites. I'll never forget the fear I felt for leaving her, thus knowing first-hand that the heart is tricky.

After all the traumas with Tony's heart, along with his going in and out of the hospital, seventy-two hours after the angiogram, Tony told me to go home. "You need to get some rest, and a good night's sleep."

Telling the nurse "Don't let my wife back in the room so she'll go home and get some needed rest."

I was exhausted from all the stress, and sleepless nights I'd been through by staying at the hospital day in and day out.

Tony seemed to be improving, so against my better judgment, I gave in and left. Tony didn't give me a choice about leaving; because the nurse wasn't going to let me back in his room.

When I got home I took a quick shower, then I called the hospital to make sure Tony was doing okay. I couldn't seem to relax though. The last time I called was about midnight. Tony's nurse said, "He's doing fine and his vitals are staying stable." After receiving that information, I finally fell asleep, only to be awakened by the phone ringing at two in the morning. Tony had woken up thinking he had an accident while sleeping, because he felt wet. When Tony turned the light on, he was stunned by what he saw: the whole lower half of his bed from the waist down was a total mass of vivid, red blood. After seeing all that blood Tony thought the head of the horse like in the "Godfather" was in his bed.

The nurse had called to tell me what had happened. She said, "Tony's catherization site had broken lose and he lost four pints of blood by the time it was noticed." Another miracle: If Tony hadn't awakened when he did with his blood pressure dropping dangerously, he would have died. He immediately buzzed the nurse. After seeing Tony's condition she called Dr. Wilton from her cell phone. Dr. Wilton ordered her to get several pints of blood and squeeze it into Tony through his IV to immediately raise his pressure, thus saving his life. AGAIN!

Dr. Wilton told the nurse it was very unusual to have a catherization site break loose seventy-two hours after an angiogram. Nevertheless, it had. The alarm that was supposed to go off at the nurse's station in a life-threatening situation had failed; the machine was not set correctly. If Tony hadn't awakened he would have bled to death!

That whole scenario infuriated me, but I was so grateful Tony was alive that I didn't do anything about it. I was extremely upset with myself for leaving him in the first place. However, I was relieved that Tony was okay and alive. I should have listened to my intuition and never left him from the start.

Two days later, Tony was able to return home. He was still very weak from all he'd been through which made him feel as though he'd been beaten up and had been to hell and back. Because of all that had happened I was petrified to be alone with him. I was afraid something might happen that I couldn't do anything about.

Despite his improvement, the spot on Tony's lung still hung over our heads, which unnerved both of us. Now, after having dealt with so much we tried to stay focused on Tony's recuperation. We had our hands full achieving that feat, since Tony had been knocked down so many times.

He was like a downed boxer going for the ten count—it was going to take longer to get him back on his feet.

We had been back and forth to the doctor on a regular basis, and the doctors and I watched him like bulldogs watch their young.

Bout Two

Two months after Tony's surgery, as Dr. Bane examined him, she said, "Tony you should have another chest X-ray." Then she added that she also wanted a CT scan taken at the same time.

A few days after getting the tests, Dr Bane called with the results. Unfortunately, I wasn't home. I was attending a Halloween convention for the store. Tammy, Mario, and I had gone to see the new products and to place our Halloween orders. Placing those orders was very time consuming and a tremendous amount of stress. We had to make decisions on what costumes were going to sell and take an educated guess on how many, of what style, and sizes, which took a clear mind and concentration.

Joey had stayed with his dad to make sure he ate and was taken care of while I was gone, so that if Tony had a problem, he wouldn't be alone. I called periodically from the convention to check on Tony to make sure he was doing okay. I also had my cell phone on me. In case of an emergency, I could be reached right away. I didn't like the idea of leaving Tony, but I had no choice. That convention was important, because Halloween was one of the busiest times of the year and when we made the most money.

When Dr. Bane called the house she asked, "Is Mary Lou there?"

Tony said, "No, she's at a convention." She apologized as she usually did and notified him that the spot on his lung had grown! Saying, "I need to find out what's going on." Tony needed a bronchoscopy, "right away." She hated to have a bronchoscopy done so soon after surgery, ideally, waiting six months would have been better, but it couldn't be put off any longer.

Later that night I checked in with Tony from the hotel, but he didn't mention the doctor's call. I found out by accident. Mario had called Joey from our room and he told Mario the bad news.

Tammy, Mario and I shared the same room. Tammy and Mario

thought I was asleep. When Mario got off the phone he told Tammy what Joey had said? I wasn't asleep though. After I heard what Mario told Tammy I jumped up and asked them what was going on? Mario repeated what Joey told him.

I immediately called Tony and questioned him about what Joey had told us. Tony said, "I didn't tell you, because I didn't want to worry you. There isn't anything you can do and I didn't want to upset you while you were working."

My heart sank and my insides whirled around like a milk shake being whipped. I was sick to my stomach, and I felt awful that Tony had gotten such devastating news, alone. I was terrified by the news. I just wanted to die for not being there with him. The empathy I felt sickened me and I was filled with anguish, along with being angry with myself for not being by Tony's side. I was scared. I could feel my emotions erupting throughout my body, and I felt the nerves in my spine tighten.

I couldn't get home from the convention fast enough; seconds seemed to tick slower, minutes like an eternity, and we still had one more day left to finish the buying. It was difficult for me to stay at the convention. I could only imagine the anguish Tony was enduring by himself, and my heart and soul went out to him. I wasn't able to concentrate or make the important decisions—mentally I wasn't there at all. Tammy and Mario had to do the purchasing. I should have gone home in a cab; I was absolutely, useless that day.

When I finally got home, Tony told me that Dr. Bane was going to call to let us know when the bronchoscopy would be done. Once again, our family was in an uproar and frightened.

Day of Horror

D r. Bane called to let us know the bronchoscopy was scheduled for Thursday, at seven in the morning. Tony and I would need to be at the hospital by six-thirty, so he could be prepped.

Thursday morning Tony, Tammy and I went to the hospital as scheduled. Tammy and I braced ourselves for what we might hear later that day. Another round of hugs, kisses and well wishes were given as Tony disappeared. Anthony had to work a couple of hours at the beauty shop that morning, but he was expected to arrive before the test was over.

The procedure was supposed to take about forty-five minutes. Tammy and I waited impatiently. My imagination ran ram-pet. Normally, I was a very positive thinker, but with all the past horrors, we'd been though, I was terrified. But, I fought to stay focused on the positive. However, the negative crept in and kept popping up; forcing horrid thoughts in my brain. My mind bounced back and forth like a ping-pong ball—my emotions were up and down like a teeter-totter, as I suffered a title wave of negative thoughts.

When Anthony got there, we went outside to have a cigarette to help calm our nerves. After a few drags, I got nervous. It was almost time for Dr. Lucas to be finished, and I didn't want to miss him. I told Anthony, "The doctor should be done shortly. We need to get back upstairs." We quickly went back up on the elevator. As the doors sprung open, I heard Tammy say, "My mother's going to flip out!" Tammy was leaning up against the open waiting room doorway with Dr. Lucas standing in front of her.

I ran up to them, frazzled, and asked, "What's the matter?"

"The test is over, Tony's fine," Dr. Lucas said. "However, the prognosis is not good. Its small cell, oat cell Cancer!" *The big C!* Something about that word "cancer" stuck in my craw. My heart pounded two forty and my legs went weak. I felt like I was going, to pass out!

I flashed back, "Is it operable?"

"No, because of the type of cancer it is, along with Tony's past lung surgeries, and having emphysema. Surgery would only impair his breathing even further, and would compromise his quality of life."

Dr. Lucas explained, "This type of cancer spreads very rapidly. There is no cure. The only thing we can do is try to keep him as comfortable as possible and pain free. Of course, we'll need the pathology report to be absolutely sure. We should have that report by Monday." I was in total shock. I had feared a cancer diagnosis, but for it to be, inoperable was alarming. This was a death sentence.

Dr. Lucas said, "Tony has approximately three to six months to live." I was stunned, I couldn't even speak to ask more questions, and the doctor left. I stood there dumbfounded taking a few minutes for all of what had been said, to sink in. Tammy got hysterical and started screaming no, no, no… then Anthony… then myself. The nurse came running out to offer us a room where we could have privacy. I also worried that Tony could hear us, since he was outside the door around the corner in the recovery room, just few feet away.

I tried to stay strong and solid like a plank of wood, and remain in control, because our children were hysterical and falling apart. That news hit us like a run away truck.

Our family had been concerned about getting that kind of diagnosis from that very first day that we heard there was another nodule. But now, Dr. Lucas had verified our fear—and it was more than we could handle. Doctors normally tell you what they suspect. Then you have to wait for the results, but he had given us a prognosis right then, and there. That was something we *were not* prepared for, even though we should have been. Anthony, Tammy, and I cried our hearts out, trying with all our strength to gain control of ourselves. When we finally gained our composure, we discussed the results and decided that we wouldn't tell their dad yet. We were going to tell Tony we had to wait for the pathology report to come back, to spare him a weekend of hell!

Shortly thereafter, the nurse came in to tell us Tony was starting to wake up from the anesthesia. We could go in to see him, so we pulled ourselves together wiped our eyes, threw cold water on our faces to camouflage the redness and tears. Then we went in to see Tony, with smiling faces and broken hearts.

We pulled it off. Tony never suspected a thing. He accepted our explanation of having to wait for the results. That wasn't anything new. He'd been through the routine before.

The minute I got home, I ran upstairs to call Dr. Bane. I couldn't wait to tell her what Dr. Lucas had said. "I don't know how Dr. Lucas could give a diagnosis without a pathology report, she replied. That may have been his opinion; I can't speak for my colleagues." She agreed, I shouldn't tell Tony because we wouldn't know for sure until the pathology report came back. I didn't want Tony to worry, he had enough to deal with, and recuperating from the heart surgery was enough.

Finally, Monday we got the results. However, there wasn't enough tissue taken for pathology to make a positive diagnosis.

Now, Tony would need a CT biopsy with contrast dye, Dr. Bane said. Tony was a nervous wreck about having that test, he'd had that test done before with the first lung cancer, so he knew exactly what to expect. Tony couldn't be sedated for the test because he had to be coherent, to hold his breath so that when the needle was in the area of the spot, the doctor wouldn't hit his other organs. A CT scan was a painful test. However, it would be another milestone to over come for Tony. There wasn't any other way around taking that test; the doctors had to find out what the spot was, so he could be treated. My heart ached for him; he had already suffered so much.

Dr. Bane called with the schedule for the CT scan; Tony was scheduled for that following Friday. He told her, "I'm not having that test done." Dr. Bane assured Tony he would be somewhat sedated and he would also need to fast the night before.

On Friday morning, Anthony, Tammy, Tony, and I were off to the hospital. They took Tony in right away once we got there; the nurse explained the procedure and why he <u>could</u> <u>not</u> be sedated. Tony was ready to walk out when he heard that, we had to practically sit on him until he calmed him down, to explain the importance of taking the test. He finally, agreed to take the test, in the end.

The nurse explained why the test was going to be so dangerous. It was because the spot was so close to his heart and the doctor had to make sure he got enough tissue that time. We would <u>never</u> get Tony to take that test again, I was positive of that. During the test the technician had the pathologist come up to the CT department to make sure he'd gotten enough tissue and they were satisfied he had. After the scan, they kept Tony for a while, to make sure there wasn't any bleeding, and that his lung hadn't collapsed. Shortly after, Tony asked the nurse, "Can I leave, I want to eat, and I'm starving." He wanted to get out of that hospital as fast as he could. She asked Tony to drink a little juice, and wait ten minutes to be sure he didn't get nauseated. If he was okay after ten minutes she'd let him leave. She explained the precautions of bleeding, or a problem with breathing with pain. If he had any of those symptoms, he should go directly to the emergency room, because that department would be closed for the weekend.

After being released, Tony seemed to be relieved and doing fine; the test was behind him and we left to get something to eat. While we were eating, we asked Tony about the awful experience he'd just gone through.

"It wasn't that bad and not too painful." Tony could endure a lot of pain. "But I wouldn't want to do it again." We didn't blame him, how could anyone blame him? He'd had it with the whole gambit of tests, hospitals, doctors, and all the medicines.

Then we had to play the game of waiting for the results. Again!

Farewell

That Friday evening we planned to have dinner with my cousin Joe and my Aunt Lottie. She was moving to Oregon to be near her son Joe on Sunday. We wanted to say our good-byes and farewells and offer good wishes over dinner before she left. But it depended on how Tony was feeling after the test. We ended up going; however, Tony wasn't feeling all that great. He was coughing and just wasn't himself?

Since Joe was a naturopath in Oregon, I questioned him about oat cell small cell cancer. He said, "It isn't good, that type of cancer spreads quite rapidly." I was devastated over hearing that, but still bound and determined to keep a positive attitude. All in all our evening was as enjoyable as it could be under the circumstances, and Tony had been a trooper. After dinner, we went straight home.

Wedding Day

On Saturday, the son of our friends Greg and Loraine was getting married. We weren't sure if we'd be able to attend due to Tony's condition. We called them to let them know our situation, and Tony's status. After explaining, we told them we weren't sure we would get to the reception. However, if he felt better we'd be there.

On Saturday morning, Tony still felt sore. Nonetheless, he decided we would go to the wedding. I ran to the beauty shop to get my hair done. It was extremely windy that day, and the wedding was downtown in Chicago; where it would be even stronger down there. Since, Tony was having; a difficult time breathing as it was, I was concerned that the wind would take his breath away, but he insisted he'd be okay.

When I arrived at the beauty shop, I told Anthony where the reception was and how worried I was about the extreme wind and his dad's breathing. Because Anthony was very familiar with the downtown area, he gave me exact directions on how to get there. He said, "There's a parking lot directly across the street."

When I got home I told Tony what Anthony said. He looked relieved to hear that there was parking so close to the reception hall.

While we prepared to leave, I saw that Tony was still sore by the way, he moved. He just wasn't feeling that great, but he was determined to go anyway. I was apprehensive about taking him at all, so we decided we'd stay for dinner and excuse ourselves early.

When I drove downtown, the directions Anthony gave me were perfect. As we walked through the parking lot, I noticed Tony was limping. I asked, "What's wrong?"

"I don't know, my hip is bothering me all of a sudden," which had periodically in the past. I grabbed Tony's arm tightly as I guided him across the street, trying to rush to get him inside as fast as we could. Just as we expected, it was windier than hell. By the time we got across the street, Tony was breathless and his hip hurt him even more. We rested once we got into the building. I thought he was going to pass out. Quickly I opened up Tony's jacket, and loosened his tie. "Take some deep breaths to calm down," I told him. Persisting with, we didn't have to go to the wedding, they would understand. We should just leave and go back home.

Tony assured me he'd be okay and said, "We're here now." We continued to the elevator up to the forty-seventh floor. "We made it." The wedding reception room was lovely. We entered a gorgeous room surround by windows, overlooking the city. The view was breathless, with all the colored city lights, twinkling brightly. Tony sat most of the evening and talked to the guests at our table. After we ate; we danced one dance; then graciously excused ourselves and left early. I was anxious to get Tony home, comfy, and close to the hospital.

When we got home Tony went straight to bed. He was still having, a terrible time breathing, and his hip still hurt. I was concerned that perhaps his lung had collapsed. I knew that could be very painful, and would also cause him to have a hard time breathing. I suggested we go to the hospital for an X-ray to have it checked out, but Tony got very distraught and frustrated with that suggestion, and convinced me that we should wait until morning to see if the pain subsided.

By morning, Tony was in excruciating pain in his chest and shoulder, and breathing had gotten even harder. I felt assured that his lung had either collapsed or he had a blood clot that was causing the pain in his shoulder.

Nightmare

We rushed to our favorite place "the hospital." Tony tried to explain to the emergency room doctor the pain he was experiencing. The doctor saw by his face that he was in excruciating pain. X-rays were immediately ordered, but they didn't show a collapsed lung. Next, a CT scan of his chest was ordered. Dr. Bane was contacted and she had Tony admitted to the hospital. She came in shortly thereafter; put Tony on a morphine drip, and ordered a cot for me. I felt weak in my knees when she did that. She had never, in all the times Tony had been in and out of the hospital; ordered a cot for me —and I had slept on many a chair.

The whole situation scared the hell out of me. I thought to myself, *this is it Tony's not going to make it. He's going to die.* I was horrified, and petrified all at the same time. I didn't know what to do run, cry, or scream. Every nerve in my body reacted and I was ready to jump out of my own flesh, the intensity was incomprehensible.

It was Sunday morning the day my Aunt was leaving for Oregon. I called her from my cell phone to say good-bye and wish her a safe trip, and I expressed how much she would be missed. Then I asked to talk to Joe. I told him what was going on with Tony, and that I was worried. I had read into the situation and said, "It doesn't look good to me," as I explained about the cot; morphine drip; pain in shoulder and chest; and it not being a collapsed lung or blood clot. I told Joe they already know its cancer and their treating it as such. Joe's response was, "They may very well have that knowledge or assumption. Joe told me, "Be prepared—the prognosis isn't good."

I didn't say anything to my Aunt; I didn't want to upset her on the day she was leaving. She absolutely adored my husband. In addition, she had lost my uncle a few years earlier with liver cancer. On top of that, she was leaving Chicago after living there all her life, which was hard enough without that awful news, to add to her sadness. I felt that it wasn't necessary right at the moment, she'd know soon enough.

After talking to Joe, I broke down and cried endlessly as I prayed silently. More like pleaded with God, to please be good to Tony and stop his pain and suffering. After drying the tears, I went back up to Tony's room, trying to be positive, and cheerful.

When Tony was hospitalized, he always had a private room, so I could stay with him. But, the room he got that time was huge. We didn't know how much we were going to need it, for what lie ahead? The room would be filled with all twelve of us, Tony, our four sons, daughter, her husband, our twin granddaughters, Paul Anthony's partner, Michael's girlfriend Lisa, and myself, plus visitors.

Worst Nightmare

*E*arly Monday morning Dr. Lucas came in and dropped the "dynamite." The results came back from pathology—the diagnosis was confirmed Tony indeed had "Small Cell Oat Cell Lung Cancer." He repeated what he had told the children and me the previous week. However—Tony was hearing it for the first time. Tony went into Shock—and Denial. He was horrified and terrified, as our worst nightmare had just been confirmed. Dr. Lucas continued, "This type of cancer it is inoperable. Surgery will impair your respiratory situation, and that isn't a good idea, this type of cancer spreads very fast." Then he said, "Your prognosis is eleven weeks without treatment. Chemo maybe radiation will be used to control it. The oncologist will be in later to talk to you. She'll tell you what kind of treatment that will have the best effect on this type of cancer."

With my very being crumbling, I tried to keep Tony focused on the positive, as I died little by little inside. I pointed out every positive thing I could possibly think of to Tony; how lucky we were that the weather was changing summer would be there soon; we wouldn't have to bundle up with all the winter clothes; how fortunate we were we wouldn't have to travel, far being the hospital was so close to our house. So we'd have to go to the hospital for treatments a few hours, so what, at least the cancer could be treated. I can now see with hindsight that I was totally in denial. For the better I focused on the positive. That was my way of coping with that evil situation.

Dr. Bane came in shortly thereafter and reiterated all over again what Dr. Lucas, said. She apologized for having such grave news. Saying, "We have to jump on treating the cancer right away, now that we finally have a confirmed pathology report."

Tony told her, "Have the morphine drip removed, the pains gone." I couldn't understand? Was the pain really gone? Or was he in denial? Dr. Bane told us, "The oncologist will be in to see you today." She then said, "I suggest Tony have a port put in a vein in his shoulder to administer the chemo through. Chemo tends to burn out the veins, and the port will make getting the chemo much easier. Especially since Tony has such terrible veins to begin with, and is more scared of the hyphen locks than any surgery he's ever had." On several occasions, we even had to get a special phlebotomy nurse to find his veins. Dr. Bane scheduled the surgery for the next morning, it wasn't considered major surgery, and would only take about forty-five minutes. A surgeon, who had operated on Tony numerous times before, would be doing the surgery. Later that day the surgeon came in to explain the procedure.

Tony was extremely upset with Dr. Lucas's bluntness. He felt the doctor just blurted out his prognosis with no finesse and was too matter of fact. Saying, "Dr. Lucas is cold and unfeeling!" Tony had always been an emotional person. He said, "I feel like a piece of meat for them to butcher and chop up and everyone is in on a moneymaking scam." I didn't blame him for feeling that way. I felt the same way. Tony had heard all that devastating information all at once and he had a hard time processing it all.

"I feel like I was just hit in the head with a brick." It was his worst nightmare. "I wasn't scared that it might be cancer, because I thought if it was cancer they would just do surgery like they did the other two times. But not being able to have the surgery and having to get chemo is another story." The bulk of awful realization of what had just been said was just too much to swallow that fast. I kept going in and out of the hospital constantly, to have a cigarette, trying to calm my frazzled nerves.

After having a cigarette as I was waiting for the elevator to go back to the room. I ran into Dr. Lucas. He could see I'd been crying. He put his arm around me to comfort me saying, "You know doctors almost always deal with statistics, and that's exactly what they are "statistics." There are miracles; maybe Tony won't be a statistic. There's always hope! Never give up! It's in God's hands!"

I hung on to his every word of hope.

Every time I left Tony 's room, I'd walk around the halls dazed, crying, and desperately praying; trying to get a hold of myself so I could be strong for Tony's well being. If he saw me upset that would throw him for a loop. "I needed to be his rock." If I kept myself composed, I could make decisions that are more sensible on Tony's behalf, and be more positive for his sake.

I walked around the hospital weeping, when one of the male nurses saw me and said these very comforting words to me. I'll never forget them. "Ever!"

"Have faith ma'am" as he looked at me with the most comforting eyes. I thought *what a wonderful sweet thing to say*. That brought my mind back to faith and prayers for strength. Faith, that's exactly what, had gotten me that far. To hear "have faith" couldn't have been more appropriate.

Later that day Dr. Even the oncologist came in to talk to us. She said, "Tony you need Chemo immediately, this type of cancer is very aggressive."

"How many people have you cured?" Tony asked.

"I had a lady that went into remission caught in the early stages." I was thrilled when I heard that.

As she left she said, "I'll be back later to talk to you more." When she left I focused on the positive.

Tony said, "Did you hear her, one person out of how many?" I was silent. She had also told us that Tony would lose all his hair, which concerned him. He didn't have much hair, but he was always vein about the little he had left.

At that point with all the decisions that needed to be made, and the closeness of our family, I called all our children. We needed to be together to discuss and decide on what we all thought and felt about what was the best thing to do about the awful horrific situation we were faced with.

We asked them to pick up fried chicken with all the trimmings for dinner. That's when the huge room came in handy. When they arrived, we ate picnic style, sprawled out all over the place; who sat on the cot, on the radiator, on the edge of Tony bed, even on the floor. As we ate, we discussed what all the doctors had told us, and the recommendations that were given throughout that day. We discussed the port being put in, and chemo treatments needed. We all agreed the port was a good idea, and better in the long run, plus less pain for their dad to deal with. We were all fond of Dr. Bane had a lot of faith in her. That was somewhat of a comfort to us. I really felt she had kept Tony alive all these years, and had never left a stone unturned in the past.

Dr. Even came back to talk to us again later that evening.

"I'm going to give Tony Cispaltin and VP Sixteen, that's what is used for this type of cancer. It's not a cure but hopefully it will hold the cancer at bay for a while." She stated that she wanted to start the chemo the next day, with that she left.

Tammy stayed with Tony and I that night, she and I slept on the cot together. Anthony was coming back early the next morning for the surgery. Our emotions were at a peak with the unknown yet to evolve. We had an awful lot to handle in a short amount of time, there was no time to chew and swallow what was going on, just react. Time was of the essence!

Dr. Bane came in early the following morning to check Tony. He told her, "I changed my mind; I'm not going to take the chemo, or have the port put in."

She told him, "It's your choice but you will only have about eleven weeks without it." That quickly changed his mind. After she left I asked him, "Why did you say that to her?"

"I wanted to see what she'd say."

A few minutes later the phone rang Anthony called to tell us Tony's mother had accidentally overdosed on pills. Somehow, she had gotten confused from taking so much back pain medication, we presumed. She was found semi-conscious. Anthony told me he had to go to her house right away, and couldn't come to the hospital. Tony's sister, Aida was in Florida on vacation. Aida had their Cousin Debbie checking in on her mother daily, while she was gone. When Debbie didn't get a response from Tony's mom when she called that morning, Debbie was alarmed and went to check on her before going to work, to find out why she hadn't answered the phone? When she got there, she found her on the bedroom floor semi-conscious and half dressed. Debbie was hysterical over what she faced all alone. She immediately called Anthony to ask him what she should do. That's when he immediately called to tell me what had happened, to explain why he wouldn't be able to come to the hospital. He had to go be with his grandmother, help Debbie, and see what happened. I was very distraught that he couldn't be with his father that morning for moral support, but certainly understood. Thank God! Debbie found her. Anthony called an ambulance when he got there. She was rushed to the hospital just in time; her blood pressure had dropped to the dangerous level. She would have died she had taken so many pills. She had been getting quite confused the past few months, between the pain pills making her groggy, and the confusion she suffered, she had taken too many pills.

Now, we had her in one hospital, Tony in another, both in critical condition. I didn't tell Tony about his mom right away. There wasn't anything he could do anyway, at that point, and he had enough to deal with. I decided to tell him later after his surgery.

Shortly after Anthony's call, the transporter came and took Tony to surgery. The doctor had explained that she was going to make a small incision, and a button like object would be inserted and connected to a main artery under the skin then sutured. That was all that was involved, on the skin's surface it would look like a small bump. The port wasn't that noticeable on his shoulder, the surgery was a success. One trauma was down!

After the surgery, Dr. Even came in to talk to us again.

"Tony you will need about six months of chemo, then we'll see where were at. The chemo will be started tonight. You'll be moved to the third floor."

We asked, "Can't we stay where we are."

"No, you have to move. The third floor is the cancer floor, and the nurses were familiar with ports and are specially trained to administer chemo." Then we asked, "Can we get a private room up there."

"Yes, but you have to wait for a room to vacate, a room should be ready shortly"; I packed everything that we had accumulated over the past couple of days as fast as I could; thinking time was of the essence. Only to wait, and wait, and wait, our nerves were frayed. I was worried and scared about how he was going to handle the chemo. Finally, I asked very nervously about Tony not getting the chemo, right away. I was told the patient in the room Tony was being moved to, was waiting for a ride. The staff wanted to put Tony in another room until the patient left, but I didn't think two moves would be a good idea. Our nerves were frazzled as it was, over the unknown. It was going to be a whole new experience, and I didn't feel moving all around would be in our best interest. One move was all we could handle at that point. Wondering if I'd made the right decisions. I was a total wreck. Not knowing if rapid growing cancer meant hours, minutes, or if waiting could be deadly? We had waited hours by then, and getting more agitated every second, my patience wore thin, along with being terrified for Tony's life. The whole situation was, hurry up and wait deal.

I remembered what Tony had said, that it was nothing more than a moneymaking scam, and he was the piece of meat they were going to feast on. It was an awful sick feeling. We were in the system and had no choice but to be bounced around, like puppets on a string.

The transporter finally came and we were on our way, to what felt like

With Death Before Us

the chamber of horror. We traveled the halls both scared to death of the unknown and what was to transpire, on the "third floor."

When we got to the room it was one-fourth the size of the one we had left. Getting that a cot in the room was a challenge. It was very tight with all our belongings, but the important thing was, I could be with Tony, and I didn't have to sleep in a chair. I could at least lie down. Tammy decided to stay with us again. I was grateful, two heads were better than one. My mind was in a tailspin and I felt more comfortable with Tammy there. I felt, if I missed something that was said, "Hopefully" she would catch it.

A little later, after settling in, the nurse came in to introduce herself. Her name was Jenny, she was a sweet young girl and very pregnant. "I'll be the nurse giving Tony the chemo. I will give you a full explanation of what is about to transpire, before I start the chemo. A class as to what the procedure was going to be: what type of chemo would be used, side effects that may occur, along with the precautions that should be taken like, hygiene, and how important it is and why."

"People think chemo is a money making scam, but it really isn't. It's about saving lives' that's the most important thing," she said. I thought *she must have been reading our minds.* I couldn't believe she said, verbatim, what we felt the whole thing was all about; did they have the intercom on?

Jenny went through our lesson, and the chemo IV was started. We were scared. We didn't know what Tony's reaction would be to the chemo. Jenny stayed and watched Tony very closely, constantly taking his blood pressure and vital signs, all through the treatment. Tony seemed to be handling the chemo with no problems at all. We were very thankful: no instant vomiting, nausea, or side effects of any kind, he handled the chemo perfectly. His treatment called for three days of chemo, one day of intravenous and two days of oral, which consisted of seven, pills per day an hour apart.

The next day was a full day for Tony with more extensive tests, an MRI, Bone scan, Blood tests, and X-rays.

We all were doing anything and everything to keep Tony's spirits up. Anthony told his dad "I'll bring you Filet Mignon and Lobster Tail (Tony's favorite meal) for dinner tonight." Tony was excited and looked forward to it. He also loved all the attention he was getting and ate it up like a kid. We felt that was the least we could do, give him lots of love, and attention.

The next day we went down to see Tony's mother. She had been transferred to the same hospital she also had Dr. Bane as her family doctor. When the accident had occurred the ambulance drivers had to take her to the nearest hospital. After they stabilized her, Aida had her transferred. Aida had returned from Florida after hearing about her mother's accident, cutting her vacation short.

It upset Tony to see his mom like that. He had tears in his eyes when she didn't even know who he was, that tore his heart out. Tony's cousin Sandy had come to visit him while we were visiting his mom. When Sandy found we weren't in his room, the nurse told her where to find us. She had brought us both chocolate malts, which was thoughtful. Greg and Loraine also came to visit Tony. The nurse had to also tell them where to find us. Not wanting to disturb Tony's mom, we decided to go to the visiting lounge, where we visited for a while.

After everyone left we went back to Tony's room. By that time I was just so exhausted from all the emotions, nerves, being on edge, and crying, I took a nap. The stress had taken a toll on me, along with not having much sleep for days. I fell asleep almost instantly. While I slept with one ear tuned in, I could hear that Anthony had arrived with the steak, and lobster. I smelled the food, but I was much too tired to care.

The more I smelled the food the more nauseated, I got. At first I thought it must be my imagination. Why would I be getting sick all of a sudden? Dismissing the feeling I tried to keep sleeping. When they asked if I wanted to eat I said sleepily, "No, I'll eat later."

I could clearly hear they were eating. Smelling the butter made me sicker with every second that passed. Finally they were done, Thank God!

I said, "Put the food away, please!" All of a sudden I jumped up and ran to the bathroom. I didn't quite make it; I vomited all over the floor, the toilet, and myself, I made a mess, I was so embarrassed. What had come over me all of a sudden?

Anthony called the nurse to have her call housekeeping right away. The nurse asked, "What's the matter with you?"

I said, "I don't know I was fine, all of a sudden I got ill for no reason. I explained that I thought maybe it had been the malt I drank? Maybe the machine was dirty and had bacteria in it because, I was fine."

The nurse said, "You should go home, because Tony's resistance is very low from the chemo, and you could make him sick." I was reluctant to leave Tony, but I left. Anthony brought me home and stayed at the house with me that night.

The next morning when I woke up I felt great, like I'd never been sick at all. I took a shower and went straight back to the hospital. I was sure it was the malt or nerves. I remembered it was more than likely nerves, because

Tony drank the malt and he didn't get sick. I also wasn't sore, didn't have a fever, or anything connected to the flu, and felt okay quickly.

Tony seemed to be doing fine all that day, but the doctors had told us, typically that type of cancer travels to the bone, and brain first.

Stage Four

*D*r. Even came into Tony's room to check him the following morning. I was alone with Tony. Tammy had gone home, after staying with us a couple of nights. When everything seemed to be going okay, she left. She had to take care of her family, and the worst was over. Tony seemed to be doing fine, we thought!

Dr. Even advised us, she had good news and bad news, the good news was no cancer showed up in the bones. She had warned us earlier that cancer could still be in the bones, but it was too small to detect yet, that was good news. She was going to keep an eye on it though. Then the bad news was that, something showed up in back of Tony's head. She continued, "It could just be arthritis, but I ordered a brain scan." I was frantic. I didn't elaborate on it not wanting to stir or upset Tony more than he was already.

After she left Tony said, "Now it's in my brain."

I told him, "Don't jump to conclusions right away," repeating that the doctor had said, "It could just be arthritis." And reminded Tony that he had been diagnosed as being loaded with arthritis in the past; telling him, "Don't worry until we have something concrete to worry about. You need your rest, and stress isn't good for you." He agreed, took my advice, and tried to get some sleep. I went down for a long overdue cigarette to think things out and calm my nerves. On my way back up, I ran into Dr. Even in the elevator.

I asked her, "Is this something I should be very concerned about?"

She replied, "I just want to be sure nothing else is going on." She thought it could be arthritis which he was loaded with, and to get some sleep.

I also asked her, "What's the prognosis with chemo?"

"Up to twelve months. Everyone is different it's hard to say," she replied.

The next day Tony went for the brain scan… now the waiting began. I felt like I was sitting on a fire but, I couldn't move. I waited for the results trying desperately not to worry. Running everything through my head repeatedly that Dr. Even had, said, and I convinced myself that it wasn't cancer it was arthritis. Nothing else went on that day, except Tony took the second day of oral chemo, and he was still tolerating it beautifully.

At about one-thirty in the morning Dr. Even came in. She was straightforward and shot from the hip. She said, "It already spread to the brain, it's malignant, and Tony will need radiation on it immediately. I'll send Dr. Tray in to talk to you this morning. He'll explain the procedure, and schedule Tony for radiation right away.

She continues saying, "I'd also like to do a bone scan."

She now called Tony's diagnosis "STAGE FOUR CANCER" the worst stage it could possibly be, it had rapidly spread to the brain from the lung. She wanted to make sure that it wasn't in the bones too.

Now as one could only imagine, Tony felt totally defeated, he kept saying, "I'm a dead man." When it all finally sank into my brain, I realized this couldn't be good.

Tony said, "God only knows where else it is."

I comforted Tony as best I could by telling him the doctors caught it right away; it could be treated, and that was positive. I told him, "It's normal to be scared, I'm scared too. You should try to not worry we're in this situation together, and have to handle it one day at a time." I told Tony, "You should try to get some sleep, and rest. It's very important for you to get a lot of rest." He finally fell asleep. How I don't know, probably from being on overload for days, or not wanting to think anymore. It was one or the other! Who could blame him?

Tony did sleep; I on the other hand was going absolutely, totally out of my mind with anguish. My mind was spinning and reeling out of control, but I had to hold firm and focused. Thinking *what exactly did all that mean? Would that shorten his life? Was he going to die now? Would it be sooner?* I didn't sleep one wink. I went in and out of the hospital all night smoking my brains out, thinking, and thinking. My father had always said, "Things are never that bad that they can't get worse." That cliché had saved my sanity many times at tough moments. Thinking *it really could be worse. The doctor could have said it's in the brain and there's nothing more we can do!*

I was going absolutely crazy with all the unanswered questions. I finally cornered Tony's nurse and asked her, "Will this shorten his life?"

"I really don't know."

"How long do people live with this type of cancer?"

"Everyone is different. However, it's very important for Tony to have a positive attitude." She was very kind, pleasant, and compassionate, but she really didn't give me anything solid to hang on to, one way or the other. I needed answers, someone to talk to, and something concrete to go on.

I debated calling all our children to inform them of the tragic horrific news. It was about two-thirty in the morning by that time.

I knew Dr. Bane came in very early daily, between six and six-thirty. I decided I'd call our children about five-thirty, that way they would have had some sleep at least. They all lived close to the hospital, and could be there within minutes.

I'd give them the grave news, and then ask them to come to the hospital, so we could have a conference with Dr. Bane. They could all ask every question they had and they'd get the answer first hand, as this affected all our lives. It would also save me from going over the gruesome situation over and over with each of them. Or have them asking me questions I didn't have answers to, because I hadn't asked that question. I felt that was the best decision for all of us. I needed someone with me right then, and there though; I was scared to death and half out of my wits. I called Mario an hour later, and told him what had taken place, and asked him to come to the hospital to be with me. He came running. When Mario got to the hospital I discussed the whole drama with him, and how I had decided it was the best decision for all concerned, he agreed.

At five-thirty I started phoning the other children. They could tell by the tone in my voice that I was extremely upset. I gave them the dreadful—awful—news—and asked them to come to the hospital for a conference. Of course, they all immediately agreed to come. It concerned their father, and they were very much involved, and very supportive.

They were all there within minutes, very upset and shaken with the new problem we were faced with.

I told the nurse to please let Dr. Bane know we were all there, and that we would like to see her as soon as she got in. I felt she would be forewarned that way and have time to brace her self for the riddling of questions that would be shot at her. In addition, she'd have a chance to look at Tony's charts to see what his status was. I knew it would be hard for her, as she adored our family, especially my husband. She had also been there through most of the surgeries Tony had through the years.

Conference With Dr. Bane

*I*mpatiently, we waited in the tiny room; which had six small straight back chairs, three on each wall left and right across from each other. In the middle of the wall facing you as you entered, was a magazine rack attached to the wall. It truly was a miniscule room, barely enough room for six people to get into, much less seven. There was so much tension in that room that it could have blown the walls out! We didn't have to wait long; the doctor was there early just as expected. When she came in one of the boys gave her his chair, as he sat on the floor. The questions started shooting at her one after the other from all angles, like a machine gun. With our hearts breaking, and tears flowing endlessly, the doctor very patiently, and calmly, answered each question in a quiet, compassionate, and honest way, one by one.

Stating, "The prognosis isn't good now that the cancer has metastasized to his brain. Reiterating, Tony now has, STAGE FOUR CANCER! The worst kind of cancer and the fastest spreading there is." Tony has about a year if there weren't any other complications with his heart or chemo." She explained, "There isn't a cure for this type of cancer, and with chemo we can only hope to prolong his life, being one of the fastest spreading, on the other hand the most treatable. It *'does,'* respond to chemo."

"It saddens me to have to share this awful prognosis, everyone wishes it were different." Repeating, what Dr. Even said, about the radiation to the brain; Tony had to start radiation as soon as possible to stop the cancer from spreading any further. If Tony didn't get chemo, or radiation he would only live eleven weeks, 'if we were lucky'. In the end, they would keep Tony pain free, and as comfortable as possible." Not one of us focused on that comment! We let it go over our heads—. We did not want to hear that or believe it—.

For us that conference could not have been more overwhelming, dreadful, traumatic, or horrific torture, we were all <u>stunned</u>. It was surreal.

We asked if the cancer spread even farther in the brain what would happen. "It's in the area of the brain that could cause seizures, he could go blind, lose his equilibrium, and or his speech could be affected." That alone was just too much to comprehend. After I heard that information my brain automatically turned off. I could only accept so much horror before my body started to shut down, protecting itself from the trauma. I wanted to pinch myself and wake up from the awful nightmare, but quickly I realized it was "no" nightmare. It was real; I had to deal with it, make decisions, and keep a cool head. Most of all I had to have a positive attitude for my dearly loved Tony to cling to.

After that meeting, I went to my car and sat there completely stunned, forcing myself to collect my thoughts. I started screaming, crying uncontrollably, and pounded on the steering wheel in anger, as I prayed like crazy. I pleaded to God please, please; please just give me a year with Tony. Let me get him back to Florida, and Maui. I had been in my car quite awhile, when our children looked for me. They came up to the car to see what I was doing. I did not want them to see me crying like that, but I couldn't control myself. I was crying, and telling them I wished, I had known this was going to happen. I would have danced with him all night at the wedding reception, just two days prior. I thought *I'll never have the chance to do that again.* I was a total complete wreck. I tried to collect myself and went back into the hospital with our children. Our children decided to stay for the meeting with Dr. Tray.

I did not want Tony to know all our children were there, or he would have suspected things to be as terrible as they were! I wanted to protect him from that torment—.

When I explained to our children, how I felt. We all decided it would be best if they went to the cafeteria until it was time for the appointment with the Dr. Tray. Then come back to Tony's room for the appointment.

When I went back to the room after composing myself, I told Tony our children were going to come for the appointment with Dr. Tray. That way we would all hear what he had to say.

Our children came back to the room just before the appointment as planned. When the time came, we went down to the radiology department together. We were all put in a teeny, tiny, pink examining room not large enough for two let alone all of us. We squashed ourselves inside spilling out into the hallway. Anthony had to leave disappointed that he couldn't stay. He had to go to work, everyone else stayed. We waited impatiently to hear what Dr Tray had to tell us.

When he came into the room, Dr. Tray shined from head to toe. His shirt was fresh and crisp, his tie, belt, pants all coordinated, and his shoes were immaculate. He looked very professional, confident, and projected himself in that manner. I felt that he knew what he was talking about. At least, I hoped he did.

Explaining, "The brain can't be biopsied where the spot is. I'll radiate the part of the brain where the mass is because; chemo doesn't go to the brain. The brain has a protective shield that protects itself from chemotherapy."

Continuing, "The reason for radiation is to kill the cancer cells in that part of the brain."

Tony wouldn't be able to drive because of the treatments. He would need fourteen consecutive treatments, five days a week.

Dr. Tray stated, "Another radiologist might recommend sixteen or seventeen treatments, but my belief is that the extra one or two aren't necessary. The only way we'll know if the radiation worked; would be if Tony doesn't get any symptoms—seizures, loss of balance, affected speech, or blindness. "If I ordered another brain scan after all the radiation treatments were completed, it would only show scar tissue and a mass in the brain."

I kept praying, *Please God let the radiation work don't let any of those devastating symptoms creep through.*

He explained, "Tony will look like he has a suntan on his head."

How Tony endured that entire dreadfulness I couldn't even guess! Seeing he wasn't fully recovered from all the trauma of the open-heart surgery, let alone everything else he had been through.

We prayed and hoped the doctors had caught the cancer early enough for the radiation to do what needed to be done—kill the cancer cells. We feared those dreadful, frightening symptoms *could* show up. God help us and him!

Tony was put on steroids to keep the swelling down in the brain. My poor husband was getting shot down from all angles. The radiologist even kept Tony in the hospital for the first four radiation treatments; watching him very carefully.

Finally, on Friday Tony was released. I was frightened to death to take him home, with this new situation. It certainly wasn't anything like recuperating from surgery. As far as what to expect—I was panic-stricken—.

I didn't show my concern or, worry in front of Tony. As we left the hospital, I was on edge though. We stopped to pick up the prescriptions that he was going to need, on the way home. Tony was thrilled to be going home, at last!

Home at Last

$\mathcal{W}$ e hadn't had dinner yet, and Tony did not want another famous hospital meal before he left, so I suggested we go out to dinner. Tony got excited about that idea; it was about five thirty in the evening by then but with all the settling in—fixing his pills and freshening up. It was getting late. Ardine stopped in to see how Tony was doing, so it got even later. By then Tony, and I were super anxious, hungry, and at each other's throats. I could feel emotions erupting, trying my damnedest to control them.

By the time we left it was eight-thirty, and we were starved. On our way to the restaurant, I explained to Tony that I had to have everything organized and under control before I could go out to eat, and relax. I apologized for my shortness and anxiety. He did the same. It turned out to be a lovely evening after all. It was an evening we both relished and enjoyed. I truly treasure those memories.

Tony had been in the hospital eleven days and had five radiation treatments while he was there. The next day, we had to go to the hospital to continue the radiation treatments; then go back Monday through Friday until he received all of fourteen treatments.

That Tuesday Tony had an appointment with Dr. Bane. She wanted to check him after being hospitalized.

She rechecked Tony's heart and lungs, then said, "Everything seems to be going okay." Tony complained about experiencing a lot of pain in his back."

Checking his bones she stated, "If there was cancer in your bones, you'd be in excruciating pain, when I thumped on them."

I was grateful he did not experience that pain.

Then on Friday, we had an appointment to go to the cancer center. That was Tony's first visit as a patient. Tammy and I had gone down to the cancer center previously to check it out when he was in the hospital. So, we could explain the center to him, to prepare him, on what to expect. Then, when we went down to see the radiation doctor; we wheeled Tony into the cancer center so he could see it for himself.

However, it was much different that day. It did not seem as pleasant as it had when we looked in. During that visit, it seemed like a pleasant, colorful comfortable room with soft gray leather contour chairs, and many cheerful pictures. Each station had its own TV to pass the time, and curtains to surround each section for privacy.

That Friday, Tony was only having his blood checked. They wanted a CBC test to see how his blood levels were after the chemo treatment.

"Tony's blood results are still okay," the nurse said.

I thought, *"Still okay? What did that mean?"*

We had to return Monday for another test to make sure his blood levels were still high enough to receive his second chemo treatment, on Tuesday.

Twenty-one days had already passed since his last chemo. I could not believe it! His blood levels were okay that Monday. I thought *'Whatever' that means! What were they looking for? It was all- new to me.*

We made the chemo treatment appointment for the next day, before we left. That particular day, the cancer center seemed to have a different light on it. It did not seem pleasant at all. Just going down on the elevator to start with, gave me an eerie feeling. I also noticed there were no windows. That specific day it felt as though we were going into a dungeon or, worse yet hell! I don't know why I had that feeling, I can only presume it was the fear of the unknown—

Never did I mention my feelings to Tony; keeping them to myself, always being positive, upbeat, and encouraging all the time. I looked at the situation in a different light, and protected him as much as I could. Tony being the patient, he seemed to look for the most comfortable way to cope. At that time he never said, or, acted like he wanted to give up. He rolled along with whatever had to be done, being a total sport.

The cancer center had two private rooms with beds available to patients receiving chemo if requested. Tony had asked for a bed the day before because, of the pain in his back. Otherwise he would have had to sit between three to five hours, while the chemo was being administered through the port in his shoulder. The treatment would take too long for him to endure sitting, without experiencing back pain, even in a contour chair.

Dr. Even was walking a fine line with Tony just having open-heart surgery, and the entire staff watched him cautiously.

That day of chemo I passed the time by walking around the hospital, and looking in the gift shop. Tony preferred to sleep through the treatment. It seemed to be going as expected, when I checked on him periodically.

Dr. Even came in to see how Tony was feeling about halfway through the treatment. She examined him; listened to his heart, lungs and thumped on his back. "If there was cancer in your bones you'd be in excruciating pain when I thumped on you like that." I was so grateful to have two identical opinions. I was mainly concerned about the bones because, of what she had stated earlier, about the cancer cells being too small to detect, but could still be there. With the close observation Tony was getting, I felt confident that nothing was growing in his bones. I still prayed for that to be true.

For the next two days Tony would also take the oral chemo; seven pills per day an hour apart. He would be home with me alone—and I was terrified about what could happen. It was exceptionally frightening. If he had any reaction at all I wouldn't have known what to do; except rush him back to the hospital.

We had been going daily Monday through Friday for the radiology treatments at the hospital. That next day Wednesday, we had an appointment with Dr. Tray to find out Tony's status. He once again repeated the symptoms he spoke of before. He checked Tony's reflexes, strength, and said, "You have three treatments left; do as much for yourself as you can, it's important, for you to try and stay as active as possible for every day you're down, and do nothing it will take two, three days to come back." Explaining, that the muscles get weak very quickly, this wasn't very encouraging. Tony could hardly do anything before; now; he was even worse from being shot up, with poison and radiation.

He was exceptionally weak because, I had been doing everything for him since the open-heart surgery. He never actually had a chance to recoup, and bounce back. In the past with the other surgeries I was used to doing everything for Tony until he got his strength back, but this cancer case was a complete new experience for us. I realized I had to push Tony to do things for himself, even though it broke my heart. I preferred to help him, than to see him struggle. But, I knew it was in his best interest to do things himself; the less he did for himself the worse it would be. I felt like I was between heaven and hell.

Besides taking care of Tony there were the normal everyday things that had to be done: laundry, grocery shopping, cooking, cleaning, just to mention a few. Since I had to drive Tony back and forth to the hospital it didn't leave me much time for the rest. I was always rushing to get things done. While our children were always at our every beck and call should we need them but, I hated to bother them unless it was absolutely necessary.

Before we knew it, it was Friday and we had to have Tony's blood tested again. I didn't understand what all those blood tests were for or, what they were looking for, for that matter. I had sent for literature from every organization I could find, for small cell lung cancer and brain cancer.

I'd seen a program on television about cancer in general, and had learned from the program that the best advocate was an educated advocate, so I started to educate myself as best I could. I'd always been a person that wanted to know the why's and, how comes, that happened to be an asset to the position we were in. I learned that the nurses looked at the white blood count, the red blood count, hemoglobin, platelets, and neutraphils to make sure they were high enough to administer chemo again.

It was close to the end of April already, and we asked Dr. Even if we would be able to travel at the end of the month.

She flatly responded, "No!"

She explained that Tony needed to be watched closely, and he was far too weak to travel! In the past, we had always gone to Florida during that time of year, but we had to cancel our second trip! Tony's health was of course of utmost importance. Canceling wasn't a problem; nevertheless, we were terribly disappointed.

Monday morning we had to go for a blood test again to check his blood levels. They were low, now Tony would need injections of Neupogen, to build his white blood cells— Warning us that, "Neupogen has side effects; causes pain in the bones since white blood cells are made in the bone marrow, it could be quite a painful experience."

It did cause pain! We were concerned because; we weren't sure whether the pain was caused by Neupogen or, bone cancer starting? With everything that was going on; it all being new to us, it was quite unnerving, in reality we did not know what was going on. Tony just listened and did not say a word. He seemed to go by my reaction, so I had to be careful about how I reacted.

Once he was started on Neupogen he would need a series of three shots, one a day for three consecutive days. Then he would have another blood test to check where his blood levels were to see if the count had risen. If not, he would need the Neupogen injections Monday, Tuesday, and Wednesday. Then Thursday, his blood would be tested once again. The levels where still low, which had us going back three more days for another series. So that on Monday, Tony could receive the chemo treatment, providing his levels had gone up. That Monday when the nurse checked his blood, his levels were high enough to receive chemo. Another twenty-one days had passed; the days just flew by, with us going to the hospital every single day.

At his third chemo treatment, he'd handled the chemo treatments well thus far, and with no nausea or vomiting. Thanking God he didn't have to deal with that problem.

The oncologist ordered a pill for nausea that Tony took three times a day, six a.m., two p.m., and the last at ten p.m. as a precaution, to warrant off getting sick on the days he took the oral chemo. It helped immensely. Tony was still very weak but, he was a trooper. He did exactly as he was told, even though it was difficult. Just taking that amount of medication was a feat in itself.

At night after I'd help Tony to bed. I would sit downstairs and cry my eyes out. Seeing him go through that was slowly killing me. It truly was torture!

Wellness House

*W*hile we were at the cancer center getting his chemo one of the nurses told us about a place called Wellness House, in Hinsdale near the Hinsdale hospital. Wellness House offered cancer patients support, and she highly recommended we attend.

"We'll check into it." I thought it was a great idea. We were both so frightened with the whole cancer situation. I felt it sure couldn't hurt to check, and see what Wellness House was all about. We were desperate for some support somewhere, and decided to go to a meeting. Feeling it would be good for both of us.

The first session we attended was called welcome to Wellness. We were greeted and hosted by two former cancer patients who were in remission. One was a man that had been diagnosed with lymphoma and had been given six months to live, that had been nine years ago. The other was a woman who had breast cancer, and that had been over six years ago. It was an inspiring experience for us. The hosts said, "Doctors aren't always right, there's always hope, and miracles every single day." That alone was something that got me through a lot, the hope, and knowledge of miracles. I personally felt I'd experienced many miracles just in the past few months alone. We both left Wellness House uplifted, feeling hopeful again, and we relished in that feeling. That was the first positive thing we'd done in months and we both needed it desperately. Wellness House also offered massages, pain therapy, hypnosis classes, exercises, and a lot of other different sessions. You could donate but, it wasn't a necessity.

The welcome people continued to explain the sessions that were available, and what they consisted of, some were available daily, and some weekly. For other sessions you had to give them some personal information to attend. They offered groups for cancer patients and caregivers, which Tony and I were interested in.

There also was a session called Connections; it was a four-week committed program where you were only committed to attend four weeks, if interested at all. We signed up for the first four weeks. They taught us many different things about cancer; what cancer is, what happens when you get it, all the emotions you go through, like fear, anxiety, frustration to name a few, and how to handle your medical team, which consisted of doctors, nurses, oncologist—. The staff talked about the miracles that had occurred and no one knew why, or how, there was no logical explanation.

Wellness House helped us immensely. I highly recommend it to anyone going through the unpleasant trauma of cancer. For me it was my shot in the arm of hopefulness. There are many people, going through the same thing with the same feelings. Wellness House offers a place to identify with, instead of feeling like a leper; it was an encouraging positive experience.

The committed groups were private groups, once you registered to attend that four-week period. No new people are added. Tony and I were in separate groups, he was in a group for cancer patients, and I attended one for caregivers. It was great for me because, I could talk openly about all my fears, anxiety, and frustrations, as everyone did and that enabled me to express feelings that I was going through without upsetting Tony or, our children. We shared our intimate feelings in that group, and found out how other people felt, either the same or similar to what you were feeling.

Tony on the other hand felt sorry for most of the people in his group. Tony's group was all women; most of them had small children, with all the chores that go with being a mother, and homemaker. He actually couldn't identify with them because we were at a different stage of our lives. He could however, identify with being a cancer patient, so he did get something out of it. Saying, "I realized how lucky I am that you do most everything for me, and I don't have small children to care for, or go to work." I felt, that even if we didn't learn a lot every time, if we got just a little something every time we went, we learned something, whatever that something was or how small it may have been. We would be better people for it, plus we may have shared something that might have helped someone else, so it was a win, win situation.

Wellness House also offered many other special events, magicians, special speakers; garden walks, along with all kinds of other activities—.

Wellness House was our salvation, and still is too this day.

Lake Geneva

*F*ive months had already passed and we had canceled two trips. We both felt the need to get away. So, we decided to take a drive to Lake Geneva, which was not too far, being only one and a half hours from home. I wanted to break up the monotony, do something normal, and expressed getting away from the cancer scene, instead of living, eating, and breathing cancer all day every day. The drive-up was beautiful; it felt good to be getting away. I felt like a kid running from the monster.

We made a stop in a quaint little country town for breakfast on the way, and then continued. When we got to Lake Geneva we checked into our hotel, and we found it to be more than we expected; lovely and homey, it was like a condo with a kitchen, bedroom, living room with a fireplace, and sliding glass doors overlooking the water.

Tony's arm swelled from his elbow down to his wrist while there. We didn't know what the swelling was from, and it hurt him. Later that evening Tony took a Jacuzzi, and could not get out of the tub. I struggled to hoist him enough so he could sit on the edge of the tub before getting out. We were both frightened and alarmed by his weakness and swelling. Nevertheless, we made the best of things, but I was particularly concerned. I did not elaborate on it, so as not to upset Tony, keeping the concern to myself. Tony's stomach was upset. He wasn't feeling all that great; either but, the scenery was different, we were away together, and that's what was important to us.

We went out to dinner and that turned out enjoyable, on the other hand, went right back to the room afterwards. He was absolutely exhausted. He was taking the oral chemo during the two days we were away, and that took a toll on him. It made things even more terrifying.

The next morning we stayed in the room until it was time to check out, then we went out for breakfast. He still wasn't feeling great that morning either. He was still very tired, and beat up from the intravenous chemo, so he rested in the car. He insisted I shop a little while he sat in the car so I literally ran in, and out of the little shops checking on him every few minutes. I couldn't relax nor enjoy shopping. I was too worried about him, so we left. We left late Thursday afternoon for Lake Geneva, and by Friday at three we were on our way back. It felt good to get away, but both of us were anxious to get home. I was frightened the whole time we were gone, but I never let Tony know that. I worried about the swelling in his arm, especially since we weren't close to the hospital if something should happen. On the other hand, we had enjoyed it as much as we could, under the circumstances. Our children were frantically worried about us, and weren't happy that we had gone that far from the hospital.

It starting pouring sheets of rain on the drive home; seemed we couldn't get back fast enough. Tony was incredibly tired, weak, and anxious. As we got closer to home we decided to stop for a hot dog for dinner, by then the rain had stopped, we ate, and left, right away to get back to our, 'home sweet home' where we'd be safe, and sound. Tony had been as anxious, as I was, but neither of us shared it with the other. If something would have happened while we were away from the doctors, cancer center, and hospital, I don't know what we would have done. Tony felt safer at home close, to everything, and so did I.

Monday was back to the hospital to have his blood checked, and it was good. We showed the nurse the swelling on his arm, she looked at it but, didn't know what it was either; there was no explanation. That was very frustrating, and upsetting to me. When things like that came up, and the medical field couldn't explain what was happening, it aggravated me to death. I felt there should be answers and explanations. I thought *why didn't they know? Was it out of the ordinary? Didn't that happen to anyone before, ever? If not, shouldn't we find out what it was, instead of just blowing it off!* That made me angry—!

Back to Our Doctor

That Thursday, we had an appointment with Dr. Bane. We showed her the swelling in Tony's arm also. She looked at it but, didn't have an explanation either. Tony also had a headache in the back of his head. She replied, "That's common with radiation to the head." His neck was swollen and his head looked as though he had been in a tanning bed. Just as Dr. Tray had told us would happen. His head was dark, and peeling just like sunburn. The nurse suggested we put aloe on it to keep it moist. Tony's head was also swollen too, almost twice the size, and he had gained a lot of weight. Dr. Bane said, "The swelling and weight gain is from the steroids, it's a side effect from the radiation." Tony's legs were also still swollen. In truth, Tony was a mess but, alive and fighting like hell. Dr. Bane stated, "I haven't received any reports from the cancer center." She told me to talk to the cancer center coordinator; to get the reports sent to her. As she examined Tony's abdomen, she said, "I don't like the swelling there. I'm going to order a CT of his chest, and stomach I'm worried about his liver." We kept going from one thing to another, up and down, back, and forth, like "Rolly Polly's.

When we went back to the hospital, I talked to the cancer center coordinator about the reports being sent to Dr. Bane.

She said, "Ask the receptionist in the cancer center." After I talked to the receptionist, I presumed the reports would be taken care of; and never gave it another thought.

Monday Tony needed his blood levels checked again. His levels were low; he'd need the Neupogen shots again. The nurse gave him a shot that day and we went back to the hospital the next two days for the others.

On Wednesday, Tony was scheduled for the CT scans of his stomach and chest per Dr. Bane's orders. There I was again filled with anxiety awaiting the results, worried about what they may find? It was taxing, agony for all of us. This time it was his liver!

Memorial Day

onday was the Memorial Day holiday, one our family use to look forward to. I tried to keep as much normalcy as I could. I went grocery shopping and prepared food for the holiday as I usually did. We always had the barbecue and swimming at our house. We tried to put the worry and frustration out of our minds as we waited for the test results. I noticed my back had been acting up with the slightest movement of my foot, leg, or neck the last few nights. It would cause my back to spasm, and wake me up. The pain I felt was kind of like a Charlie horse only in the small of my back. I had hardly slept the last few nights between the anxiety, stress, and Charlie horses. I thought it was from helping Tony get up, and down out of the chair, thinking that the pulling and straining probably caused it, but it was getting worse and worse. I guessed all the grocery shopping, along with lifting heavy pots and cooking I had done didn't help. By Saturday evening, I had not slept at all, so I went downstairs, not wanting to disturb Tony. I tried sitting in the recliner; chair, and even laying on the floor. Nothing seemed to relieve the pain, every time I moved my back spasmed. I was up, down, sitting, laying nothing helped; didn't matter how I moved or, what I did, the spasm wouldn't release. I thought I was going to go absolutely crazy, in extreme pain. I was so drained and tired by morning all I wanted to do was sleep but, couldn't. I finally decided to try the heating pad, thinking that might help, but that made it even worse. I was desperate. I tried muscle relaxers, and pain pills. That didn't help either. At seven that morning; I woke Tony up, and told him, "I have to go to the hospital. I've been in relentless excruciating pain all night, and haven't slept." He suggested we call the doctor first. "You have to call the doctor, I can't talk." I paced the floor, back and forth, like a crazy caged tiger. When Tony called Dr. Bane, she was off that weekend. Naturally! The covering doctor told him, "I'll order her muscle relaxers, and pain medicine. Put ice packs on her back to see if that works, before coming to the hospital."

Tony told him, "She already tried those medicines, they didn't work."

After hanging up Tony said, "The doctor said you have to take "two" pain pills, a muscle relaxer, put ice on your back, stay off her feet, and get in bed. Try that before coming to the hospital."

Right at that moment; with me in tears from the pain, our sons Michael and Joey came walking through the door. They were there to do some repairs on our fence. They saw that I was crying and in terrible pain, still pacing like a rabid animal. I explained that I'd been up the entire night, and I couldn't stand the pain another minute. Anthony called just then and he said, "I'll go pick up the prescriptions." With that being taken care of, Joey ran upstairs and got an old back brace Tony had from another injury. He put ice in a towel; laid it inside the brace, put it on my back, and closed it using the Velcro strip. By then Anthony was there with the pills; I took them, and went to bed. After taking the pills; the ice pack on my back, I finally fell asleep. Every four hours I took more pills like clockwork, they knocked me out, and I continued to sleep. I was petrified to move for fear that the pain would return. The boys took care of us both all day, along with fixing the fence.

Anthony came back later that day and took all the food for the barbecue to his house, there was no way I could have had the holiday. I'd be lucky if I could get to his house to celebrate Memorial Day. By the next morning I felt better, but still took the pills. We went by Anthony, but I didn't do a thing while I was there. I was petrified to death the pain would return. I had never experienced pain in my back like that before. Nor, did I want it to reoccur, so I babied myself.

Seeing Dr. Even

Wednesday we had an appointment with Dr. Even for a check up, and the results of the CT scans. We could have gotten the results earlier, I knew, they'd be in. However, we decided we didn't want to know until after the holiday, for fear of what kind of news we'd get.

Anthony insisted on going with and I was glad. It was always good to have someone else there, what one didn't hear or, remember the other one did. Under stress, sometimes your mind just shuts down. When Dr. Even came in the room, she said, "I have good news and bad news, it's not in the liver, but remember all the back pain you were having? Well it metastasized to the bones." I was stunned, and stood there in disbelief, speechless—.

But, she continued, "The lung is significantly better."

She pulled out X-rays of his lungs from the last test, to show us the difference between them. The new test did show that the lungs had improved by three fourths that was terrific. When she showed us the bone scan, it showed white spots that she said, was cancer. I was livid at that point. I said, "Dr. Bane and you both said, "The thumping on the bones with no pain meant there was no cancer there. If cancer were there, Tony would have been in excruciating pain. I wasn't worried about the bones; I was worried about the liver." I got so angry right then, that I could not utter another word.

She said, "This is the lesser of the two evils."

Continuing, "The lung is much better." Nevertheless, Tony, now, had cancer in the bones, and she wasn't so sure whether one of the other cancers came back, or, if it was a different cancer altogether.

She said, "We're going to watch it." At that point, I thought *they're all full of shit, contradicting them selves.* The situation kept getting more confusing by the day. With all that anxiety building, I felt like my brain was going to explode out the top of my skull. I could tell by Tony's quietness, that he felt, he couldn't handle one more thing either.

I put on my happy positive attitude, and assured him that the chemo would kill the cancer in the bones or, Dr. Even would change the chemo to kill it, don't worry.

I reminded Tony about the woman we met at Wellness House that also had bone cancer and she was doing fine. We had some hope, and we would get through it together.

Literature

I had received all kinds of literature from every cancer organization I could find, that pertained to the type of cancer Tony had. When Tony went to bed a night, I'd read through it. None of it was hopeful. There was a ton of literature coming in every day, and I'd read some each night, crying my eyes out every single night, telling myself repeatedly, that these are only statistics like Dr. Lucas had said, that first day. I kept telling myself, they're not talking about Tony in particular. After all the staff at the hospital was calling Tony "Miracle Man!" Praying harder and harder each time I prayed, asking God to help heal Tony and give me the strength and patience to do what needed to be done, to help him through the nightmare. I had many sleepless nights, my mind shuffling through all I had read. I never shared with Tony what I read, or the frightening, sad statistics.

Every single day I would only focus on the positive; hope, how good Tony was doing or, how good he was eating, how fortunate we were that he was handling the chemo, and how lucky we were the hospital was so close and on and on. If, Tony came up with a negative it got shot down with a positive. Always praying and Thanking God for all he'd done thus far, which was the many miracles that kept me going.

It was now June, and the following Tuesday, Tony was scheduled for his fourth chemo treatment. He had an X-ray taken before they did the chemo, I wasn't sure why? Thinking *so far so good, the doctors were still watching him like hawks.* Tony was still swollen like a balloon ready to pop, from the steroids, but he hung on.

We'd been at the hospital almost daily since January, sometimes twice a day. Depending if Tony had to have tests, shots, or both.

On Friday Tony had his blood levels tested and they hadn't dropped. Thank God!

Then on Monday he had them checked again, they dropped a bit, but not enough to need Neupogen.

The following Thursday, we each had appointments with Dr. Bane. Mine was at eleven forty-five; Tony's was at twelve. She had whistled me in for my yearly check- up. She wouldn't give me my estrogen patch prescription until I had my checkup; I was way over-due, so I had no choice but to make an appointment. I made the appointments at the same time so we would accomplish two things at once, making it easier; since I had to be there with Tony anyway.

Our Doctors Appointment

Since my appointment was first Tony, waited in the waiting room until our Dr. was ready for him. I was taken in for mine; Dr. Bane started examining, first my heart, then blood pressure, going through the basic exam. I mentioned the back problem I'd had. She said, "Stress could have also attributed to it." Then she took a Pap smear and continued to check my breasts. In total silence, she examined my breasts, and finally spoke, "I feel a lump in your left breast." I just about went through the ceiling, with fear. I actually felt the blood rush to my head, as my thoughts quickly took over—.

Emphatically I said, "You have got to be kidding. God! I can't handle that now. I've got my hands full. Not now, I don't have time for that!"

The Dr. quickly responded, "It's not uncommon for the caregiver to get sick. You have to take care of yourself or, you won't be any good to take care of Tony."

Telling the nurse, "Call the hospital; and make an appointment for a mammogram, back X-ray and chest X-ray for her." Then instructed me to have them hold me at the hospital until, they talked to her with the results. She left no stone unturned, and was very thorough. She comforted me by saying, she thought it was a cyst, but we had to be sure. I was concerned because, she requested the mammogram to be done the very next day. In addition, the read, and hold part frightened me. Besides, I certainly couldn't handle that problem now, Tony was far too ill.

Dr. Bane then started to talk to me about Tony, she told me that what he had was a horrible disease, and that we should have a living will done. Continuing with, "I have one myself everyone should, to alleviate problems later." Suddenly, the nurse came running in, saying, Tony's very ill in the waiting room. Dr. Bane had a close circuit TV in the waiting room, so the nurses could see the patients waiting, in case of an emergency. Like This!

We all ran to see what was happening to him. I asked, "What's wrong?"

"I have to go to the bathroom." The nurse gave me the key to the bathroom so I could take him; there were no other patients waiting, Thank Heavens. After I got Tony in the bathroom, I told him, "I'll wait right outside the door until you're done." The nurse let me keep the key in case I had to get back in there in a hurry. I stood outside waiting a few minutes. Then asked, "Are you okay in there?"

"Open the door." When I opened the door, he was half unconscious. At that precise second the nurse came to check on us, just as Tony said, "I'm going to faint." The bathroom was, tiny with just a toilet and a sink. We both were holding Tony up, on the toilet, when the other nurses came running. One nurse was on one side; one on the other, another giving him smelling salts, with the doctor in the doorway telling everyone what to do! I'd gotten pushed out of the way, and was trying to see what was going on. There we were with the bathroom door wide open; Tony sitting on the toilet with his pants down around his ankles, and all of us standing in the doorway around him, doing what we could. Thankful that no other patients were waiting! The smelling salts brought Tony around, while another nurse ran, and grabbed an office chair on wheels. We got Tony to a standing position I cleaned him, and got his pants up. Then we got him on the chair to wheel him back to the exam room and sat him in a chair there so, he could rest. That was a scary fiasco!

By then, I was shaking from head to toe. Dr. Bane said, "Tony had viovagle, caused by diarrhea, and his blood pressure dropping." The nurse gave him some crackers, juice and let him sit in the exam room for a while. His blood pressure started to come up. The Dr. had me call Anthony to help me get his dad back to the house. When Anthony got there, we told him what had happened. Dr. Bane told him, "Your mother needs a mammogram tomorrow, I found a lump. Could you go with them tomorrow so you could stay with your dad while she has the tests done?"

"Yes, of course." The nurse then gave me some smelling salts to have on hand in case I needed it later, and we left.

At that point, I thought *did I dream that or what?* That was too much to handle all at once. Suddenly my father's favorite cliché flashed to mind, *"Things are never that bad that they can't get worse?"* Couldn't have been at a more appropriate time! Things could have been much worse, I wasn't sure how but, I was positive they could have been. Quickly releasing that thought, to focus on the positive, NOT the negative—.

I was worried about Tony—Anthony petrified for us both. He followed us home, and made sure we got in the house safely. Then ran out of the house like his rear end was on fire, left so quick I couldn't understand what the hurry was. Later, I found out why he couldn't get out of the house fast enough. He went straight home to call Dr. Bane right away, in concern for me. She told him, "The reason for the hold your mother until they had the results, and call her order was to get a faster answer. That way, she wouldn't have the extra stress of waiting for the results over the weekend. Otherwise, she wouldn't get the results until Monday." She knew, I was about to have a, breakdown. She knew me all too well to know I was almost over the edge; pushed to the limit, at my wits end, and ready to flip out. Knowing Tony and I had handled a lot in a short amount of time.

More Tests

We went to the hospital early in the morning, that Friday. Anthony came as planned to help. I thanked God, for him he was a God sent at times like that. Anthony and his dad went to the cancer center for Tony's blood test, while I went for the X-rays and mammogram. The X-ray was a snap, and fast, the mammogram on the other hand was horrid, because I had dense breasts, they're more difficult to X-ray. The technician had to take quite a few X-rays to make sure she got good pictures. Then left saying, "I'll be back in a few minutes; I need to check them to see if the film is satisfactory for the radiologist." Only to came back saying, she had to take more. I thought she was going to pull my breast off my chest it hurt so badly. She informed me that dense breasts hurt more than others, because they had to use more pressure to get good pictures.

"Aren't I lucky?" Reminding her about the orders from my doctor, she didn't seem too pleased with that.

"I'll have to tell the radiologist who's reading them."

"Whatever, I'm not supposed to leave until you call her." A little while later she came back saying, the radiologist said, "You should make an appointment for an ultrasound."

She continued, "I think everything's okay but, just to be sure, you also need the other test." I left right away to make the ultrasound appointment. While I was gone, my doctor called to talk to me, I anxiously called her back. She said, "I'm really not worried. I talked to the radiologist, he didn't think it was anything serious either, but thought it was a good idea to have the ultrasound, just to be sure. I'm almost sure it's cystic!"

"I already made the appointment for the ultrasound."

"Don't worry."

I really wasn't worried because; I knew if she had the least bit suspicion, there was a problem; she would have had the ultrasound done immediately. I erased it from my mind since I couldn't get it done right away, and she didn't seem too concerned. A few days later, I received a letter stating the mammogram was abnormal, and that I should have an ultrasound, which I already had the appointment for.

Hospitalized Again

nthony told me, "Dad's blood levels were low. He'll need the Neupogen again. The nurse gave him one of the three shots today." That meant we'd be going back to the hospital the next two days. Tuesday I took Tony for the CBC blood test to check his blood levels, after having the Neupogen series. He started to experience difficult breathing, so, I asked the aid to check his oxygen level. The test showed his oxygen intake was low, and he was in pain. The nurse called Dr. Even to inform her, and she ordered oxygen for Tony, and the nurse gave us a tank to take home. Tony was so weak, and in so much pain, Dr. Even wanted to run another battery of tests the next day. She was in the hospital; so, she ran down to see Tony for herself. She made the decision to keep him in the hospital to run the tests because; of all the pain he had, plus the breathing difficulty he was experiencing. She ordered a CT scan of his chest, and abdomen. Tony was experiencing extreme bone pain. I was baffled as to what was causing the pain. *Was it the Neupogen, 'Or'—?* The next day, Wednesday, they gave Tony a blood transfusion then a MRI, but he was in so much pain he couldn't lay flat for the length of time it took to take that test. They scheduled him for another MRI the next day; Dr. Even ordered pain medication to help him last through the MRI. He made it through the test but, in the middle of it, they had to give him another shot for pain. We got the results Friday night when Dr. Even came in to see Tony about midnight. She said, "I'd like to biopsy the lower pelvis area because, the MRI was not inconclusive." Tony was not happy about that one bit; and we had a terrible time convincing him that it needed to be done. Who could blame him, he'd been through the mill. However, I felt, we needed to know what, if anything was going on. Dr. Even wanted to do it right away, but she needed a special licensed nurse to assist her. She promised Tony he wouldn't feel a thing. She was going to give him Versaid, explaining that it's a drug that works like amnesia, and he wouldn't remember a thing. He finally agreed. She personally was going to do the biopsy, in his hospital room. Changing her mind she came back to let us know she'd do the test in the morning when she was fresh. We asked what time she said, she didn't know it depended on what time she got out of the hospital, maybe around ten or so. I told her, "There's no hurry get your rest we'll be here." Where else would we be! She informed us we could go home about three hours after the biopsy. Tony was thrilled to hear that, he was sick, and tired of hospitals, and so was I.

The next day Dr. Even came about one. Tony was getting very antsy he wanted out of that hospital. He'd been there too many times and was extremely sick of the food, tests, and everything else that went with it.

The nurse prepared Tony for the biopsy; that was going to be done in his room, including closing the cot, to make room for all the equipment. The nurse brought in the; electro paddles, blood pressure machine, heart rate monitor, pulse ox monitor, and the cardiogram machine. It all looked frightening, but I felt assured they would know immediately should there be a problem. I was asked to leave. I probably could have stayed had I asked, but I was certain at that point I couldn't handle it. The doctor said, "It will take about twenty to twenty-five minutes." As I left, Dr. Even assured Tony that he wouldn't remember, or feel a thing. I hugged my honey and told him I'll be right outside the door.

Another milestone how many more could we handle; I waited, afraid for Tony, and myself as to what would be found. I went outside to smoke, and chatted with the friends I'd made in the smoking hut, they all knew me well by then, and all about Tony. They were my support group since I spent so much time at the hospital; they had been extremely helpful, knowledgeable, and comforting to me.

I told one of the aids that worked on the cancer floor that I would have liked to stay with him. She assured me that I wouldn't have. It's awful doing that part of the pelvis area; during the biopsy, you hear a pop, she had watched the procedure, and stated she could hardly handle it, even being she was studying to be a nurse. I was definitely glad I hadn't stayed. Thinking, poor *Tony my heart aches for you!*

By the time I got back upstairs, the door should be opening any minute. A couple of seconds later it did, I'd timed it perfectly. I was frightened and scared in fear of what I might see or worse yet—hear from Dr. Evan.

Then the door opened, "Everything went well you can come in," Dr. Evan said. As I entered, I saw slides with blood and chips of something; I presumed it was bone fragments. It made me nauseated; I hurt for Tony, and worried that he'd be in pain. I asked the doctor, "Will he be in any pain?"

"Not really maybe a little sore?"

I thought *Yah! Right! She wouldn't be feeling a thing.*

Tony was waking up already. She said, "Tony I want you to remember a pink polka dot giraffe, it's really important. I'm going to ask you about it later." As she turned to me, "Now's the time to ask Tony questions or, ask him for something like furs or, diamonds. He won't remember promising them to you." We laughed a little, even though it really wasn't a laughing matter.

"He'll be a little groggy, and maybe sleep awhile. Once he has eaten something, been watched about three hours, and walked with the walker, he'll be able to go home."

The nurse came in, and moved all the surgical equipment out. Afterwards I opened the cot up so I could lie down: I was wiped out from the pent up stress.

I watched Tony's face to see if he showed any signs of pain, asking him if he had felt pain. "A little pressure is all." I felt relieved.

Tony hadn't been out of bed for five days since being admitted. The therapist had brought in a walker the day before, and showed Tony how to use it; then she came back with one for him to take home, set the height, and told me, to put his name on it, and the oxygen tank. "Things sometimes disappear accidentally, and with his name on it, we'll be able to track it down." I put Tony's name on them right away. She told me, "Call the Oxygen Company as soon as you get home. The tank we gave you will, only last five hours, and he needs the oxygen continually."

It was raining furiously; an absolute miserable day, you could hardly see, the rain was so heavy. I hoped that it would stop by the time we left. We had acquired a walker, and oxygen tank on top of all the other stuff we had, and I was nervous about getting all of it to the car, and then in the house. I wasn't in any hurry to leave in that storm.

As Tony became more coherent, I asked him if he wanted to have dinner there. He instantly answered, "No!" Just then, the nurse's aid came in to get Tony out of bed to walk him with the walker. I could not bear to see him deteriorating like that. It felt like I was dying myself, bit by bit. My heart pounded so hard I thought it was going to burst out of my chest, as I saw that Tony could hardly stand he was so wobbly, and weak. The aid confirmed my feelings by saying, "He's not stable." It was a horrendous sight to witness my loved one walk with a walker it tore at my inner soul. I had to hide the tears; I fought to hold back.

A little later I said to his nurse, "We'd better wait awhile before releasing him, he's still very wobbly." She didn't seem to like that suggestion.

"Ask the aid that walked him." She also said, "He's still weak." What the hurry for Tony to leave was, I didn't understand.

I explained, "It's pouring outside, and I'll have to get him into the house, beside the fact that it's slippery."

I knew I had to be our own advocate like the books had warned. I wanted to avoid any chance of something horrible happening.

The nurse stated, "Then I'll have to call the doctor, and she will probably want to keep him another night." I'm sure she knew how bad Tony wanted out of there, and she had said that as a threat.

"Hold on let's wait thirty minutes to an hour to see how he does, maybe he'll be more coherent and stable by then," Tony <u>was</u> <u>not</u> happy with me for saying that, but I was trying to be sensible. He was angry with me, nonetheless. He wanted to get home, and eat some real food.

Sure enough after waiting an hour when we got Tony up, he was much stronger, more solid on his feet, and much more coherent. Yeah! We did get to go home. Thank God or I would have been in big trouble. The social worker came in to make sure I remembered that I had to call the Oxygen Company as soon as we got home. We'd need the oxygen delivered before the other tank ran out. She was exceptionally concerned about that, I assured her that, I would call right away. Tony was exceptionally weak from being in bed all those days, and would need a lot of help going up and down the stairs. I told Tony it would take some time for him to bounce back again. I had been pushing him up the stairs under his butt, but now our children worried that I wouldn't be able to push Tony up anymore because, of my back or, that we might both fall. I had investigated getting a stair lift, but Tony did not want one.

Anthony had told me, "Call me when we you're leaving, so I can meet you at the house to help you with dad." We had accumulated a ton of things that needed to be carried in: flowers, books, oxygen tank, walker, clothes, it was like we were moving. I should have been used to that with all the hospital trips we'd had, but I wasn't. On top of all that I felt a lot of pressure because, I also had to make sure I had the prescriptions filled that Tony would need once we were home. With so much on my mind, when we got to the driveway, I realize I'd forgotten all about calling Anthony. I called him right away from my cell, as we pulled in the driveway. It only took him a few minutes to get there. After getting Tony in the house; I still had to prepare his pills, which were numerous, and make sure they were ready for that evening.

It was a tedious job. He took different pills one to three times a day; some a.m., p.m., and at bedtime, and some even had to be cut in half?

When I was done with that feat; I had to order the oxygen, and bring all the stuff from the car in, and put it away. But most of all I worried about being able to handle Tony, and take care of all his needs. I had to be sure I had everything I needed in the house because, Tony couldn't be left alone. It was a terrifying situation.

Home Again With Oxygen

*A*fter getting everything settled, Anthony stayed with me until the oxygen was delivered. Thank God. I was uneasy about not being able to remember everything. The oxygen man brought a brand new unit that made its own oxygen for the house, with a fifty-foot hose, the maximum length that could be used safely. I was so pleased because, it reached all the way up upstairs to our bedroom, and to the bed. Tony would be able to sleep in our bed. This had been a big concern to us wondering. We had no idea if that was going to work out; since we had a colonial type house with all the bedrooms upstairs. Plus the fact that we'd have to be careful that he didn't trip on the hose going up the stairs, or worse yet get tangled at night in bed, as the oxygen would get cut off.

The oxygen situation worked out perfectly though. Except—the sound of the oxygen machine made me sick to my stomach. I don't know why? Whether it was the gnawing sound reminding me that Tony was sick—or the fact that he had worsened. The sound was a constant pusssssssh, swwassssssssh, pusssssssh, swwassssssssh, sound all-day—and all-night—day in—day out—non stop, relentlessly. I was a constant reminder that illness lurked in the house.

The portable oxygen tank was another decision we had to make. Medicare would only pay for one tank holder so I had to choose between; either a five-pound tank with a pushcart or a two pound that I could carry over my shoulder in its bag. We could get as many tanks as we needed, that wasn't a problem. Anthony didn't want me to get the heavier tank that lasted three and half-hours to carry over my shoulder because, of my back. The oxygen man was particularly helpful at that point. "You can try it, if it doesn't work out, you can change it." I took the two-pound tank with the shoulder strap. I thought I'd try it; for transporting Tony for all his appointments, it would be faster, and easier. Then we'd use the five-hour tanks for visiting. We'd keep extra tanks in the trunk of the car, as a precaution that way we'd never be without oxygen.

Then the oxygen man taught us how to put the hoses on, change the tank, turn the valve on and off, and how to change the nosepiece. He showed us everything we needed to know for the oxygen to work properly. That lesson was an experience. I didn't think I would remember everything, except the important things, like making sure the oxygen was on, and coming out. To put me at ease he said, "We have a twenty-four hour phone service, if you need assistance." I was comforted to know that because; I was terrified I would make a mistake! And I had Tony's life in my hands—.

Tony's fifth chemo treatment was that following Tuesday. With every chemo treatment, Tony got knocked down farther, and farther, and he got weaker and weaker. I saw that the stress of everything was taking a toll on him, but he still had the fight in him. He was a resilient man, how he did it, I don't know? That must have been when God carried him, like the prayer "Footsteps," states. It's one of my ultimate favorite prayer's.

The bone marrow biopsy came back "negative." Yeah! Another miracle, both sides of his pelvis had been tested, that was wonderful news, and music to our ears. We were very happy but, still confused, as were the doctors. Dr. Even had also had a PSI test done for his prostate which came back, negative too. We were on a roll of good news for a change instead of the up, and down of a rugged ladder.

July Fourth Holiday

On July 4th, we had all our children over. The weather didn't get hot enough to swim. It turned out not be a good day. Tony didn't spend much time outside with us that whole day. He wasn't feeling well. It actually was a sad day, and a lot of tears were shed! With Tony being so lifeless and ill, we were all affected by it. He wanted to go to bed right after he ate which was quite early. The boys helped him up to bed to fulfill his wishes

We all took turns checking on him. I had bought a portable intercom and set one up in the bedroom, kitchen, and basement, so if Tony needed something, I could hear him no matter where I was. It saved a lot of running up and down to find out what he needed, and a big help, along with a comfort to both of us.

Our evening ended early. As everyone was saying, they're good-byes and goodnights; somehow, we all ended up in bed with Tony sharing thoughts, fears, sadness, and crying. We told Tony he had to stay positive, and keep fighting, we understood that it was hard, but he could do it. That was easy for us to say and an emotional day for all.

Back and Forth to Hospital and Doctors

That Friday we went to the hospital for Tony's blood test. His blood levels once again were low he'd need another series of Neupogen. That day the nurse also decided to start Tony on Epoetin, which was used to build the red blood cells that carry oxygen through the blood, to the body. I was excited about that because, I hoped Tony wouldn't need the oxygen as much. The nurse said, "It takes quite a few weeks before you'll see any results." I felt anything that helped Tony in anyway, I was all for it.

That following Thursday evening, as I was getting Tony ready for bed, he said, "I want you to call the doctor tomorrow morning."

"Why?"

"It's personal."

"I don't understand why you don't want to tell me." I thought *he wants to give up*. I prayed some more. I explained, "If I talked like that, you'd want to know what was going on with me? It's not fair for you to shut me out like that." Tony finally broke, and shared with me that he was having suicidal thoughts.

"I need to see the doctor for some medicine. I dreamt I was in the garage with the car running and I woke up with you standing over me with the doctor." After hearing; that, I became frantic, and worried that he might do something stupid. 'Like follow through with his dream'!

I got out of bed extra early the next morning to call the doctor. I was more than concerned, and saddened that Tony was feeling that way. I asked the nurse if they could possibly squeeze Tony in that day. I told the nurse, "Tony wants to see the doctor alone, it's personal. Stating, he needs to see Dr. Bane right away this morning."

"I'll call you back after I talk to the doctor." I waited impatiently for the call, when she finally called back saying, "I squeezed Tony in, bring him in at eleven-thirty."

I ran upstairs, and gave Tony the good news. I rushed, giving him his shower, dressed, and breakfast just in time to leave. When we arrived at the doctor we went right in; the doctor came in shortly thereafter. Tony explained how he was feeling, and his thoughts of suicide. The doctor was very sympathetic, and understanding. She explained, "After all you've been through, that isn't the thing to do. You have depression; I'll give you medication to help with that. Telling him, "Don't give up the ship now, and with what everyone has gone through with you. You have a loving family, and it wouldn't be fair to your beautiful granddaughters or, your family."

After she gave Tony a pep talk along with the depression medication, she told me, "Get Tony a personal trainer to help build his muscles, strengthen him, and get him in the pool to exercise."

"He constantly makes excuses not to get into the pool, he says; it's too hot, too cold or, too breezy. I'll get a heater so he'll go in the pool to exercise."

More Tests

The following Thursday, Tony was scheduled for a CT bone biopsy, another needle in the haystack. He was frightened to death about that test. He remembered the CT lung biopsy all too well; it hadn't been that long ago that he'd forgotten. He was pretty much fed up with all the prodding, and poking he'd been through. I certainly could understand why, he was truly a miracle man, going through all of that rig-a-marrow, and torture. I could barely handle it, and I was only witnessing it all.

I did however; want to know for his sake if he did in fact have cancer in his bones, so that it could be treated right away. I got the feeling Tony didn't much care anymore. He agreed to have the test, but, only if he could be sedated; he even went as far as to call Dr. Bane, and told her his decision. Dr. Bane and Dr. Even promised Tony that he *would* be sedated. Dr. Bane told him, I could stay with Tony and if the doctor doing the test refused to sedate him. He always had the right to walk out that's what convinced Tony to even consider taking that test.

He remembered very clearly that when we had gone for the CT lung biopsy, the doctors promised him he'd be sedated, but when it came right down to doing the test, they couldn't. It was understood and very "clear" why Tony had apprehension!

Anthony went with for the test that day. We had to go down to the cancer center first so Tony's port could be accessed. All Tony kept saying while we were there was, "If they don't sedate me, I'm walking out." The nurse in the cancer center over heard him, and had Dr. Even paged. She was going to meet us in the CT scan department. By the time we got upstairs, Dr. Even was already there. "Tony you're going to be sedated with the same medicine you had with the bone biopsy. All doctors aren't comfortable using that drug. I use it all the time; I'm going to talk to the doctor doing the test about using it." Tony was relieved to hear he 'was' going to be sedated, and so, was I. I was anxious about the test, hoping we'd find out why Tony was having the pain? My thoughts were *"God" I pray it's not malignant.* At last, they took Tony in for the test. Anthony and I went for a cigarette to kill some time, and calm our nerves, while we waited for the test to be done. They told us it would take about an hour. We were uneasy as we waited for it to be over. I hoped it was painless for Tony as they promised, and not as bad as he had imagined. I felt just horrible about Tony's suffering, and what he had to go through. It was incredibly hard to watch my loved one go through all that torture, and pain. I hoped against hope, that I had made the right decisions on his behalf.

On the way back, we ran into Mitch a friend of the family, who we saw often because, we were there so much. He worked at the hospital in admitting, and had helped us get Tony a private room many times. He came over to kiss me as he always did, when we say hello. Then proceeded to tell me, he saw the invitation to my party. I looked at him befuddled! T Thinking, *what party?* He knew from the look on my face I didn't know what he was talking about. When he realized what he had just said, as Anthony flashed him a look? As if to say you just blew it, he quickly, changed the story saying, "Oh!" "It wasn't for you, and walked away." He was embarrassed for blowing the whole thing, I'm sure he could have kicked himself for spilling the beans.

My Surprise

After Mitch left I looked at Anthony and said, "What's going on? What have you children got up your sleeves?"

"Nothing!"

"Tony I'm not that stupid. What's going on?" I had told our children earlier that I didn't want a sixtieth birthday party especially with what was going on with their dad.

Anthony finally said, "Okay Ma we're just going to have family over Sunday." I didn't want to make him feel bad. I knew all our children meant well. As we walked back to the CT department, I thought *I'm not happy about the party, but their hearts were in the right place.* We continued to wait for the test to be over. Tony was done shortly after we returned. We asked him how the test went. "It wasn't as bad as I thought it would be." I was thankful; all the praying evidently paid off. He was hungry, and wanted to eat he hadn't eaten since midnight. After he was released, we went straight to a restaurant in town.

A few months back when Tony, and our children, asked about my sixtieth birthday. I expressed that I would like a cocktail ring like one Anthony had gotten in Maui a few years earlier, only on a smaller scale. I just loved his ring.

A couple of days later Tony said, "I want to talk to you." I thought *Ah! Oh! What's he going to say? Is he going to say he didn't want to get chemo anymore or, something to that effect?* Instead he said, "I want to get you the ring myself. I don't want our children to contribute towards it. I want it to be from me, but I want you to get a big diamond like you've always wanted."

"Oh, Hon, that's really sweet of you but I really want a ring like Anthony's. Besides a ring like you're talking about will cost a small fortune."

"I don't care; I'd like to take the money out of my profit sharing. I've never touched that money and that's something I want to do for you it's important to me. Please let me do that for you,"

"We'll see I won't get a ring without you, and you're too sick to go shopping."

I hide my feelings of disappointment. I really wanted the cocktail ring like Anthony's I even suggested to Tony that maybe we could get bigger diamonds in that style setting. Tony insisted he wanted me to get one big diamond. I felt awful about that, I felt, like he felt, he needed to buy me that ring because of all I did for him, like it was payment. Presuming that was the reason, I told Tony, "It's not necessary one bit." That had actually upset me, and did not make me happy at all. What I did for Tony was because, I loved him, and I didn't need to be paid for it! It was an insult to me, if that was the reason.

Under normal circumstances, I would have been ecstatic beyond words, but under those circumstances, it was different—much different.

Nevertheless, as sick as Tony was we did shop around, and he did get me the diamond ring. We went to the jeweler and chose the diamond together, and had it made. Which is absolutely beautiful, and I adore it. It's something I'll treasure for the rest of my life.

After Tony got out of the hospital we went to pick up the ring. When we picked it up I cried it definitely was an emotional time for me. It was a sad moment because, of the situation, I wished, if only it could have been on different terms.

Thinking back *I know he wanted to get me that ring because, it was something he wanted me to have and it had given him pleasure to do that for me.*

Tony still wasn't feeling all that great. I started to notice he got worse the eight to tenth day after chemo. That's when his blood level would drop. It would knock the hell out of him, with each chemo, he got worse!

On Saturday, we had a play to go to. It was touch, and go for a while, I didn't know if we'd get to go or not. Tony had waited until the last minute to get ready. Because, of all the swelling from the steroids his feet were swollen, and he couldn't get his shoes on that matched what he was wearing so he had to change all his clothes. By that time; he had totally used up his energy, was frustrated, and angry but, we went. Reluctantly! We were both frustrated with the whole situation.

When we got to the play we ran into a problem, we had always been seated at a front table being subscribers, and had been since the day it started. Somehow; someone goofed, and because we were late, it couldn't be rectified so, we didn't get our regular front table. Tony was livid, and so was I. We were going to just leave, and attend another night but, our son-in-law Mike was already there, and Tammy was on her way. We decided to stay, still very upset about the mix up but, we made the best of it as we waited for Tammy. A little later she called from her cell to tell us there was a problem with the water tank at the townhouse, we had just rented. She was going to be late, and we should have her dinner put aside. Of course, this upset us even further, but it couldn't be helped. Mario finally got there, late as usual. Tammy called again saying; she'd be even later, the battery in our van had just blown up. I couldn't believe what I was hearing. Her brother Michael was with her though, that was a blessing. He had gone with her, so he could check the water heater for her. He went right away, and bought a new battery. Thank God, she wasn't alone. Tammy finally arrived about one forth of the way through the play, and it ended up being an okay evening after all. However, Tony was freezing and fatigued the whole evening. (Being cold and fatigued are the most complained about side effects of chemo.) His situation got sadder and scarier by the day. I put my arms around him trying to keep him warm. So, he could enjoy the play. Neither of us could wait until we got home.

We were taught at Wellness House to take the situation on a day-by-day basis. I had to keep reminding Tony and myself about that. It was the only way to live with it, if you thought ahead, your mind would run away with you, and that was frightening

When Tony got cancer there were no more future plans; just day to day existing—. Sometimes it was only moment-by-moment. It was really hard to deal with. Our whole world and life stopped—dead in its tracks.

Our family sprung on me, "We're going by Anthony's house for the family get together tomorrow, to celebrate, your sixtieth birthday."

Sixtieth Birthday

S o, on Sunday, after we got up I showered, then helped Tony get showered and dressed. I made him breakfast, then he rested before going by Anthony's. It was a gloomy morning, but warm; but I noticed on our way over to Anthony's that the sun had come out. I pointed it out to Tony saying, "Look the sun came out for you."

"No, the sun came out for you" I didn't understand that comment. As we turned the corner to Anthony's house, and got closer, I noticed a lot of cars parallel parked on both sides of the street. It looked like a parking lot, but Anthony's driveway was empty, not a car on it. I couldn't figure out why all the cars were parked that way. When we pulled into the clear driveway, our son, Michael came out to help me with his dad.

I asked Michael, "What's with all the cars in front of the house."

"The neighbor across the street is having a big party, and they asked Anthony if they could use his front yard to parallel park the cars." Just then, Tammy pulled into the driveway behind us.

I really didn't give it another thought; I was too focused on getting Tony in the house safely. As we proceeded to go inside, the moment I stepped into the foyer, everyone shouted.

"Surprise!" I was totally stunned, actually shocked! There <u>was not just our family</u>, as I expected. There was extended family; cousins, aunts, and most all of our friends. I was flabbergasted; really, truly, totally, SURPRISED!

The further I got into the house, the more flabbergasted I became, the house looked absolutely beautiful with all the decorations. Anthony had done a great job. When I approached the back of the living room; acknowledging everyone and saying hello; as I moved through room to room and reached the dining room. When I looked out the picture window that over looked the back yard, it looked like a wedding or, a party for a movie star. They had a tent with all the tables covered in bright cheery colors, centerpieces, and a balloon arch over their deck. Our children had done a great job that took my breath away. Throughout that day, all I kept saying was, Oh My God, over, and over. I was overwhelmed, I couldn't believe my eyes, I didn't know where to look or who to say hello to first. It had turned out to be the hottest day of the year, most everyone stayed in the house, it was so sweltering. Some of the many guests preferred to eat inside where it was cooler near the air conditioning. Anthony and Paul have a big ranch style house on a half-acre of land; people were everywhere inside and out.

All our children had helped with the party; who got the booze, decorated, helped set up, sent the invitations, the planning was a family effort. Anthony had made all the food; he had been cooking for weeks, and freezing it. From the HorDerves down, to the fruit, and everything in between, Anthony had ready. The HorDerves he made were incredible, and delicious. Not a thing was left out. It was absolutely fabulous. What a joyous day it was with all my loved ones around me. It truly was a day I'll never forget. Ever! Beside the lavish party; our children gave me the most gorgeous diamond bracelet that has seven links with five diamonds in each link one for each of our children. The seven links symbolize my five children, and two granddaughters. In between each link is an X link symbolizing a hug from each of them, it truly is the most beautiful sentimental gift I'd ever received from them. I will treasure it forever. Then of course the 'Outstanding, Beautiful, Diamond, Ring,' my husband Tony bought me. 'It was the Frosting on the Cake'. I announced, "I certainly, feel like a star for a day." I will always have these treasures to remind me of that day and their love. Those gifts mean the world to me, and I'll forever treasure them.

Back to Real World

*T*he next day Monday was back to the real world. Tony needed the CBC test and Neupogen shot. Later that night we had dinner at Anthony's house again. Tony still wasn't feeling well. He was having back pain, and pain in his chest. "The pain goes from the front to the back," he explained. Dr. Bane had put Tony on liquid morphine for pain, with pain pills in between. As the week progressed, I went crazy trying to remember what pain medicine I had given him last and how much of which one. I finally made a written list and carried it with me at all times to keep track. With all his other medicine he took, it was very confusing. I had to be cautious. I was very nervous about the liquid morphine, fearing I would make a mistake and overdosed him accidentally. That scared me to death. The rest of the week went like that; a nightmare, one hell of a week, and the mental anguish was at a peak.

By Friday, Tony was in a lot more pain. We had gone to the cancer center for another CBC and I told the nurse, "He's in a lot of pain."

"I'll call the oncologist that's on call, explaining Dr. Even was still out of town." The oncologist on call told her, "I don't know Tony's case, call his family doctor." Because, Tony was having chest pain, she was afraid to treat him. The nurse called Dr. Bane and she also was out of town. Figured! But the doctor on call for her told the nurse, "Have an EKG (electrocardiogram) and chest X-ray taken to be sure it not his heart." After Tony had the tests done, they found it wasn't his heart, Thank God! The nurse told me, "Increase the pain medicine, if necessary, to keep him comfortable, and call Dr. Bane on Monday."

Pool Heater

On Monday, during that afternoon, I finally found some time to work on getting a pool heater for Tony. After investigating the different kinds, and prices, I found that I got the best deal at the pool store we bought our supplies from. The owner knew us and said, "I'll deliver it today, no charge for delivery." That was a load off of my mind and kind of him to do that for us.

Our son Michael said, "I'll install the heater tomorrow, Saturday it won't be a big deal." Well that was not the truth! It turned out to be a nightmare of a mess, with digging up the yard, to put the gas line in, but there was no turning back once he started. Michael, Joey, and a friend of Michael's worked their tails off to get it all done. I thought it *was a big deal, a mess, and a lot of work.*

Anniversary Dinner

That Saturday, Tony had asked Anthony and Paul out for dinner. They had just celebrated their anniversary. Tony wanted to take them out to celebrate, since they'd had us for dinner practically every night. We'd been at the hospital so often I didn't have time to grocery shop or cook. Being Anthony took that pressure off of me; Tony wanted to treat them, for all they did! We planned to go even though he still wasn't feeling great and suffering with pain in his leg. I didn't think it was a good idea but; Tony kept insisting. He had to walk with a cane because, of the pain.

Anthony and Paul came earlier that night to help me with Tony and the oxygen tank. Then we went together in my car; we were excited to take them to the Greek restaurant that, our friend, Tom managed. Anthony and Paul had never been there before, so the evening was going to be even more, special.

When Tom saw us, he was shocked knowing how sick Tony had been, but was happy to see us. Tom told me, "One of your girlfriends is here with her husband." I couldn't believe it. It was my girlfriend, Joann, and her husband, Angelo, so all of us went over to say hello. She hadn't made it to my party; she had a wedding to go to that day. I hadn't seen her in awhile. We hugged and kissed then continued to our table to sit because, Tony had a hard time standing.

We ordered a drink, appetizers, and then Anthony and I then went to the bar to have a cigarette, while we waited for our drinks to arrive. When we saw the drinks and appetizers arrive we went back to the table. We clanged our glasses toasting their anniversary, shared the appetizers, and exchanged small talk, and then the waiter came to take our order. It was an enjoyable evening. Up to that point! After finishing our appetizers, Anthony and I went back to the bar to have another cigarette. We stopped to chat with our friends. They had finished dinner, and were on dessert and coffee.

It was Joann's night out. She had her hands full too with her husband's father who had dementia. They took care of him every weekend, to help her sister-in-law out, who had him throughout the week. Once a month they had a free weekend, and it was their free weekend. They were having dinner, and staying at a hotel that night as a reprieve.

Ambulance Ride

As we were talking to them, we saw our dinner arrive. We excused ourselves, and went back to our table. We had just about started to eat; we hadn't even taken a bite yet. When Tony said, "Take me to the hospital, I'm in excruciating pain." I had never heard or, seen Tony act that way before. EVER! I immediately gave him the liquid morphine, and tried to calm him.

"I'm having a heart attack."

I tried to console him saying, "You're not having a heart attack. I know what a heart attack looks like, and you're not short of breath, no loss of any color or cold sweats. The pain medicine will work quickly." But Tony insisted he needed to go to the hospital, telling us to call an ambulance. That was extremely unusual for him to *ask* to go to the hospital. He really hated the hospital. As Tony got up, and headed towards the front of the restaurant, he handed me his money and told me to pay the bill. Tony had all of us frightened, and the matr'd called an ambulance.

By the time I paid the bill, the bus boy had the food packed up and ready. By then Tony was at the front of the restaurant standing next to, the matr'd. The matr'd had been giving the ambulance driver directions; and an explanation of what was going on. However; Tony was still very anxious, in excruciating pain, and told the matr'd, "Tell the paramedics to just get here!" We brought Tony to the restaurant entrance to lie on the couch, out there. I could tell the pain medicine was starting to work, as Tony got calmer. By the time the ambulance got there, the pain was gone, and Tony had the oxygen on. We had asked Tony earlier if he wanted the oxygen. He said, "Yes." So, Paul ran to the car to get it, when all the commotion started. People that were leaving the restaurant were giving us their blessings. Which I appreciated tremendously we could use all the blessing we could get. Joann and Angelo consoled me and gave us their best as they left. It was so unlike Tony, totally out of character, we were terrified for him.

When the paramedics arrived, they asked a lot of questions about what happened. I explained, "It's not his heart, its cancer related. I gave him liquid morphine when he got the pain, and that seemed to have helped." The paramedics stabilized Tony so that they could transport him, then we proceeded to the hospital. Anthony and Paul had gone ahead with my car. I went in the ambulance with Tony.

Anthony and Paul arrived at the hospital way ahead of us, by at least thirty minutes they got worried because, we weren't there yet. They wondered what could have happened, and why it was taking us so long. Poor guys! We finally arrived at the hospital and went straight into the emergency room; Tony was totally pain free by then the morphine must have kicked in. All our children were notified about what had happened, and Tammy came running to the hospital.

The emergency room doctor wanted to take an EKG and chest X-ray. I told him, "Tony just had those tests yesterday; the pain is cancer related it's not his heart. Naturally, the doctor had to test his heart just to be sure, but the test came back negative. I told the doctor, "Look at Tony's records on the computer. He just had a CT scan, and it showed something in the T-4, and T-5, vertebra. The pain he's having is in that location."

The doctor went to the computer, and pulled up Tony's file. He looked back and forth, first at Tony, then back at the computer, shaking his head.

I got nervous over his reaction, not knowing what he was thinking or, worse yet saw on the computer.

When he finally came back I told him, "Tony's oncologist couldn't prove he had cancer in his bones. He also had a bone, and bone marrow biopsy, that came back negative, and if I rub the area the pain is in, the pain goes away.

"Is it possible to rub bone cancer pain away?"

"No."

"Tony has been on a muscle relaxer before maybe that will work?" He never really answered me, but he gave Tony a muscle relaxer and a prescription for them. Tony did not want to stay in the hospital that night. It was the weekend and nothing would be done anyway, so we went home.

When we got back home, the boys were still working on the pool heater installation. We reheated our dinners in the microwave. However, by that time we had lost our appetites, and all Tony wanted to do was get in bed. I didn't blame him he'd been through hell once again. Anthony and I brought him up so, he could relax, and hopefully fall asleep.

Sunday we went by Anthony's for dinner again. Tony was still in pain, I tried the muscle relaxers, but they didn't work either, so I went back to the liquid morphine, along with the pain pills. We didn't stay by Anthony very long after dinner, Tony just wanted to get home in bed, he was so uncomfortable, and miserable.

Same Routine

Monday we went back to the hospital for another CBC. Tony was supposed to get chemo that day, but we had decided to wait twenty-eight days, instead of the twenty-one. We wanted to give him one *good week*, but that didn't happen. It was a vicious circle, very nerve racking with him, having the pain, with no explanation. Obviously it wasn't caused by cancer according to the test results. We told the nurse what had happened over the weekend, and the visit to the emergency room. She advised us to call Dr. Bane to let her know. When I called Dr. Bane to tell her, she ordered pain patches for Tony. The patch was a narcotic, so we had to get a written prescription, before it could be filled. Anthony had to go to the doctor's office to pick up the prescription; then go to the drug store to get it filled, and then bring the prescription back to our house so I could apply it. Dr. Bane wanted to see Tony the next day, but the only appointment she had open conflicted with the cancer center appointment for the CBC. Anthony, Tony, and I decided to go to the doctor on Wednesday instead of the cancer center. She insisted he be put in the hospital to see what was actually going on, and to get the pain under control. The patches for the pain hadn't done a thing. "Tony needs a lot more pain medication, and it has to be done under supervision."

Back to Hospital

Tony was put back in the hospital that day. I asked her to please get a private room, and a cot. We went straight to the hospital from her office.

Tony was put in a two-bed room. We were told as soon as a private room opened up probably by that afternoon he'd be moved. Just as we were getting ready to settle in that room, the cleaning lady said, "I just cleaned a private room." By then we knew all the nurses, aids and cleaning ladies, we'd been there so much, so they switched us right away, which worked out much better. Instead of settling in one room only to move again, it worked out to be much easier since we *had* to be there, again!

Tony was immediately given a morphine drip to control the excruciating pain he was experiencing. More tests were scheduled for Wednesday and Thursday. Wednesday he had X-rays of his body, and spine. Then on Thursday, he had a CT scan of his dorsal spine.

On Friday, Dr. Bane sent an orthopedic doctor in to see him. He said, "Tony has osteoporosis of the spine with two-compressed vertebra. That's what is causing the excruciating pain, but I'd also like a CT scan taken."

"Tony just had a CT scan taken yesterday check the computer at the nurse's station."

The doctor went back to check the computer, only to come back saying, "I want a different CT scan." He ordered the scan; it was to be done that day. Continuing with, "I'm sending someone in to measure Tony for a brace."

Tony was still on the morphine drip, and really didn't know where he was. At one point he said, "This room is nice at the Hyatt." I couldn't stand to see him out of his mind like that, it tore me up inside. However, at the same time I was grateful he wasn't suffering. My emotions; were in turmoil, and my stomach in knots. Tony was really out of reality, and in the "ozone." The doctor kept increasing the morphine until Tony was comfortable, and pain free. Here, I had been afraid of over dosing Tony. At the hospital, he was getting twenty times the amount I was giving him at home. They did however have an injection attached to the morphine machine in case of an overdose; so it could be counteracted immediately.

The man to measure Tony for the brace came later that afternoon. He said, "I'll have the brace back by Monday," as he left. I presumed the brace would be elastic, with stiff stays in it, or something of that sort, to support his back.

Later that day a substitute oncologist came to see Tony; Dr. Even was still on vacation. The substitute had a pleasant personality; was down to earth, and we liked her. I debated the fact that Tony ever had bone cancer according to the test results. I was told today, "That it was osteoporosis."

"Even if it is osteoporosis, and not cancer we'd still keep the same procedure with chemo. It really doesn't make a difference one way or the other."

Actual Birthday With Tammy

It was Saturday July 22, 2000 my actual birthday the day before. Tammy had scheduled us to go to a psychic the next day. I had mentioned to her sometime earlier that I'd like to do that, but I had told her earlier in the week we couldn't go. "Let's play it by ear and see."

She said, "Joey will stay with dad so we can go."

"I don't want to leave your dad."

"Dad will be taken care of, and there won't be any tests taken on Saturday anyway."

"If your dad is doing better maybe, we'll go." I didn't want to commit to going anywhere. I was not leaving Tony.

I really had no more interest in going to a psychic then running a marathon. Nevertheless, Tammy called early Saturday morning, and said, "Joey's coming get ready, dad will be okay for a couple of hours."

She told me to make a list of things I wanted to ask the psychic, then get dressed she'd be there about one. We had a two o'clock appointment, and had to drive to St. Charles, IL. I showered and got dressed to go, Joey came while I was still in the shower getting ready. Tammy came soon thereafter, and we left.

After our psychic reading; Tammy took me out for lunch, as she drove, we discussed the readings, and compared notes, about what she had said. I shared a few things the psychic said, "Tony's going to be okay. He's fighting like hell, and he can beat this if he wants to. You're going to have a reason, to celebrate, what I don't know, and you will be traveling, she told me.

After she said all those positive things, I asked her, "If you knew what Tony had, would it make a difference?"

"It doesn't make a difference."

It was fun after all, and I was glad Tammy had insisted on taking me there. Then we went back to the hospital. I needed that break, and it was a *good break,* it did sidetrack me, while we were gone at least.

The weekend at the hospital wasn't very productive, weekends never were. The only thing that was being accomplished was keeping the pain at bay for Tony. That day they tried to wean him off of the morphine, only to have to increase it again because, the pain was still too severe. On Sunday they tried to wean him again. That time they gave him morphine pills so the pain could be maintained when he got home.

On Monday when Dr. Bane came in she said, "I'm going to increase the morphine to stabilize Tony's pain for when he goes home." That didn't make any sense to me at all. Why increase the morphine for home? If the amount of morphine he was taking relieved the pain why more would be needed, once again confused me—.

The Brace

*O*n Monday afternoon the man, that had measured Tony for the brace delivered it. I was appalled, and upset, when I saw it. It was made of heavy plastic, and it looked like a 'Viking Vest.' Only in white with a front, and back instead of silver, held together with Velcro straps on the sides. As he put it on Tony I said, "It's cutting into his legs." It went from high up on his chest, down to his groin. I asked him, "How's Tony going to be able to use the toilet?"

"He'll be able to."

"Not if the circulation is cut off, in his legs," he can hardly even sit let alone go to the bathroom. Then he adjusted the brace by heating it, and bending it to relieve the cutting.

"His port needs to be accessible."

"The brace won't be in the way, it will be okay."

I was so frustrated and scared for Tony. I thought *how the hell is Tony ever going to wear that thing? He could hardly hold his own weight up. How was he going to handle another ten pounds? At least that's what I thought that thing, they called a brace weighed. I thought of it as more like a straight jacket being all bound up; heavy, hot, and uncomfortable. That awful goofy brace! Not knowing how long Tony would have to wear it weeks, months, or forever, had me nuts. That didn't make it any easier. I felt so bad for Tony I just wanted to scream!*

Every time I went for a cigarette, in the smoking shed. I complained about the brace, to my personal support group (some of the medical staff). They had gotten to know me from my being there so often. In fact, at one point, they thought I worked there. They convinced me that the brace worked and did do the job. I felt much better; about that contraption, they called a brace. I expressed my frustration about the bones—its cancer—its osteoporosis; I was so confused, and frustrated by the whole mess. The medical staff said, "The bones are a 'very gray' area to detect cancer in, to be sure exactly as to what's going on is difficult!" Later that evening I asked Tony's nurse, "Is there a machine anywhere that could tell us whether it's cancer or osteoporosis?"

"No, as sophisticated as the machinery is, there's only so much they can tell."

Dr. Bane came in early Tuesday morning as usual, and spotted the brace. Tony wasn't wearing it. "We don't know what to do with it," I stated.

"It works though." She could tell I was frustrated. "The orthopedic doctor will be in later to see Tony."

When the orthopedic doctor finally got there, he said, "How do you like the brace," in an upbeat tone.

I said, practically in tears. "I hate it."

"But it works. Tony only has to wear it six to eight weeks. And he only has to wear it when he's up, and walking around." I was happy about that. The doctor had a sense of humor saying, "It will be Tony's best friend," as he chuckled.

By Tuesday, I had hardly slept with all the anxiety, even though I had the cot. I must have been just beat; and finally dozed off into a light sleep. I could still hear Tony rustling but, I really didn't pay much attention. I thought *he's just stirring in his bed.* Within a few seconds, he had gotten out of bed, next thing I knew he was on top me, on the cot. Thank God, the cot was there God only knows what would have happened to him.

I was livid, asking, "Where are you going."

"To get my breakfast tray!"

"Why didn't you ask me to get it for you?"

"Because, you were finally sleeping and I didn't want to wake you."

"Don't ever do that again, ask for help you could have hurt yourself." I was so angry; not that he fell on me but, because he was so drugged, and weak he couldn't even stand up, I worried about how he was going to be able to do physical therapy, once back home? Moreover, I was frightened about how I was going to take care of him at home, by myself. With all that whirling through my head, I was petrified, and a nervous wreck. That started the morning off, and it progressively got worse. Tony ate some of his breakfast but, his appetite wasn't all that great, and that bothered me. Especially since, he had been a great eater. After breakfast I got him cleaned up; and then put on the brace. He hated the brace, because it was uncomfortable, hot, and stiff, just as I had feared. Thinking *I hope he wears it, without putting up a fight daily.*

Dr. Bane came in earlier on Wednesday morning and said, "Tony maybe you'll be going home tomorrow. I'm going to increase the morphine pills." I really didn't like that idea at all. He could hardly talk, walk, or stand as it was. I was scared because of what was taking place, and what might happen to us once we got home. In addition, he was weak from not being out of bed, on top of being drugged out of his mind.

The therapist came in a little later to work with him. He could barely stand. "I don't know how I'm going to take care of him at home." She informed me Tony could go to rehabilitation. Rehabilitation to me meant a nursing home. Tony and I had promised each other, we'd never put the other in a nursing home, so that was not going to happen. Period! I was beside myself and tremendously frustrated, I had it by that time the whole situation had gotten the best of me.

Its cancer—its osteoporosis—he's drugged out of his mind—the brace—I doubted he even had cancer in the brain? Do the doctors even know what the hell their doing? Was this a joke or a horrible nightmare? Someone pinch me so I could wake up.

Hostile Situation

I said to the therapist, "Absolutely not, I went ballistic saying, "There will be no nursing home or rehabilitation. Tony walked into this hospital, and he's going to walk out of the hospital. I don't care what it takes. How's he supposed to be able to do anything with all these drugs?"

"Would you like to see a social worker or, priest?"

"No." I think she knew I was on the verge of cracking.

When the nurse came in, I told her what had just transpired when the therapist was there. I told her, "I want all the drugs stopped. Take Tony off the morphine, this is ridiculous."

"I'll call the doctor."

In the midst of all the chaos, Tony's friend Greg came to visit. He must have thought I was losing my mind. I was—. I was terrified; frustrated, and crying. As Greg entered, he heard me say, that I wanted all the drugs stopped. With that, I stormed out of the room still crying.

I was so aggravated. I thought the blood vessels in my head would explode. I went right to the nurse's station, and repeated, "Tony walked into this hospital and he's going to walk out of it. I didn't care who I have to talk to, the manager of the floor, or the president of the hospital whatever it takes. I was totally out of control; with fear, anxiety, anger, and all those emotions were wrapped into one. The whole situation just didn't make common sense to me. Expecting Tony to be able to walk; do therapy, with the brace, all screwed up on drugs, was unbelievable. I blew my top!

Afterward I went outside to cool off; get some fresh air, calm down, and have a cigarette. As long as Greg was with Tony, and he wasn't alone, I could relax a few minutes.

In the interim, the nurse called Dr. Bane. When I came back she stated, "Dr. Bane said, 'The morphine <u>won't</u> be increased.'" She's going to send in a pain management doctor, to talk to us, regarding a permanent pain pump, to help manage the pain."

Later that day they sent in a priest to talk to us. "Tony how are you feeling,"

"Okay."

Then he looked my way suggesting, "Why don't you go home for a while; maybe take a bubble bath to relax, and you might want to bring your own bed pillow you'll rest better." He was trying to be comforting, and it did help somewhat. I did take his advice, and took a relaxing bubble bath after he left. I was fortunate this hospital room had a tub in the bathroom; not all rooms had tubs.

I then went down for a cigarette; I needed a break from the whole nightmare, a breath of fresh air, and different scenery.

When I got back, Tony was trying to talk to the pain management doctor. The doctor told me he had just looked at the charts, and needed more information. "I'm not quite clear as to what is expected of me."

I explained, what had been going on with the morphine, and tests. "I don't blame you for being confused about all the tests." He explained that a compressed vertebra was very, painful and that the, pain was caused by the nerves having pressure on them. Once he understood what was going on, he went over different pain management procedures. He talked about an epidermal pump, what it entailed the good and bad about it, and that it would be permanently implanted. First they'd try it manually to be sure it worked for Tony. The downside was that there was a chance of infection, and we'd have to go have the pump filled once a week. It really didn't sound like it was worth all the trouble of maintaining it, along with the risk of infection. Tony certainly didn't need any more problems than he already had.

He suggested that Tony try this pill first. "It's a pill that was used for depression, but we've found that it works on the nervous system." Tony agreed to try it. The pain specialist was great and had spent over an hour with us explaining everything calmly, and thoroughly. I was very grateful and pleased that he spent that time with us.

The orthopedic doctor had also put Tony on a pill to help build his bones. Tony had to take the pill on an empty stomach with a full glass of water every morning. Then he had to sit up for at least a half-hour before eating anything or he'd get very bad indigestion.

The next day between the brace, and the new nerve pill, Tony finally got a good night sleep for the first time in days, and the pain seemed under control, and better too. Thank God!

It was Tuesday and we had been in the hospital a whole week. Since he was scheduled for chemo at the cancer center that day; instead, he had it in his room. I was so grateful, and excited that the brace, and nerve medicine worked for him, I could have jumped for joy. Tony was pain free at last! I was convinced that if the nerve medicine and brace worked for him, there never was cancer in his bones.

With everything working out for Tony, I was elated for once, and couldn't have been happier. With the exception of Tony being extremely weak and he'd also been in bed and off his feet for another week. I worried about all the days he was in bed; that it would take two to come back, like we were told. He had been shot down left and right for months. I don't think I could have felt any sorrier for him, and what he'd been through, it stirred my emotions deep down in my soul.

I was worried about the brace situation though. I feared Tony would never get out of bed if he only had to wear it when he was up moving around. He had spent too much time in bed as it was. Therefore, I had him wear the brace while he was in bed, during the time he was in the hospital. I figured maybe that would encourage him to get up, and move around, and it worked.

That next day, Wednesday Tony took the oral chemo, without a problem. He still didn't have any back pain either— and he was wearing the brace—. The therapist came two times a day to work with him. Tony knew he had to walk before he could go home. Since Tony didn't have pain, Dr. Bane said, "Tony you can go home tomorrow after you finish the chemo." That was a heavenly sound, "HOME."

HOME AGAIN AT LAST

The next day Thursday Tony was to be released, but he wasn't excited to be leaving! He feared the pain would return. That was the first time in Tony's entire life—that he <u>did</u> <u>not</u> want to go home. When Dr. Bane came in she said, "The CT Scan is negative, and it's not malignant." YIPPEE! I was so thrilled to hear that, it was the most exuberant news we had had in a long, long time. When I ran into our doctor in the hall she told me, "I wouldn't be surprised if Tony has pain when he gets home."

"Why?"

"Because the hospital has become an umbilical cord to him," sure enough, he did have pain that night after we got home, just as she stated.

Entering the Pool

I was told to get Tony in the pool to exercise, and keep him moving. That was a difficult and frightening task. I knew if he fell he could be injured badly because of the osteoporosis in his bones, but I tackled it anyway, and I succeeded by pushing him up the ladder under his butt. Even with the heater, and the water being warm, Tony still made excuses not to go in. He was still extremely weak; and on all that pain medicine. I thought if I got him off that stuff he would be more alert and have more strength, how could he be strong, with all that medication making him unstable

On Wednesday, August 2, 2000, we had to go to the cancer center for the CBC, and to see the Dr. Even; she had returned from her vacation. I told her, "Tony hasn't had any back pain, and I'd like to cut the morphine down." At that time, Tony took sixty mg two times a day. She gave me a prescription for fifteen-mg pills, and told me, "Cut down to forty-five mg at night instead of sixty. Then give him three, fifteen mg pills at night, if he does all right with that, cut them down in the morning every other day, and cut the dose down a little at a time. I then told her, "He got weaker with the last chemo."

"I'm not so sure it's the chemo." I knew what she meant, but I did 'not' want to hear it.

"I don't know if Tony can handle another chemo treatment—but I don't think I can!"

Everything seemed to be going good except for the weakness. He could hardly do anything; he was thoroughly wiped out.

On Thursday we went to the hospital for the Neupogen shot, his blood had dropped, again. The fatigue was relentless, and ongoing, no matter how much rest he got, it didn't matter. He had a terrible time getting around; I didn't know what was causing, it the brace or what?

Friday he got his other Neupogen shot, the last of three. The following Monday he needed another CBC. His blood was still low, so he needed another series of three Neupogen shots. Then on Thursday, Tony got Neupogen and Epoetin. All we did was run back and forth to the hospital constantly.

That particular Thursday we also had an appointment to see Dr. Bane. She was pleased with Tony's results. His heart was super, and his lungs sounded great. "We're also going to be seeing the orthopedic doctor today.

"Tony's doing wonderfully. He's going to make it. Typically six treatments of chemo, maximum ten are needed to make sure we got every last cell. You have literally kept Tony alive by taking such good care of him, with all the love and help; it helped him fight this awful, horrible, devastating, disease." I was so excited I could have kissed anyone and everyone. I was so happy; I was flying high on the clouds. Hallelujah! It had been a long haul, but we finally at last—received some phenomenal news— we could sure use it. She continued, "After five years you're considered cured." I was on a high, my emotions overflowed.

I immediately called everyone to tell them the good news. Our children were all elated and excited. Everyone was thrilled, to hear the good news, even though we didn't exactly know what, 'he's going to make it,' meant. One year—Two years—but I didn't care. Just hearing those words 'he's going to make it' was music to my ears. Even with Tony being weak and having a hard time walking, we could deal with that, it was no problem.

Directly after the appointment with the doctor, we had an appointment with the exercise director at Wellness House. We were going to find out what could be done to help strengthen Tony. The exercise director was very knowledgeable, and tactful. He explained, "The exercise we do here is aggressive and would be too hard for Tony at this time. We want people to be successful in what they do and not feel defeated. Tony's not quite ready for excessive exercises yet. What he needs is therapy until he gets to that stage. I'll have a trainer set up an appointment to see you." He also mentioned a machine they were getting to help build the muscles around the lungs for lung, cancer patients. It was a machine that athlete's used to strengthen their lungs. When the machines came in, he'd have someone call us.

"The doctor mentioned getting a personal trainer for Tony." He warned us, that we should make sure they were certified. Some places had people that really don't have credentials to be doing that type of training, check the kind of credentials they have beforehand.

When we went to see the orthopedic doctor, he said, "I'm going to order home therapy for Tony to help strengthen him." I thought that idea was awesome and I was thrilled. I thought *good things are finally happening*. Tony's going to make it, and now he's going to get built-up and, strengthened too. I thought Great! Super! "The therapist can start weaning Tony off the brace in three weeks."

"Tony's been pain free since the brace was added." I told you the brace would be your best friend. Make another appointment for six weeks from now." The doctor gave us the order for the therapist to build him up. Tony was weak from being off his feet for so long. We left there tremendously excited about the therapist. That would take the place of a personal trainer; in addition, the therapist would be educated in that field. Like the exercise director at Wellness House told us; to get so Tony would be doing the exercises that pertained to his situation. He would now be able to strengthen himself in the comfort of his home with no running around that was great for both of us. Tony was finally going to get the help he needed, and it all pretty much fell in our laps, and came together! Another Miracle!

We had an appointment for the Epoetin shot on Friday. He now needed one every Friday since he started them.

He was scheduled for another chemo treatment the following Tuesday. I dreaded seeing Tony go through the chemo, getting weaker, and all that went with it. We had thought about, and discussed waiting the twenty-eight days for treatment that time, because he hadn't bounced back from the last chemo. He was still extremely weak, but Tony was afraid to wait. I could see how weak he was but, I was also afraid to convince him to wait for fear that something might backfire. Then I would feel guilty for postponing his treatment, so against my better judgment I went along with Tony's decision. After all, it was his body, life, and ultimately his decision, not mine, so we proceeded with chemo on Tuesday.

Tony instantly got diarrhea after the chemo before we even left, which made him even weaker. I immediately gave him anti-diarrhea medicine to help control it right away. It was very hard for Tony to get to the bathroom with that brace, and to get his pants down, he had limited mobility because of the stiffness of the brace. It was quite a fiasco for him, to go to the bathroom. With all that going on, he still wanted to go out to eat, before we went to Wellness House for our Connections meeting. He wanted to go to a restaurant in Oakbrook, but I said, "We won't have enough time. It will be super busy at dinnertime and we'll never make it the meeting." The nurses in the cancer center told me to call and make reservations to be sure, we could get in right away, which I did. We rushed out of the hospital so we could get to the restaurant in time.

It was very difficult, and impossible to move fast with Tony because of him being so weak, it took us forever. By the time we got to the car, we both knew we'd never make it. We decided to just have dinner at a little Italian restaurant right around the corner. It turned out to be a good thing that we didn't go to Oakbrook, because in our rush the nurse forgot to give us Tony's two days of oral chemo pills, so we had to go back to the hospital. I called the cancer center from my cell phone. I told the nurse, "You forgot to give us the oral chemo; we'll come back after we eat to pick them up." Fortunately we were still in town, because we didn't think we'd have enough time to go to the other restaurant."

After dinner, I agreed to call the hospital when we got there. The nurse said, "I'll run the pills up to you, " that sounded good to me as the whole bathroom episode, and rushing had Tony and I fatigued, especially after we ate, and we still had the Connection meeting to go to.

On our way back to the hospital Tony said, "I have to go to the bathroom again. " That meant I had to take him into the hospital. I quickly parked the car and ran to find a wheelchair, and took Tony down to the cancer center where the bathrooms were big enough to fit a wheelchair. I finally got him down and on the toilet. Time was ticking away and at that point, we were trying not to be late, by then I was stressed to the max. I ran to the cancer center to get the pills, while Tony was in the toilet. "I would have brought them out to you,"

"Tony had to go to the bathroom so I just ran in to get them." I ran back to get Tony off the toilet so we could get on our way to the Meeting.

As we entered Wellness House we ran into the exercise director, and he helped me get Tony into the meeting. He was so weak. I was having a horrible time, and very grateful for the extra help. We shouldn't have gone there. We got to the meeting a few minutes late by the time I parked the car, got the walker out, and walked Tony in, but it was okay they did not mind.

Lately Tony had been cold and freezing so, I made sure we always had a jacket, and blanket for him. "I'm cold." I just ran to the car and got his jacket. The meeting was very informational and helpful but Tony really wasn't well that night. He was just wiped out, from the chemo, plus all the hustling.

After we were there a few minutes Tony said, "I have to go to the bathroom again." I knew I had to be quick because, of the diarrhea. I tried to rush him, poor thing couldn't help passing gas on the way out. I freaked. I was afraid he wasn't going to make it to the bathroom. We did though. Whew! I had to go into the bathroom with him; to help because; he could not wipe himself with the brace, which wasn't a big deal for me; I'd been doing that for him since he got the brace. None-the-less it was humiliating for him.

When he finished, we went back to the meeting, but the group was in a relaxing session, so the door was closed, we had to wait until it ended. By that time Tony had, had it! He was completely wiped out, and fatigued. "Let's go." That was a direct order. When he talked with that tone, I knew he meant business.

We excused ourselves, and left. On our way home, it hit me. I realized I was wiped out, and relieved to be on our way home too. We called Anthony to meet us at the house, so he could help his dad in, and upstairs to bed. The boys had been taking turns helping Tony upstairs for some time now but, it was mostly Anthony that helped. He was the biggest of the boys and Tony felt safe with him. I felt awful that we had to depend on them all the time; they were afraid I'd hurt my back again, Tony would fall or, worse yet, we'd both fall. Then we would really have big problems; I understand their concern, being afraid myself. Anthony said, "I really don't mind," but I knew what an inconvenience it was. Thank God, he lived close by, and was able to help. Fortunately, for us, Anthony had moved about five minutes away a couple of years earlier. Actually, all our children lived close, and we were grateful for that.

That night Tony said, "I feel nauseated." That was something he hadn't experienced. I was taken back by the instant diarrhea and now the nausea. That hadn't happened to that extent before, and I was frightened. Thank God, I had the medicine, and it worked like a charm, but somehow that Chemo was different. It wiped him out instantly, where before, it wasn't too bad until eight to ten days later, but never that bad. I thought *maybe it's a build-up of all the Chemo treatments he already had?*

Twins Birthday

That Saturday Tammy was celebrating the twin's birthday. It was to be a small family party, but she had invited more than I had expected. She invited my sister-in-law Aida, her husband, my mother-in-law, her friend, and caretaker.

Tony was weak and not feeling well at all that day. Of our children house's; Tammy's was the worst to get Tony into because, it was a raised ranch. There were nine stairs up to the front door, and then another seven, into the house. It was very difficult for Tony to go there. We brought him in through the garage and let him rest in the lower-level recreation room for a while. That rest helped; it was easier for him than going up all sixteen stairs at once.

We went there early so I could help Tammy prepare. Tammy had a sleep-over for the twins with some of their friends the night before, so she needed some help organizing.

After Tony rested awhile, we brought him up to the den area off the kitchen for a while, so he could watch us preparing. Then he wanted to go lie down in Tammy's bed, until everyone arrived, and we were ready to eat.

When we were ready to eat, we got Tony to the table. He was so weak though; my heart just ached to see him like that. It tore me apart inch by inch little by little. I couldn't even fathom how he felt, or what he was going through, along with everyone feeling sorry for us, and what were going through. I didn't like people feeling sorry for us, and I didn't like talking about the situation either. There was really nothing to say, and no benefit in talking about how awful it was, except to make matters worse.

I was very upset with myself, and concerned that we'd made an awful mistake, by not waiting until Tony was feeling a little better before we shot him down again, with Chemo. I was feeling guilty for not insisting to wait because, I should have known better, but the damage was done. Tony got even weaker than he had ever been in the past and I was terrified. What was going to happen to him? I certainly hadn't done him any favors. I really felt that particular Chemo treatment almost— killed him. Literally!

Therapist

I kept wondering when the therapist, was going to call. Finally, the following Friday I got a call from the home health nurse. She said, "I have to come out first to see Tony and get information, I'll be there about eleven thirty."

Then the therapist called, "I'll be there about twelve thirty."

"We have to be at the hospital at two o'clock for a CBC test, and Tony's weekly Epoetin shot."

"We'll have enough time."

The nurse came to take the information she needed, then the therapist. The therapist introduced herself as Lita. She was just as sweet, and cheerful as she could be, as she did a few exercises with Tony. I immediately took a liking to her. She explained, "Tony will be getting therapy every Monday, Wednesday, and Friday for the next six weeks, and that it could be extended if necessary. Tony also took a liking to her and also worked well with her. She had that special something, not everyone has, that work with the ill.

The previous night Tony had peed on the carpet accidentally, he couldn't get out of the recliner fast enough, by himself. The brace was too cumbersome, plus he didn't have the strength to push himself out of the recliner. I got angry at him because, I had just asked him if he had to go to the toilet before he sat down. But, he didn't want to get back out of the recliner. I had run upstairs to take a quick shower, and wasn't there to help him. In reality I was probably madder at myself for leaving him, and wasn't there to help him when he needed me. When I came down he was all wet, ashamed and apologetic, which made me feel even worse

On Wednesday, we went to see Dr. Even again. Tammy went with us that day I told Dr. Even, "Tony had a difficult time with the last chemo, and I felt it almost killed him. I don't know if he can take another chemo treatment, but I don't think I can! Tammy and I felt his weakness was due to the last chemo treatment it had totally wiped him out." I also explained the accident Tony had.

"I'm not so sure it's the chemo, and not the disease." That quote upset me, horror ran through my body down to my toes, and made me shiver! That wasn't something I wanted to hear. I questioned her about the bones again.

"The next set of tests, should tell the tale, about the unanswered questions, whether it's osteoporosis or cancer."

"Tony's also pain free, and off all the morphine.

"I love it." She recommended keeping a urinal next to Tony in a pretty tote bag so no one could see it, and he wouldn't be embarrassed about it. I reminded her that the last chemo was his seventh chemo treatment. She suggested a hospital bed for our home, because Tony was having such a terrible time walking even with using the walker. Tony wouldn't hear of that at all.

"Our sons help Tony up the stairs, and that seems to be working."

"We'll test him again in about two, two and a half weeks from his last Chemo. We need to wait until then to get the best results. Because Tony's blood had to be at a certain level before we can do them." Tony also needed a CBC, and a Neupogen shot again that day

Anthony couldn't be there with us that day; because he was working on a movie and couldn't get away. That upset him because he liked to hear what the doctors had to say for himself with his own ears.

That day was also Tammy's and the twin's actual birthday, August 23, we decided that after the doctor appointment we'd all go out for dinner to celebrate. Tony barely made it into the restaurant, and to the table, with the walker he was so fatigued. I felt so badly for him, and what he was going through. I would have given anything if I could have taken some of his pain and suffering away. We had a decent time however eating, and being with each other. Tony got restless though, when he was finished. He wanted to leave immediately he couldn't sit another minute, so we hurriedly left the restaurant.

We were going to look for a new contour recliner for Tony after we ate but, that was out of the question. I had tried to accomplish that task many times, but hadn't succeeded yet. Tony didn't want to go look, he just wanted to get home in his bed, and so we went straight home. Six months had passed, since we started with the whole nightmare. Where had the time gone?

The next day Tony had to go to the hospital for another Neupogen shot, it was the second of the three. After that, we had an appointment at Wellness House to pick up the breathing machine, to help build Tony's lungs. I had a hell of a time getting him in the building; he was so weak we barely made it. I was concerned about how I was going to get him back to the car; we'd had such a hard time. He most definitely was in worse condition than he'd ever been. The volunteer explained how to use the breathing machine, clean it, and gave us a chart to record Tony's progress. I was exceptionally excited about the machine, anything that we could use or do, to help with his recuperation, I was thankful for it. Tony however, could have cared less! I had a terrible time getting him back to the car, just as I had suspected. What little strength he had was used up. It took every ounce of energy he had, to accomplish all that running around. We went straight home, when we were through, Tony was absolutely positively spent. It was; and had been for quite sometime, more difficult, to get around with Tony! I was always scared to death Tony might lose his balance fall—and I wouldn't be able to prevent it.

That next day Tony had an appointment with Lita. He was so good about doing what she asked of him, and expected him to do. He actually shocked me, as to how he would exercise with the therapist, and work hard at it. I couldn't get him to do any exercises at all— and that frustrated me. I knew the more he exercised, he'd get stronger quicker, and he'd feel better about himself. But, he did exercise with Lita at least it was something, that was better than nothing.

Then it was back to the hospital on Friday for the Epoetin, and Neupogen shots.

Saturday we had to go to the hospital again; he needed another CBC to check his blood levels. OMG! His levels were low once again; he'd need another round of Neupogen shots. The nurse told us, "You'll have to come back on Sunday and Monday to finish the series. Tony's blood is seriously low.

On Sunday we were suppose to go to Mario's house for dinner. Our children were taking turns having us for dinner weekly so our whole family would be together every weekend. That weekend Tony was so sick, and weak we ended up not going. That was the first dinner we had to cancel. It broke my heart in a million pieces, not being able to do a thing to make things better for Tony, except be there for him, love him, and comfort him as much as possible, and do as much as I could.

On Monday, Tony had therapy again. Cheerful Lita would be coming. He was really doing well with her, and getting a tiny bit stronger. I asked Lita, "Will he ever get stronger." She assured me that he would in time; Tony just had to keep it up. She also suggested that we put a railing on the wall going to the upstairs. "It will help Tony immensely to help pull him self up the stairs. He'll gain more strength by doing that, by using his own muscles. Do you have anyone to do that for you?"

"I'll call the boys, it won't be a problem at all

After they were finished with Tony's therapy, we also had to go to the cancer center for the last Neupogen shot. The nurse said, "Tony also needs a blood test for a platelet count." We found that Tony's platelets were so low, that was why he was getting black and blue spots all over his arms and hands. The skin, over the marks, was so thin, it was like tissue paper; the spots would break-through, and bleed at the slightest bump. It looked like he had some kind of awful creepy skin disease.

"The blood gets so thin when the platelets are low you have to be very cautious about the bleeding," the nurse warned.

On Thursday, Tony needed another CBC to find out where his blood and platelet levels were, and if they came up. I asked the nurse, "If Tony's platelets are okay, can we schedule him for the CT scans?"

"I'll have to call Dr. Even."

After she called, she said, Dr. Even said, "Yes." The tests were scheduled at the hospital at nine in the morning for that Saturday.

The next morning when I got up, I bathed Tony, got him breakfast and went back upstairs to get myself ready. Michael had come early that morning to cut the grass for us. As I was coming down the stairs, I saw Tony going out the door. I started hollering; I didn't know Michael was with him. Michael thought I was hollering at him. He didn't know, that the day before his dad had gone outside by him self, and could have fallen and gotten hurt. Poor Michael, he thought he was doing a good thing by taking him outside for a while. I became frantic with worry when all I saw was Tony, going out the door; I thought he was pulling a fast one. I thought I had told him the day before, to never take a chance of going outside alone. It was too dangerous to do that by himself, with the possibly of falling.

More Tests

On Saturday, the CT scan was to be taken and Tammy came to help me with her dad, since Tony was so weak, and Anthony wasn't available. I had to have help I couldn't handle him by myself anymore. Tony actually seemed to be a little stronger that day, his blood levels were coming up, and that seemed to make a difference.

Tony was a nervous wreck about the test, wondering what they were going to do to him that time. What type of CT scan were they going to take? Tammy and I explained, "There isn't going to be any pain involved at all." We had to go to the hospital early, so the nurse in the cancer center could access his port first, other nurses didn't have that training. After she accessed his port, she gave him the barium to drink, which he absolutely hated. The nurse saw that Tony was a wreck over the tests.

"You're only going to get pictures taken, no biopsies, don't worry."

The nurse in the CT scan department wanted to give Tony an enema, but that's where he put his foot down. Noooooooooo enema! When the tests were over, he was relieved. At last, that ordeal was over, and Tony wanted to eat. He had to fast; and hadn't eaten a thing since midnight. Tony asking to eat was music to my ears. Just hearing him say he was hungry thrilled me. I knew a good appetite was very important for him to get strong.

Tony was ecstatically happy once the tests were over, and he could finally eat!

He decided he wanted to go to; another favorite restaurants in town. It was close by, convenient, and the food was good, so off we went. The handicapped parking was taken so we had to park a few spaces farther away, but we made it. With the weather being so humid, Tony had a hard time breathing When we got there Tony decided he wanted to walk-in without the walker—that was very scary to me; with him not being real steady on his feet. Tammy and I each took his arm one on each side, and helped him walk in <u>without</u> a walker, or cane. We had really lived dangerously taking that chance. Tony plopped down on the chair just as soon as we got to the table though. Even though it was a very hot and humid day, Tony was always freezing, so I still kept a jacket and blanket for him in the car. His appetite was okay but not the way it usually was. He was generally a good eater; he lived to eat, <u>did</u> <u>not</u> eat to live, but the last chemo had affected his appetite tremendously; it hadn't up to that point! He did however, eat well that day in spite of it. We ended up having a nice lunch, as all the pent-up stress was behind us.

Movie Dilemma

I mentioned, "Maybe we could go to the show with Mario later on this evening?" "I'd like to go." I called Mario when we got back to the car from my cell, to find out if Mario was still interested in going with us? "Yes." Mario was as excited, to go to the show as we were. I needed someone to go with us, I was still afraid to handle Tony alone. I was so very excited about going to the show, we were finally going to do something not cancer related like normal people did. It was going to be a treat for both of us. I thought!

After we got home, we discussed what movies were playing, where, and at what show. I asked Tony, "What do you want to see." He made his decision. The movie he wanted to see was playing at a show close by. The plans were all set; we'd need to leave by six in order to get there on time. Everything was in order; Mario would be here by then, and we'd leave.

In the meantime, Michael stopped over to visit. That was something our children did now and then, to spend time with their dad. I thought it was great that they took the time to do that. I told Michael excitedly, "We're going to the show tonight." He thought that was a great idea too.

Tony said, "We'll take the wheelchair." However, I was determined to get Tony back on his feet, not wheelchair bound.

"No, I'll drop you off at the door with Mario, then I'll go park. You really don't need the wheelchair, it's more work than it's worth." Using that as an excuse for him NOT to rely on it!

"Then I'm not going"

"Yes, you are, you'll be alright you can do it. It'll be okay, hon." Nothing more was, said. Michael and Tony continued talking until Mario got there.

When it came time to leave, Tony said, "I'm not going, you can go with Mario!"

Angrily I said, "That wasn't the plan, why aren't you going all of a sudden?"

"I want to go to bed." I totally lost it. I went ballistic at that point!

"You had no problem going to the restaurant; because that was something you wanted to do. But now that I want to go to the show, it's different."

We had rented a wheelchair for the next day so Tony could go to the Italian Feast in his hometown. The feast was something he had always gone to every year. As a matter of fact, the house he grew up in was across the street from the church, it was directly in the middle of the feast. He liked going there every year to see all the people he hadn't seen through the year, it was a part of his heritage. I didn't feel the same. I didn't like the crowds, so Anthony was going to take his dad. Being there was no way Tony could walk around hence, the reason we rented the wheelchair.

That comment he made, hurt me. It made me feel horrible; deserted, betrayed, let down and like shit that Tony didn't want to go to the show, with me—. I felt Tony really didn't want to go, so he wasn't going, it didn't matter, what I wanted. My feelings didn't count, and I was more than upset and hurt!

I felt like he should have given a little, and gone out of his way for me once in awhile at least. The same way I went out of my way to do everything I possibly could do for him. I told Tony, "Maybe that's why you're going through what you're going through, to learn to do things for other people sometime." That was something he wasn't used to doing; unless it was convenient for him and something he wanted to do. He could be very self-centered at times. I didn't want to go to the show with Mario; I wanted to be with my husband in a normal setting for a change. I told him, "If I wanted to get out, and away I could have done it many times. I want to do normal things with you." Things got heated; blown out of proportion, and one thing led to another.

I was sobbing uncontrollably by then; I was so crushed and hurt over his not wanting to go to the show with me, I took it personally. I felt like he knew how excited I was about going to the show; he must have wanted to hurt me. It wasn't even the movie that wasn't the issue, the movie wasn't one I was interested in seeing. It was the fact that it was something fun, different, and an escape from the cancer scene. Period! An escape! I was so beside myself; hurt, angry, I even went as far as to tell Tony he could take the diamond ring, and he knew where he could stick it. I went on to say, "Material things don't mean a damn thing to me. I'd appreciate you thinking of my personal feelings more often. I'm living a life too," I continued to rattled on, and on out of control, saying all kinds of stupid, childish things.

Mario finally said, "We're going for a ride so you could calm down."

I told Michael, "Stay with your dad." Michael was upset with me for talking to his dad like that and got involved when he shouldn't have. "Don't worry about my dad he has enough money to be more than taken care of!"

With all the stupid things said, Mario and I took off. He wanted to get me out of the house; and away from the situation. My pent up emotions were erupting like a volcano—.

Mario said, "I still want to go to the show." I on the other hand didn't give a shit where I went. In reality, I didn't know where I wanted to go or what I wanted to do. I was so miserable and hurt, I felt like I just wanted to die. The movie we were going to see had already started. I didn't want to see that movie. I told Mario, "It's a movie your dad wanted to see."

I drove around aimlessly; I was so frustrated, angry, and sad. We drove past another show but, we didn't like what was playing there either. Then we drove back to our neighborhood. We went past our local theatre but, by then the movie I wanted to see had already started too.

After the driving fiasco, and not knowing where to go, we decided to just go to Denny's for coffee. I asked the waitress, "What kind of pie do you have "I had a taste for hot apple pie with ice cream. They didn't have any apple pie. Figured! I got even more frustrated and agitated. "Let's go." I felt like a bomb with a short fuse about to blow, so we left.

Mario decided we should just go to the local video store; rent a couple of movies, and go back home.

While Mario and I were gone, Michael had his girlfriend Lisa, come over. When we got home Michael and Lisa hung around for a while. Tony had gone to bed like he wanted.

Michael asked, "What can I do for you?"

"Nobody can give me what I want because, want I want is my husband well again, and my old life back." I think what had happened was I had a minor breakdown from all the emotions I'd had pent up inside for so long. By then, I was sobbing uncontrollably again. None of that whole turmoil really had anything to do with going to the show. Michael, and Lisa stayed until I calmed down, then they left.

After Michael and Lisa left; Mario and I proceeded to watch the movie, he had rented. I fell asleep as soon as the movie started. I was as beat up as one could get, along with being exhausted, and depressed. Mario started to watch the movie, and fell asleep too. We both slept on the couch that night, Mario on one side of the living room on the loveseat, and I on the other side, on the couch.

The next morning Anthony came over, and talked to his dad. The night before all our children had talked and came over, which I didn't know a thing about. They all knew what had happened. Anthony said, "Dad wants to go out for breakfast."

Reconciling Breakfast

I had called Tammy that morning, and told her about the fiasco the night before. Not knowing she already knew. Tammy said, "I want to take you out for the day." I wasn't in any mood to go out shopping or, to do anything else for that matter.

"I'll let you know."

I decided I'd go out to breakfast with Anthony and Tony. Unbeknownst to me our children had talked; and decided to join us at the restaurant, after breakfast Anthony was going to take his dad to the Italian Feast for the day as planned—with the wheelchair!

Driving to the restaurant I explained, "I took it personally when you didn't want to go to the show."

"I felt too weak, I needed the wheelchair."

"Instead, of standing up to me, saying, "We take the wheelchair or I don't go, because, I'm weak," I would have understood that better rather than simply saying, "I'm going to bed."

I interpreted that as, he just didn't want to go, even if it made me happy, and I felt hurt. I felt he couldn't even do that for me, when I did anything and everything for him. The whole situation had gotten totally out of proportion. We both had learned at Wellness House, to be explicit, not implicit which was exactly what had happened The misunderstanding could have been totally avoided, had we each been explicit, not implicit. I explained, "I could have gone to the show many times, if I really wanted to go without you." The whole idea was I didn't want to do anything without you. I only wanted to do things with you that weren't cancer related, something normal for a change. The problem was discussed and we completely understood one another, after the discussion we immediately dismissed it. Tony then said, "I'm happy you're not angry with me any longer." The whole wheelchair thing amounted to, I didn't want Tony to become dependant on a wheelchair when I was trying to help him get well and become strong, and independent.

When we got to the restaurant, our children started to arrive one at a time. We ordered and took our time eating. I told Anthony, "Take my car to the Italian feast from the restaurant. It'll be easier because the wheelchair is already in the trunk. I'll go with Mario in his car, and do something to keep busy until you come-back from the feast." We were all going by Anthony for dinner, later that evening.

After breakfast, we went our separate ways. Mario and I went to a couple of stores. My mind really wasn't on shopping we just looked around. Then we went back to our house for a short swim before going to Anthony's for dinner.

Although I hardly left Tony's side, and never wanted to, I couldn't have done it all if it were not for our children, plus with all their help including my son-in-laws Mike, and Paul. Plus of course all our friends; family, calling us, taking us out to dinner, and hospital visits. It meant a lot and was greatly appreciated by Tony and me.

Our children took turns every Sunday having dinner for our whole family. The boys took turns cutting the lawn, trimming shrubs, planting flowers, and vegetables for Tony so, he could watch them grow. That was something Tony loved to do. Our children thought if they kept everything up he wouldn't get upset, and he could still enjoy seeing the growth of the flowers and vegetables, which he did.

Our children, had all been at our fingertips, if I needed them to go to the hospital, help with showers, shop, anything at all, they were there. Every single night one of the boys would come over to help their dad upstairs so he could sleep in his own bed. They repaired things; put up the railings, so it was safer and easier for their dad. Anything and everything, needed they were right there. I could go on, and on about them and how fortunate we were to have such loving children every one of them. I applaud each of them we were blessed—.

The following Wednesday, Tony had an appointment with Dr. Even. That day was to be D-day—. We were to get the results from the CT scans; I was holding my breath regarding the results.

I also had an appointment that day with the surgeon for the lump in my breast. I had put it off for months. I was much to busy with Tony to go, until Dr. Bane called me to ask if I'd ever gone to see the surgeon. "No."

The nurse told me, "You need to take care of yourself, so you'll be healthy to take care of Tony." That prompted me to make the appointment with the surgeon.

Unheard of Remission

*A*nthony and Tammy had gone with us to see Dr. Even that day. I needed help getting Tony there, plus our children wanted to hear what the results were themselves. Dr. Even pretty much said, "I feel Tony had cancer of bones, and the chemo treatments stopped it." I felt differently, but it may have been wishful, thinking. The whole bone cancer situation was a strange turn of events.

Dr. Even went on to say, "Tony needs to decide what he wants to do. The chemo made you weak, but you had a lot of disease as well. The lungs look better, lymph notes look better, kidney, liver, pancreas all look good. But he had extensive small cell cancer. The lumps went away but will not stay away, it will regrow. However, the lungs are better." She presumed with all her knowledge, that Tony did have bone cancer. She continued to tell us, "This cancer isn't curable. We could stand back, and do nothing, but we could not expect the cancer to be controlled. It will come-back sooner rather than later, with, or without treatment. Tony could choose to be kept comfortable with hospice, which is what would be next if we chose no treatment. The cancer was better, she couldn't say cured, or that it would stay away. Tony would get morphine for pain, and be kept comfortable. This type of cancer has median survival. Tony has responded to treatment. Radiation isn't in order, because he isn't having pain, and the lumps in his lungs are gone."

Then continued with, "Take a week to decide what you want to do."

Then suggested, "Maybe monthly chemo, to see if we could keep the cancer at bay, long-term survival is rare. All total, he's much better than he was in March when we started. The cancer is gone, and right now I couldn't prove he has cancer." He was in remission, and it wasn't common for anyone who had that type of cancer to go into remission, and live that long. Another Miracle! Thank God.

"I don't know when or, where the cancer will come-back. I don't have a crystal ball."

Anthony and I were ecstatic about that information, focusing 'only' on the positive. "Tony Was In Remission And Cancer Free." That was all I heard—. Words I'd been waiting to hear for months—had finally been said. I couldn't have been happier than I was at that moment—Tony and Tammy focused on the negative. There was no cure—no—long-term survival—and hospice—was what they focused on. Tammy was down; and Tony was crying. That really upset me because; I had to leave Tony with Anthony. Tammy and I had to go to the surgeon for my breast. Not a good time to be taking care of myself, but I already had made the appointment. The doctor waited after hours for me, because of my situation with Tony, she had made an exception for me. Anthony was taking his dad home while Tammy and I went to see the surgeon, above all times to have to leave Tony, that wasn't the time.

When we got in the car, I jumped all over Tammy about her negative attitude. I explained, "We just got good news, go with it don't focus on what could happen. Take one day at a time, like I am, I need to do that to go on. That's what has kept me going all those months."

She commented, "I'm worried about you hoping for too much. You're not being realistic, and you're going to fall apart when dad starts to fail."

"I'm going to fall apart when dad gets worse, and expires, and you aren't going to be able to protect me from that. I don't believe you're ever ready to accept that, and I have to live one day at a time. It's the only way for me to cope." I truly believed that Tony would rally, like he had so many other times, and that he was going to make it in medical books. Wishful thinking, along with a positive attitude kept me going.

My Surgery

We finally got to the surgeons office and they were waiting for us. The doctor knew my circumstances. She had put Tony's port in. As she checked my breast, she said, "The lump has to come out. I don't think it's anything awful at this point but it should come out before it turns into a problem." We scheduled the surgery for the following Monday to get it done as fast as possible, while Tony was in remission. He wouldn't be going to the cancer center daily so; right at that time was perfect. Another Miracle!

"What could happen if I wait?"

"You'll only be asking for problems."

"The lump already shrunk."

"If the lump hasn't gone away totally, in three months, most likely it won't. Don't fool around, and just get it removed."

I had already called my cousin Joe in Oregon to ask him his opinion about the surgery before going to the surgeon, and he agreed it should be done, not to fool around.

The next step was to get pre-op tests before Monday. The surgeon called Dr. Bane while I waited, to have the tests done there but, Dr. Bane was going out of town. I was going to have to go to the hospital for the pre-op tests. The surgery was going to be done as day surgery, in the medical building the surgeon was in. She convinced me, that it would be better, more intimate, I'd get better care, and I'd be in and out faster without all the red tape, so I agreed.

I wasn't really worried about myself. What I was worried about was how I was going to handle Tony; taking care of him while sore, and recuperating Since I had to lift Tony up from the recliner every time he had to go to the bathroom; kitchen or out, wherever, I feared I wouldn't be able to do it.

After the doctor visit, Tammy, and I went to get something to eat. We talked about her dad, and the up-coming surgery. I was in a whirlwind by then, everything happened so fast. I called home while we waited for our food to come on my cell. "Dad's in bed." I was livid hearing that. I assumed Tony was depressed, and focusing on the negative, and I wasn't there to pick his spirits up which made me feel awful. Anthony assured me that he had tried to tell his dad to focus on the positive, pointing out the positive things Dr. Even had said. But, Tony insisted on going to bed, and that was that. I tried to talk to him but, he was unresponsive to me also. That affected me; and I became distraught over it, those emotional turmoil's were difficult. I felt I had to get home to be with Tony as soon as possible.

While we were eating and talking, I decided to call Dr. Bane to talk to her about what Dr. Even had said Dr. Bane always seemed to have a way to lift Tony's spirits up: he just adored her, and had a lot of faith in her. So, I called her from my cell. Naturally, I got the answering service; it was after office hours by that time. Since it wasn't an emergency, I hoped she would call me back, and she did.

I explained to her what transpired with Dr. Even that day, and the hospice talk. She on the other hand was as optimistic as I was regarding Tony. I told her, "I know you're going out of town, but I would appreciate it if you could see Tony if at all possible, before you leave." She had that magic touch, and positive attitude, he needed.

She also said, "Tony being in remission is excellent news. We should go slower with the Chemo treatments, maybe three, or four more, to pursue a longer remission. Maybe it will come back maybe it won't. It may never come-back. There's no need for hospice. I don't understand Dr. Even talking about it at this time. Considering the tremendous good news you got." I couldn't understand either.

"It would be well worth at least two more chemo treatments, or a maintenance situation. I'll call Dr. Even in the morning to find out her thinking." She didn't understand Dr. Even, except she said, "Oncologists see a lot, and aren't as bubbly." I thought *they have to cover their butts.*

"Lets face it, cancer is a business, and maybe it was to scare him into taking more chemo."

She quickly responded, "I know for a fact, Dr. Even doesn't make a penny on the chemo or medication. She only gets paid for office visits, so that couldn't be the case." *Dr. Even has since this writing opened her own chemo clinic?*

She advised me, "Call my office in the morning to see if Tony can be squeezed in, I know I'm already double booked. That was nothing unusual for her.

When I got home that evening I told Tony that Dr. Bane wanted to see him the next day for a follow-up visit. I said all kinds of positive things to him. He on the other hand didn't want to discuss anything at all. I let it rest, counting on Dr. Bane to get him through it.

Visit to Our Angel Dr. Bane

I didn't sleep again that whole night. I finally got out of bed to start calling the doctor's office. I'd gotten up so early that they weren't even open yet. The answering service told me to call back at eight forty-five. When I called back, the line was busy; I kept hitting redial on the phone trying to get through. When I finally did I told the nurse I had talked to the doctor the night before, and she told me to call to see if Tony could be squeezed in. The nurse said, "I'll see what I can do. I'll talk to the doctor." I prayed from the moment I hung up the phone, that the doctor would have the time to see Tony before she left.

I waited for what seemed like an eternity.

As for my surgery, our children had it all worked out. Tammy would go with me for the surgery. Mario would stay with his dad. The party store was closed on Monday so that worked out. Then Mario would stay a couple of days to help me with his dad's showering, and needs. So, I wouldn't have to be lifting Tony up, for a couple of days.

Finally, the phone rang. I answered before it even rang a full ring. It was the nurse my prayers had been answered. Tony was to be there about twelve thirty, one. I thanked the nurse, "See you soon."

Excitedly I ran up the stairs to wake Tony up. I needed to get him showered, fed, and ready for the appointment. "I want to go out for breakfast." Michael came over just about that time with a juice maker, and all kinds of fresh fruit, and vegetables. He wanted his dad to have fresh juices hoping it would help him to recuperate faster. I expressed how thoughtful that was. I told him, "We're going out for breakfast, and then we have a doctor appointment."

"Can I I hang-out with you."

"Of course!"

"Why aren't you working today?"

"I told my boss I wanted to spend time with my dad." His boss understood, so Michael went to breakfast, and to the doctor with us.

We went to a restaurant right around the corner that Tony had gone to daily for coffee, and to read the paper, before he got sick. All the waitresses there just loved him, like everyone who knew him did. We went there to give them the good news. After we ate, we went on our way to the doctor. I was grateful for having Michael along; being Tony was so weak from the last chemo I really needed help. But, I hated to bother anyone more than I had to. They had already done so much, and of course had there own lives, working, houses.... It was a blessing that Michael had shown up, just at the right time. *(As I wrote this I wondered if our children hadn't planned it.)*

When we got to the doctor's office, the nurse took Tony right in. She took his vitals, and asked a lot of questions, what medication he was taking, how he was feeling.... Then the doctor came in, being her bubbly self. She told Tony, "I heard the great news, how, wonderful." She re-iterated what she had said to me, the night before.

"I'm glad you scheduled the surgery for yourself,' she said to me. I also think it's a cyst, but better to be cautious than not."

"Your wife is going to need your help after her surgery." Her thought was, maybe Tony would snap out of it, if he felt he needed to help me. Tony told the doctor, "I'm weak; fatigued, tired, just plain wiped out."

"You need a couple of weeks of rest. Get the rest you need, do the therapy, and you'll get stronger soon."

I asked, her if she'd like to make the money for the pre-op tests since I was there. "I'll only do them to save you the trip of going to the hospital because, Tony is exhausted." That worked out great; we wouldn't have to make another stop.

Tony went to wait with Michael in the waiting room, while I made another appointment for him in two weeks. Michael kept walking in, and out, and back, and forth not wanting to miss a word the doctor said. The doctor was joking back and forth, about me, doing everything for Tony. She had lost her own father to lung cancer twenty years earlier. I asked her, "How long did your father live."

"Seven months."

"Did he have the same type of cancer?"

"Yes. "

"He had small cell oat cell cancer."

"No small cell."

"That's what Tony has?"

"No, he has small cell oat cell."

"I don't think so, and had the nurse pull up the pathology report to make me a copy." Once again, I was ecstatic.

"So, it's not as bad as oat cell?"

"No, it's treatable." I was so excited I could have flown… I was so high. We thanked her, and left.

It was lunchtime by then, so on the way home we stopped to pick up some Popeye's chicken, Tony had a taste for that. When we got home we ate, and I was pleased that Tony ate pretty well. Then he went to his recliner to rest.

After lunch Michael cut the grass, when he was finished he said, "I have to go home for a while. I'll be back later to help dad up to bed."

Later that night when Michael was on his way back, he called from his cell to tell me, "I pulled small cell oat cell cancer up on my computer, and it wasn't good."

"I'll read the literature I received later." That was a mistake the literature said, 'small cell cancer was previously called oat cell".

What a rude awakening; we were still dealing with the same deadly disease. I became depressed immediately, and on a downer. I couldn't believe it; we were, back to square one. Tony's cousin Sandy called just then all bubbly she had gotten the good news. I must have sounded like hell, because her voice immediately came down about five octaves. I felt bad, but I just couldn't for the life of me be excited at that moment. I didn't want to go into explaining what the reason was at that time, I just couldn't. She must have thought I was nuts, had totally lost my mind, because we had just gotten good news. We thought?

I should have called Dr. Bane back, but I couldn't deal or debate another thing. We just went on with our lives with the good news we had gotten. As if I'd never read that literature. I totally believed Tony was going to beat the cancer, fool all the doctor's, and go into medical books.

Grand Opening

That Saturday evening we went to a Grand Opening for Tony's cousin Earl, who had opened a Shrimp House. We decided to take a ride, to support Earl's exciting night. When we got there, I pulled along side the curb to park because; Tony was far too weak to go in. The family saw us arrive and everyone came out to say hello. It was a sad moment because; we weren't able to join the celebrating inside.

Joey often hung around with Earl and had gone there earlier to see if he could help. When he saw us, he came to the car with a menu, so he could place our order for us. We talked with the family while our order was prepared.

After Joey delivered our food, we left right away. Tony wanted to get home before the shrimp and baked clams became soggy and cold.

After we ate, I asked Tony, "Would you like to play cards." Much to my surprise he said, "Yes." Playing, five hundred rummy, was something we use to do when we first got married to pass time. Tony beat me every game just like he had back then. It brought back fond memories, of years passed. I wished silently that we were still at that same time in life.

Joey came later that evening to help his dad upstairs to bed.

We were all going to Joey's house for dinner the next day. With Tony still being very weak, he laid in the recliner most of that day sleeping and not saying much, when we got there. He did talk a little when he came to the table for dinner, which I was happy for. Right after dinner however, he wanted to go home, and get in bed. Mario came home with us that night, to help his dad up to bed. He stayed over night, because I was having surgery at nine the next morning.

Tammy came to pick me up around seven thirty so we could be at the medical center by eight. I had to be there an hour before the surgery so they could prep me. The surgery went as scheduled, and we were out of there before twelve that afternoon. I told Tammy, "The surgery actually wasn't bad at all. I didn't have any pain or a problem of any kind." I was pleasantly surprised and happy about how it had gone.

I felt so great afterwards that Tammy and I went right out to eat, then, actually shopped a little. We got back home about three. By then I felt, a little funny, woozy, and sore. The medication had started to wear off. I went directly to bed when I got home and got up at eight thirty when Tony came to bed. I went downstairs to chat with Mario for awhile, as I wasn't tired after sleeping. I stayed with Mario for a bit then went back to bed.

The next morning I felt perfectly fine. I was just a little sore. Mario stayed with us until Friday, because I wasn't supposed to do any lifting. When Tony needed help getting up Mario was there to help him.

The following Wednesday we resumed our group session at Wellness House. Being able to talk to people that were in our position, helped us both. That night we signed up for a comedy show on Friday, and looked forward to a fun evening.

After our session, we went for a hot dog. I was going to get the hot dogs and bring them to the car, but Tony wanted to go inside to eat. He knew he couldn't pull himself up on me because, of the surgery, so he asked a man that was going in if he could help him. It was rough going in, and I was alone bringing him out, but we made it. I wondered where and how I got the strength, and guts. I guess you just do!

On Thursday, we got the results from the surgery, and everything was negative. It was a fibroid cyst *not cancer*. I thanked God, for all his blessings.

Friday, we went to the cancer center for the Epoetin shot. I asked the nurse to do a CBC, and full blood work up. I was sure Tony's blood levels had dropped way below normal, because he was very, very, weak. But, his blood checked out fine. I wondered, *why all the weakness? Was the cancer growing again, draining him of all of his strength or was the weakness the results of his last chemo? If so, what would the next chemo do to him,* Fear, anger, and anxiety, welled up in me over the abyss—.

After the hospital, we had planned on going out to eat; then to the comedy show.

Restaurant Fall

When we arrived at the restaurant Tony said, "I don't need the walker."

"Are you sure because, if your legs give out I won't be able to hold you up." My breast is still sore from the surgery."

"I'll be okay."

I parked right outside the restaurant door in handicap parking, and thought it was close enough that he should make it. Besides, I didn't want to discourage him from doing something positive, so I went along with him. I helped him get out of the car; held his arm firmly, and walked along side him. That was a, BIG mistake! We did fine, until—we got to the door and I opened it. Neither, of us noticed the little step about two inches high. Tony went to step inside; and tripped, DOWN HE WENT! Down to his knees; now, there we were, in a pickle filled with fear, frustration, and anxiety. Tony could not muster up the strength to get back on his feet, and I couldn't lift him up to his feet. I thought my breast was going to burst open with all the pulling, inside. I kept hollering my breast, my breast, at that moment a waitress just happened to be going to work. She appeared behind us, as I hollered help me—help me—. She said, very assured, "My grandfather has been sick, and I've helped with him a lot, it won't be a problem, I'm used to it."

"Are you sure? He's dead weight; won't be able to help you, he doesn't have the strength."

"I'll be okay." She grabbed Tony around his waist to pick him up but, because, he was dead weight, and couldn't help her at all, she couldn't lift him either.

"Wait here," as she ran inside, and came back with two big guys to help.

The two guys had a difficult time getting Tony up, and sat him on a bench that was thankfully, right inside the door. By then, Tony was all shaken up, and embarrassed. We both sat there a few minutes to collect ourselves and calm down. It was a traumatic accident that shouldn't have happened. Blaming myself; for his not using the walker, in the first place.

"Do you want us to call 911 for an ambulance?" I assured them he would be okay his legs were just weak, and he didn't have the strength to pull himself up, but okay.

I then asked Tony, "Do you want me to get the oxygen, and your walker?"

"Yes," so I ran to the car to get it for him.

"How are your knees you fell on?"

"One of them is sore."

"Do you want to go to the hospital?"

"No."

We decided since we were already there, and inside the restaurant that we'd go ahead and eat, we got to a booth without to much trouble because Tony had the walker to lean on. We ordered dinner; but I was a nervous wreck, and couldn't calm down. Of course, the comedy show was out of the question. I would be petrified to go any where with Tony alone after that fall. We had just experienced what I had, feared all along. Tony then asked the waitress, "Could you help me back to the car?"

She was kind enough to say, "Sure no problem." But, she went, and got a big guy to come along to help. We got him to the car okay, but as he walked, I noticed blood on his pants at his knee. I knew then he had really hurt him self—. How bad I didn't know?

On the way home as I drove I told Tony, "Call Joey at work, and explain to him what just happened, and ask him if he could please meet us at the house. So, he could help me get you in the house." Joey was happy to help.

Once Joey got there; we got Tony in the house, settled, and I immediately took off his pants to see what had happened to his knee. He had just scratched it, but, because, of the blood thinners it bled like he had cut it wide open. I was afraid to look for fear of what I'd see; but it wasn't that bad, I cleaned and dressed it right away. Then Joey helped his dad up to bed. It was still quite early and I was upset that Tony wanted to go to bed, but I was too frazzled to fight with him.

On the other hand that's why Tony wanted to go to bed. He was also frustrated, and anxious that he just wanted to relax. After getting him all comfy and settled, I went back downstairs.

I stayed downstairs crying my eyes out, not knowing what was happening to his legs. I felt he should be getting stronger not weaker, with all the therapy.

Ruminating in my mind, like a record gone out of control. *He's not getting better with the therapy. He's still weak. What's going on? Tony had also complained about having blurred vision. Was his brain causing that problem because the cancer had come back?* I was going absolutely crazy over the unidentified reason—.

Then that Monday, he had a terrible time doing his exercises he was just so weak. He had only exercised Saturday on his own. He didn't have it in him on Sunday, and fought me about doing them. So by Monday it was even more difficult for him. I had noticed a big change in him; it seemed he'd gotten much worse. If that could have even been, possible? The therapist also noticed he was weaker. I expressed my frustration, fear, and concern to her. She asked me right out, "How are you doing."

I replied with quivering lips, "I'm okay."

"Maybe you should get some help with showers—?"

"I'm okay; I'm just scared about the chance of Tony falling."

"We'll talk about it more, later."

Tony and I discussed maybe going to the Morton Arboretum that day after therapy. He needed some activity and to get out of the house for a while. I wanted to keep him busy, as he was starting to show signs of depression.

By Tuesday when the therapist came, we discussed that Tony was even weaker. However, he had to still keep trying and do what he could to keep his muscles active. We already knew if he didn't use them, he'd lose them "quickly." That was something Tony didn't want to happen.

Tammy came over to stay with her dad while I went for my after surgery check-up. I asked Tammy, "Ask the therapist when she comes if all the exercising is fruitless. Dad just seems to be spinning his wheels, and failing quickly."

Everything went well for me at the doctor, and checked out okay. Thank God. "The incision looks good. Keep the steri-strip on until it falls off. Before you leave; make another appointment in two weeks."

I called home from my cell to see how everything was going. Tammy said, "Dad is sleeping, take a couple of hours to shop and relax to get away from the situation." I did go shop for a while, but I had to get back for an appointment Tammy and I had made, with a Realtor. We were going to put the business up for sale, which we did.

After the realtor left I asked Tammy, "What did the therapist say?'"

"He's getting weaker but, still needed to exercise. She wasn't going to paint a pretty picture, it's going to get worse, and it wasn't going to be easy."

She then told Tammy, "I'm not as worried about your dad, as much as I am about your mom. It's very difficult being the caretaker."

I knew that, Tony needed a lot of assistance with everything. He wasn't well enough to be left alone, since it all started. Now, he couldn't do anything independently. Not that I minded one bit, because I didn't, that wasn't the issue at all.

That night Anthony came over to help his dad up to bed, Tony just dreaded going up the stairs, it was so very difficult on him.

Lita came at ten thirty the next morning just after Tony's breakfast. She started right in with the exercise routine, Tony wasn't feeling well again, and didn't want to exercise, but she coaxed him into doing some at least. Lita told Tony, "Tammy and your wife shared something with me, that you told them."

Tony had told Tammy that he had a repeated dream that he went to the garage—turned on the car—and started it—trying to kill himself, but I had found him. He woke up with Dr. Bane standing over him in the hospital. He was very angry, that I found him, and saved him. Tammy had shared the story with me when I got back from the doctor.

The therapist said, "I feel that's a sign of depression. I need to get a new work order to continue working with you, plus I also have to do a report for the doctor. I always discussed with my patients what I'm going to put in the report. I like to be up front with my patients." We both agreed on what she was going to put in the report. Then she showed me the correct way Tony should be helped up the stairs, to make it easier for all of us.

After Lita left, I took Tony for a ride to the Morton Arboretum, as we planned. It was a nice get away, and a beautiful day outside. After about an hour Tony got anxious, and wanted to go home. He couldn't sit any longer, he was uncomfortable.

We stopped to pick up some prescriptions, and I got a few groceries while I was in the store. Tony waited in the car while I did the errands

Anthony came right after work that night to help his dad up the stairs. I was already upstairs preparing the bed for Tony. I was at the top of the stairs telling Anthony how to assist his dad explaining what the therapist had taught us that day, so that Tony would use his own muscles.

They tried doing it the therapist's way, but Tony was so weak his legs just gave out and Anthony had to literally carry his dad the rest of the way. By the time Tony got to the top of the stairs, I thought he was going to pass out; he was actually shaking all over, breathing very heavily, and scared to death. Tony swore that night he'd never go up the stairs again. He was also wheezing that was something he'd never done before. I truly felt sad and compassionate for him my heart bled for him. Tony had also been having a difficult time getting on and off the toilet, and recliner. He needed a lot more assistance those last few days. He didn't seem to have too much trouble getting out if the recliner was high, and firm enough though. I had tried to put a cushion from a chair in the living room on it, to heighten the recliner seat, and it did help, but Tony said, "It's uncomfortable for me to sit on."

By the next day Tony could hardly stand; it was a very difficult day for him, and I was pretty much beside myself, declining very rapidly, I didn't understand it, at all. If the cancer was in remission, could the cancer have come-back so vehemently, so quickly? *Was I going to lose him—? Was he going to keep getting worse—and worse— and worse?* I couldn't bear to think of that happening, and I was scared to death! I was also very frightened that he'd fall; really hurt himself or, worse yet break his bones or, fall and crack his head or, kill himself. Tony had gained seven pounds in a week. He was to heavy for me to control if he lost his balance, that would be a disaster for both of us

Every night I'd just cried, and cried, and cried, I was so afraid of losing Tony. Never discussing with him about how scared I was.

When Lita came the next day, I told her about the night before. How awful hard and scary it had been for Tony, going up the stairs. I also told her I was going to investigate getting a stair lift for him. I didn't want Tony to ever go through that trauma again. I told her he had made a promise to himself that he'd never go up the stairs again; it had been that scary for him. To lose your breath, and not be able to catch it had to be the most awful, horrible, scary feeling for him. Tony was just shaking, gasping for air, and wheezing. It had taken about fifteen minutes for him to calm down. I also did not want to see him go through that again. Ever! Lita thought if Tony got a lift, he'd use it wither he needed to or not, and she didn't want him to become dependent on it.

I was also worried that both him, and Anthony might fall. On the other hand, Anthony could hurt his back, if his father buckled under him, because he'd be dead weight. Or, if all of a sudden Tony lost his balance with both of them on the stairs they'd both fall, a complete catastrophe.

I asked Lita, "Could you order a toilet seat riser for Tony, because he's really having a hard time getting off the toilet."

"I'll find out, for you." It was getting more difficult for me to lift Tony off of the toilet, because of it being so low.

"Have you given any thought to the help I suggested? About having someone come in three times a week to help you with showering Tony."

"I think it would be helpful having someone professional, because I'm fearful of Tony falling."

"I'll have a social worker call you."

She then asked, "Could I have Friday off? My husband and I just bought a boat, and I would appreciate it if I could come Monday, Tuesday, Wednesday or Monday Tuesday Saturday."

"Of course go, enjoy yourself while you're young, and can do all those things." We had an appointment to see Dr. Bane on Thursday of the following week, and on Saturday, we liked to go out to breakfast with our children. I didn't want to tie the weekends up at all, if possible either.

Monday, Tuesday, Wednesday worked out for all of us. Then she left saying, "I'll see you next week on Monday."

After she left, I got on the phone to research the stair lift for Tony. What the costs were, the different manufacturers, functions, color sizes and warranties. How invasive it would be; if rentals were available, and buy back policies. It was quite a fiasco. I also wanted to know how long it would take to get one and have it installed. In between making calls, I was running to help Tony on and off the recliner to the bathroom, on and off the toilet, back to the recliner, I was running back, and forth. Even with the walker Tony couldn't do it alone he was too wobbly on his feet. The walker would help him catch himself, but if he were really off balance, he'd go over completely walker and all. I was very anxious that day, trying to take care of Tony's needs, make calls, wash clothes, make meals, and make sure he took his medicine at the correct time, along with other everyday upkeep.

Downhill

As for myself, it was a very emotional time for me. I had a lot to swallow, my brain was going in all different directions, and I was on a speeding roller coaster journey of thoughts. *Was it going to be downhill from here? Was Tony going to gain strength and be okay? What was our future? Are we ever going to have a future again?* I could feel the fear building in me like an erupting volcano. I got angry with Tony that he wasn't trying hard enough. *Was he lazy, giving up, or really just too weak?* I couldn't stand to see him digress; it was literally tearing my guts out. *I'm not going to be able to handle it.* Not the labor of taking care of him; wasn't the problem, that didn't bother me in the least. It was watching him get worse, and worse, that I couldn't handle, and I died a little with him day by day. There wasn't a thing I could do, to make it better; no matter what I did, us how hard I tried, it just didn't seem to make a difference. Except—to pray very hard, *please God, give me the strength, and patience I need to help Tony get better. You got me this far in my life.* I knew it was only through him that I'd been able to do what I'd done thus far.

The doorbell rang, ding-dong—ding-dong—it was the deliver man delivering the toilet seat riser the therapist ordered. Tony's aunt had one she wasn't using, as she was in a nursing home, and didn't need it. Tony's cousin brought that one over for him to use too. One problem down, and solved. Yahoo! We'd have a toilet riser for both bathrooms one for the upstairs bathroom, and one for the downstairs powder room. I wondered how many more problems we'd have to tackle, and face.

I had bought the movie 'Jesus' the day before when I picked up the prescription at the drug-store. They had the movie on display right at the counter, and I thought it would be a good movie for us to watch. We both sure needed "A Higher Power" with us at that time; something for us to look forward to.

We had decided to have dinner and then watch the movie, and that's exactly what we did. Dinner was a quiet one. I was still very angry about the situation of the night before though; trying to get my point across to Tony. Tammy came in just as we were finishing dinner. She had borrowed her dad's car to go on a job interview to sell industrial real estate. Then she had to go downtown for a personality test for an interview she'd been on the day before. I asked her, "Do you want to eat," at first she said, "No." She could feel the tension in the air. I convinced her to eat it while the food was still warm, there was plenty. She finally agreed to sit down, and eat.

I was storming up and down the stairs, washing clothes, folding clothes, occasionally going outside to smoke. Giving Tammy time to talk to her dad, I just didn't know what to do with myself. I just really wanted to die literally!

Tammy the poor thing didn't know what to do for either one of us. Having compassion for both of us asking, "Is there anything I could do."

She asked me, "Do you want to talk? Do you want to get out for a while? Do you want me to stay for a while? Do you want me to leave?"

"I really don't care what you do." That poor kid, didn't know what to do I had her in such a turmoil.

What I wanted, she couldn't achieve; I wanted her dad; well again, and for everything to go back to, normal. That, no one could do, but God—; I kept asking and pleading for him to do just that over and over again. When Tammy and her dad finished eating, I did the dishes, and we went to watch the movie.

"If you don't need me I'm going to leave, I have a lot of things to get done." We all kissed and she left.

The Movie Jesus

We settled in the living room, and I started the movie "Jesus." How perfect I thought, as we talked about what was going on in the movie. It wasn't an easy movie to follow, especially, since our attention wasn't totally focused. At one point I asked Tony, "Should I back the movie up."

"No." Instead, I stopped the movie and we discussed, exactly what had happened in the movie up to that point.

Then I apologized, for acting like an awful, raging, asshole. Explaining, "I can't stand to see you like this, it's killing me. It makes me very sad, and it's painful to see your loved one slipping through your fingers. It's almost like seeing your loved one drowning right in front of you, and you can't keep their head above water; no matter how hard you try—.

By that time, I was standing over Tony, stroking his arm, crying uncontrollably. I felt so bad for the way I was acting and the way I was treating him, totally out of control as to what I could do to make everything okay, and all better.

Tony's response was, "Hon; I'm not going to make it; your problem is you're in denial. You won't accept it. It's part of life; everyone dies at sometime in his or her life. It will be okay. You won't have to work. It will all-work out.

"You have too positive of an attitude".

"You have a negative attitude and we need to meet somewhere in the middle."

As we were talking I looked down at Tony's feet. I noticed his feet seemed unusually swollen, larger than usual. His feet had been swelling, but that night they looked like balloons. "Let me take a closer look at your feet."

I took off his sock, when I did, the ribs of the sock was deeply imbedded in his skin at the ankle. When I pushed on the top of his feet, my thumbprint stayed pressed down in his skin. I then pushed his sweat pants up, pushed on his legs, and the print stayed pressed down in his calf. Then I looked at his arms, and hands they were swollen too.

I immediately started putting all the pieces together; swelling, wheezing chest, nausea, seven pounds in a week, and weakness. He's got congestive heart failure! Oh! My God! I'd been so busy fretting about what's been going on, and being frustrated. That I was blinded as to what actually was going on; not thinking or acting with a clear head at all.

"I'm going to call the doctor. I don't think we should wait until tomorrow; you could drown in your own fluids." It was seven in the evening; I hated to bother the doctor, but felt it was an emergency. I picked up the phone to call, to ask her opinion whether we could wait until the next day, as we had an appointment with her then.

Earlier that day I had called about the watch I had bought Tony for his birthday. The band was too big for his wrist, and was being shortened. I was supposed to have it back the next day, that was four days ago. Being in the mood I was in already; ready to kill the first person that got in my way. When I called about the watch I said, "If I don't have the watch back by tonight, I wanted my money back. Tony's birthday is tomorrow, and I want him to have it for his birthday."

The doctor called right back. I explained the situation as to what I thought; was happening, and why, and that we had an appointment with her, the next day. I asked, "Should we wait until then."

She explained, "I haven't seen Tony in two weeks." She couldn't diagnosis over the phone, naturally. He should be taken to the emergency room for them to make a diagnosis. If it's nothing we could come back home; but at least we'd know for sure. If we didn't go, she said, "I know you, won't get any sleep or; if anything should happen to him. You'll never forgive yourself." She was sure right on, about that.

Back to the Hospital

$\mathcal{W}$e immediately were on our way to the emergency room. Just then Tammy's brother-in-law Jeff showed up to bring the watch back, and he helped me get Tony into the car.

I called Tammy to let her know where we'd be, so she could call all the boys. She asked if I wanted her to come to the hospital with the twins.

"No, I'll be all right; the twins have school in the morning." Anthony called just as we were walking out the door. He was calling to let us know he was coming to help his dad up to bed. I told him not to come as we were just leaving for the hospital. I thought his dad had congestive heart failure. I had called the doctor and she said to go to the hospital emergency room, to get a diagnosis.

On our way to the hospital, I stopped to get cigarettes first, in case we got held up there by being admitted to the hospital. I didn't expect him to be admitted but, I wanted to be prepared, just in case. If that happened I'd need my cigarettes, which were my sedatives, tranquilizers and antidepressants all in one. My cell phone rang just then. It was Mario, "I'm at the hospital waiting for you, where are you?"

"I stopped for cigarettes."

"How did you know we were going to the hospital?"

"A little birdie told me." That could only have been Tammy. I asked him to have a wheelchair ready for his dad I'd be there in a minute.

When we arrived at the hospital Mario was waiting with the wheelchair, and Anthony was already there too.

"Where were you? I went to your house to help you, and you were gone." I explained I had help from Tammy's brother-in-law then, I went for cigarettes. He asked if his dad would be admitted.

"I have no idea; whether he's going to be admitted or, will be able to go home?" Anthony "Go home, you worked all day and you're tired, Mario will stay with me."

Anthony then asked the nurse. "He'll probably be admitted at least overnight." So Anthony left, as he had to be up very early to go to work the next day.

The emergency room doctor ordered a chest X-ray, and electro cardiogram, the routine for heart patients. The X-ray looked real good the doctor informed us. However, on the other hand Tony's heart was beating very fast, and he was having a difficult time breathing. He was diagnosed with having congestive heart failure. "Another Miracle"! It had been a message from God, I'm sure; that I was able to put all the pieces together, and recognize that Tony was having congestive heart failure. He was also experiencing pain in his lower abdomen. The doctor ordered an injection of morphine for the pain. That worked. The pain subsided.

Tony was admitted to the hospital, and put-on the heart patient floor; thrilled it wasn't the cancer floor. I hoped Tony psychologically would realize he was in remission. They immediately gave him a diuretic to rid him of the water he was retaining. I had Tony settle in a private room with a cot, by that time it was our usual procedure. Mario stayed the night with me, so I wouldn't be all alone.

Tony's Birthday

$\mathcal{T}$he next day was Thursday, September 21, 2000, Tony's birthday! The next morning when Dr. Bane came in, she said, "I'm going to change some of his medicines for starters." She ordered an echocardiogram and was going to send in Dr. Wilton, the cardiac Dr.

"Tony has a little bronchitis—nothing cancer related, just some gunk in his lungs." She ordered respiratory four times a day to loosen it up.

Tony received a lot of calls from friends, and our kids checking on his status, and wishing him happy birthday. It was an awful way for him to have to spend his birthday.

I asked the doctor how long Tony would be in the hospital.

"Until the middle of next week at least," I couldn't believe it. I thought we'd only be there a day or two.

"Tony's heart is enlarged a little too." And she also wanted to get some CT scans taken. I explained to her that he had CT scans done on his abdomen, chest, and pelvis September 2.

"I'll call for the reports on them."

That afternoon Dr.Wilton came in to check Tony. He explained that his heart was beating rather fast. That he'd like to slow it down. Then give him some medicine to make it pump harder to push the fluids out, of his body. We'd have to wait to do that until his heart settled down first. That afternoon Tony's Mother, caretaker, Sister Aida, our family, and Greg came to see Tony for his birthday. We tried to make Tony's birthday as pleasant as we possibly could under the circumstances.

The next day Mario stayed with me again. Joey called to see if he could bring us anything. Tony wanted Burger King, so Joey brought all of us Burger King for dinner. Anthony then brought his dad a birthday cake. Which Tony didn't want to eat he wasn't feeling good.

The next day the doctor came in and said, "I'll be off for the weekend. I'll have another doctor look-in on him, and Dr.Wilton will be around if Tony needs anything."

Dee and George stopped to spend some time visiting with us. Tammy had been there earlier; she brought me some clean clothes, and personal items. Anthony had also stopped on his way home from work.

Tony continued to have pain in his lower abdomen, and was taking pain medicine for it. Tony explained the pain as a pinching or, like sticking

113

him with a knife at times, and it also shifted from side to side. He was kind of out of it, from of the pain medicine. He'd been having that pain the past couple of weeks. I had attributed the pain to the pill for the osteoporosis that strengthen his bones that he took early in the morning; which was notorious for indigestion. Obviously that wasn't the problem.

The next day a male doctor that was relieving Dr. Bane came in to examined Tony. The doctor asked, how the pain was, how long Tony had it, and if the pain medicine was helping.

"Yes. " After checking Tony he left. It was a male doctor relieving our doctor.

Greg and Loraine called to see if they could bring Tony anything as they were coming to visit. Tony asked them to bring him a bagel with vegetable spread. They arrived shortly after calling with the bagels, and vegetable spread. They'd been so good to Tony, and I through the whole nightmare; taking us out to dinner, visiting, and calling with concern. Greg had visited Tony constantly through all his hospital stays almost daily. We couldn't have asked for better friends with all their support. We were visiting with them when, out of the blue, Tony asked for the phone. He wanted to call Joey at work, I asked what for?

"I want him to pick up a fish sandwich; I have a taste for that." He still hadn't eaten the bagel with the vegetable spread he'd asked for earlier. I wanted to shoot him on the spot because, now he wanted a fish sandwich. Loraine jumped up and said, "I'll go for you, it's not a problem, Honest. I'll run real fast; it's close by don't call, your son." Off she went in a flash. Tony's wishes were all of our commands, anything to make him feel better, eat, and get well, was our goal.

Loraine had been gone a long time; we were getting a little worried. She finally came back, after being gone quite awhile.

"You'll never guess what just happened to me, as I was on my way back. There was an accident; I was a witness so, I stayed because, it wasn't the ladies fault, and I wanted to make sure she didn't get blamed for it." The police had called an ambulance and the woman was then brought to the same hospital Tony was in. Loraine was quite shaken up over the accident. She said, "I had to slam on my brakes or I would have been involved in the accident."

Tony said to Greg, "Your wife is really going to hate me." I don't feel good, and I can't even eat the sandwich now.

"You've got to be kidding. They brought bagels you didn't eat, then she runs for the sandwich and now you can't eat that." I was embarrassed, and felt bad, that Loraine had gone through so much trouble.

Greg said, "Don't worry about it Tony. "

I jokingly said, "Loraine almost gave her life to get you that fish sandwich, and now you're not going to eat it. I'll feed you the sandwich if you'll at least try." Tony agreed to try, and he did eat the whole sandwich after all. I was so happy that he at least had eaten something, and ate all of it to boot.

Tony continued to have the pain in his abdomen though. The nurse said, "I'm going to call the doctor about it." When the nurse came back she said, "The doctor ordered a CT scan to see if it's diverticulitis."

"He just had a CT scan September 2nd, and he does have diverticulitis." It's never bothered him before now and actually I'd forgotten about it. The nurse called the doctor back to let him know.

"He'll do an ultra sound to check the kidneys for kidney stones; he'll be in later to assess him."

Greg and Loraine had spent about five hours with us that day. This was great; as we talked about all kinds of things, and then they left. Their visit was greatly appreciated; it helped pass the time faster.

The doctor did come back later saying, "I'd like Tony to fast at least until tomorrow, to see if the pain goes away." Tony wasn't happy about that at all. Tony was a very good eater normally, so he was quite upset about that, but he was in pain, and willing to go along with it. Besides he was taking a lot of pain medicine, and wasn't totally with it, so the fast started.

Joey stopped by later that night and he and I went to the cafeteria, to get some dinner. Tony rested while we were gone. When we got back Joey stayed awhile, visited with his dad, then left.

I was pretty anxious about all the pain, Tony was having. The unknown was again very scary. Thoughts kept creeping into my mind no matter how hard I tried to dismiss them. *Was it cancer of the stomach, liver, panaceas, kidney, or what?*

I was up half the night worrying about what could possibly be going on with Tony, seeing how weak he was, and all the trouble he was having breathing. It was the weekend again, our doctor was off and not much was being accomplished. Of course I would have liked everything done right away, worried that time was wasting, or knowing what was happening to him!

I finally fell asleep about one thirty that morning. I could hear the nurse's through the night going in and out. Then I heard Tony say to the PCT he'd missed the urinal, he was apologizing, telling them how sorry he was. They had to change him, the bed, the whole works. I didn't want him to feel worse so I pretended to be sleeping. I could see it all through silted eyes though. The rest of the night nurses continued coming in and out checking, his blood pressure, temperature and pulse.

Sunday morning started a new day. Just as I was coming out of the bathroom after freshening up, I saw the food tray by Tony's bed. I thought to myself, *why did he get a tray?* Tony wasn't suppose to eat he was suppose to be fasting. I looked above his bed there was no sign saying nothing by mouth. I was confused. I looked at what was on the tray. There was a small amount of breakfast food; stamped on the menu it said, "Carry up." It wasn't what I had ordered for him the day before either, I was puzzled, and by then Tony was hungry since he hadn't had anything since lunch the day before.

I tried to find someone to find out what was going on and to ask whether I should give him the tray or not! When the PCT came in, I asked her. She said, "I'll ask the nurse." No one ever came back to let me know. I asked the PCT again, "Oh! Let me ask the nurse." When a nurse finally came, she said, "Your nurse is at breakfast, I'll check." She never came back. I was really getting very agitated by then.

Finally I said, "The hell with it" and gave Tony the tray. I got him set-up; then left to go have a cigarette I needed to calm my-self after all the confusion. Just as I was leaving his nurse came back from her breakfast. "He can't have the tray," I was so angry by that time! I already gave him the tray I can't help it if your people are incompetent and can't get it straight. I don't give a damn what you do— I'm not taking that tray away from him! If he can't take the test you'll have to answer for it." As I kept walking away to go have a; well-deserved cigarette.

It's really important to stay with your loved one to make sure their getting well taken care of, the hospital system isn't what it used to be. No one gave a damn; was consistent anymore, or did they want to take the responsibility for the work their supposed to be doing, they all passed the buck. I'll give them the benefit of the doubt as far as being short staffed; overworked but, the ones that are there should take pride in their work at least. I thought *what ever happened to pride in a job well done?* That was the number one reason, I never left Tony. And when I did leave him, shit happened! Tony was way to sick too take any chances so; I guarded him like a watchdog.

When I got back to the room, I asked him if they took the tray away. Tony said

"Yes."

"Did you eat anything?"

"No, I was just getting ready to, when they took the tray away." I told him I was sorry, and angry that had happened. The staff wasn't on the ball, or with the program, it was their job to follow the doctor's orders. If I hadn't been there he'd have eaten the food, screwed up the test, and it would have been postponed until the next day. Tony was hungry, and I didn't have the heart to take that tray away from him. After numerous tries to straighten it out, I finally relented, and gave him the tray.

Later that day Anthony and Joey visited. They both commented that the room smelled of urine.

"I didn't notice it." I usually can smell urine; I hate that smell however, I hadn't noticed an odor at all. I thought maybe the urinal or, potty-chair smelled, and maybe since I was staying there I was immune, to the smell. I couldn't figure it out, I sniffed all over the room trying to detect where the smell was coming from, but never did find out.

Tony was still having pain, and taking morphine shots to kill the pain. I was still very anxious and wound up likes a time bomb with worry about what was going on with him. Scared to death that the cancer, was back.—!

I didn't feel Tony was in that much pain to warrant getting morphine shots. I felt it was more a physiological withdrawal from what was actually going on, plus the pain. I asked Tony what the pain level was, "five or six" the regular pain medicine had controlled that level previously, so why morphine now? I constantly racked my brain trying to figure out what could be wrong with him!

When lunchtime came Tony he got another tray. But, still hadn't gone down for the test yet, I reported to the nurse he'd gotten another tray. She came to take the tray away, I asked her to leave the tray; that I'd eat it later. The PCT said, "The nurse said, she didn't understand why he had kept getting trays, she's going to call down again to notify the kitchen of the mistakes."

At dinner he received another tray, which consisted of soft food that time. Again they said,

"Don't eat any of it." I asked them to leave it I thought maybe our granddaughters would like some of it. The tray had a shake, and pudding, on it; I knew they liked to eat what was on the tray, if Tony didn't want it.

Then the nurse came, to give Tony some kind of citrus drink to clean him out for the test.

Tammy and the twins came a little later that evening to visit, we'd been expecting them. The twins wanted no part of the tray though. They wanted to go to the cafeteria to eat; they thought it was a fun thing to do, so I told them we'd go down later.

Tony had to go potty just then so, it was a good time to give him some privacy. I asked the nurse to help get him on the potty. I told her we were going to the cafeteria to give him some time alone. Well be back soon and we left.

We each got a little something in the cafeteria then went outside so I could have a cigarette before going back-up

We had been gone at least an hour, by the time we got back. Tony was still sitting on the potty, I saw RED! Asking him if he had the light on for the nurse?

"Yes." I asked Tony, when he had put the light on?

"Right after you left." At that point I was fuming—.

"And no one came in since then?"

"No!" All the aggravation piled up. Getting angrier by the minute! (You can see what I meant about leaving your loved one that was for only an hour away!) I went and got the nurse to help transfer Tony back to his bed, and got him settled for the night.

After Tony was all settled Tammy and the twins said, good night they had to get home. The twins had to go to school the next day; I walked them back down them so I could watch them go to their car. I decided to have another cigarette; they stayed with me until I put it out. Then I kissed them good-bye; watched them go to the car and leave.

When I got back to the room, I heard him asking for another pain shot. I asked, "What the pain level was. "About a five," I confronted him as to the reason he was asking for a shot, do you want to go into the ozone? "Yes." I knew it—. Because, the pain pill had controlled that level before; Tony didn't want to deal with the anxiety of the tests to be taken the next day, or deal with the no food situation. It was an escape for him, and no reason medically for that shot. On the other hand, I certainly could identify mentally what he must have been going through!

I couldn't blame him but; still no reason to get a morphine shot, when a pain pill would have done the same thing, relaxed him. I became frustrated, over that.

When the doctor came in he put Tony on a clear liquid diet; but was able to have Jell-O, Popsicle's, juice, and liquids of any kind. That was Tony's dinner; thinking that the doctor wanted to see how he would do with liquids, first. Later that night I asked Tony; if he'd like some more Jell-O; a Popsicle or, juice, since he hadn't had a thing since dinner. "Yes." He ate two more servings of Jell-O, and a Popsicle. Then he was ready to go to sleep.

I on the other hand was to wound up over all that had happened that day, and what we had ahead of us the next day. Tony really had not been with it; he had been pretty much; out of it, from the morphine, not dealing with all the reality, as I was. Being restless; I kept going in and out to smoke until about twelve-thirty. When I decided I'd better try to rest. I finally fell asleep about one thirty in the morning.

About two in the morning, I heard Tony calling my name. I asked very sleepily, "What's
Wrong!"
"I have to use the urinal, and I can't reach it; Hurry!"
I jumped up, out a sound sleep, and ran to the other side of the bed where the urinal was. Grabbed the urinal, and as I lifted the sheets I smelled the stench. The smell was awful I asked him, "What smells?" Ignoring me he said, "I want to sit on the side of the bed it's easier for me to urinate that way." I put the call light on for the nurse; I needed help lifting him. I lifted Tony up to a sitting position; which I didn't want to do because, of the breast surgery but, I was desperate to help him. No one was coming—so I tried to get him to a sitting position myself. Worrying about him slipping off or, falling off, the bed knowing very well I would "not" be able hold him up if he slipped, at the same trying to get the urinal placed where it belonged. Every time I turned to reach for the urinal with one hand, Tony fell over. I'd sit him up; he'd fall over when I let go of him with the other hand. I was yelling by then, "TONY YOU'VE GOT TO HELP ME. HOLD YOURSELF UP WITH THE BARS ON THE BED. I can't do it myself; I need your help." He was like a wibbly, wobbly just falling back, and forth, from side to side, still no one came—. Finally I said, "I can't do this myself. I've got to get help." I laid Tony back down; by that time I was shaking like a leaf. No one ever answered the call light. What the hell was going on?

I ran into the hall for help. No one was in sight, I stormed to the desk, and shouted I need help Tony needs to use the urinal I can't help him myself he's too weak, finally someone came. They laid him down, put the urinal in between his legs, and put a blanket on top of the urinal, so it couldn't move.

I was wide-eyed by then from all the commotion, even though I'd only slept a half-hour. I was shaking like a leaf. I felt awful, and angry with myself that I had gotten upset with my poor husband because; he wasn't able to help me, when all he wanted to do was pee. Perturbed with myself that I wasn't able to help him; I felt guilty, helpless, useless, sad, and frustrated. I had so many emotions rumbling through my mind all at once.

I went outside again to have a cigarette, cool off, and tried to calm myself. It was about two thirty in the morning. I smoked a cigarette, and went right back up, Tony still had the urinal between his legs, but hadn't peed. "I couldn't pee anymore." I certainly could understand that I couldn't have peed either after that trauma. I waited for the PCT to come back to remove the urinal. "Did anyone check-in on you since I left?"

"No." I was waiting for them to come back, so I could tell them I wanted Tony washed up as he reeked of urine. Obviously; they hadn't cleaned his privates that morning or, he wouldn't have, smelled!

I then remembered the boys complaining about smelling urine earlier. I realized it was when they had bent down to kiss Tony, that they smelled the urine. I then put together what they smelled was the urine that had fermented on him from the night before when he had missed the urinal and peed in the bed. I was livid— still waiting—no one came—. I waited until three, one hour later. I went storming to the desk again, I was so angry by that time I couldn't see straight. I was seeing red, yellow, purple and orange. I was like a bull just out of the gate. I said to the nurse, "I want towels, soap, washcloths and powder. Tony stinks of urine, and I'm going to wash him right now. The aids left him with the urinal, for over an hour, and never came back. I was going to talk to them, about washing him then, but they never came back.

"We're short-handed, I'll help you."

"I really don't need your help I can do it myself." She insisted on helping me. She was apologizing all over the place, explaining how awful it was Tony was left, and how they only had two PCT's for fifty patients. The hospital kept cutting the help and the PCT's and the nurses couldn't give the patient the care they'd like to have given, because of not having enough time.

"Administration is going to hear from me in the morning. This is ridiculous! The rates keep going up but the patient care keeps going down." She had brought in the soaped disposable washcloths that were not heated. I was so anxious to get rid of that smell; poor Tony was getting a shock treatment with the room temperature washcloths. The poor thing when I think about it in hindsight, I feel awful that we didn't take the time to make them warmer. He never even complained about them, he was probably relieved to be getting freshened up.

When I went to wash his groin; in the cracks, I could actually see the urine from the night before rolling off. Trembling with rage, and verbalizing uncontrollably to the nurse how distraught I was, over the whole situation. She had a lot of empathy about what had happened. Plus I'm sure she was worried about her own job being threatened but, I actually wasn't personally angry with her.

I knew she was an excellent nurse because we had her on the cancer floor, and she had been a very attentive nurse. The cancer floor was a whole different thing. The patient's care there was impeccable up there, which made me even angrier; you had to be in a dying situation for good patient care. Bullshit! It should be like that all over the hospital not just on the cancer floor. We finally got Tony all cleaned up, and powered. Fresh, clean, and smelling like a human being again. I tucked him in, and he fell asleep like a baby. My baby!

I wasn't able to sleep by then; I was just so frustrated, after that whole mess all; I kept milling the situation over, and over in my mind.

Going in, and out smoking my brains out all night—morning couldn't come fast enough—. I finally laid down about five thirty knowing Dr. Bane would be there in about an hour. I couldn't wait!

Finally six thirty came, right on time; Dr. Bane was in the hospital. The nurse from the night before came in and said, "Your doctors in the next room. She'll be in to see you shortly." She told me that she had told the doctor what had happened the night before. She again apologized; just at that moment the doctor came through the door.

The doctor was also upset saying, "I heard what happened last night." Agreeing; that it was awful, ridiculous, and something needed to be done. Administration doesn't listen to the nurse's, PCT'S or, even the doctors for that matter. Complaints had to come from the patients or, their families. She told me who to call, and complain too.

"Call at eight-thirty. I've been receiving a lot of complaints lately." She went over what was going to take place that day. Tony was going to have an ultrasound of the kidney, pancreas, and liver, then a nuclear bone scan. "Tony also has bronchitis, and I'm going to change the nebulizer to ventilation therapy to help loosen up the mucus. I'm ordering an EMG test and having a neurologist look at him. I'm also stopping the Adivan Tony was sleeping too much, and changing the anxiety and depression medicine, switching medicines around." Continuing with, "His blood work was looking good but, I don't have the results of the echocardiogram yet." When she was leaving she encouraged me to call the head honchos, and complain.

Eight-thirty couldn't come fast enough either. I kept going in and out of the hospital until finally it was eight-thirty. I called at exactly eight thirty five, the lady that answered the phone said,

"The VP is on the phone." told she would call me back. I thought sure I'll never hear from her, but I was wrong, about twenty minutes later. The VP did call— I told her what had happened, and that the hospital was worse than a nursing home; how ridiculous it was to expect the staff to handle so many patients. It was humanly impossible to do all that was expected of them, and it wasn't their fault. They simply needed; more staff. Period!

I told her, "I'm not new to the hospital. We've been coming to this hospital for thirty years." I'd seen the care go downhill, drastically since the beginning of the year, and gotten progressively worse. I told her Tony had open-heart surgery back in January, from then until that day medical care had fallen terribly. I also mentioned the situation regarding Tony's practically bleeding to death in ICU, *(Intensive Care Unit)*. The only reason I hadn't complained then was I was so thrilled, he was still alive—I blew it off. Nevertheless it happened, and should not have. I also commended the cancer floor, and told her every floor should be like that one. It was a dirty shame you had to be on your deathbed to get the care you needed. It wasn't fair. I then told her about the food situation, and that I had complained to the charge nurse about it.

I didn't stop there; I called the pride line to complain to them too. The pride line was for complaints, because they wanted their patients to have excellent care. Ha! Ha! How? With limited help, I didn't think so, and expressed just that!

I was on the phone with the pride line when the charge nurse came in. She was armed with pencil and paper she wanted to know what had happened verbatim. She was jumping through hoops to make me happy. She had the cleaning woman cleaning the whole room, and scrubbing the mattress. The transporter had just taken Tony for the ultra-sound, they had been there earlier, but he was on the potty due to the physic, he had the day before. The cleaning-lady was cleaning everything in sight, vacuuming, washing cabinets. She then said, "I'm going to have the carpet shampooed." That was very impressive; but all I really wanted was, Tony to be taken care of, and more staff put-on the floors. I had been assured that would happen. I also overheard the charge nurse asking the VP whom she should call; I assumed she was talking about more staff. They did however have more staff on the floor that night. I guess that old saying is true. *(The squeaky wheel does get the oil.)*

All the nurses and PCT's were happy that I had complained. The nurse's had been trying to tell the head honchos the situation, but their response was, work harder and faster. One can only work at a certain speed when working with patients who need care. One patient may need more time than another. Insurance and hospital rates kept going up, but the care less desirable.

When Tony came back from the test, I told him what had transpired while he was gone. He was shocked, with all that had been done

He was having a rough time from the physic he had, the diarrhea was relentless and making him miserable. Everything had to be done at once, or else, he'd have an accident, and he didn't want that to happen.

I was upset about the physic Tony had, he was quite uncomfortable from it. I questioned if he even needed it for a kidney ultrasound. I was assured he did to get better pictures without contrast dye. I had explained the day before the test; that if he was to have contrast dye, he would need prophylactic medication, he's allergic to contrast dye, so without contrast it was necessary to have the physic to get better pictures. I guess one has to do what they have to do. Nevertheless, it had disturbed me to see Tony so uncomfortable and miserable. Poor guy enough was enough.

Since Tony had gone over a lot of hurdles; he'd overcome throughout the years; a lot of the staff knew us, from tests, different floors he'd been on, for different reasons. In addition, I'd met a lot more in the smoking shed through the last few times he was in the hospital. We had been at the hospital excessively that year especially. When I'd walk around the hospital it wasn't uncommon, for people from different departments to come up to me, and ask how Tony was doing. They were my support system while I was there and I Thank God for them. You can't even imagine how much they had helped me through a lot of tough times. I thank each and every one of them from the bottom of my heart.

When the technician came up to inject the nuclear medicine for the bone scan; being done later that day, she happened to be one of the technicians that had taken care of Tony many, times over the years. She told Tony he'd be able to have lunch, get some rest, then he'd be going down about two thirty for the test. *(Nuclear medicine has to be in your body about three hours before the scan can be done.)* Afterwards he'd be done with tests for the rest of the day.

The diarrhea continued throughout the day making Tony weaker and weaker.

Throughout that day Tony also got inhalation therapy four times to clear his lungs.

By that time dinner was near, and he didn't want hospital food.

"I want ribs. " I asked the nurse if he could have them and she said, "He can have whatever he wants."

"He deserves a reward after what he's gone through." She agreed!

Tony called Joey to see if he would go get him some ribs after work. Joey's was more than happy to do that for his dad

When Joey got to the hospital we all had ribs for dinner. It was great to see Tony, have an appetite, and eat well. After he ate he pretty much crashed. He was however; still sleeping a lot, I was sure the morphine contributed to it. He was exhausted though he'd had a full day of the works; tests, therapy, and diarrhea. Joey left shortly after we finished eating; I pretty much crashed too after, the last night we had.

The next day we were awaken by the cheery voice of Dr. Bane saying, "Good morning. I hate to wake you up this early but you could go back to sleep when I leave. I've got good news." She examined Tony telling us, "The tests came back CLEAN—. There's 'NO CANCER,' and the "BONES" are fine."

"I don't believe he ever had bone cancer?" She agreed with me and said, "I don't either, his kidneys, pancreas, and liver are all okay too.

"Thank You Jesus, Another Miracle!" As I make the sign of the cross. She went on to say, "I'm going to order an EMG *(Electro muscle graph)* to see what's wrong with Tony's legs, and why he was having such a hard time walking, and was so weak." I was happy to hear we were finally going to get to the bottom of things. She asked if the Dr. Even had come in yet.

"No, I haven't seen her. Maybe she's mad at me, because I called you instead of calling her when Tony got sick this time."

"I notified her that Tony was in the hospital, and I requested her to see him."

Then she continued saying, she'd like a neurologist to look at Tony. She was discontinuing the IV because it wasn't doing anything except, make him shake. She was also going to reduce the heart medicine, and add another she didn't care what Dr.Wilton said. She mentioned maybe-sending Tony to rehabilitation to build him up. I mentioned the rehabilitation in the hospital. However, she replied that was only for short term, and Tony would need a longer; length of time.

To say that we were more than elated with the good news is an understatement. Next, was waiting to find out what was wrong with Tony's legs?

We had waited all that day for Tony to go down for the EMG test. I didn't know what that test was for so; I asked my support group in the smoking shed about it. It was explained that the EMG test was to measure how much muscle Tony had in his legs. I asked where the test was done, as I'd never seen that department before. They told me, it was in the outpatient rehabilitation area. There's a special doctor that did the test and it was usually done when the doctor was called in on an emergency, the doctor wasn't there all the time. Which explained why it wasn't a scheduled test, Tony never did have the test that day.

Tony finally got called to go down for the EMG test the next day. I went with him to the rehabilitation department. The nurse took him right in we didn't have to wait. They wheeled the gurney Tony was on into a tiny office having a hard time fitting the gurney in, and closed the door.

I had asked if I could stay with him, but the doctor said, "The office is too small, there isn't enough room." I really wanted to see for myself what kind of response Tony would get from them putting needles in his legs. I also wanted to hear for myself what the doctor had to say. I certainly saw with my own eyes, that the room was in fact too small; the test would take about twenty minutes. I ran outside for a cigarette while Tony was tested. I got back just about the time they finished. He was just being wheeled into the hall as I got back. The transporter was there waiting for Tony's chart, before taking him back to his room. The doctor was writing his evaluation in it after finishing the test. The clerk then gave the chart to the transporter. I asked the clerk if I could talk to the doctor, she told me the doctor was on the phone when he got off the phone she'd tell him I wanted to see him. I told Tony, "I'll meet you upstairs; after I talk to the doctor, as he was being wheeled back to his room. Since Tony couldn't remember what the doctor had said. Tony was screwing the whole thing up; I couldn't make any sense out of what he was telling me. When the doctor finally came out to talk to me, I asked, how Tony had done with the test, and what the conclusion was? "The nerves in his legs were damaged from the chemo. That's why he's having a problem walking."

'Is the damage permanent?"

"As long as Tony continues with chemo; it will not get better, it would only get worse." I explained that Tony was in remission, and hadn't had a chemo treatment since August.

"If he doesn't get anymore chemo the nerves will repair themselves with therapy." I was delighted to hear that news was more than encouraging.

The doctor asked me about Tony's history, I went through it all; the three open-heart surgeries, two thoracotomies, the lung cancer, and that it was his third type of lung cancer Tony had; and how it had metasized to the brain, and supposedly the bones. I continued, telling him Tony had whole brain radiation, and seven chemo treatments. He asked if I knew what kind of chemo Tony had gotten, I quickly rattled off VP 16 and Cisplatin, one day of intravenous chemo, and two days of the oral chemo. "I'll write my report for Dr. Bane."

He then said, "I'm considering a rehabilitation center for acute patients. There they would teach Tony how to sit, getup, walk, get in and out of the car, plus much more; so he could be self-sufficient when he got home." I explained to the doctor that we already had a walker, and toilet seat risers at home. I thanked him for his time, and went back upstairs, to explain to Tony, what the doctor, said.

When I got back upstairs, I explained to Tony exactly what the doctor had said to me. Tony said, "I thought I heard the damage wasn't repairable, and maybe I'd be able to walk.

"On the, contrary."

The doctor said, "The opposite as long as you didn't get chemo. It was repairable and reversible." Nevertheless, negative Tony always focused on the negative. Or did he hear correctly? I told Tony the doctor talked about a rehabilitation hospital. Tony then expressed his wishes, by saying he wanted to go back home to do the therapy. *(God do I wish I had listened to him now; hindsight is terrible.)* I explained to him that it was going to be intensive therapy, that he couldn't get at home, and how important it was to follow through. It wasn't going to be easy on him, but on the other hand, it would be a piece of cake, after what he'd been through. I reconfirmed, "You want to walk don't you?"

"Yes."

"Then that's what needs to be done to achieve that goal."

Again at dinnertime Tony did not want hospital food, so he called Joey. Tony wanted Buffalo wings that night. Good old Joey said, without a quibble, "Whatever you want dad."

Tony's wishes were our command for the last nine months, anything to make him happy; and as content as we could. I can't say enough about our children. They had been there every step of the way. Supporting us in any way they could. Through an awful horrible situation they sure have made me proud. We are blessed, I know, to have all our children stick together, and be there for us. Many people had told us how great our children were. I must say I couldn't have done what I did without their help. I surely would have crashed months before.

When Joey got there we discussed through dinner what transpired throughout the day. We talked about the EMG test, and Tony explained how the doctor had put needles in his legs to see if he felt them. When Tony had felt the stick the doctor would say, good, explaining to Tony it's good when you feel the needles. If you hadn't felt them, that would be bad. Tony was grateful he had felt all the needles, and so was I. I assumed that meant the nerves weren't dead completely. Tony was tired after dinner, but more aware than he had been; now that he wasn't taking quite as much pain medicine. Some of the swelling was also going down; so things were looking much better. We had continually gotten great news; the anxiety and tension was starting to dwindle. At last! We both needed a breather from all the stress and sadness. After nine months of intense terror, with an awful situation that seemed to get worse daily. We deserved a break. I certainly was on the verge of cracking.

Dr. Even finally came in that night. I was kind of waiting for her; I had run into her earlier in the elevator. I asked her if she was going to come in to see Tony. Dr. Bane kept asking if she'd been to see him yet. When I ran into her she explained she had been off that weekend. She had just recently opened a new office and was very busy with that. I asked if she was chalking us off her list. She laughed saying, "No I'll be in later." It was late when she arrived; about twelve thirty in the morning. I had been doing my nails to kill time while waiting for her. Tony had been sleeping on and off all day, and was sleeping when she came. She said, "You're up?"

"Yes, I was waiting for you." Tony woke up when he heard her voice. She started asking him questions about how he felt.

I told her he said, "For the first time today, he doesn't want anymore chemo." We were told the problem with his legs was; a side effect from the chemo. She hadn't said much, and then she left. I was sure she thought at that moment; to each his own! I followed her out to tell her the bone scan came back clean. She replied that the last bone windows she saw showed otherwise. Her professional diagnosis was that there was bone cancer. Although she couldn't prove it by the two biopsies Tony had.

I was still very confused, who, and what, do you believe?

That evening we were finally; going to be able to go to bed, without all that pent-up stress, both exhausted after seven days of intense anxiety. I felt like the air had been taken out of my tire. The elephant had been lifted off my shoulders. Relieved at last!

Dr. Bane came in bright and early the next morning as she always did. "There isn't much more we can do for Tony at this hospital. Tony's stable, I'm going to get the rest of the results, and have a social worker look into the rehabilitation hospital. That's what Tony needs next. That's the next step after I get all the results."

Relieved Tony ate a real good breakfast that morning. We were both in great moods, feeling somewhat alive again, which neither had felt in a long time.

Tony was still getting inhalation therapy four times a day to loosen the congestion in his lungs.

Then the neurologist came in to talk to us, and check Tony over. He ran Tony though a few different tests. I guess to see if anything had affected Tony's brain. He had him touch his nose with each hand, and then he pricked Tony with a pin all over his legs to see if he felt it. The neurologist tapped on Tony's feet, ankles, and knees, with his little mallet to see if Tony responded. I told the neurologist Tony's nerves were damaged from the chemo; it was a side effect from it. He said, "Don't say anything about the Dr. Even in this hospital she's like a God here."

"I'm not angry with Dr. Even on the contrary, I'm very grateful to her. She has put Tony in remission, and I'm very happy about that." He went on to say, she's a personal friend of his, and she was very devoted, and worked day and night. (Which was a fact!) He didn't know how she did it. He worried about her. Saying she couldn't keep up that pace, she's very highly regarded.

I responded, "I personally have not heard one bad thing about her, only good, and praise."

"With cancer you're between the devil, and the deep blue sea. Without chemo you expire, with chemo there are side effects." I repeated that I was very appreciative, and grateful to her "after all" she put Tony in remission. As a matter of fact, I even hugged and kissed her for it.

A bit later, Dr. Wilton came in, and advised us, "All Tony's heart problems were chemo related, there's nothing wrong with his heart. His heart was amazingly strong with all he had gone through." He was even pleasantly surprised how well the heart was functioning. I told Dr. Wilton, Dr. Bane, and Dr. Even said, "I'd literally kept Tony alive." He was writing in Tony's chart at that point. He stopped looked up at me and said, "I agree." I guess I was looking for an explanation as to how; I had accomplished that feat. Not quite understanding 'how' I possibly could have accomplished that, I felt they were just patronizing, all I did was take care of the 'man of my life', the best I could. He also went on to say, "Dr. Even did a great job with Tony," and I agreed.

As I was coming back from having a cigarette, the social worker stopped me in the hall. She said, "The exercise doctor will be in to see you. Look for the good-looking Greek," and chuckled.

"Okay I will, and chuckled back."

Later that day the exercise doctor came in. Low and behold it was the same doctor that did the EMG. I was shocked actually, because I hadn't gotten his name the day before. I had no idea it was the same doctor. We went over Tony's medical history again. He said, "I'm thinking about the rehabilitation hospital." Asked us what we thought about it. I was all for it, I felt it would be beneficial to Tony's, recovery, quicker. He said, "I was very impressed that you knew the dates regarding Tony's history. However, I was stunned when I asked you what kind of chemo Tony was on and you spit it out without hesitation." He remarked that most people don't know that. They only know their getting chemo, with no idea as to what kind.

I learned early on the best advocate was a knowledgeable one. So I made it my business to know all I could, and then some.

The EMG doctor said, "It will take Tony some time to get back on his feet. After all it took ten months for him to deteriorate." The rule of thumb was it takes three days for every day you're off your feet. I'd heard that before, so using that scale it would takeover a year to get Tony back to normal.

Nevertheless, we were so pleased to hear, Tony could get better time, didn't matter. We had all the time in the world. We were very happy with that news for a change, finally were on an upswing and it felt, wonderful. Prayers were being answered—.

Later that evening Tony wanted corn beef for dinner. He called Joey again and asked him if he'd, please pick it up for him. Joey again said, "It'll be no problem at all." When Joey got to the hospital we told him the great news, he was excited too. Our poor kids were affected as much as we were, and I kept them abreast, every step of the way.

That night Tony and I were still exhausted from the entire trauma. I felt for the first time somewhat relieved; we both went to bed early, feeling as though we'd been beaten with a whip, every bone in our bodies ached, positive it was from all the stress, and tension we'd experienced. Tony felt the same.

The next morning when Dr. Bane came in saying, "All the news is good." Again she repeated; that there wasn't anymore that could be done at that hospital. She was going to have the social worker call the rehab hospital to see if there was a bed, and they'd be moving Tony as soon as there was one available.

When she left I went down for a cigarette. On my way back to the room the social worker caught me in the hall again, she said, "I was waiting for the rehabilitation hospital to call me back to let me know if they had a room. I'll let you know when I hear something. If there's a room he'll be moved sometime today; he'll need clothes for the week, sweats would be best because they're easy to put on and off. He'll also need gym shoes, sox, and underwear. The patients dress daily; it's part of the therapy. They don't stay in bed all day like a hospital. In addition, he'll need his own toiletries, as Medicare doesn't pay for those items."

When I got back to the room I quickly called Joey at work. I asked him about the clothes he'd taken home the night before. He was going to wash them for his dad. He said, "I only washed the sweats, not the underwear." I told him to bring the sweats when he came after work. Later that day I was coming back from having a cigarette again when the social worker caught me.

"I was just in to see Tony and explained all about the rehabilitation hospital to him."

The doctors said, "He'll be there a week to ten days. The rehabilitation hospital just called, they'll have a bed about two thirty, three today. You'll need to be ready to go by then. I'll order a Med. Car for that time."

"Could I drive Tony myself? I think he'd like that better."

She asked, "Will you be okay?"

"We'd been fine. I've been transporting him until he was hospitalized without a problem." She advised me that when we were ready to leave, I'd have to bring papers, regarding the transfer. I thanked her for all her trouble. Of course I wouldn't be able to stay there with Tony like I did at the hospital. "Will you be okay with that?"

"I'll be fine." She went on to say it would be good for me too; I'd have a little break from all the pressures.

"The only reason I'll be able to handle this is; it's in Tony's best interest to go there. I felt he'd get better faster, with the fulltime intense rehabilitation as opposed to part time at home so, I was all for it.

I immediately called Joey back to ask him if he could go to our house at lunch and get more clothes, underwear, and gym shoes for his dad. He was going to be going to the rehabilitation hospital about three that afternoon. Joey said, "I could do that." Thank God for his help. That would sure made it easier for me, that way I could pack up the room, get Tony dressed, and ready to go. Then take all the stuff we accumulated over the last eight days, flowers, candy, cards, Tony, and our clothes. We had a ton of shit to pack up; I felt as though I was moving, I had to make several trips to the car, I couldn't carry it all at one time. My packed car looked like we we're living out of it, like vagabonds there was so much stuff.

Joey brought the clothes, during his lunchtime. Tony had lunch, then I got him dressed, we were ready to be on our way. I got the papers from the social worker we had to turn-in when we got there. We said our good-byes to all the staff that had come to know us well, and off we went. The PCT got a wheelchair and brought Tony down; while I went ahead to get the car so I could pull up to the curb to make it easier for Tony.

Rehab Hospital

$\mathcal{W}$ e were finally on our way. I asked Tony how he felt about going there. "I'm okay with it." Tony was anxious to walk, and he thought the rehabilitation hospital would be good for him.

Our goal was to be able to go to Florida in a couple of months. That gave Tony a deadline to shoot for. Tony said as we were driving, "I want a malt before we reach the rehabilitation hospital," so we stopped at a drive through to get one.

Then he said, "I have to go to the bathroom."

"There's no way I could possibly get you in, and out of the car, and in and out of the bathroom alone. You are going to have to hold it, hon. I will get there as fast as I can." *Maybe I should have let the medical car take him after all. I was a nervous wreck.*

I knew the general area the rehabilitation hospital was in however, I did not know exactly where it was located. Anxious about finding the sign; it could be seen from the street the social worker warned us. Then we had to turn onto a winding street covering four acres of land with multiple buildings to find the hospital. I had to make sure I went to the right building, and the emergency entrance. Once we arrived the staff would come with a wheelchair for Tony. We found the right building without any trouble; I thought we would never get there though it had taken so long— much longer than I anticipated. I went in to get help; the staff brought Tony into the hospital, while I went to park the car. I hoped I would be able to find Tony once inside the building, I did not know the layout of hospital. It was not hard to find Tony; the frazzled nerves had been in vain, I guessed being anxious about the unknown; and not knowing my way around.

After finding Tony, the staff and I got him settled in bed right away. The nurse explained the routine; the rules then brought Tony his dinner. That he enjoyed since eating was important to Tony's rehabilitation. Thank God! The food was not bad at all. I joked with the nurse that she had won Tony over by bringing him food right away. We all chuckled. Asking Tony how he was feeling, and if he was comfortable, "I'm okay." *However, I could sense his anxiousness.* The nurse explained, Tony would be kept busy all day, going in and out of different kinds of therapy, and over the next couple of days, they would be accessing him.

One of the rules, I needed to leave when visiting hours were over. It was important because they had the patients up early in the morning, and they needed their rest. The nurse said, "They work the patients hard." They were also going to give Tony a shower that night. He had not had one in the past eight-day's only sponge baths. That would make him feel good, once freshened up, and he was looking forward to that.

As they took Tony for his shower I kissed and hugged him said, good-bye. "I will be back tomorrow afternoon."

I felt terrible leaving Tony there, but good at the same time, because I felt we made the right decision. Having mixed emotions as I drove; knowing that I'd be lonely, and frightened to death to be alone! However, by the time I got home, I was so tired, and exhausted I could not even think anymore. I just went to bed, immediately fell asleep, almost before even hitting the pillow, I was that tired.

The next morning when I woke up; umpteen things had to get done. I hadn't been home in eight days. The mail looked like I'd been away a month. I had wash; bills to pay, and clean the refrigerator of rotten food that had grown green stuff. YUK! Then straighten the house though it wasn't dirty, no one had been here to dirty it, just dusty. I dusted, gathered some fresh clothes for Tony, and called him about lunchtime to see how he was doing. He was homesick, stating, "They are not doing anything for me that I can't do at home." He wanted to come home, and told me to come get him.

"You haven't even been there a day you have to try it, give it a chance."

"I'll take a cab home." I ignored that comment. Telling him, "I'll be there in a little while."

"Don't bother to come."

"Okay." I hung up the phone, and finished the things I had to get done. Then I took a shower, got dressed, and left. All the while my heart was breaking. I had stopped at a store, when I came out; I called Tony from my cell.

When Tony answered saying, "I walked eighty feet, the therapist was amazed that I did so good." I was so happy for him, I could have cried with joy. Tony was excited, heard it in his voice. He said, "I could come home when I walk, Right?"

"Yes, of course."

If Tony had only known in my heart of hearts I was torn to pieces, and that I was dying inside. To be without him, was like being without my arm. My heart was breaking; I missed him so much, but I couldn't let him know that, I had to be strong for his sake. I'd have given anything to have been able to go get him; bring him home but, that would not have been a good idea or good for him—. It tore me up to have him think I didn't want him home. He was my darling, the love of my life, my world! If only Tony knew—how sick—lonely—depressed—and scared—. I really was—over that situation. However, I had to keep my feelings of crumbling to myself, for his sake. I had to stay "strong"!

"I'm coming to the hospital even though you said. "Don't come.""

"I changed my mind," we both had a little chuckle.

I was at the hospital within a few minutes. Tony's attitude had improved. He'd felt a sense of accomplishment; I was so pleased for him, and with him.

Inspirational Story

When I arrived at the hospital Tony and I went to the sunroom. It was just down the hall a few feet from his room. The sunroom had windows all the way around, floor to ceiling, offering a beautiful view of the grounds. The sun was shining that day, and it pleasantly warmed the room, as we chatted

There was a woman in a wheelchair (obviously another patient) talking to a couple. After the people left she turned to Tony, and asked, "What are you in here for?" He also was in a wheelchair.

"I had lung cancer, I'm in remission, and the chemo damaged the nerves in my legs so, I have to do extensive therapy to strengthen my legs again."

"Maybe I have a story to inspire you. I also had lung cancer that metastasized to my brain; I had chemo, and full brain radiation. The doctor's gave me six months to live. I was fifty-three then; which was three years ago. When it was in the lungs I had a five- percent chance, when it went to the brain I had a one- percent chance of survival." In awe; my mouth hung open I bet! I turned to Tony, and said, "From God's mouth to your ears—if that isn't inspirational—I don't know what is. What were the chances of that woman of all the patients in that hospital to be in that room, at that time, and giving 'you' her personal testimony?" "Another Miracle!"

I was so touched by that woman's story, after hearing her recap, verbatim, exactly, what Tony had gone through himself the past year. Her testimony, stirred the emotions, deep in my soul,

I hung onto her every word as Gospel.

Dee and George had called that evening saying, "We went to visit Tony, but we went to the other hospital. Only to find out that he had been transferred." They were going to try to get there before eight.

They were having a house built in Florida, and had to go there to check on something. They needed to inspect something for approval, so the construction could continue, and they wanted to see Tony before leaving.

They did make it before eight; and spent a few minutes with Tony at least. They were leaving the next morning, and would be gone for a few weeks or so. They gave me their cell number in case I'd need them, or they'd call us when they got back.

The next day was Sunday, all our children came to see their Dad, except Mario, he was working. Anthony was bringing mostoccoli for Tony he had a taste for that, of course he would enjoy home cooking better, then hospital food, couldn't blame him, who wouldn't?

Anthony was supposed to be there about four or five. Tony usually had dinner around four thirty so that would be perfect.

I had picked up our granddaughters at the Halloween store on my way to the hospital, so Tammy could work in peace. She was going to meet us later at the hospital, and have dinner with us

When we reached the hospital, I left the twins sitting downstairs in the waiting room, while I ran up to get Tony, to bring him down. I let the twins wait downstairs knowing there was a guard by the door watching out for them. After I brought their Papa down the twins were all over him, as we visited, waiting for Anthony to arrive with dinner.

It was getting later and later and Tony and the twins were getting hungry and impatient. I was starving myself. Anthony finally got there around six, by then my patience were frazzled, and we were beyond hungry. I told Anthony not to cook anymore because it was a hassle for him and caused too much anxiety for Dad. Though the thought was heartfelt, it turned into a fiasco.

Tony was done eating; he wanted to go back to his room, and go to bed. He looked exhausted! The twins had worn him out.

Our family had all met in the large visiting room where we ate, and visited together. The hospital only allowed two visitors on the floors, and children weren't allowed up there at all. The huge lounge area worked out great, there was a TV, and it helped to keep the twins busy while we talked.

Tammy finally called saying she was on her way, and wanted her dad to see her new truck she had just bought, but by that time, he was too tired to wait. He couldn't have cared less at that point; Tony's endurance was gone. He didn't care about seeing anything but his bed, to tell the truth, I was ready for bed myself. I found it amazing how emotional stress could drain you.

Shortly after eating our children said, "Good-bye." I had taken Tony up to his room to get him tucked in when, Tammy got there. She ate real fast, talked with her dad a few minutes, and then we all went on our way.

The next day I went to the hospital around one, to meet with Tony and the physiologist, she was going to test him.

Tony seemed confused on a couple of the tests, but nothing too serious.

Some of the questions on his health, how long had he been sick, his age, date of birth, year, what, where, and when; Tony had never been able to answer some of those questions; he always relied on me, so that didn't seem different. He did however, have trouble with putting pieces to a puzzle together. After the tests were completed, we met with the caseworker. She introduced herself, and then explained that she would be meeting with all the staff working with Tony that would be assessing him. And she would let us know his prognosis, and when his expected discharge date would be. We made an appointment for the next day to go over all the assessments that were done that day.

The next day Anthony had talked to his dad, and told him he was bringing him ribs, but didn't commit to a time. That hospital wasn't as easy, fast or, close to get to, as the other hospital in our hometown. It took a minimum of thirty minutes if not longer to get there. Anthony had however, brought the ribs before dinnertime. So at least Tony didn't have to wait to eat, that was great. Anthony stayed for a while, visited with his dad, then left.

That night Greg and Loraine called to say they were coming to visit. They asked if they could bring Tony anything. "No, thank you though. Just come." They got there about thirty minutes later. We visited for awhile when, Tony said, "I'm tired, you'll have to excuse me, but I have to go to bed."

They had gotten him up early at the hospital, to dress, eat, and then off to therapy, so he'd had a full day. Greg and Loraine said, "Good bye." I stayed and got Tony back in bed, his clothes ready for the next day, kissed and hugged him, then left. I was drained myself by then, I didn't know if it was from all the stress I'd been under or what but, I was extremely exhausted. I couldn't wait to get home in bed.

The next day I had the appointment with the social worker, to get Tony's medical assessments, and discharge date.

I was rushing to get ready to leave, when a friend who had also suffered with cancer stopped by. She had heard Tony was back in the hospital. I explained he had been, but was in the rehabilitation hospital then. She told me I needed to take care of myself, and take time for myself. How important it was for me to do that, with all the stress I was under. I should take a day or so off, and go somewhere with my daughter. Tony's in a good place, and was being well taken care of. When Tony did come home, I'd have my hands full; I knew that to be fact. She then said, "Tell Tony I send him my best" and left.

Reprieve

A s I readied myself to leave for the hospital, I thought about what she had said, knowing she was right. People kept telling me I needed to get away from the tension at times, to take a break. But, I wouldn't think of leaving Tony that was out of the question.

As I was driving, I thought maybe I should take advantage, if only one night. I called Tammy from my cell, and told her, we're going to Lake Geneva for an overnight reprieve— to arrange for it— we were both excited—. When I got to the hospital I told Tony of my plans he wasn't for that idea at all. I told Tony, Tammy and I we're going to leave the next day right after my appointment to have my breast checked. I explained, "We'll only be gone over night, and I'll be back the very next day. The boys will come to the hospital to visit, and I'll call to check on you while I'm away." But, Tony still wasn't crazy about that idea. However, I knew I needed to get away from the stress— if only for a day!

During our appointment with the caseworker, I told her I wanted to take Tony home the following Sunday on a pass. We were going to celebrate Paul's birthday that day, and I wanted to bring Tony there for the party.

She explained I'd have to go through training with a therapist before I could take Tony out on a pass. I had to learn how to transfer him, even though I'd been doing it for months. It was a hospital rule. I could understand that since they were liable for his safety. I didn't like that idea but I went against my gut and went. I was willing to learn anything to make things easier on Tony and myself. She said, "You can go for the training Friday for his Sunday pass." Continuing with, "Tony's discharge date will be October twenty fifth. Tony's psychological test showed there's some brain damage, either from the cancer or, radiation, but considered to be very mild."

I explained that I was going to Lake Geneva the next day and I would be back by Thursday night. I would be there at nine-thirty sharp Friday morning for the training class with Tony.

I stayed at the hospital all day until late evening after getting Tony all settled in bed. I reminded Tony that Anthony was coming on Wednesday and Joey on Thursday. I'll return Thursday evening and that I'll see you early Friday morning, for the training. Tony said, "Have a good time."

"I'll call you tomorrow." Explaining that my doctor's appointment was in the morning; and then Tammy and I were leaving! We would only be away one day, then I hugged and kissed Tony and left.

When I called the rehabilitation center the next morning Tony sounded good. I knew he missed me already, I missed him, and I hadn't even left yet. I felt guilty about even leaving him at all. However, I knew it would do Tammy, and I a world of good just to get away. If only for that one day!

We went to see the surgeon early the next morning, as planned. The surgeon said,

"You're doing fine come-back in three months for a follow-up." By then it was lunchtime, so we stopped for lunch. As we got back in the car Anthony had called on the cell and left a message. He wanted me to look at a couch he had seen, and wanted our opinion. The furniture store was just off the highway we were taking, so we stopped before leaving for our trip. After looking at the couch, we called Anthony back to let him know we both liked it. At last we were on our way to Lake Geneva, our final destination. By then it was late afternoon, and the traffic was getting heavy. *(Anthony did end up getting that couch.)*

We had run into a terrible car accident, which delayed us, even longer. We finally arrived about six that evening; and drove around the town while it was still light out. I showed Tammy a cottage her father had helped his uncle build many years ago. We noticed the whole town closed up at dusk, and there wasn't much to do. We decided to have dinner, then go see a movie

We had dinner in the restaurant that was adjacent to the hotel. Starting with a couple of cocktails, relaxing, and talking, about our trying drive, and horrible accident we had just missed being involved in by a few minutes. We knew we didn't have much time, before we'd be back on the road home. We tried to savor every minute we had by trying to relax as best we could. My mind was wandering thinking and worrying about Tony. It felt good to get away, but my heart was back home with Tony.

After dinner we went to the show, which happened to be a horror film. We had no idea it was three flights of stairs up to the theatre. We were shocked; we had never been to a movie where we had to go up three flights of stairs to get to. Not to mention that we were the only ones in the whole show. It was spooky! Then just as the movie started, two guys came in. Tammy and I both turned around simultaneously to look at them. We were both scared, and unnerved, neither of us letting the other know how scared we were. Through the whole movie, we each kept looking back trying to see what the two guys were doing. *Did they have to sit behind us? Couldn't they have sat in front of us where we could see them?*

The movie was very good. However, I couldn't wait for it to be over; so we could get the hell out of there.

When that movie ended immediately both of us; at the same time, jumped to our feet! Turned around and Tammy addressed the two guys saying, "So what did you think?" They mumbled something, as they continued leaving; neither of us understood a word they said.

We were however behind them as we left but, by the time we got to the stairs. They were nowhere in sight. They had, it seemed, to have totally vanished into thin air. Just then the strap on my purse broke. I had to stop to get a better grip on it before I dropped everything all over the stairs. I grabbed my purse tightly against my body as quickly as I could, as we ran down the stairs, out the door, and right to the car. We were scared— two-woman out alone —late in a strange place—. We locked ourselves in the car immediately, as we looked around to see if we were being watched or what— No sign of them—. We were paranoid, and shaking in our boots. We couldn't figure out where they had disappeared.

We continued back to our room watching, looking back making sure we weren't being followed. Whew! We weren't! That was creepy.

Back in our room we got our pajamas on to relax, safe and sound. We went through books of sales, and things to do the next day.

We decided we would get-up early the next morning, and go for a massage. That would be relaxing, fun, and something we both could use and enjoy. Tammy had checked the brochures for the best places to go. Then she made a few phone calls to check prices, what was included, appointment times, and all the particulars.

The next morning we drove to the resort we had chosen for our massages. It was very classy, secluded way off the main drag. In fact, I thought we'd never get there. As we entered the road, the grounds were pretty over looking the golf course as we drove through. When we finally got there, we parked the car, and went directly to the girl at the counter to inform her we were there for our appointments. Then we walked around the gift shop while we waited to be called. When we were called they gave us each a big; plushy Turkish robe, and a pair of rubber massage flip-flops. It was a posh place and quite a treat for both of us. First we went into the hot tub to relax and wait our turn for our massages. Next came the massage, it was fantastic, and really did us a lot of good, to un-stress our bodies. After the massages we took showers to freshen up and left. When we got back to our room we dressed, packed up, and checked out.

Our next step was where to eat. We decided to try a unique restaurant that served Swedish food. Neither of us had ever eaten at a Swedish restaurant. It turned out to be good and different. After lunch we were off to our shopping excursion.

We each bought several duck outfits for the seasons, for our outside ornamental ducks. We bought candy to bring home as gifts for several people. And I also bought the book that was recommended by the woman we talked to in the sunroom titled: Love, Miracles, and Medicine.

Then we decided to stop at an outlet mall that was on the way home, by then it had started raining, and gotten bitterly cold. We hadn't planned on it getting so cold, nor did we have the proper clothes. It had been beautiful out when we left, but with the drastic weather change we were freezing.

We literally ran in and out of the stores there, my teeth were chattering, I was so cold. It was ungodly, nasty out, and we both agreed that part of the trip was not enjoyable at all. *(More like torture.)*

As we got closer to home I called Tony to see how he was doing. Joey answered the phone and said, "Dad's sleeping already, he didn't eat much, he wasn't feeling well, he missed you." The feeling was mutual. I missed Tony immensely too, and was anxious to see him. It did us good to get away, though. Nonetheless, couldn't wait to get home to Tony! We still had to pick up the twins, stop and eat dinner, and then get home. We we're both pooped it had been a full day, and a half. I was tired; and had to be at the hospital at nine the next morning for the training. So that I'd be rested for the next day, I went right to bed.

I got up early to get to the hospital by nine. When I got there Tony still wasn't feeling well, and had refused therapy that morning. I made it clear to him that if he didn't do the transfer therapy, he wouldn't be able to leave Sunday for the party. We needed to learn it!

He finally agreed to try therapy that afternoon, if he felt better. By noon Tony was feeling somewhat better, and did go to therapy. The rehab center had a huge room that was sectioned off into different departments. Filled with equipment for therapy; machines, stairs, even a half car and a full bathroom like the one in a house might be. Tony actually did very well; I was amazed at how good he did. I learned the correct way to transfer him in and out of the car—on and off the toilet—in and out of the tub— and the proper way to go up and down stairs—.

Afterwards we met with the caseworker; again she mentioned the mild brain damage, Tony had encountered. Stating it was nothing to worry about; it wouldn't affect his daily living at all. Thank God for that! That day ended on a better note than it started on.

The next day Tony was still feeling nauseated, and had diarrhea. However, he did go to therapy. He'd been ill Thursday, Friday, and Saturday. What was happening to him, since I'd gone to Lake Geneva? I talked to the nurse about my concern with the diarrhea; that was making him weaker, asking about his medication, and the side effects of each one. For some reason they had increased the anti-depressants. She said, "I'll look-up the side effects of that medication." Sure enough, the side affects for the antidepressants were nausea and diarrhea. Bingo! I assume that could be the problem because, Mario had taken those pills over the years. I had some insight when, I suggested that maybe that's what caused his problem. She called the house doctor, and he did cut that medication back to one a day to see if that helped. The nurse said, "The doctor also ordered a stool sample to make sure there weren't bacteria in his system." Tony had had a bowel movement already, but he had put toilet paper in the toilet, which contaminated the stool, therefore it couldn't be used. That afternoon Tony had another bowel movement. When I told the nurse she said, "There isn't a written order for that test, so I can't take it." I was totally confused! *What the hell was going on* I thought to myself? I adamantly told her, "Well there was an order, where did it go? " She just repeated, there wasn't an order, there may have been one, but she didn't have one in 'her' charts. There was nothing she could do. How could there have been an order earlier? That made absolutely no sense! I was confused!

The next day was Sunday and the day of the party. I had to pick up Tony because I was the one that was trained. I was anxious about being alone. All our children were busy; Joey was painting his house outside trying to beat the winter weather. Michael was working on a job he had to get done. Mario and Tammy were at the Halloween store. Hence the busiest time of year— Tony was making dinner for the party. Plus the hospital wasn't close; it was at least an hour there and back. Maybe more by the time I got Tony in the car. I had to challenge it alone! I was sure if I had asked, someone would have gone with me. *I said, bravely to myself you could do it alone.* It was a mistake—.

I had called the hospital before I left. I could tell Tony was anxious to leave. It would be his first time out of the rehabilitation center since he was transferred, over a week ago. "I'll be there in an hour." Tony wanted to be picked up by ten. I got there as fast as I could by eleven I could tell he was disappointed. That hour had seemed like days for him. We were both on edge before we even started to leave. I had talked to Anthony before I left; and we had decided to meet for breakfast. We wanted to give Tony some variety and a change from the hospital food. I was all stressed and shaking by the time we got to the restaurant.

I was taught by the therapist in rehab to put a plastic garbage bag on the seat of the car, to make the transfer to the car easier. That idea was, "Not Good." It made the seat so slippery Tony slid right back out, onto the edge of the car doorframe for starters. I finally got Tony back in the car, with the grace of God. Anthony had bought his dad a rotating swivel seat to make it easier for him to swing around, but Tony complained that the seat was hard and hurt him.

"You'll have to get back out of the car again to remove it." I couldn't pull it from under him, as it had sunk into the car seat from his weight.

"I'm not getting out of the car again."

"There's no way I can remove it with you on it." That started what was supposed to be an enjoyable day. As we started on our way, Tony started. He said, "My back hurts I need a pain pill."

"I don't have any medication with me. I took it out of my purse."

Tony got sarcastic with me, saying, "You shouldn't have taken it out of your purse."

"Even if I had it I couldn't give it to you. You can only take the pills the hospital gives you." Tony wasn't happy about that at all.

"Knock it off. Today is supposed to be an enjoyable day. Not a horrible, miserable one."

I then told Tony about the plans to meet Anthony and Paul for breakfast. His answer was, "No one told me about it."

"I'm telling you now." He was irritable, and miserable, saying, "I feel nauseated." It made me sad to hear he was sick but, I ignored the comment. There wasn't a thing I could do for him. At the restaurant, Tony hardly ate.

After breakfast on to Anthony's house, when we arrived there we got Tony comfortable and resting on the couch. He was extremely tired, and worn out, I was sure from all that had taken place. I knew I was; the stress alone was excruciating.

Anthony and I canned hot peppers, while preparing the dinner.

Then our children started to arrive for dinner, and Paul's birthday.

Tony hardly ate again. With him normally being a great eater that upset me. I was concerned about him being nauseated. Thinking what's the problem? Why was he sick and nauseated? Lots of questions with no answers caused stress—on top of stress—.

We left shortly after coffee, and cake. Tony had to be back to the hospital by eight or, he'd lose the privilege of another pass. I rushed to get him back to the hospital on time; but we were still about ten minutes late. Mario had gone back with me, I'm sure our children knew it had been a bad idea that I'd gone alone that morning with all that had happened. I was grateful to have the help, Mario helped me get his dad undressed, and settled in bed. I laid Tony's clothes out for the next day, and took the dirty clothes home to wash. Visiting hours were over at eight and they enforced it. I then had to fill out forms about Tony's pass, before we left. They asked, about how the day had gone, what we did, who we spent the time with, and on and on. It had been an awful day all the way around, and that's the way I reported it.

Mikey and Ardine

When I got home that evening I called Ardine to see how Mikey was doing. Mikey had a heart attack the Sunday before. "He's not doing too well. He's very sick; had to be put-on a respirator, and had a feeding tube put in. The doctors told her he was a very sick man." She also said, "Mikey needs surgery. The valve in his heart isn't working properly. He's too sick, and weak to do anything now they have to wait, and build him up first."

That poor woman sure had her hands full. She had been diagnosed with breast cancer at the same time I was going through my mammogram, and ultra-sound. She was getting her results about the same time, except she wasn't as lucky. She also had to have the lump removed; it was cancerous. She had to get chemo, and radiation. A few months earlier, Mikey had also had a mild stroke. Then she was in, and out of the hospital herself; having her own problems, and had a problem when she had the port put in. It was leaking blood into her system for some reason. It was causing her so much pain in her chest; she had to be hospitalized for it. Then she had a horrific problem with the Epoetin shot. It had caused her awful pain in her bones, it was so excruciating; she was hospitalized. To top it all off, she had a problem with her leg and back. We cried on each other's shoulders. I tried to pacify her and she me.

The next morning I called the nurse's station to see how Tony was feeling; she told me he hadn't eaten or gone to therapy. I guessed there wasn't any improvement as far as the diarrhea and nausea. I was very upset, but didn't know exactly what to do about it. I was also worried about the diarrhea making him weaker, and him not having therapy to get stronger. The whole deal at the rehabilitation hospital to get stronger was backfiring.

I called the caseworker to set up a meeting about what was going on with Tony. I made an appointment for later that day.

I quickly got a few things done around the house and washed Tony's clothes to bring back. Then made a lot of phone calls looking for the special equipment Tony was going to need when he got home. I called on the stair lift, transfer bench, and grab bar for the tub. Then I was off to the hospital for the meeting.

At the meeting the caseworker asked about the equipment, and what I had found out. I explained, "I found out you have to do your homework. I called several places and the prices varied. If people only called one place they really could get the shaft on price." I was pleased that I had taken the time to call several places, as I saved quite a bit of money doing so. Tony cut in expressing, "I'd like a transfer bench with a hole in it. Like they have at the hospital, so my butt can be cleaned easier." I was glad I hadn't bought one at that point. I thought Tony's suggestion was a great one, anything to make it easier and more thorough for us. You would think the hospital would have suggested that one. "How did the pass go?"

"It was horrible, the diarrhea and nausea continued, and it put a damper on the whole day." None of us liked to see Tony so miserable.

She then said, "I'll set-up an appointment with the therapy doctor so I can discuss it with him. I'll meet with Tony's therapist for an update on his progress."

"I want to talk to the doctor myself."

"I'll make an appointment for you, and let you know when it will be." Our meeting was over; I was to wait to hear from her for the appointment time.

Later she found us; she told me the meeting with the doctor was at eleven the next day. Tony was still not eating much that day. I tried to coax him; so he'd eat as much as he could. Tony was also complaining that he had pain in his hip. My thoughts; fleeing again—was *the cancer back? I was going absolutely crazy wondering worrying praying for God to guide, and help me, help him.* Tony was, not happy there, and expressing just that. I stayed until visiting hours were over as usual, and then went home. It was so difficult for me to go home alone. I extremely missed Tony not being home— In addition, I didn't feel at ease leaving him there either—

I felt between a rock and hard place trying to do the right thing for him and by him, but was I? I wasn't happy about anything that had happened there thus far. When Tony wasn't happy or healthy I wasn't happy either. He was my whole life. We had been together since I was fifteen, and married for forty-two years. Through thick and thin we'd stuck like glue.

It was October 10, 2000, and I had an appointment with the therapy doctor that morning. Before I went to the hospital I ran a few errands. Then I called Tony to check on him. He asked, "Could you stop and pick up tacos for lunch?"

"Sure."

When I got to the hospital I had a hard time finding him. He wasn't in his room, so I went down to the therapy area. I was looking all over when a therapist told me where to find him. He was in a back room doing exercises with his therapist. When I found him, Tammy was there much to my surprise, I didn't know she was going to be there. I was very happy to see her. My philosophy was always better to have two to make sure nothing was missed.

We hadn't stayed very long; he was busy doing his therapy. I told Tony we'd see him later, back in his room after we talked to the doctor. He asked, about the tacos I told him they were in his room.

Tammy and I proceeded to go see the doctor. First we had to go back upstairs, to meet with the caseworker that was waiting for us. Then all of us went back downstairs to meet with the doctor. Once in the office with the doctor I explained that Tony had been sick since the previous Thursday. I didn't understand why they hadn't given him Imodium AD, or something to stop the diarrhea, that is what I would have given him. He explained, "If Tony has an infection we need it to come out of his body. A stool sample was taken, and it was negative, but ideally three stool samples should be taken to be sure. Sometimes bacteria could be missed."

I asked the doctor about the recliner we had at home, and explained the difficulty Tony had getting in and out. He suggested raising it by putting it on a platform, five or six inches off the ground, could make the difference or, try putting a pad three to four inches thick on it. I then told him about the pain in his hip. "I ordered an X-ray of the hip to see if there's a problem there. I also ordered pain pills and a sleeping pill for him." Tony had been having a hard time sleeping; the doctor also had put him on an antibiotic, and told us a wheelchair was ordered for him. I then asked him about a chair lift, if I should rent one, or buy one, he suggested rental. He went on to say, I needed to get the other equipment for baths. Then he slipped away, leaving us with the caseworker to talk to. She talked about giving me a list of people, and agencies to hire for extra help, should I need someone when Tony got home.

After the meeting Tammy and I went back to Tony's room. Tammy left after a few minutes of talking to her dad; she had to get to the store. I stayed and went to therapies with him. He seemed to do well with the exercises. The therapist was pleased with his progress.

That evening Greg and Loraine visited again. We were all talking, she was telling us she had bumped her toe, and tore off her big toenail. Expressing how painful it was. They were leaving for vacation, and she was worried she wouldn't be able to walk.

They had brought Tony lotto tickets, something he normally loved. They were so good to Tony; I could never thank them enough. Greg had been there practically daily bringing Tony candy and lotto tickets all the time. Plus all the dinners, they would never let us pay. Just wonderful people and friends, we're so fortunate to have had their help.

While we were talking I noticed Tony was holding his hand funny, like a stroke victim. When I questioned him about it, he moved his hand, and I didn't give it another thought. I thought he had just laid it on his chest funny. He said, "I'm tired." I had been there all day and visiting hours were almost over anyway, so we all decided to leave, so he could rest. Greg and Loraine were hungry and asked me if I wanted to get something to eat with them. I thanked them but declined, I was tired. I just wanted to get home in bed. I was beat-up from going back and forth to the hospital. It would be another thirty to forty-five minutes before I'd get home. All the traveling and stress took a toll on me. I went straight home, and got right in bed.

A Stroke

I got up early the next morning and tried to call Tony before he started therapy. There was no answer. I kept trying, finally Tony answered, I asked, "Why, didn't you answer the phone before?"

"I couldn't reach the phone." Tony was having a hard time hearing me for some reason, I told him, "Switch ears." Just then the nurse came on the phone, and told me, "Were sending Tony back to the other hospital." I was stunned!!!

"Tony wet the bed twice last night and didn't want to go to therapy. We had the house doctor come because, he was disoriented this morning. The house doctor is going to call you." I was horrified. What the hell was going on there? I was so scared, and thrown for a loop; I just didn't know which way to turn or, what to do first. Cry— Scream— Run there— or, what?—

Once we hung up I immediately called the caseworker. She didn't answer, so I had her paged. She didn't answer that either and I left a message. She called me right back.

"What's going on?

"I don't know." She asked, "Did the house doctor call?"

"No, I only talked to the nurse."

"Hold on I'll get the nurse on the phone." Instead the house doctor got on the phone. She explained in broken English, I could hardly understand, "Were sending your husband back to the hospital, because of the bed wetting, disorientation, not eating, and not going to therapy."

She continued, "I'm not sure if he had a stroke or, if the brain metastasis has anything to do with it. I had blood work, and an EKG done which all checked out okay."

I was thrown for a loop again, stunned, and speechless, as I look back now I'm sure I was in shock. The caseworker asked if I was going there.

"Yes, I'll be there as fast as I can." I couldn't get there fast enough. Wishing I had wings—. I didn't know what to think, and I was scared to death about what I had to face when I got there. The caseworker said, "Tony won't be transferred until five or six this evening because, Dr. Bane can't see him until then." She also suggested I get a hold of my daughter to go with me. I'm positive she knew I was beyond, beside myself. Torn with emotions resembling a breakdown!

147

I immediately tried to reach my daughter; I couldn't find her anywhere. All the other children were at work. I didn't know what to do or which way to go. I tried calling Mario, and he answered Thank God! I told him what had happened, by that time I was crying hysterically, and uncontrollably.

Telling him, "I don't know what's happening with your dad, and the caseworker suggested I go to the hospital with someone."

"I'll be right over." I called him back to tell him not to rush, but he got there almost in the time it took me to hang up the receiver. I then called Tony to let him know I'd be right there.

Mario and I decided to take two cars, in case he had to leave to help Tammy at the store. Figuring that would be better. We left right away; we wanted to get there as fast as we could. When we got there, I asked Tony what had happened the night before.

Tony repeated what the doctor had said.

Then he said, "The psychologist came in to see me and asked me if I was giving up, because I didn't want to go to therapy." I told him, don't worry about that. Thinking to myself *Are these people goofy? Can't they tell if he had a stroke? It was a hospital, there were doctors, how could they, NOT know? What the hell was going on? Pinch me am I having a bad dream, or what?*

Tony went on to say, "I don't feel good, I want to go to my own doctor. She'll have me up and about in two days." He seemed okay to me, talking perfect sense. I wanted him out of that place too, the sooner, the better, wouldn't be quick enough! Mario and I started packing Tony's things. I was in a tailspin; I didn't have my head on straight. Thank God I had Mario with me. We went to have a cigarette, and called Tammy. Both Mario and Tammy said, "If Dad did have a stroke there's a medicine they could give him within the first three hours, to prevent it from getting worse." We knew about that from when Tony's aunt had a stroke. Tony was complaining of tingling and numbness in his arm, and hand. In addition, his one arm was colder than the other from the elbow down to his hand.

I then asked the nurse about the potassium episode from a couple of days earlier.

I had questioned the pills they were giving Tony, they were potassium pills. I asked how that could be when; the nurse had given him medicine a few days before saying his potassium level was high. She said, "That must have been a mistake, the reading must have been off, because his potassium is low." That particular morning, when I got to the hospital, the nurse was in the room trying to give Tony some medicine. She said, would lower his potassium. His potassium level was high and Tony was refusing to take the medicine because it tasted awful. Maybe you can convince him to take it, because it could be dangerous if we don't get it down. He told me, "You drink it."

"If I taste it and I don't think it's that bad will you drink it."

"Yes." I tasted it and said it's not that bad. Try and drink it."

"He could also take an enema if he prefers." Tony opted for the enema. *Did that episode have anything to do with the stroke? I'm saying to myself what the hell's going on?* Too much contradictory information; I didn't trust any of them, by that time. The left hand didn't, know what the right was doing.

The doctor that suggested this hospital was behind the desk when we got back from having our cigarette. He never came in to see or, talk to us, which I found awfully peculiar.

Back to the Hospital

*M*ario and I continued back to Tony's room to finish packing his dad's clothes, and everything else he had accumulated there. Suddenly, the nurse came in and said, "We're going to transport Tony now, the ambulance is waiting. The therapy doctor thought Tony was gone already. He obviously saw us coming back from our cigarette. Did he not want to talk to me? I smelled a rat, but I was grateful Tony was going back to the hospital under Dr. Bane's supervision. Where he would be SAFE!

We were on our way back to the hospital, happy, and relieved. I called the hospital as I was driving, to ask Mitch for a private room with a cot. I was never going to leave Tony. Ever again! Not for a minute!

When we got back to the hospital as we were going down the hall the nurse told us, "Your rooms ready, and the cots on the way." When arriving to the room we made Tony comfortable in the bed.

The nurse came in to assess him. Tony told her what had happened, and that something was wrong with his hand, he could not use it. "You had a mild stroke." He could use his hand, but the fine motor skills were affected. "It will come back in a short amount of time." Your doctor won't be in until tomorrow morning. I was shocked hearing he'd actually had a

STROKE! She said, "Dr. Bane ordered, all kinds of tests for you. A MRI, carotid artery ultrasound, echocardiogram, and a neurologist will be in to see you."

Tony wanted food from another one of his favorite Italian restaurants, in town. We called and ordered the food. They wouldn't be open until five but, they took our order. It would be ready for pick-up at five-fifteen. I was thrilled that Tony was even asking for food of any kind. Period! As I've said, we would have gone to the end of the Earth for whatever he wanted.

Mario had something earlier at the rehabilitation hospital. He didn't want anything from the restaurant. Plus he said he couldn't wait that long he was starving. He decided to eat right away at the hospital café; then run to get Tony's food. He had until five–fifteen anyway, before the order would be ready.

The nurse came in to tell us they were coming to take Tony for the MRI. Tony refused to go until he ate first. Mario couldn't get back fast enough he was taking forever. He just had to go around the corner; finally, he made it back! By five Tony was famished. He ate a few bites at least. He had just finished when they came back to get him for the MRI, it worked out perfect. We had both eaten, and still had leftovers, the portions were huge.

Mario and I then went to have a cigarette while Tony went for the MRI. We also ran to see Mikey (Ardine's husband) in the Intensive Care Unit. Ardine was there visiting too. Mikey looked terrible with tubes, and hoses coming from every orifice of his body. Of course, he couldn't talk, with the tube down his throat. You could see from his eyes though that he was happy to see us. He grabbed our hands to his chest and squeezed them. He mouthed to us, "How's Tony doing?"

"He's okay, he had a mild stroke." He gestured to us with both his hands fisted, as if to say they both had to fight like hell. I repeated those words to make sure that's what he was gesturing. He shook his head yes. "I'll make sure Tony gets the message," telling him to follow his own advice.

Mario and I gave our love, prayers, and told him to rest. We'd be back later he needed his rest. Telling him we just wanted to stop to say hi, and let him know we were all pulling for him. As we were leaving we assured him he'd be okay. It was pitiful to see Mikey like that. Ardine was beside herself and fatigued, her hands were full too.

Tony came back from the MRI just as we got back to his room. The timing worked out perfect.

We told Tony about our visit with Mikey, during his test. Mikey had worked with my mother years earlier, which was where I met Mikey. Then my Mom got Tony a job there before we got married. That was how Tony met Mikey, over forty-five years ago. We gave Tony the message Mikey had sent him; 'that they both had to fight like hell'! We told Tony how sick and pitiful Mikey looked. Having had a heart attack, infection in his lungs, and then his heart valve was damaged and leaking. However, he was too weak to have surgery at that point. They were trying to clear up the infection, and build him up before they could even think of doing the surgery.

Tony was very saddened, and upset to hear that about Mikey. It seemed as though all we had was, sadness and stress around us.

Dr. Bane did come in to see Tony that evening after all. She checked him thoroughly saying, "His right side is definitely affected." Tony was still confused; and he didn't know his right from his left, while she was testing him. "I'll have the results of all the tests tomorrow." But, reiterated that he'd probably had a mild stroke; she also went over all the tests he'd be getting, and told us a neurologist would be in to see him that night. She kept Tony on the same medicines, but was going to add aspirin to thin his blood, and add medication for cholesterol.

Mario stayed with us that night. We went to bed early; it had been another trying day. To put it mildly—

Dr. Bane was in at six the next morning. She informed us, "It was in fact, a small stroke in the parietal lobe of the brain. With little damage, he was already bouncing back." She advised us, his hand with therapy would come back thoroughly. The MRI was good. "No Cancer!" Thank God! That was the utmost question in my head; regarding what was going on with him. No tumors and the brain cancer was history, GONE! There was something on his left ear maybe a mastoid? She was sending an ear, nose, and throat specialist in to see Tony and check the MRI. "The lungs looked real good, echocardiogram was good, and his heart was remarkably good." She still wanted a carotid artery ultrasound done yet, and she was ordering physical therapy for him.

"The nausea could be from the antibiotic, I'm going to discontinue it today." It was the weekend again and she was going to be off. Another doctor would be looking in on Tony. Tony and I both hated when she wasn't there. She assured us she'd be around if she were needed she could be contacted.

Shortly after she left the neurologist came in. It was still early in the morning. He tested Tony to see the severity of the stroke. He agreed Tony had a mild stroke. Repeating almost verbatim what Dr. Bane had, said. He even went, as far as to say, without therapy his hand would come-back just by using it but, don't tell the therapist he'd said, that as he kind of chuckled. "Ideally it would be a good idea to take him off as much medicine as possible but, Tony needs most of it unfortunately for his heart. However, he'll be all right in the end." He also went over the MRI, and all the tests. Reiterating what Dr. Bane had, said. That was also good news to have another doctor give the same diagnosis. "Good News" at least!

That emotional up, and down could drive you nuts, the up and down of he's okay, he's not okay. Was it cancer? No, it's not cancer. You're so wrapped up in what's going on trying to stay, and wanting desperately to believe that. I personally think now, with hindsight you see only what you want to see and hear. On the other hand you handle what your mind and body can handle when it's on overload.

That next morning Tony took a bath but, didn't eat much breakfast. Complaining about the nausea as the reason for not wanting to eat; poor appetite I just couldn't understand why he was so nauseated. I knew the doctor said, "It could be the antibiotic." But, he was nauseated way before he started taking that. There we were once again starting yet another day of whom, knew what?

Tony had a hard time using his hand to eat; maybe that was why he was nauseated? *Was it nerves, and or side effects of having a stroke?* I thought to myself. He couldn't control the fork or spoon. I felt so bad for him, my heart bled for him. God only knows what he was thinking and feeling. To watch someone you love struggle, and going through that frustration of trying to use their hand, and it not working right, was an excruciating site my gut was tied in knots. Knowing that, what I would have liked to have done wouldn't have been in his best interest. Which was to take him in my arms; cuddle him, feed him; to save him from the frustration and anguish he was going through? Not being able to do that was just killing me little by little, bit by bit—.

When I saw he was just so frustrated he wasn't going to eat, then I'd fed him as much as I could get him to eat. Telling him he needed to eat to gain strength. I did, and said, whatever it took to get Tony to take another bite. Almost to the point of saying like you would with a child, here comes the airplane. Open up!

The ear, nose, and throat doctor came in to examine Tony's ear. "I've looked at the MRI. Sometime MRI'S show too much (*What did that mean, why hadn't I asked.*) If you're not having any trouble with that ear, it should be left alone." When he checked the ear he didn't see any problem. That's the way it was left. He advised us to make an appointment to see him after Tony was home, for another check-up. I asked myself a check-up for what? If there was nothing he could see. I assumed when he said make an appointment that he meant if Tony had a problem when he got home. Otherwise, why would we need to go see him?

Then the occupational therapist (OT) came to assess Tony's hand and give him exercises to do. The exercises were to stimulate, and exercise the different nerves and muscles in the hand to strengthen it. She was also optimistic that the use of his hand would all come-back in time. That was encouraging to have the same diagnosis from so many different professionals.

Then the physical therapist (PT) did a few exercises with Tony in bed, and then got him up to walk. He walked well considering he'd been in bed the past few days. Of course, he was wobbly and weak, with having diarrhea, and nausea all that time, not to mention the stroke, it had all taken a toll on him. If he would do a little, every little bit helped to gain strength.

Tony's sister Aida stopped in that afternoon to see him. He asked her if she'd go get him a hot dog. She right away ran to get it for him. When she got back she wanted to feed him, he was having trouble eating it; I understood her feeling like that. Naturally! But, told her to let him do it himself. It was very hard to watch him have to struggle but, Tony had to try or, he'd never learn. It was much easier to feed him but, he'd never learn then, to use his hand or, gain the confidence that he could, if we kept feeding him.

When he gave in to frustration, I did feed him, just to make sure he ate something. He wouldn't eat much but, something was better than nothing.

Mario had left by then, as he had to work that afternoon to help Tammy at the Halloween store.

That night for dinner Tony called Joey again at work, and asked him to pick up Buffalo wings. Of course, Joey did but, Tony didn't eat much of that either. Now he was complaining that his mouth was hurting, his gums were sore.

And, that evening Tony's niece Dina; came to see him, she brought him a Hacky Sack ball; for him to squeeze to exercise and strengthen his hand, a very thoughtful gift that he could really use.

All through the days in between Tony's doctors coming in, and out, I'd go see Mikey upstairs. I'd wet his lips because, with the breathing tube in his mouth, and not eating or, drinking, his mouth was always dry. I ran up when I could, as Ardine had to leave, to run some errands.

The next morning started another weekend and Tony was still nauseated. Even though the antibiotic was discontinued? He was complaining and said, "I have sores on my gums." He had both upper and lower plate; and soreness under a plate can hurt like hell. A tiny sore could make you miserable, and very difficult to eat. Consequently he didn't eat too good again

Being the weekend he only had physical therapy. I was thrilled he at least got that. At least it wasn't a total waste.

Our brother-in-law Dave (Aida's husband) came to see Tony that day. Dave and Tony visited for a while making small talk, and then Dave left. I was grateful Tony was still getting visitors at all, with being in and out of the hospital for months. It was wonderful that people were still coming, and I was happy for him.

The doctor filling in for our doctor came in to see how Tony was doing. I asked her, "Is diverticulitis aggravated by spicy food? Or can it cause nausea."

"Not really." *What's casing the nausea?* I asked what kind of diet he would need to be on for diverticulitis.

"He'll have to stay away from nuts, peanuts, poppy seed, pop corn, any type of seeds, things of that nature

"His gums are sore, and causing him to have a hard time eating. Could you order a swish and swallow, numbs it, or Origel. He needs something that will numb the pain."

I was still going up to see how Mikey was doing, when the chance arose. Also to check on Ardine who was still getting chemo. I was worried about both of them. Her daughter had previously scheduled a trip to come in from Colorado for four days. Thank God she'd at least have some help. Ardine had just recently started driving, but only in town, within a limited distance. She had appointments she needed to get to, and her daughter would be a help.

I was getting pretty sick of the hospital scene myself. I could feel myself being drained by the whole depressing, awful, situation. With sadness all around us, I kept trying to keep my chin up but it was getting harder, and harder. Tony's situation wasn't making it any easier either. Everyday there was something new although we had gotten terrific news, Tony wasn't responding to it. I couldn't figure out if it was psychological or what. All I knew was something had to give. Soon!

Finally, I told Tony if he didn't change his attitude, and get-up in the chair at least, soon. I didn't consider that living. If he wanted to give up that was up to him but, I wasn't going to be a part of it. I told him I was going to have a cigarette, he should think about what I said. I had done all I could for him. The rest was up to him.

When I came back Tony was sitting in the chair. (I guess that worked). That made me feel good. I explained to Tony, he couldn't just lie in bed and expect to get better. It took hard work, which wouldn't be easy, and that only he could do it. I couldn't do it for him; I could only support him.

When Joey got there that night Tony even walked the hall with us. At least he was trying; doing something instead of just lying there.

I told Tony we were going to Florida in November so he had a goal to strive for. I told him, I was going with— or without him—. That of course wasn't true I would never have left him. However, he needed a purpose and a fire under his butt, to get him to do the right things, a reason to do what he needed to do, to get better.

Being at the hospital on Sunday, and the weekends was hard with nothing being accomplished. The weekends dragged endlessly. Tony didn't want to get up early the next morning. I had to coax him up. He didn't eat much again, as his mouth was still sore. When the doctor came she told me the pharmacy didn't have numbs it. I asked, "Is there something else you could order?" She did order some kind of numbing medicine, but it didn't help.

I was disgruntled about Tony complaining over everything, when he was cancer free. I felt he should be more grateful that the cancer was gone. If it wasn't one thing it was another. Day after day—. It was starting to wear on me. No matter what I'd do or how hard I'd try, it was still always something. It wasn't totally his fault; he had legitimate gripes nonetheless, all the negativity was very hard to listen to.

Still very frustrated over the rehabilitation hospital; wondering if in fact it had been their fault; that he had the stroke, by changing his medications. The potassium episode—the extra antidepressant pills—! Waiting too long with the nausea and diarrhea? I guess I'll never know or prove anything?

The phone rang just then taking my mind off of thinking about that. It was Anthony he was calling to see if his dad wanted spaghetti. I asked Tony, and he said, "Yes." Tony was going to bring it to the hospital for dinner that night.

Joey was busy at home finishing the roof on the addition. It needed to be done before it snowed. He did however; stop by later that evening to visit with his dad. When he got there we asked the nurse if we could take Tony up to see Mikey in ICU. "Yes" We got a wheelchair and off we went to take Tony up to see him. Mikey and Tony both cried when they saw each other. It was a sad moment. Tony got upset seeing Mikey hooked up to all the machines. It was an emotional turmoil for all. We visited for a while, and then Tony wished Mikey luck, and told him to fight. Telling Mikey he'd be all right as we left.

Mario and Tammy were working at the Halloween store

Michael had gotten five jobs, which had to be done by a deadline.

Everyone was busy if we had a problem and I needed them they'd be there. However Tony was fine and they had things that needed to get done? They all had been so good, putting their lives on hold running all around with us for months I certainly understood, we couldn't complain. Tammy did call to say she, and the twins were coming later that evening. I told her, Anthony was bringing spaghetti, and that she could eat with us. "I'll have some when I come."

When Anthony brought the spaghetti at dinnertime; Tony ate the most he's eaten in days. He wasn't able to eat the meat though his mouth still hurt, at least he ate the spaghetti. I was so happy to see him eat. It made me hopeful that all the nausea and diarrhea was behind us.

Anthony didn't stay too long he brought the spaghetti and pretty much left. He was also exhausted; we were all burned out from all the running and stress. He had been working on a movie, working all kinds of crazy long days. He was beat; I told him, "Go home and relax everything is fine with us." We appreciated the spaghetti especially being as tired as he was; and still did that. He was happy to see, and hear that his dad had at least eaten the best he'd eaten in days. Tony's eating was a long-awaited inspiration; we'd been waiting for.

Tammy called shortly after Anthony left. I asked her if she'd mind picking up some Ora-Jel for her dad's gums, and a deck of cards. The therapist had explained to us that playing cards was good exercise for Tony's hand. The shuffling, and holding cards, and controlling them would be good. It was also something to do all day, and a good pass time.

When Tammy got there with the twins, they were full of piss and vinegar. Just as antsy as they could be, on the chair off the chair, on the bed off the bed, they couldn't stay still.

Tammy and I decided after she ate, to take her dad for a walk, to get some exercise. I was amazed at how far Tony walked. He must have been showing off for his granddaughters. We were all very happy for him, and he was as proud as a peacock. He really had done terrific. I told him, if he kept that up he'd be walking better, and better real soon. He even told his granddaughters he would be riding his bike next year with them. It was the first positive thing he'd said in eons. It was exceptionally inspiring to hear him talk of the future. I got a hopeful feeling I hadn't had in what seemed to be an eternity. Hearing Tony with a positive attitude was terrific, and uplifting.

The twins finally pooped out, and they still had homework to do when they got home. I told Tammy, to get them home before they fell asleep, they need their rest. When they left I went down with them to make sure they got to their car okay. I had a cigarette while I was downstairs. I needed just a few minutes to myself to relax and get some fresh air.

Then when I got back to the room, Tony and I decided to wrap it up, and get good nights sleep. The doctor would be there early, at the crack of dawn. Literally! We called it a night and went to bed early for a change.

But first I ran to check on Mikey once more. He was going to have the open-heart surgery in the morning, and I wanted to give him our love, and best wishes. I was glad I went he needed his mouth swabbed. I told him to fight like hell, that he'd be fine, it was almost over, and all the waiting was coming to an end.

Sure enough at the break of dawn—our wonderful doctor was there—she came in, her usual cheery self.

Tony she said, all good news. We're going to spring you by, tomorrow! Everything looks good. There's nothing we can do here for you anymore; the rest is up to you. "I'm going to send in the social worker, order the therapy, and have it all set up. By tomorrow it will be set-up, and you could go home. How does that sound?"

Tony just about jumped out of bed with glee, "Can't I go home today."

"I don't know if all that can be done by days end." In addition, she wanted to see how he did throughout the day. Tony practically pleaded with her to go home. He told her, "I hate the food, and I'm tired of the hospital, I'll do better at home."

She relented saying, "Okay, I'll let you go home tonight if all goes well throughout the day. There's not much done at the hospital after five anyway."

I asked her right out if she thought it was the rehabilitation hospital's fault that Tony had the stroke. "It's hard to say, Tony has hardening of the arteries, heart disease, and a lot of complications. It's really no ones fault. It's just one of those things." I accepted that answer what else could I do? But, my gut told me different, I didn't believe it.

She said, "I took Tony off all the antidepressants, and pain pills. I only want him to take the pills he was taking for his heart, aspirin, and cholesterol pill, nothing else." I was glad to hear that, all those pills have side effects. I felt the cure was worse than the illness at times.

Remembering Mikey was having his open-heart surgery that morning. He'd been in ICU for two weeks. They had waited to clear up the lung infection first, and tried to build him up at the same time. That day was the day they decided he would be ready, and strong enough to withstand the trauma.

It was about seven in the morning and Mikey was scheduled to go about that time. I ran up to see if I could see him before they took him. I got there just before they took him, but he was already sedated. I blew him a kiss and left.

Ardine and Mikey's son went down to have a cigarette so I joined them, and we talked briefly. The doctors said, "It will take about six hours for the surgery." Mikey's son and Ardine decided to get some breakfast while Mikey was in surgery. I told them I had to get back to see if Tony was up yet. He was still sleeping when I left.

When I got back Tony was still resting comfortably. I went back down, and had breakfast with them in the cafeteria. Afterward we had another cigarette together. Then they said, "We're going back-up to take a nap."

"I'll see you later."

When I got back Tony was just waking up and I helped him with his breakfast. He ate decent that morning, and did everything right. It was amazing when he had a goal, and wanted to accomplish something, how well he could do. Tony wanted to go home, and he wasn't about to screw that up if it killed him.

I personally didn't think he was strong enough, but maybe it would be best, and he would do better at home. I gave him the benefit of the doubt that he would. He'd probably eat better for sure, because, I'd make him whatever he wanted. I must admit I was worried about the weakness, and his hand wasn't working that well yet.

Later in the day I ran back to see if they'd heard anything about Mikey yet. To my surprise the surgery was over. They were waiting for the doctor to come to talk to them. Mikey was in the recovery room, and the doctor was checking him, then he was coming to give them the update. Just then the doctor came in and said, "Everything went well and the valve is replaced." They had finished a whole hour earlier because it had gone so well. The first twenty-four to forty-eight hours was the most crucial time. They could go in, and see him in a few minutes. Of course he'd be sedated and full of hoses. We were all relieved and hugged each other. "I'm going back to tell Tony the good news."

"Tony may be going home tonight; I'll be back later to check on you before we leave."

Tony was thrilled to hear all went well, it was over, and that Mikey was in recovery.

Tony continued doing everything right that day so he could get out of the hospital. He kept asking me if he was going to be able to leave. "I don't know the answer to that yet."

The nurse said, "We have to give the doctor more information at five. It's up to her after she gets the reports she's waiting for."

Finally, finally we got the go-ahead—they were going to release him. They just had to get the paperwork in order. I told Tony I was going to go see Mikey before we left. I knew I wouldn't get to see him once we left. After we were home I wouldn't be able to leave Tony.

When I got to the waiting room; Ardine said, "Mikey's doing okay, but he's still sedated." I asked if I could peek in and see him. "Sure." I told her I had to get back to get Tony dressed he was getting released and was anxious as hell to get out of there.

I peeked in to see Mikey. He looked as good as could be expected; naturally he didn't know I was there. I said, "Good-bye" to Ardine and left.

When I got back I got Tony dressed. Then he sat in the chair waiting to be released, it wasn't official yet, and he was very antsy to leave.

At last the nurse came in saying the doctor said, "You can go home."

I had already packed everything up, and we were more than ready to get out of there. Except they had forgotten to remove the needle in Tony's port; so we had to wait for that to be taken out, finally we were FREE to leave.

In Route Back Home

e had talked to Anthony earlier, and had planned to go out to dinner. He said, "I'll have the twins Tammy's working at the Halloween store."

"That's great, dad will love seeing them. I think it will be better since I haven't been home and it would take too long to cook anyway."

I was supposed to call Anthony after I'd picked up the prescriptions that had to be filled. When I got them, I called Anthony from my cell to have him meet us at the restaurant, with the twins. It was very difficult getting Tony into the restaurant that evening; Thank God Anthony had met us, and helped a blessing I would have never been able to do it myself. Tony was far too weak for me to handle alone. It was good we went though, it was a change of scenery for Tony, and he did eat a little. After dinner we went to our house. Anthony and the twins helped me empty my car, and get Tony in the house. We must have had ten days of clothes, since we went directly from one hospital to the other. We had Tony's clothes from rehab; plus all my clothes our children had brought me, as I hadn't left the hospital.

The twins helped me empty the bags, sort things out, and put them away. That really helped and saved me from running up and down the stairs. They also seemed to enjoy helping, our big helpers.

After we got all settled Anthony helped his dad up to bed. I fixed his medicine for the week. Then I wrote two lists of all the medication with the names, and milligrams, and how many times a day he took what pill, and when. One for the house and one I kept in my purse for emergencies.

When I was done with that I started straightening the house. I really hadn't been home to do anything for three weeks. I did go home at night when he was in rehabilitation but I had only done Tony's laundry, and went to bed. The next day I would go back to the rehabilitation hospital again. Then when Tony got transferred to our hospital I never left him. I had a lot of catching up to do. The mail alone was a chore I had a ton of it; you'd have thought I was president of the United States.

I did a few odds and ends and decided to go to bed. I couldn't wait to sleep in my own bed with Tony next to me. I decided to finish what I didn't get done the next day. As it turned out I still didn't get to bed until about one.

Tony was happy to be home, in his own house, and in his own bed again too.

The next morning I immediately got up at eight-thirty sharp to confirm the appointment with the stair lift Company. Then I called for the transfer bench, and grab bar for the tub in our other bathroom. Then I would be able to give Tony a shower in the tub sitting down. That bathroom was much bigger, and would be safer, especially with the medical equipment. It didn't have glass doors like the one off of our bedroom, and I wouldn't have to worry about him falling through them. I had been using a lawn chair in that shower stall for him to sit on. I started using the lawn chair after the open-heart surgery, because he was so frail and weak. He had a hard time standing for any length of time.

Our second day home we got up and I gave Tony a shower. He hadn't had a full shower since the Saturday before he was transferred back to the hospital. He said, "It really felt good to take a shower at home." He was a little wobbly, and I was frightened to death he'd fall, but we were very cautious, and took our time. I tackled it because; I knew he'd feel like a million dollars afterward.

Anthony called just as I was going to bring Tony down; he wanted to come, and help me. "We'll be okay." However he insisted on coming over; afraid to let me do it alone.

I already had the appointment with the stair lift company. I wanted to see exactly what needed to be done, and get a firm price for our stair situation. They had advised me that after it was ordered it would take about a week to get it installed. That meant we'd need to help Tony up, and down the stairs for another week.

When Anthony got here he got Tony down, and I made him breakfast. But he really didn't eat that much, his gums were still hurting him.

Dental Trauma

*A*nthony had already made the dentist appointment for Tony. Anthony was going to take his dad for me. He went to the grocery store for me while his dad tried to eat breakfast. When He came back with the groceries they left for the dentist.

While they were gone I was running around the house like a mad woman trying to get everything done. Mop the floors, dust, clean bathrooms, washed clothes, and put groceries away and clean the refrigerator before they got back, and trying to put some stuff away outside before winter set in. Then I got myself ready for the appointment.

The home health nurse called saying, "I'll be there between two, and four."

I told her, "Tony might still be at the dentist." She gave me her beeper number and told me to beep her when they were on their way back. I called Anthony on his cell and left him a message to call the nurse on his way home.

Anthony called me when they were on their way back. He said, "Dad wants to eat when he gets home his mouth is better." I gave him the nurse's beeper number again. He said, "I already beeped her."

I hung up the phone with him and the stair lift sales representatives called. He said, "I'll be there about two."

The nurse called back again saying, "I'm on my way over."

I explained that, "I already have an appointment with the stair lift company, and he's coming at two."

She said, "That's okay I'll need two hours anyway, it'll be all right."

At that point I was tired and frustrated. Tony would be coming in any minute wanting to eat. And I still had to get myself ready. By then the chair lift salesman and nurse would be here. Everything would be happening all at once. It was too much for me to handle at the same time. I was rattled!

We had been home less than a day and I'd been running around playing catch up from the minute we got home.

Anthony and his dad had gotten here within a few minutes. Anthony said, "Dad had a little accident while we were gone." Tony hadn't quite made it to the bathroom, and he needed to be cleaned up. I was a little upset, because I had told Tony before they left to go to the bathroom. However, he didn't want to take the time to go then. I knew the trauma Anthony had experienced. I'd lived it many times myself. It was an awful situation trying to rush with Tony and he wasn't able to walk fast with the walker? Not being steady on his feet, he couldn't take his own pants down. He was so weak. You're trying to rush to prevent an accident, only to get there too late.

Tony said, "It wasn't too bad dad just soiled his shorts a bit, we'll change him after he rests a few minutes." Anthony went on to explain the whole bathroom trauma. How he had parked the car diagonally on the corner right in front of the door of the doctor's office, so his dad didn't have too far to walk, to make it easier—only it was in vain with his car blocking the entrance. I felt bad for him as I could picture the whole scene. The car parked illegally by the front doors, with his dad saying hurry, as he barely moved and your trying to make sure he doesn't fall. Then after getting him to the bathroom and the trauma of getting his pants down, if you didn't make it in time after all that you feel even worse, as though you failed.

Anthony said, "Come by me for dinner tonight." I told him about the appointments I had. He could see I was frazzled to the blowing point. I complained to him that I didn't know how I was going to talk to two people at once and how upset I was about it. It seemed we were all having a bad day.

By that time I was exhausted from running up, down, all around, and anxious about the two appointments.

I made Tony lunch right away but he hardly ate anything. That upset, and disappointed me on top of everything else that had gone on so far, that day. Tony's not eating added to the stress immensely and concerned me. He had always been such a good eater before. My anxiety and exhaustion was at a peak.

Just then the doorbell rang; ding-dong— ding-dong— it was the salesmen for the stair lift. We went into the kitchen to talk about the lift. Then the phone rang, it was the home health nurse saying, she was on her way and needed directions. "I'll be there in a few minutes."

"The salesman is here."

She continued, "It's okay I need to be there awhile to fill out papers anyway." I could hardly wait to fill out all the papers. I can truly say I was not happy.

Within a few minutes, the nurse was at our door. I brought her in into the living room by Tony. Then I went back into the kitchen. I was trying to listen to what she was asking Tony, and not fully paying attention to the stair lift salesmen.

Nurse Intake

The nurse interrupted us to ask if I had a chair, so she could sit next to Tony. Why she had to sit so close was beyond me. I said, "No," I didn't." I was ticked by her interruption, since I had a whole living room full of places to sit. Then I remembered the stools I had, and gave her one. Still upset by her interruption.

The main question I had for the sales representatives was how fast could I have it installed, because Tony was already home. The salesmen checked saying, "Thursday at nine-thirty in the morning was the soonest." I said, "Great," signed the contract, and he left.

Then I went into the living room so I could concentrate on what the nurse's questions were, some of which I found to be quite intrusive. Question after question after question, I got more frustrated by the minute. Since this was the fourth time I had to go through the intake. Except, she was asking questions, I'd never been asked before. It was making me angry. Finally I said to her, "Why are you asking about our children, how many, names, who helped more, their ages, where they lived." That did it I blew up. I said, "What difference does all that make?"

She explained, "They just like to know."

I told her, "I'd never been asked in detail so many questions about our children before." I wanted to know why it was necessary now! She immediately stopped asking any more of those questions. She could have gotten a job with the FBI. She surely qualified for one. However I never did get an explanation of why, she had asked all those questions?

She asked about the bruising on Tony's arms. Why how came, what was it, how long. Now being a nurse. I would have thought. She would have known and be telling me. Not the opposite! I was getting angrier and angrier by the second.

She then asked me for a thermometer. That did it, I blew up—.

"I would think a home health nurse would have one of these"

"I do but I'll have to leave it, because I can't use it again on anyone else. Most people don't like them anyway, patients usually have there own." I thought that sounded lame to me, as I went to get our thermometer. Years ago we just used alcohol to clean it, and that worked just fine in the past. I was in no frame of mind to deal with that pushy, intrusive unmannered, so-called nurse.

She then took Tony's blood pressure stating; she couldn't hear it in the first arm; she then checked the other arm. As she was checking his pressure she heard, kept hearing a ting, ting, ting, noise. "What's that tingling?"

"I don't hear any tingling. " Then it happened again, I remembered the thermometer did that when three minutes were up and the temperature was registered. She had forgotten to shut it off, so it kept tingling. As she was taking Tony's blood pressure I quickly ran and got our blood pressure machine out, to compare ours to hers to see if it was accurate. Ours was ten points off according to her reading, "But close enough," she said.

Then she wanted to check his feet for swelling. She asked about his legs having any breakthrough like on his arms. I said, "No" because he didn't. I had given Tony a shower that morning and had just cleaned him again an hour earlier. She checked his feet they were okay, but noticed blood on his leg, "What's this."

"I don't know," in shock as I jumped off the couch to look; there was a lot of clotted blood inside his wind breaker pants. I couldn't believe my eyes. Not only was there blood, but also Tony didn't feel it or know how it happened. We finally saw two tiny scratches. "All that blood from those" I said. It hardly seemed possible. I cleaned him all up and put another set of clean clothes on him making sure not to get blood on the recliner or carpeting. She asked if I had a tegadirme patch, which Tony had on his hand. I told her, "No." I hadn't wanted to use the ones I had for fear of when I needed them, I wouldn't have any. Beside, thinking she was the nurse and should have those supplies? By the time I got Tony changed into clean clothes again; and ran up and down the stairs multiple times, I was so tired, and upset, that I couldn't see straight anymore.

The nurse was then telling me she was going to come three times a week for the next two weeks. And Tony was going to get PT (physical therapy) four times a week a PCT (patient care therapy three times a week to help with his shower. In addition, an OT (occupational therapist) and sometimes there would be two people there at the same time.

That did it!

Scheduling Dilemma

I said, "Wait a minute first of all he doesn't need a nurse three times a week. I know how to take care of Tony plus he's seeing our doctor regularly." There also will not be two people here at the same time. Tony could only do one thing at a time, and I won't allow it. The times have to be set-up where there's one person here at a time. He couldn't possibly be taking a bath, doing physical therapy, or occupational therapy, and talk to a nurse at the same time. Right about that time, I could have SCREAMED! I said, my peace and that's the way it was going to be. Period!

Lita the therapist called while the nurse was still here to tell me she'd be here at ten-thirty the next morning. I was happy we'd gotten her back. I had requested her.

The nurse was ready to leave at last. She said, "I would be getting a call from the other people as to when they would be coming." Then she left Thank God, and good riddance.

Tony had to go to the bathroom then. I tried to get him up. He could hardly get out of the recliner, and had been having a hard time all that day. Since he'd left the hospital he seemed to be having a hard time and I couldn't figure out why? Tony couldn't get off the toilet, recliner, bed, or kitchen chair. His strength was totally kaput. I prayed the therapy would help.

After changing Tony three times, playing catch up, the appointments and the bathroom episode I'd had it. I was worn to a frazzle ready to come apart at the seams, and my back was killing me from pulling Tony up.

Just then Anthony called to find out when we are coming for dinner. I said, "We're not coming I've had it." I felt his dad had come home from the hospital too early. He couldn't do anything on his own. He was much worse than he was before and I couldn't do it. I felt he relied on me because it was easier on him, and he wasn't going to get better if I keep doing everything for him. "He was okay, and did everything to get out of the hospital, but now that he's home he can't do anything suddenly."

Feeling terrible about the whole situation and blowing up, but the fear anxiety, stress and exhaustion all caught up to me. I felt as if I was ready to flip. On overload; stressed to the max!

"He needs a lot of rehabilitation or something until he's better or we'll have to stay in the house, because it's too dangerous for him to go out." I was afraid to take him anywhere by myself; for fear he'd fall and I wouldn't be able to hold him up. He could also hurt himself badly or break bones. We certainly would be in a pickle then and we didn't need that to happen! He had come too far, that would surely do him in, and me too.

Anthony ended up bringing the whole dinner to our house for all of us to eat together; a nice gesture, but again Tony didn't eat much. He was eating just enough to keep him alive, and I was very upset over that. I couldn't understand why he wasn't eating, and I was worried that he'd get weaker and not have the strength he needed to walk. *What do I do? How can I do it? Was it a physiological thing?* Was it because he was, truly sick? My mind was reeling out of control trying to figure out how to correct the problem. Since the nausea, in the rehabilitation hospital, then the stroke his appetite had declined tremendously I was trying desperately to fight death with all the power and ounce of strength I had.

After dinner Anthony took his dad up to bed, got him settled, and then left.

I was up awhile finishing the wash that had all piled up and did some other errands, then turned in. We had the therapist coming in the morning.

That next morning I was up early. I got Tony bathed and dressed; then made him

breakfast. I had him ready early enough so he could rest before the therapist came.

Intense Therapy

ita was on time and very happy to see us again, and vise-versa. She said, "Tony you look terrific, much better than you did before. You're much more awake, aware, and your color is good." He must have gotten the hint, and did the therapy with enthusiasm. Anthony had told him, "If you don't get it together we're going to Florida without you?" He had set a goal for him to meet. I would never have gone anywhere without Tony, however we felt it was necessary to give him the push to work hard with the therapist. It was true however that we couldn't take Tony the way he was he was much too weak.

Tony did very well with the therapist. He told her, "I have a goal. My wife is going to go to Florida without me if I don't get into shape." I winked at her. I knew she knew me, well enough to know I would never do that. Ever! Not for one minute let alone a week.

The transfer bench and grab bar was delivered early that morning and installed.

I had asked Lita if she could order the above equipment since she had gotten us the raised toilet seat she'd said, "I'll check it out for you."

"I'll take the other equipment back if you can."

I asked Anthony to pick up a showerhead with a hose for the shower, to go along with the rest of the bathroom equipment. I hadn't had a chance to get one or the opportunity to get out. I was delighted Anthony was going to pick that up.

Lita and Tony finished the therapy. She couldn't praise him enough he had done terrifically and worked very hard. I asked her about the stair lift and told her it was being installed the next day. She advised me to call them and hold it off for another week to see where Tony was, at that time. "I don't want Tony depending on it; it's good exercise going up the stairs and will help strengthen him."

Tony seemed to be a little stronger; I challenged going by Anthony for dinner that night alone. We made it there fine. Our granddaughters were there Anthony was watching them, so Tammy could work in peace at the Halloween store. Tony's sister Aida and his cousin Debbie also came by Anthony's house for coffee that evening. After the store closed Tammy came to pick up the twins. Mario and Paul's sister had also stopped to say hi. The whole evening turned out enjoyable.

Anthony had fallen while working and hurt his neck, and shoulder, so he was in pain himself. But he still helped me everyday by making dinners and helping with his father.

Anthony insisted he follow us home to help his dad up to bed. That was the nightly ritual the past few months. I felt bad about the inconvenience but Anthony agreed with the therapist, if we had the stair lift installed. Tony might depend on it, by using it when he didn't need, to taking the easy way out for sure.

When we got home there was a message that the OT wanted to come at the same time as the PT was going to be there. I was hoping she'd call first in the morning so we could change the time. They were not going to play their games on us, with all of them being there at the same time was ridiculous—.

The next morning the therapist did call. I explained, "You'll have to come later. The other therapist is going to be here at that time." And we changed the time for later that afternoon.

When Tony got up that morning I bathed him, and made him breakfast. However he ate very little. Again! "During the night from four to six I was having a hard time breathing, and he felt nauseated."

"You need to wake me up, if that ever happens again. It's important that I know things like that."

I was calling the doctor anyway that morning. I wanted to ask her about giving Tony pills to help increase his appetite that I had heard about at the cancer center, and make an appointment for next week. I explained to the nurse what had happened to Tony during the night. "Give him the oxygen at night. As for the pills, you can give him one to one and a half."

We had just gotten done with Tony's bath and breakfast, when Lita arrived. Tony had done excellent and worked very hard for the second day. That was always encouraging to me and made me feel hopeful again. As I look back now; I could see most of the stress was caused from the hopelessness I felt, the not knowing or admitting (Being in denial) to what actually was going on.

Right after Lita left the OT came, she assessed Tony and they did some fine motor skill to exercise and strengthen his arm and hand that was affected by the stroke. He did really well with her too. However he still was having some difficulty holding a fork, and spoon. It was getting better than it was though. "It will get better in time."

She then went upstairs with me to check the bathroom equipment to see if it was safe. "Return the grab bar there isn't enough room for Tony to swing his legs into the tub with it there. The transfer seat has a bar to grab on it so, the other one isn't necessary." What I thought was a large bathroom had shrunk with all the equipment in it, plus the chair for Tony to sit on while getting dressed. He was still too weak to stand while getting dressed. After that the therapist said, "I'll be back tomorrow" and left.

Anthony invited us for dinner again. Tony wanted him to bring it to our house again. I said, "It's too hard for Anthony to bring all the hot food here. " Plus it would be inconvenient for him, I convinced Tony to go there.

I'd been having a very hard time getting Tony in and out of the recliner for quite some time. I'd had been looking for a new one ever since he had the open-heart surgery. Every time I had Tony in the car and we tried to go get one. I'd leave Tony in the car and I'd go look. If I saw something I thought he'd like I'd get him to look at it. But he was always either to sick, too weak or in pain and didn't want to go in. The couple of times I did get him in the store; he either couldn't open or close the recliner himself, which defeated the purpose for getting a new one. Since he needed one he could get in and out of by himself. He just plainly didn't have the strength or mobility to get one opened or closed him self.

The one we had was a swivel rocker and had a very low seat (which made it harder for him to get out of). When I helped Tony get out of it, it would swivel, and rock which made it a nightmare of a problem and dangerous for both of us. Between him not having the strength to stand and being wobbly, and the chair swiveling and rocking didn't help one bit. He needed a stable, firm, solid recliner, with a higher seat. The one we had was broken in, and it was easy to open and close but he still needed help even with that one.

I decided that day was the day to go look for a new recliner. I couldn't stand the old one, one more second. I felt if we could find another one to fit our need, it would make our lives a little easier at least.

After lunch off we went on a recliner hunt, Tony wasn't too keen on the idea, but we went anyway.

New Recliner Search

The first store had a nice recliner; but Tony wasn't crazy about it. It was quite a fiasco; getting him in that store; with the oxygen tank cart, walker, him barely having any strength and not steady on his feet! We struggled getting him inside. We made it. Though! Whew! After trying it; He said, "I want to think about it!" I thought it was a decent recliner but; he's the one that was going to be sitting in it. We went across the street to another store; much to my surprise, Anthony was there waiting for us. Shocked actually to see him, not knowing he was going to be there. I explained, our experience from across the street; that his dad wanted to think about it so, we came here to check out our choices.

He said, "I already looked; there isn't anything here either," and he left reminding us we were going by his house for dinner.

However, being there already, I ran inside to give a look at least. I ran around the store very quickly, as Tony waited in the car. I did see a couple of recliners there though. I didn't know why Anthony had missed them? And when I noticed that they had wheelchairs, I thought perfect, we wouldn't have difficulty getting him inside either. I went up the salesperson; asking him if he could please, get me a wheelchair. He quickly got one for me and I went to the car to get Tony. After he sat in it; got in and out of it, Tony wasn't crazy about that recliner either. On the other, hand I thought it would work perfect for his needs. IT was stable, firm, with a higher seat that he could get in and out of easier, and would make our lives much easier. Just like the Dr. at the Rehabilitation Hospital had recommended. We decided to buy it with thoughts that when he got better we'd get one that he really wanted, once he was stronger. The soft, cushy leather kind he wanted, but one like that would never have worked at that point. Not until he got stronger. We bought that one, plus at a good price, hoping it would be an asset and make our lives less stressful.

Then we called our son Michael to see if he could pick it up with his truck. He said, "I can't, I have a rush order I need to get out, but Joey could use my truck to pick it up." That will be great. Asking Michael, "Would you like to have the old recliner?"

"Yes, I would."

"Good, when they bring the new one to the house, they can take the old one for you." On our way to Anthony's house; we dropped off the receipt at Michael's house, so Joey would have it when he picked up the truck. Then we proceeded to Anthony's house for dinner.

Dinner was good as usual, it had worked out at least; I didn't have to worry about cooking that day. Anthony then followed us home to help his dad up to bed. The nightly chore—.

Joey came just as we walked in with a friend of Michael, to deliver the recliner. They brought the new one in and took the old one out. It didn't take long to switch them. One, two, three, one in, one out, it was practically that quick.

What a day that had been. I was glad it was over. Tomorrow would be a new day. Feeling we had finally accomplished a long awaited feat. In addition; hopefully, would make our lives more enjoyable.

The PCT called then and said, "I'll be there at nine; nine-thirty tomorrow morning for Tony's shower."

The next morning I got-up in enough time to get myself ready and Tony's clothes ready, before the PCT arrived. I was nervous because the OT was going to be there at ten-thirty; therefore we had to rush Tony's breakfast, so he'd be ready for the appointment. I was against rushing Tony from thing to thing.

As it turned out; rushing wasn't necessary. The OT didn't get there until eleven-thirty. Talk about promptness, but Tony got to rest for an hour; that worked out better.

We went from running to the hospital daily; to a hectic daily schedule at our house.

The OT went over some new exercises with Tony, and then did some of them with him. In the mean time, the phone rang.

It was Ardine she said, "I've got bad news." I thought she was going to tell me about the problem she was having with her arm since her breast surgery, but, that wasn't it! Instead she said, "MIKEY DIED!" I was in total shock. It took a few minutes for it to sink in. MIKEY DIED—NO—! Instantly stunned, taking a few minutes for it to sink in; I thought *she has to be kidding, but she wouldn't be kidding about something as serious as that, would she? No, that wouldn't be funny; or nice—, she was Serious—.* I got hysterical; yelling Noooooooooooo! I couldn't believe it—! *This couldn't be happening. Someone pinch me. It must be a dream.* But, it wasn't a dream, it was real! All the while! We had been worrying about Tony and Ardine for months and within three weeks her husband was gone. Just that fast— Unbelievable!

I had been outside having a cigarette when she called—.

My poor husband Tony was in the house wondering what could have happened. When he heard the shrilling scream! He thought something happened; to one of our children. As I went back in the house, I said, "Tony, Mikey died." He was crying; and I was crying, we were just beside ourselves. The therapist said, "He doesn't have to do the therapy." She could see we were both distraught, but felt it better they continue, instead of him dwelling on what happened, to help keep Tony's mind busy. They finished the session, and she left saying, "I'll be back tomorrow."

After she left we both kept repeating over and over we couldn't believe it. OMG! Mikey's Gone—! Both in shock—!

Tony had some rest in between the therapist's sessions, which was good. That seemed to work out better. Then Lita came, she had already heard of the loss; and gave us her condolences.

Then asked, "How are you doing, Tony, since your fall?"

The fall happened a few days earlier when Tony was on the toilet and tried to get up him self. He had lost his balance and fell up against the wall in the corner of the bathroom. He was in the powder room downstairs;

which was small, a wall on the left side, and one right in front of him. It was a lucky thing for him that the walls were there. He could have gotten hurt a lot worse. If the walls hadn't broken the fall, God only knows what would have happened.

"I'm Okay, but sore." He went through the exercise routine with some pain, but did most of it. Going up the stairs was still very hard for him. She told us, "Another therapist will be here Saturday, I have Saturday off. I'll be back on Monday."

We were having lunch when Anthony stopped after work to check on us. Tony had eaten well that afternoon. We asked Anthony if he wanted to go to dinner with us that evening. He said, "I'll check with Paul and let you know."

He called back later saying, "Yes, we'll go out to eat."

"Great." Letting Tony rest while I ran upstairs to get ready, then came down freshened him and put clean clothes on him.

Not being able to get Mikey and poor Ardine out of my mind, wanting to do something; for Ardine and her family. Deciding to have a tray made up, but found out it was too late to order one. Then after made up my mind to stop at the grocery store and pick up a few things to make my own tray, which I did. When we got home, Anthony took his dad up to bed, and left.

While I finished preparing the tray, and got everything together to bring by Ardine; I called Joey to see if he could come over for a few minutes so I could run it over to Ardine. "I'll be right there." Then, when I ran it over to them, I was happy I made the tray. It was greatly appreciated. Being; Ardine hadn't had a minute to shop, since, she was at the hospital with Mikey, plus going for her own treatments, so it all worked out well for them.

The next morning started with another bang. Our son Michael was supposed to come to help his dad down the stairs, but called from the hospital! Lisa had gotten another collapsed lung. She had been sick with a cold and her lung collapsed from all the coughing; also had collapsed a couple of months earlier. They doctor admitted her. "I called Joey to come and help you with dad." Joey did come to help get his dad down the stairs.

Tony ate a decent breakfast that morning. Thank God! The therapist came for his exercise session, and then Tony rested for a while. We had decided to take a ride to bring the grab bar back. We weren't able to use it and thought taking a ride just to get out of the house for a bit was a good idea. NOT!

The Fall

*G*etting Tony ready; scarf, coat, and walker, we stood by the front door. Just as I turned around to grab his hat, before I knew it, he lost his balance. Down he went, straight back like a log, flat on his back in the middle of the foyer. I saw him going over out of my peripheral vision; immediately grabbed him, trying to prevent the fall. But, all I did was break the fall; he still fell flat on his back. I was petrified to move him for fear of broken bones or worse. I let him lay still while I slowly and cautiously checked for movement in both legs then arms. He was saying, "I'm okay, I'm okay." There was no-way I could get Tony up from that position, alone. Both stunned by what had just happened, he said, "Call the neighbor to help get me up." I didn't want to call the neighbor; for fear she wouldn't know how to lift him, or be careful enough, even maybe make matters worse. Wanting to call an ambulance; knowing that would really freak him out and make matters worse. My mind fled with different thoughts on how to handle this serious situation. Praying for answers, as I checked his sides, hips, and head, saying, "I'll get you up." He then insisted I call Michael to come help him up; which I did. While we waited for Michael to get there, I ran to get him a pillow to put it under his head, continuing checking for broken bones.

What saved Tony was his heavy mid length leather jacket; fur lining, with heavy padding, helped save him, I'm sure. He was going to be sore; no doubt, almost sure, nothing was broken.

Michael was there within a few minutes. We rolled Tony over, scooted him onto the rug in the foyer, then we got him on his knees by pulling him up with a gait belt (A belt that goes around the middle to prevent falling by someone holding the belt behind the person being helped), I ran outside and got a lawn chair, we then pulled him up by his waist, had him put his arms on the seat of the chair one at a time; we then had him on all fours, and Michael helped him get on one leg at a time, with his legs straight, to sit, as I slipped another lawn chair under him, then put the walker in front of him, and got him up to standing a position. Slowly moving him, using caution with every step, and move, we kept asking, if he felt any kind of pain, with each step. We walked him back into the living room to sit in the recliner. Naturally! We decided not to take the grab bar back. Instead we decided to go to the hospital to make sure there were no fractures. Michael helped me get his dad into the car.

On the way to the hospital, I went to a drive up to get Tony a hot dog first, he hadn't had lunch and it was after three by then. Knowing once we got-to the hospital we'd be there at least a couple of hours; if not longer. Not wanting him to wait that long to eat or miss lunch. Since he was finally eating well; and I did not want to break a good thing, Eat! Tony ate half of the hot dog and a couple of bites of tamale. Happy that he ate that much, still wishing he had eaten more. The stress of him not eating well pushed me to the limit. I wasn't able to cope when Tony didn't eat. Obsessed with knowing that was his lifeline. If he didn't eat, he'd die, also vital to his recovery and strength. Feeling like I was caught in a revolving door, spinning round and round, and not getting anywhere fast. It was an awful feeling of helplessness; taking two steps forward, five backwards. I kept saying in my mind, *if I felt that way, I couldn't even imagine how he felt.* It had to be even worse for him. Every time we thought we had a handle on things, something else happened!

Holding up when a crisis arose, but afterwards fall apart. Everyone kept telling me you're only human. I found it unacceptable behavior to lose my wits. Then I'd beat myself up about it; wishing I could have found another release, but hadn't. Anthony had called as we were leaving for the hospital. Shortly after arriving at the hospital he showed up. He asked, "Do you know anything yet."

"We just got here because I stopped to get a hotdog for dad." When they took Tony for the X-ray, Anthony and I went outside to have a cigarette and I explained what we were doing, and how the accident had happened, feeling horrible about it. My poor husband wasn't dealing with enough. Now that!

Expressing my frustration about what had happened; one thing after the other—it didn't stop—explaining I can handle the physical labor, it's the stress that's a killer. I didn't think I could take much more; we had to get off that roller coaster—.

We were all fatigued and stressed to the max. The cancer was in remission. Thank God! However, the problems hadn't ceased. We had gone from one thing to another without a break.

After our cigarette break, Anthony and I went back in the hospital. Tony was back from X-rays already. The doctor came in and said, "There are no breaks." I thanked God silently! Switched gears to the positive attitude; all the while fighting to keep them positive. Telling my self it could have been worse. (My Dad's saying.) He could have broken a hip, leg or both. Another milestone to get through that's all— Anthony was insisting I get a nurse three times a week to help me. I insisted that I didn't need one. Even if I'd had one, the fall still would have happened. In addition, I had help with showers from the PCT three times a week. Again I said, "It's not the physical work it's the stress— and no one could take that pressure away."

Anthony had come straight to the hospital from work; he was hungry and tired. I told him to go home and rest, "I'll call you when were on our way home to help me get dad in and up to bed." When Tony was released and we we're on our way back home, I called Anthony; all the tests had come-back negative. Thank God. The doctor said, He'll be sore all over from the fall."

After getting in the house, I told Tony, "I'll make you some soup after your settled." Then fixed ice wrapped in a towel, a brace to hold it on his back to help with the pain, and also gave him some pain medicine. He did eat all the soup; that of course made me feel better. That was his dinner, not much of one, but better than nothing. I couldn't entice him to eat anything else. I was pleased that he at least ate that.

All our children kept calling to see if everything was all right and we were okay.

It was wonderful that they cared, but frustrating at the same time; because every time the phone rang I'd have to stop what I was doing. Sometimes I was in the middle of changing bandages, dressing Tony, preparing his breakfast, lunch, washing clothes in the basement, or transporting him from room to room. Becoming a difficult situation; the good part was we have five wonderful children. The bad part was we have five wonderful children calling all day to get the update on everything.

With so many calls every day, I felt like I was whirling around in that revolving door; again spinning like a top out of control, round and round.

I sat there; the day of Mikey's wake, still not believing it, waiting for our children to come so we could all go together. I thought back to when I was a kid. As mentioned before; he worked with my Mom. When going to see her; I'd see him sometime. That was about forty-five, years ago. I was just a teenybopper then. It was a sad, depressing day for Tony and me.

Paul was going to stay with Tony, as he was very sore from the fall; and could barely sit let-alone stand; totally unable to attend the wake, feeling horrible about not being well enough to attend, and so did I. Even if we used a wheelchair he couldn't make it because of the sitting; he could never have sat that long, nor could he stand the entire time either. It was just a miserable situation for all concerned.

Tony wasn't eating again either that day. All he had was two Popsicle's and a glass of juice to take his pills with. Suggesting all kinds of food; he just didn't have a taste for a thing I mentioned—.

Anthony told me; he was going to make ribs and bring his dad some, with potato salad. I hoped he would eat that at least. He had to eat something; to keep his strength up.

Sometimes I think he just gave up, especially with losing Mikey. I think he wished it were him I just sensed it. Especially since; he had made the comment, "How did he get so lucky."

The Wake

Anthony came with the ribs, and potato salad. Paul hadn't eaten either. Tony decided to come downstairs he had stayed in bed since he fell, so Anthony helped him down. I said, "You and Paul could eat together." I set the table, said, "Good-bye, I'll see you later after the wake ends." I didn't want to get upset before I went to the wake if Tony didn't eat again. I wanted to get out of the house as fast as possible. I was upset enough. Just as I was leaving Joey came; he had stopped for food too; at some point our wires got crossed, regarding the wake. Joey and Paul had made previous plans to work on a resume for Joey. Now they were going to do it at our house. Joey didn't think his brother Anthony was going to cook. Anyway Joey ate the food he bought and Tony and Paul ate the ribs. Joey told me, "I'll stop by the wake later, were going to work on my resume first." It was already six, when Anthony and I left for the wake. I felt that if I went from six to nine that it would be okay. I wasn't going to be able to go to the funeral the next day, at all, because, I didn't have anyone to stay with Tony; as all our children had to work.

Joey said, "I called Michael to tell him we'll meet there about six."

Tammy and Mario were to come about the same time, after closing the store. When I had talked to Tammy earlier that day she told me, her husband and the twins had already been there.

The funeral home was very close to our house; actually, it was just down the street. Anthony and I had taken our own cars, so if Anthony wanted to leave earlier, he could, that way I'd have my own car to get back home.

I dreaded going into the funeral home. Especially since Tony had said, "That's where I want to be waked" when we were at Burger King, that day being not long ago. Not only was it a sad time, that also gave me an "Erie" feeling. Here Mikey and I had been worried about Tony and Ardine with the cancer, but instead I was going to, 'his' wake. It just goes to show you, you just never know. Only God knows, who goes, when, and how!

Once we arrived at the funeral home as Anthony and I walked up to the door. Mikey's daughter and son were standing outside having a cigarette, and greeted us as we approached them. I dreaded going in the funeral home; like the plague.

We found the parlor Mikey was in, signed in, and walked up to the front where the casket laid. I naturally was all choked up and trying desperately to contain my emotions. I couldn't believe it then and still can't as I write this, and relive it. Mikey actually looked good, like himself, even with all he'd been through. He looked just as though he was sleeping with a very peaceful look on his face. We knelt down to say a prayer, and then I patted his hair and spoke to him as if he could hear me. 'You're at peace now, we'll miss you.'

We then went up to Ardine gave our condolences, hugged her as we both cried, holding onto one another. Just babbling about what had happened, stating we just couldn't believe he was gone. Just that quick— I think we both were still in shock.

Anthony and I looked at the pictures from the previous years of the four of us, when we had been on a cruise together, and pictures from over the years. That really saddened me; but it was also nice to see the pictures again. Wishing, seeing those pictures could have been on happier terms.

Anthony stayed with me awhile then left to go back to the house to be with his dad. Shortly thereafter Tammy, Mario, and Michael came. Joey came within a few minutes of them. Ardine was pleased to see our children. They stayed awhile then Tammy and Michael left. Tammy had to get home to the twins. Michael of course had to get back to his shop. Mario and Joey stayed with me until the end.

I asked Ardine to take a break, and go downstairs to have a cup of coffee and a cigarette with me, so she could relax for a few minutes, which she did.

After the wake as Joey, Mario and I said our, good-byes I explained to Ardine, "I won't be able to attend the funeral. I can't bring Tony because of the fall and of course I can't leave him alone." She totally understood. She told me to say hello to Tony and to give him a kiss for her.

When I got home, our children told me Tony hadn't eaten a thing. As usual I got even more upset.

The next morning we had another day of?????????? The PCT came for the second time to give Tony his shower, and it did give me a break. I had everything ready for her when she got there. Somehow however, I didn't feel right about it. I felt I should be doing it and felt guilty. All the while knowing I had to let someone help me to keep my own sanity. Supposedly when things got stressful I'd be more rested and able to handle it better. So I was told anyway.

The PCT told me Tony's shower with the transfer bench, worked out good when I asked her about it. Tony said, "She did a real good job" when he was eating his breakfast. He continued, "It felt good to take a shower, but it was hard to move because of the pain." We had a real hard time getting Tony down the stairs that day. He had to actually come down on his butt, one stair at a time.

That morning I made Tony oatmeal, Jell-O with bananas and peaches, prunes and juice. He had about five mouthfuls of the oatmeal, and couldn't eat anymore. I fed him the Jell-O with peaches and bananas, then the prunes. Then he had a couple of Popsicle's. I had succeeded in getting something down him. Yeah!

Then he went to sit in his new recliner, which he hated. He said, "It's not comfortable it hurts my back, I liked the other one better." However, it was higher, stronger, but most of all stable and much easier to get him out of. Thank God. We would never have made it with that other recliner rocking and swiveling with him being so sore, and weak. It was enough of a problem; just getting him around. Let alone deal with the other recliner, which would have been the thing to push me over the edge most definitely.

I explained to Tony, "At least I can get you out of this recliner without a problem. It doesn't rock, and twist. Plus the other one was too low for you to get up from."

Lita had explained to him, "Getting out of a lower chair, you're actually using your thigh muscles to give you the push, and that's much more difficult than using the calf muscles." That's why Tony's having such a problem, and it made sense. At last something was making sense, I could understand.

Tony also told me, "I want you to order the stair lift."

"I'll ask Lita when she gets here."

"I don't care what Lita says I want it," from not wanting it, to wanting it. I assumed the soreness was so uncomfortable; he didn't want to go through the agony of going up and down the stairs anymore, and it was just too painful.

Changing the subject telling, "You only have a few minutes to rest before the OT will be here." He took my advice and rested.

In between breakfast and the therapist coming I read a book on positive attitudes to Tony as he rested.

Just then a social worker called saying, "I'd like to come out and go over some different things with you." I explained, "I have a therapist coming at that time."

She asked me, "Can I come after that."

"Okay," and we set-up a time.

When the OT got there I explained that Tony had fallen. He hadn't broken any bones, but he was extremely sore. She asked him a few questions, and then did a little therapy with him. His attitude wasn't too good that day with being sore and all.

I told her he hadn't eaten much that morning or the day before, and he was in bed, the last two days. I was sure being weak; and sore attributed to his poor appetite too.

She explained, "It's important to eat, even if you don't feel like it Tony. You need to force some food down. Not eating will only make you weaker." After they finished, she excused herself, "I'll see you tomorrow," then left.

She no sooner left; and the social worker was at the door, ding-dong, ding-dong. She was a very attractive, nicely dressed, and a well-mannered woman. She came in, sat down, introduced herself, and asked about Tony's health history. She went over agencies that were available, nurses I could hire, PCT'S, housekeepers that live in your house. So, when Medicare no longer would allow the PCT to come I'd know where to get extra help should I need it. She said, "If you need any help; or have any questions, call me I'll help in any way, I can," before leaving.

After that Lita came. By that time she was like our daughter we felt that close to her, feeling that she had the same feelings, sometime you can just sense those things. She really liked Tony and personally cared about him. I explained to her again about Tony's falling; his attitude, and the not eating.

She explained, "You need to move even though it hurts. I don't want you to lose the muscle and strength you've gained. Also by not moving even though you're sore the muscles will tighten up. You have to keep moving so that doesn't happen to you."

Tony tried but said, "I'm too sore to do anything." She did some resistance exercises while he sat in the recliner, to work some muscles at least.

Also reiterated how important it was to eat. If you don't put fuel in—the motor won't work. She finished up saying, "I'll see you tomorrow."

Tony's attitude was really negative, and I was extremely upset with him about it. Feeling he was not really trying, like he'd given up? Even went as far as to ask him, "Are you giving up?" "No." However his actions and attitude spoke louder than his words.

I had also talked to Lita about the stair lift. "It's really a personal thing." She asked if the boys were giving up. "No, but I felt it was really hard on them every morning and night."

"Try it."

After she left I asked Tony what he wanted for lunch. "I'm not hungry." Again the not eating got to me. My concern for him was growing and my frustration was at a peak. Actually I was getting very angry with him for not eating. Feeling as though we were all jumping through hoops for him and he wasn't doing his part.

Between not eating, and not trying to do his exercise, I was really losing my patience. I knew it was hard for him, but it was also hard on the rest of us.

For dinner I reheated the ribs and took out the potato salad. I put dinner on the table and helped Tony to the kitchen to eat.

He sat there playing with his food. He tried to eat part of a rib, and ate maybe two mouthfuls of potato salad. I asked if he wanted me to cut the meat from the bone. "No." He was having a problem eating with the hand affected by the stroke; along with not having an appetite. I felt so sorry for him, but at the same time I felt he could try harder to eat more. All of a sudden I heard something fall on the floor. When I looked at the floor I saw his tooth! That was the third time it had fallen out of his plate. I asked him, if he'd lost his tooth? "Yes, now I'm really screwed."

I went as far as to say, "A dead man doesn't need teeth don't worry about it." If he didn't eat I knew he would surely die. That's exactly what I was trying with all my might, to prevent from happening. That's why when he didn't eat I got frustrated, scared, and frantic.

I took Tony's plate out and repaired the tooth by gluing it in. Then I gave it back to him.

Why wasn't he trying? I threw his dinner in the garbage. Then I really lost, it I told him, "If you want to give up, I won't be a part of it. I'm more than willing to help you in everyway I can." But, at the same time I just couldn't be part of him dying. He had beaten the cancer, and was on the way, but, 'he' had to keep trying.

I tried to use every tactic, I could think of—!

I told him, "If that's what you want to do I'm going to put you in a nursing home. Because, "I'm not going to participate in any way; shape, or form to that situation. You better make-up your mind."

All our children knew he wasn't eating and they were reading him the riot act too, being they were all upset about it. We all knew too well about the ultimate outcome.

After I finished eating I brought Tony back to his recliner, still ranting, and raving out of control.

I know that sounds mean, but I was trying to bring the fight back in him; to shake him, up, back to his senses.

I put a tape in the VCR about a quadriplegic that I had gotten at a sales convention a year earlier. The man in the tape had conquered a lot of obstacles. He spoke at that convention and it was very motivational. I was so inspired; by what that man had conquered, I had to have a set of his tapes.

Thinking maybe, just maybe; if Tony would pick-up one small thing out of them he could use, maybe it would inspire him in someway, seeing someone that could hardly move; become totally self-sufficient. Maybe he'd say to himself if he can do all that. I can do the little I need to do to get through my exercises.

Just about then Joey stopped by. He had gone to the store; his father had asked him earlier if he'd pick-up some sherbet and Popsicle's for him, and said, "Sure." It was about six-thirty when he got here. I asked Joey to eat the rest of the ribs and potato salad. He asked if he could take it home, "If you want to go-ahead that's fine."

Tony took advantage of Joey being there and asked him to bring him up to bed. "It's a little early."

"I feel better lying down my back is hurting. Besides then Anthony won't have to come later." That of course was a good reason, saving Anthony a trip.

We turned the tape off and Joey and I helped him to up to bed. He actually had made it up the stairs pretty good. We got him into bed; let him rest a few minutes. Then said, "Let's do your leg exercises," much to my surprise he did them! That made me happy and pleased. (Maybe the tongue-lashing did help after all. Or was it the tape?) It really didn't matter whatever it was Tony did what he was supposed to do. Afterwards Joey said, "I have to go."

I ran downstairs with him, to grab the tapes to put it in the VCR upstairs. Then I sat, and watched it while Tony listened with his eyes closed.

After it was over, I asked Tony, "What did you get out of it?"

"To have a positive attitude and keep trying." I thought "YES," that's good for starters. Telling him that I'd told him many times before. 'If you think you can you will; if you think you can't, you won't, and there was no reason you can't? Our doctor also had told him there's no cant's, or wont's. The therapist also said, "Don't say can't say I'm having difficulty doing that." We were all on the same track. Psychology has a lot to do with a person's recovery. The person has to have encouragement, and you have to try whatever it takes to push their buttons to motivate them. Whatever worked was my motive, keep trying, and don't give up! The results were worth it, if you can get to that point. We just had to get him on track. Feeling like I did when raising our children. Always looking for that trick to pull out of my bag, to get the results wanted. Always asking God for the patience needed; to persevere.

After getting Tony settled I went downstairs to write this book. I had done that many nights; some nights, back-tracking going over the past months, trying to get up to date so, that I could write exactly what transpired on that day. That night I was finally going to get to that point. It was a good feeling to be up to date on the daily activities and much easier to write about. Not to have to worry about what I'd left out or that I had missed an important issue. Plus I had tons of notes to sort through to get to this point. I did however take exact notes to go back to for a back-up.

I had been inspired back in January to write this book; therefore I had a lot of back-tracking to do. I only know I was inspired by a higher power directing me and kept me going and that there had been a lot of miracles that had transpired. Feeling it was my responsibility to get the word out about the Miracles for all to read about.

The next morning I got Tony up, got him into the bathroom and undressed him. Sat him at the sink soaped up a washcloth gave him a towel, and told him to sponge him self off, and I left. I told him while he was doing that I was going to jump in the shower. It was too heart wrenching for me to watch him struggle. I would have ended up doing it for him. That wouldn't have helped him. I showered as fast as I could. When I went back; Tony had washed himself. I did help dress him, as he was fatigued by then. He even brushed his own teeth. Then Anthony came to help him down the stairs

Tony ate breakfast that morning very well. "Amazing" "Another Miracle!" I thought to myself, Thank You God! He still was having a hard time holding the utensils however, and got very frustrated and defeated right away. But, when that happened I'd take over and feed him. At least he had tried to do it himself. Realizing that was probably part of the problem for the loss of appetite, plus depression and fear, also played a part. I can't say as I blamed him, God only knows how I would have felt in that position. I do know though that you have to keep trying, not give up on yourself no matter how frustrating it gets. That wasn't an easy thing to do sometime either. I can personally vouch for that. I did try to keep a positive attitude myself and kept asking God for guidance and patience. So far, he hadn't turned his back on me; I couldn't have done any of it without his help all the way.

After Tony ate that morning; he got to rest quite awhile before therapy started. I thought watching the tape worked he'd made up his mind to live. He was trying.

However, he still had to throw the negative in there sometime. While he rested, I played the other tape, we watched it together it sure was an amazing tape and very inspiring.

The OT called to see if Tony was going to participate that day. "Not too much." I asked for the telephone and said, "He'll be fine. He'll do what he can."

"I'll be there in twenty minutes."

When she got there, she went over a few new exercises. I told her he was having a problem eating. He couldn't control the utensils. She asked, "Did you have lunch yet."

"No, he hasn't."

"Can you get his lunch ready? Then I could observe him eating." As he ate she gave Tony a few tips. Again, when he got frustrated I fed him so he'd eat, and he did eat. She said, "Tomorrow will be a free day. I'll be back on Thursday; you should do your exercises tomorrow on your own."

He told her, "I dread Lita coming because, she makes me work hard." We all laughed, he was kidding of course.

He had time to relax before Lita got there. Tony took a nap until then. I was so very happy he ate; I was in ecstasy, over him 'finally' eating. I hoped he was on a roll and would continue.

Lita arrived about two-thirty. Tony said, "Oh no!" as she came through the door so she could hear him. "I can't do much today.

She quickly said, "We're only going to do what you can tolerate, but you have to keep moving it's very important. Remember we don't want you to have a set-back here. We want to keep those muscles moving. If you stiffen up it will be worse." Tony did very little walking it hurt too much. She did a lot of resistance therapy with him again, with him sitting in the recliner. Tony happened to like her a lot, and that helped. She told us she had an opportunity to go to Maui, with some of her friends. Our paradise! She'd talked to us about the trip and how excited she was about it. Of course, that happened to be one of our favorite subjects. He told her about places to go to, what to do, and went on and on about it. She said, "We like to snorkel." We told her; "We'd never done that, but heard it was just beautiful to snorkel in Maui; the fish are just beautiful. That day as she was exercising him he said, "I hope a blowfish gets in your snorkel."

She laughed and said, "Tony aren't they poisonous fish?"

"Yes" and laughed. We all laughed, she knew he was just kidding around. She gave him a love tap on his shoulder as if to say how dare you but laughed. He had laughed, and kidded, that was something he hadn't done in a long, long time—. It was fabulous seeing him that way again, almost back to his normal self. Tony normally had a great personality; and everyone just loved him. He was truly a charmer.

She was leaving for Maui that next week; our most favorite place in the whole wide world—. And would be snorkeling that's why Tony made that comment about the blowfish. We also shared different restaurants to eat at, and things not to miss. Lita was a great therapist. We felt so fortunate to have had her. She's very dedicated to her job and took it personal and seriously, but she also had the knack to put fun and laughter into her work.

I told her, "I ordered the stair lift it's going to be installed next Monday." It's only ordered for thirty days; winking at her, not wanting Tony to depend on it. Saying, "The boys weren't happy with our decision to get the lift." I don't dare call the company again and tell them we'd changed our minds again. They'd think we were crazy. She laughed and agreed. Then explained my feelings of being in a revolving door going round and round, getting no place fast and couldn't stop it. She was very compassionate about my feelings and what I was going through.

She told Tony he'd have a free day the next day. She'd be back on Thursday, but to keep up his exercises. Not to slack off, to do what he could, something was better than nothing. As she left she said, "No pain no gain." She was always so bubbly saying, just the right things to him.

Tony took a nap after all his hard work. One he deserved. He had worked hard and was finally trying. Thank You, Jesus!

I called Tammy to see if the twins could come over. The OT said, "Tony has to work with play dough to work the muscles and nerves in his hand." Maybe our granddaughters could make a game out of it with him. Perhaps her husband Mike could pick up some Play Dough, on his way over when he brought the twins.

Later that day when I had asked Tony if he was hungry; "Not really but to go-ahead and cook," when dinner was ready, I helped him to the kitchen table. I had made linguine and clams. He was really having a tough time trying to get the linguine on the fork. I watched him for a while. Urging him and telling him to take his time, as I placed the fork in his hand appropriately, several times. He'd try again only to get a few strands in his mouth. Eventually he just gave up. I said, "You did well." Then I fed him almost all that was on his plate. I was extremely happy he'd eaten. Whew! We were finally getting somewhere; at least he was eating something.

After dinner we went in the living room to watch TV together.

Shortly thereafter the twins came. We turned off the movie we were watching to visit with them. The twins said, "We're hungry, so I fixed them a plate. Then they had dessert. In the mean-time Tony talked to our son-in-law Mike.

Then Mike helped Tony to the bathroom, as I was busy getting the twins fed. I had to go to help Tony though he needed to be wiped. On the way out of the bathroom, he went the opposite way towards the foyer, the opposite from the living room. "Where are you going?"

"I'm going up." I was disappointed. "The twins just got here they came to see you."

"Have them come up." He had an answer for everything. "I want to go up now, Mike can help me; and then Anthony won't have to come later." Up he went, with Mike, as Mike he had to leave to go to work.

Tony did do his leg exercises after he got settled in, and rested a few minutes. The twins came up, then to watch count, and reminded him of each exercise he had to do.

Afterwards; the twins came back downstairs, for some more dessert, and played with the Play Dough for awhile. When they got tired of that, they went back-up to watch TV with their Papa, their favorite person in the whole world. They just adored him, and he them. He was like their playmate, he rode bikes with them, took them fishing, to the park, all the things a Papa does with their grandchildren and then some.

After awhile they came back down for more dessert and watched TV until Tammy came to pick them up. Tammy ran upstairs to say hi to her dad. He told her all about the twins, counting and helping him with his exercises. He really enjoyed them helping him. She hugged and kissed her dad saying, she had to leave to get the twins home. The twins came running up to kiss, hug, and say good night to their Papa. They had school the next day; and homework to finish, when they got home.

I went downstairs and I watched them go to their car; watched TV for a while then went to bed. We had to be up early the PCT was going to be there at nine-thirty for Tony's shower.

She arrived at nine for his shower. I had just gotten Tony on the toilet and his clothes and towels were laid out.

Anthony called; he was going to the grocery store for me. Then he was going with us to the doctor. He said, "I bought frozen waffles and pancakes for dad." I asked Tony what he wanted to eat for breakfast. "Waffles," I cannot say how excited I was to have him eat, and to cook for him, just on top of the world that morning.

I wanted to try some new jeans on him he had gotten for his birthday in September. He never got to try them on to see if they fit, because he was in the hospital then. Tony had been on the toilet what seemed like forever, he kept thinking he was done, I kept wiping him, after the third time, he was finally done. We only had gotten to try on one pair of jeans; his strength was spent by then.

I asked the PCT to put on the jeans he'd tried. After his shower, I told her he was already beat! Then said, "I'm going down to make his breakfast; when you're done call me, so I can help you down the stairs." I had called Anthony to see if he was bringing the waffles soon; his dad wanted them for breakfast. "I'll be right over with them."

After some time had passed, I went upstairs to see if Tony was ready to come down. As I started up the stairs, I heard him moaning, and asking for me. As I went into the bathroom, he said, "Where were you when I needed you?" I could see through the mirror he had been on the toilet, not the raised toilet seat. The PCT had him walking out of the bathroom by that time. Tony was saying he wanted to lie down on the bed his back was hurting.

The PCT explained he had to go to the bathroom while he was in the shower. She had removed the raised toilet seat to make room for him to get in and out of the shower. So she had to put him on the regular toilet that was too low for him to get back up from. That caused more strain; and consequently, more pain getting up off the toilet. I was worried about the PCT being late for her next appointment. She'd already been here an hour and a half, and Tony was still upstairs.

Just then, Anthony walked in with the groceries. That was great timing, now he could help get his dad down the stairs. Which he did, and the PCT left. When we got Tony down instead of going to the kitchen, he went into the living room to his recliner.

"You've got to eat."

"Not now."

I went about my chores, and then asked if he was ready to eat. He again said, "Not yet."

I fed him some prunes so his stomach wasn't empty, so that I could give him his pills, and then gave him orange juice to swallow the pills with.

I told Tony I was going to take a shower to get ready for the doctor's appointment at one. After my shower, I started getting nervous it was getting late, and he still had not eaten.

Stopping what I was doing to go down to make Tony's breakfast, so he could eat before we left. As I called him to eat, he said, "Not yet." I explained he had to eat right away; we had to leave shortly, getting more anxious by the minute.

He still had to eat, and shave before we left. I told him to shave as I tossed the electric shaver to him, angry that he hadn't eaten.

Ran back-up to finish dressing myself, Anthony called to say he'd be there in a few minutes. "Okay," I'm really rushing at that point.

I called the doctor to see if she was running on time. I had always done that so we didn't have to wait in the office forever if she was backed up. The nurse said, "She's waiting for you."

"His appointment isn't until one."

"No it was twelve-thirty."

"I have the time written down.

"Hold on," she came back and said, "Just come over she's waiting for you." By then I was shaking.

Anthony came just at that time. "Anthony put your dad's coat on we've got to go the doctor's waiting for us. Somehow, someway, the appointment time got screwed up."

It was a chore just to get him to the car let alone inside of it, and it took quite awhile just to do that; I sped all the way to the doctor's office.

When we finally got there the nurse said, "What happened did you take the scenic route." I'd had it by then, my patience were totally gone. I answered, "Do you know what it takes to get him here?" She must have seen the steam coming off the top of my head. She didn't say another word. She could see how weak Tony was. I was ready to blow I was so wound up. I told her I'd had it, and I was ready to jump out the window. That's exactly how I was feeling, maxed out totally, my battery drained down to zero.

Now, I know what they meant when they said, "You need to get out and away from the situation; at least once a week. Otherwise when Tony really needs you, you're going to be spent, and won't be able to be there for him." Well I hadn't listened to them at all, now it was showing. My fuse was gone; I had no endurance left, feeling as though I was going to have a nervous break-down.

Tony was so weak and sore he couldn't even get up from the table. The nurse had him sit-in the chair while she took his pulse and blood pressure. She didn't bother to even weigh him. It would have been too difficult to get him to step up on the scale. I said to her, "Maybe we should he's losing weight. "It isn't necessary this time."

"My wife is giving up on me."

"No, she's not, that's not Mary Lou, she's just having a bad day." She hasn't given up on you at all." Shortly after the nurse was done; our smiling doctor came in. That woman is something else. How she kept it all together with all her patients, and the hours she worked, I don't know. I admire her tremendously, she's a fantastic person, doctor, and so angelic. She always knows what to say, when, and how to say it. I feel very fortunate to have her for our doctor.

"You look so tired Tony, what's going on, how, do you feel?"

"Not too good." She continued to examine him. Listening to his heart, "Your heart sounds really good." She listened to his lungs, "Your lungs sound terrific." She examined his abdomen; everything was good there too.

He's always nauseated, and isn't eating that well at all. "With everything he's been though, you should cut him some slack. What he's going through is all normal its apnea after chemo, the stroke, and all. In addition, the medicine he's taken. Some of the medicine could be making him sick." She was going to start by cutting back more medicine, and then take a lot of blood tests to see how Tony's blood was.

She looked at his arms with all the break-through. "Stop the blood thinner so that will go away." I was so happy to hear that. His arms looked awful, maybe they will clear up. I hoped so for his sake. I'm sure looking at those spots, didn't make him feel any better.

"He'll be fine; it will take about a year to get back on his feet again, but he will it's just going to take time."

She told Tony, "Use your mouth to tell them a thing or two, and how you feel. Something he's never done, only when pushed to the hilt—he'd say what he would and wouldn't do. "Don't worry about him eating. I'll put him in the hospital to feed him if he doesn't eat. You just don't feel good, and you're weak, nauseated, and fatigued. Just not feeling well and you'd like to end it all. You feel like a burden on your family and you see your wife getting very tired."

"Is that how you feel?"

"Yes." She told him, "You know Tony sometimes it's good to have a good cry it's healthy."

I told her about the fall; that it was one thing after the other, it just doesn't end. "Don't worry about that. He may fall again, and maybe break his hip. She says, "That's what sickness is, we'll fix it then, don't worry about it. We have no control as to what's going to happen. All we could do is our best."

Continuing with, "I know what you're going through. I went through it with my own father. My mother would cook and he wouldn't eat. She'd get mad, and throw it out and holler at him. The family would all holler at him. Then when something happened they all felt badly, about what they said, and did. He couldn't help he was sick."

"That's how Tony, is he can't help that he doesn't feel good. He was doing the best he can, it's important for him to exercise as much as possible, but not over-do it. He knows his own limits, and Tony you have got to speak up."

Then she said, "But you've got to promise me one thing, if you don't eat you have got to drink, one supplement a day. I don't care if it takes you all day, but you've got to do that. We have to give you some energy. Let's start with what we've discussed, and see what the blood shows."

"Can I have a beer?"

"You could have several beers. They're good for you, they have nutrients, malt, hops, and it's fattening. I have no problem with that."

She told me, "You have to get help in the house one day a week to get out for awhile. Go get your hair done, nails, or toenails, I don't care what, but you need to get out."

Tony, "Do you agree."

"Yes."

"Go shopping; go to the show, anywhere away from the situation. That's our plan for now, call in a week to let me know how Tony's doing."

Anthony took his dad to the car. While I went to the billing department to sign checks over that I had received from the insurance company. On the way there I ran into the doctor again. She told me, "If we didn't let-up, Tony was going to give up totally. I could see it on his face he was on the verge. He just wants to throw the towel in."

When they had tried to take blood the nurse couldn't find a vein (that upsets Tony) the doctor was going to send a home health nurse over to draw his blood from the port. They didn't have the right needle to do it in the doctor's office, nor were the nurses trained to access it. She'd also have the home health nurse check the break-through bandages on his arms. I asked her, "Does his port need to be flushed once a month?"

"Yes." That's another reason you need a home health nurse to come. You can't be on top of everything all the time. You can't change the future. So lighten up, he's on his way, that's what we have to deal with right now. Or you're going to drive yourself crazy."

"Okay" and we left.

I told Anthony when I got to the car, "I feel like I did with my first baby. All the recommendations are driving me crazy like they did then. The doctors told me way back then, don't listen to anyone but me! I'll tell you what to do. That's what I'm going to do now, just listen to her."

As we were just about to leave I realized after all that transpired, I didn't have the prescription or samples of the one medicine the doctor changed. I had to run back-up for it. The nurse gave me the prescription samples, and we were on our way.

"Tony, are you hungry?"

"Yes, I want fried chicken." I asked where he wanted to go to eat, "The family restaurant in town." When we arrived there I asked Tony if he could walk a littler farther than usual, the handicap parking was taken. He said, "I don't want to go in, take me home." Anthony then suggested Popeye's, as I started to drive there; I asked them what side's dishes they would like, with their fried chicken. Anthony said, "I can't eat the fried chicken with the diet I'm on."

"Tony what's your son going to eat? If we go to the restaurant he could eat too." I turned the car around again to go back to the restaurant we were at originally.

It was difficult for Tony, I must admit. Getting him into the restaurant was a fiasco, but he made it. I actually think it was good for him and his moral because, he succeeded.

When we got back home, Tony went straight to the recliner to rest. I fixed all the medicine the doctor had changed, opened all the samples she gave us. I organized all of that, and still had the groceries all over the kitchen I had left, as we hurried to get to the doctor.

While Tony rested, I finished up with the groceries. Then I went upstairs to make a few phone calls, to the agencies from the list the social worker had given me, wanting to find out what that was all about, the charges, times, minimums, and if the people spoke English. I'd never had anyone like that; and needed to get information. There wasn't that many to reach being after five by then.

While I was upstairs Tony was trying to make a phone call. So I hung up to give him the line. I had the baby monitor on in case he needed me, I could hear everything he was saying. He had called our son Michael, and said, "Joey was supposed to come but he wasn't home. He wanted to go upstairs. Michael said, "I'll be right over." After he hung up I called Joey to see if he was home, and he was. I let him know what his father had told Michael. He said, "I've been here, he never called here! It's all right just let Michael come."

Then I went downstairs to see if Tony wanted to eat anything else. "No." I gave him an Insure to drink. Reminding him that he had promised the doctor he'd drink at least one a day, to get some nutrients anyway.

It was six thirty by then, and Tony wanted to go upstairs, because his back hurt. He told me he had called Michael to take him up. It had been only a few minutes, but Tony was already getting antsy, and impatient. "It takes a few minutes to get here."

Then I asked Tony why he had told Michael Joey wasn't home? I had just called Joey, and he was home, "Joey said, you never called him?"

"I couldn't remember his number." Then he picked up the phone, and asked for Joey's number. He called, and asked Joey to come here.

"Now both of them are going to be here at the same time." Joey told him he'd call Michael to see if he was on his way. Joey called back, saying Michael was in fact on his way, and would be here in a few minutes. Shortly thereafter Michael came.

Tony then had to go to the bathroom, it was another bout of on and off three times, finally he was done. I was trying to get his pants off him and hold him at the same time, while Michael just watched sitting at the table, his father had to say, can't you see your mother's struggling help her. I think Michael was in bubble as to what actually was going on there and couldn't handle it.

We finally got Tony up in bed. Michael asked if we needed anything else, "No", thanks for getting dad up to bed."

"Bye, if you need any thing, call me." I told Tony, "We have to do the exercises on his legs." he was very cooperative, surprisingly! I finished getting him settled and went back downstairs.

To call Ardine to see how she was doing. She sounded okay but sad. She said, "Her and Mikey had our problems; (who doesn't?) it's so different, lonely, and hard to believe that he's gone." She also realized there would be no one to go to dinner with. No one to talk to— No one to share her life with—, "I could only imagine." Those were all my fears, I'd be facing. I too, had a hard time believing Mikey was gone, but she'd be all right she had to be. She went on to say she had nothing to live for. She had cancer and she didn't care if she died. Correcting her by telling her, she 'had' cancer but, no longer had it. She had surgery, chemo, and radiation, to make sure they hadn't missed cancer cells. Those treatments killed the cells. Actually she was cancer free, after the surgery. She went on to say she didn't know that. I then told her again that she'd be okay. The same words she had said to me many nights. I even pointed out that I was repeating the words she had said to me many nights, and then explained, "That her children needed her." At that point she needed to get some rest. None of which she'd gotten the last three weeks. She needed to start taking care of herself she was also exhausted. We decided to go to bed, as we said, "I love you good-bye," and hung up.

The next morning Tony and I got up later than usual. The phone rang it was Anthony he wanted to know if we were ready to go down. "Give us twenty minutes." I had to sponge bath Tony, and get him dressed. While sponge bathing him I went to do his private parts, Tony was never circumcised when he was a baby. They didn't believe in it years ago. When I pulled the foreskin back to clean his penis; it was sore and had accumulated debris under the skin. It was so raw it was actually bleeding.

I had to really clean it out thoroughly. I was livid with the PCT obviously she hadn't been doing that, or it wouldn't have been like that.

Immediately, I called the doctor to get cream to help with the soreness and to heal it. Poor guy, at everyone's mercy—, not being able to do for him self—. That alone had to be a hell in itself—.

Anthony came just at the right time, and brought his dad down. Tony wanted waffles that day. He only took a couple of bites but ate the Jell-O and half banana I cut-up in it and some juice, to take his pills with. Then he went to his recliner to rest.

The OT came at twelve thirty; I thought the PT was coming at two. Tony was going to take his dad to his house so I could get out for a while. But, the PT wasn't coming until three fifteen I screwed up; she was coming later that day. I called Anthony to let him know about the time change.

When Lita came Tony said, "Oh! No", she's here." Joking! It was a love hate relationship. He hated her because she made him work, but loved her because he knew she was making him do the exercises for his own good. She really worked hard with him, and he really tried. They finished, and she set-up an appointment for the next day, and left.

Anthony came right after the exercises were over, and took his dad by his house. We were going to have dinner there also at six-thirty.

I left a little after them. I really didn't know where I was going. I decided to go to a shopping mall. I had a gift certificate for a store there that I had received for my birthday back in July. So I went there to see what I could buy myself. I was looking for a new cigarette case and a wallet. I went right to the purse department. I thought I'd found the perfect wallet. I asked the salesperson to hold it for me. I wanted to look at the eyeglass cases. That's what I use for a cigarette case, because I smoke one-twenties. And they won't fit in a regular cigarette case. On my way over to the eyeglass department I spotted the Whiting Davis counter that has accessories to match. I ended up ordering the whole matching set in black. I had already had the silver and gold in the past, but I never had the black. I thought, I'd enjoy something different, and it could be used with any color. I was very pleased with my choice, it had given me the lift I needed.

Then I went back to the eyeglass department, to look for an eyeglass case. My other one had broken, I found one exactly like it, and I bought it. As I was paying for it, I saw what I thought was a cigarette lighter. I said to the saleswomen, "Is that a lighter?"

"No, they're reading glasses."

"Reading, glasses?" Shocked! Here was this tiny thin case about the size of a toothbrush case, with a tiny pair of glasses inside. They were the cutest things; I tried them on they were itty bitty and thin. She said, "The ladies are buying them like crazy for their evening purses; they take-up so little room, and are convenient for reading a menu, when you go out for dinner." I just had to have a pair of those, and bought those too. That made my evening—. You would have thought I found gold, I looked at my watch it was seven o'clock. I almost died where had the time gone. I knew they'd be worried about me. I started my way toward the door, and suddenly couldn't remember which door I came in from. I walked around the store a couple of times trying to remember. Finally I thought I'd found the door. I walked out, but I still didn't see my car. I decided if I walked around the building I'd have to find it, and I did. As soon as I got in the car; I called from my cell; to let them know I was okay and I'd be there in a few minutes. I explained, "The time got away from me, and then I couldn't find my car." Anthony said, "We ate but I put your dinner on the side"

"Great because I'm starving", When I got there I ate right away, I was famished. I asked Tony how he was doing. He was content lying on the couch. Tony said, "We thought you ran away."

I laughed and said, "I'd never do that." We chatted awhile then I showed them the treasures I bought. They thought the glasses were the cutest. Our granddaughters loved them too. Then Tony and I left to go home. Anthony and Joey followed us home and helped get their dad up to bed and settled for the night. I went downstairs for awhile then went to bed myself.

At six thirty Tony woke me up saying he had to pee. Sleepily I got the urinal, and helped him. When Tony was done I washed the urinal out anxiously, wanting to get back in bed right away, just as I was finishing. "I have to go to the toilet."

By that time I have to say I was a little agitated. "Why did you make me go through all that, if you had to go to the bathroom anyway?"

"I didn't have to go then." Which made no sense however; I proceeded to get Tony up. I was still half asleep, and he wasn't all that awake him self. I was trying to hold Tony up watching he didn't trip on the oxygen tube, and watched where he was walking so, he wouldn't bump himself. As he was walking he bumped his arm on the TV stand anyway, by the time I noticed, he was bleeding all over the place, because of the tissue being so thin the slightest bump ripped the skin wide open, and it bled like crazy. By then the blood was all over him, the walker, his undershirt, and the carpeting, having to clean all the blood up right away before it stained everything. Needless to say I had a mess. A series of things you don't want to be wakened to experience—in the middle of the night I assure you—.

After it was over I explained to Tony I wasn't angry with him. It was the experience, and scariness of what had happened, that upset me. Tony had never awakened to go to the bathroom before. It was something new to add to the list; however we both fell right back to sleep almost immediately.

I had the alarm set for eight forty-five so if the PCT got here at nine we'd be ready. Instead the phone rang, not the doorbell. First it was the home health center calling to tell me the nurse would be out that day. Next called back again, and asked, if I had supplies for the port to be accessed. I said, "Of course not." Then they called back again to ask if they could use a vein instead of the port. "Absolutely not," Tony didn't have the port put in, for it not to be used." Finally a nurse called saying, "I'll be there at eleven thirty." I told her Tony would be with a therapist at that time. She said, "I'll be there earlier and be done, before the therapist gets there."

The PCT didn't get there until nine-thirty, which was all right. I asked her if she had ever washed anyone that wasn't circumcised. Still angry from the day before, she remarked usually her patients wash their own private parts. I told her, "I don't care who washes it; just make sure it gets washed thoroughly." Explaining, what had happened; how sore his penis was, and how it had bled. She could tell I was extremely upset. I asked her to call me when Tony was ready to come down, I'd help her.

While Tony was getting showered, his sister Aida called. She asked how Tony was, and if we needed anything. Then she asked if Tony wanted anything, explaining she was in the neighborhood. "Ask him if he wants anything." When I asked him he said, "Yes, a bagel with vegetable spread."

"I'll be there shortly."

When Aida got there Tony was getting ready to come downstairs. I told the PCT, "I'll be right there to help you." Aida said. "I'll help them."

"No you may hurt your back," as she has a bad back.

"It's already sore it's okay." So I let her help the PCT, as I watched them from the bottom of the stairs. She meant well, and she really hadn't been around much for Tony. She had her hands full with her mother being ill with Alzheimer's, and keeping track of the caretaker. Rental property to manage she was a nervous wreck herself. The few times she had been with her brother she wanted to do as much as she could for him, which was understandable.

They finally got Tony down the stairs and to the kitchen table. I asked if anyone wanted a cup of coffee. First Tony said, "Yes."

Aida said, "No." But I made coffee anyway. Then I got Tony some grapefruit juice and laid out the pills for him to take. All the while Aida kept saying to me; go do whatever you have to do; I'll do that for him. I'll take care of him, take some time for your self. I made the mistake of saying I had to take a shower. Aida kept saying, "Go take your shower, I'll stay with him." Before I knew it, she was feeding Tony. Literally!

I really got upset I said, "Aida don't feed him let him do it himself. He's got to use that hand he had the stroke in. When he gets real frustrated, that's when I feed him if he hasn't eaten enough." Which he hadn't been lately. Aida mentioned a friend of her's father had a stroke, and was having trouble eating. They had some kind of test done and found something wrong with his throat. That's why swallowing was a problem for him; she didn't know the name of the test was though.

I was still angry that she was feeding him. I went on to say you're not doing him or me any favors by feeding him. I knew what I was doing I had enough professionals coming here I should. Aida said, "That's why I don't come here." I just didn't even comment on that. Thinking that *wouldn't be good for him, doing everything for him all the time.* I already was doing plenty for him. There were some things he needed to do for himself. I explained it would be much easier and less frustrating for me to do every single thing for him. It wasn't easy to sit and watch him struggle. It was heart wrenching, but that's what needed to be done if he was going to get better.

Aida debated it even further saying, "He exercises his hand all day doesn't he?"

I said, "No actually, he doesn't." And eating technique is much different than exercising the hand. When you're eating you're using fine finger, motor skills. She meant well she just didn't understand. I didn't need people coming to the house two, three times in ten months upsetting the apple cart. I couldn't nor wouldn't allow it. Period! I knew how hard it was for her to see her brother like that. I felt the same way, but I had to stay tough for his sake. I was already on edge from the hectic morning I'd had with all the confusion and phone calls; I was in no mood to debate anything.

Tony decided after all the controversy he did not want to eat anymore. Of course he loved the attention, of being fed and all. He liked putting on the mosses for his sister or family. He always had, another whole story, poor me act.

I did get him to eat the fruit and he drank all the juice. Aida and I then brought Tony to the recliner in the living room. I left them, so they could sit and talk, while I did some things. I was actually waiting for the nurse to come before the therapist got there. Tony and Aida talked for awhile, and then she said, "I have to leave." I walked outside with her. I told her the stair lift was going to be installed on Monday. She said, "She was going to talk to her mother. If her Mom were well she'd want to pay for it. She was going to call me about it after discussing it with her." It really didn't matter to me, because Tony was going to get it either way. Just as Aida was pulling away, the nurse pulled up in front of the house.

When I came back in the phone was ringing, Greg was calling to say, "I'd like to come visit."

"Come over any-time you want."

By then the nurse was at the door ringing the doorbell, Ding-dong, Ding-dong. She said, "I made it before the therapist got here."

"I had made a mistake or the therapist would have been here and I wouldn't have let you take the blood test, because Tony's therapy is important." She came in and got set-up. I asked her if she had ever accessed a port before. She assured me that she had many times. She had actually worked on the cancer floor for many years, which made me feel much better and more comfortable with her. I was relaxed once I was assured she knew what she was doing.

I told her, "I think the home health service stinks."

"What makes you say that?" I explained to her what had transpired over the phone before she got here. With all the phone calls back and forth, first regarding the needles, and then wanting to use his veins, then asking me if I had any supplies. She explained that some patients did have supplies in the house. "They should have explained that to me, because it sounded stupid. Why would I have supplies for the port? When the doctor had just put the order in for the blood test; Tony had never had his port accessed at home before that day." However, they should have known if I had supplies at home. They would have been the ones that ordered them.

"And the question about the vein was because some people only use their port for the chemo." Which made no sense to me, but knew for a fact they couldn't draw blood from some patient's ports. That explained the second question. If they'd taken the time to explain like she did, they wouldn't have sounded so ridiculous to me. If they used a vein any nurse could have drawn the blood. He wouldn't have needed a special nurse. At that point I notice the hand Tony had the stroke in was swollen, so were his legs, and feet. I had the nurse look at them, while she drew the blood samples she needed.

Greg came to visit; while the nurse was still there, he brought Tony candy and lottery tickets. Tony and Greg visited while the nurse finished up. When she left I apologized for giving her such a hard time about the whole mix-up. But I had quite a frustrating morning.

Tony and Greg continued to visit for a while then Greg left. He didn't stay long, he could see Tony was getting tired, and he knew Tony needed his rest to get well.

At that point Tony was extremely fatigued. I guess the stress of the port being accessed didn't help, along with all the confusion. "I feel nauseated again."

While I had a few minutes I'm going up to take a shower. I thought the therapist would be there at two. I straightened a few things got my clothes ready, then hollered down to Tony. "Are you okay, I'm going into the shower now?"

"Yes." I wasn't in the shower more than five minutes. When I came out I thought I heard Tony calling. I ran to the top of the stairs. "Are you calling me?"

"Yes, I have to go to the bathroom." I ran down in the nude, to help him right away. Then I'd go back-up to get dressed. I put the walker up to the recliner. Just as I pulled Tony up with the gate belt, I noticed his pants were wet. "Your pants are wet!"

"I know I couldn't hold it, it just came out. I think I also dirtied my pants."

"Do you still have to go?"

"No."

"I just asked you five minutes ago if you were okay, I was going in the shower."

"Yes." Not five minutes later all this happened."

"I didn't hear you." Trying to keep my cool, with my brain reeling with what to do first, clean him, get myself dressed, as I was still nude. I tried to gather my thoughts and stay calm to think. "Okay, I'm going to go up, and get some clothes on before the therapist comes to the door, and catches me in the nude. I'll be right back to change you; I'll bring you clean clothes down with me. It's okay well get you cleaned up. Don't worry about it. It's okay."

I ran upstairs threw my clothes on rapidly, as fast as I could. Grabbed Tony clean clothes, and ran back down the stairs. While I was doing that, my mind was reeling out of control again. *Did he have another stroke? He had said, "He didn't remember me asking him if everything was okay and he had answered yes?" Was he having another stroke? Was he losing control of his bladder and bowel? Was he just that sick with nausea? What was happening? Should I give Tony Imodium AD for diarrhea and Zofran for the nausea?* Saying to myself, "Stay calm." Don't let your mind take you on a nightmare tour, get him cleaned up first, handle the latter later. I got Tony out of the recliner. Now I noticed the pillow I had behind his back was also wet. We walked to the bathroom with the walker. I had Tony sit on the toilet to make sure he was done before I cleaned him all up. As I took off his socks, pants, and underwear, calming Tony telling him it's okay you'll be clean in a minute. Scared to death myself, as to what was happening to him. I let him sit while I took the pillowcase off threw that down the stairs to be washed, and cleaned the pillow and took it outside to dry, then went back to Tony, he said, "I'm ready." I washed him all up, put clean clothes and socks on him. I wanted to call the doctor before I gave him the Imodium AD or Zofran. To be sure I was doing the right thing. All the while rushing because; the therapist was going to be there any second.

Devastating Phone Call

When I called the doctor I explained to the nurse who adored Tony, what had just happened regarding the incontinence and nausea? The nausea had been going on and off for two and a half weeks, with not eating, and swollen hand, legs, and feet. I gave her Tony's blood pressure, and pulse rate, which were actually very good. She said, "I'll talk to the doctor, and call you back." Then she said, "Wait let me see where the doctor's at." She came back to the phone and said, "Are you ready for this?" (Confused)

"Ready, for what?"

"Tony's very sick and not eating, you know that's not good. The good news is he needs to see a speech therapist for testing his throat. The bad news is you have to take him to the hospital for the test." Then she went on to say a stroke was different from cancer. "It's a vicious circle Tony's taking a lot of pills for his heart. The answer is he has to eat plus he's tired of it all." You can't blame him, he wants to give up, and you my dear have to be ready for that. You need to take care of yourself. You need to get away from the situation for a while. Go to the show or shopping something, you need to be prepared if something happens. It's up to him and God now. You have done all you could and did a good job. There isn't anything else you could do. I was in a stupor—Shocked— I had called about the medicine, and she was telling me all that. What was all that about?

"Would you like to talk to the doctor?"

"Why"

"Cause she loves you that's why." Still Confused!

"Okay," as the doctor got on the phone.

"Mary Lou"

"Yes."

"I think Tony's giving up. What's happening is not cancer related at all. I could see it in his face when you were here the other day. He doesn't want to tell you that because he knows that's not what you want to hear. He's protecting you."

"I don't think so; he does his exercises and all."

"He's very tired; he's been through a lot of difficult situations. He's just plain tired. You have got to prepare yourself if something should happen. Maybe you should have a family meeting. Don't blame yourself, you've done everything you could, and you've done a good job, but it's between him and God now. He's got to have the will and he's just tired out. Be very careful with your wording. He also feels like a burden to you. He sees what your family's going through. He doesn't want to see all of you suffer anymore either."

She paused, "Take care of yourself." I thanked her and told her, "I'll keep you posted."

"You can give Tony the Imodium and Zofran for the diarrhea and nausea"

I have to say when I hung up the phone I was totally confused, just baffled, and very saddened and distraught. I had been outside having a cigarette when I called the doctor, and now I was crying like a baby. Were they trying to tell me he was going to die? If Tony didn't get some energy, and a surge of positiveness, or were they trying to tell me the stroke had something to do with him maybe dying. What were they trying to tell me? Anything could happen at any time. Naturally I didn't accept that at all—.I wouldn't hear of it!

I immediately went into the living room, and told Tony I'd talked to the doctor. I explained what she had said, about the pills, and his not eating. That what was going on was a revolving thing, the pills played hell with the stomach, and with no food they cause nausea. I also told him, "She was going to set up the speech therapy test as soon as possible."

Lita came just then. At some point I had looked at the calendar to see when she was due. She wasn't due to come until three-fifteen. She arrived around the time I got off the phone with the doctor. "What's wrong?" She could see I'd been crying. "I'd just got off the phone with the doctor. I whispered to her, what the doctor had said "He's giving up." She made a sigh to me. I also told her Tony had an accident. She went to Tony, saying, "What's going on Tony?"

"I don't want to do any exercise."

"Tony I'll be real easy on you today. You can stay just where you are and we'll do a few. She got him going, and he did do a few. She said, "He did well, do a few exercises over the weekend, have a good weekend, and I'll see you Monday," as she left.

Then I pulled up a stool next to Tony's recliner, and asked him what his goals were. He answered, "I want to walk." I explained calmly that he needed to eat to have strength to walk. Then I asked, "Are you giving up?

"No," then I asked him what he thought of the whole situation. He answered a question with a question, "How would you feel?"

I answered honestly; "I probably would have given up months ago." Then I asked if he was putting up a front for me, but really wanted to give up. "No," asking if he was being honest with me. "Yes." I was crying uncontrollably by that time, telling him he was the most important thing to me in the whole wide world. That money meant nothing without him. Telling him what good was money without you? Then talked positive, telling him he would walk again in time with a lot of hard work. We would be going on trips and everything again soon. We could do it together, but he had to eat. He needed to Force Himself!

Then I asked if he wanted to eat. "Yes."

"Do you want a chicken sandwich?"

"Yes, with some chips, and a beer." My heart soared, as I got it all ready, and brought Tony to the kitchen table to eat. He took about three bites of the sandwich ate some chips with cheese dip, and drank part of the beer. I then fed him Jell-O with fruit. "I'd like to go to the Mexican restaurant for dinner tonight." I told him, I'll get one of our children to go with us. Being afraid to go with him by myself, calling I got Michael, and Lisa to go with us. We made plans to go around seven thirty that evening. I was excited Tony wanted to go out to eat. My hopes were boosted immensely!

After lunch we went back to the living room, put a movie in the VCR, but fell asleep I was emotionally exhausted. I woke up a couple of times to answer the phone but went right back to sleep. I woke up when the movie was over and was going to get ready to go to dinner. Tony said, "I watched the whole movie, and it was a good one." Thank God he liked to watch TV; it was a great pass time for him. It had been his salvation. I'm not and never have been a TV person.

I went upstairs to freshen up. When I came back down, Tony said, "Call to see where they're at?" When I called Michael's cell they were just around the corner from our house. We got Tony in the car, he was fatigued by then and still pretty weak, even with all the exercise, still difficult getting him in the restaurant. Nonetheless, we made it, and he ate pretty well. Thank You, Jesus! Not a whole lot, but he ate. We all enjoyed the evening very much. I hung on every encouraging positive thing I could. That's what kept me going, enjoying every second I could with him.

When we came back Tony went right to bed. He was surely spent, by then it was about ten, and he was beat. No exercise in bed that night, he was too tired after he was all settled.

I went back downstairs for a while and called Ardine to check on her. She was doing the things she needed to get done for herself. Nevertheless, it was very difficult, and lonely she admitted.

I had cried for months myself, worrying about losing Tony, and being in that position. I, knowing I wouldn't want to live without him. We had been together since I was a kid, and I loved him so much, more than life itself.

The next day was Saturday; no one was coming that day. Wanting to stay in bed so bad, but I had made a hair appointment. Dee and George were coming over to stay with Tony, so I could go. Which I thought was awfully nice of them, such good friends. We were very fortunate. It would also be good for Tony to do something different. I really didn't like the idea of leaving him though. Hoping he wouldn't have an embarrassing moment. Praying he'd be okay until I got back. Leaving him with our children; was tough enough however, leaving Tony with friends, was another story, even though we had known Dee and George for many years. They had been best man and maid of honor at our wedding, if he had an accident in front of them, he would be humiliated. For that reason I left Tony as little as possible.

Anthony and I brought Tony downstairs, and then I fixed him cereal, juice, Jell-O with fruit, and gave him his pills. By then Dee and George were there. I told them there is food in the refrigerator for lunch. I'll call before I leave the beauty shop, to see what you want to eat later for dinner, then left.

It took longer at the beauty shop than expected. I had gotten bumped. If Anthony was busy, his customers came first. I knew I was going to be late getting home. So, I called to see how everything was going there and told them I'd be later than expected, because Anthony was extremely busy. Finally, when I was done, I called to see what they wanted to eat. It was dinnertime by then. We all agreed on barbecue, which worked out great because the barbecue place was right next door to the beauty shop. I picked that up, and rushed home so it would still be hot. We ate as soon as I got home with the food. Dee and George had to be somewhere at five thirty. I thanked them for helping me out. Tony had enjoyed their company, too. After we ate, they left shortly thereafter.

My sister-in-law Aida had an appointment at the beauty shop that day and she brought a video to watch later. After Dee and George left, Tony and I went into the living room to watch the video, when I realized I'd left the movie, in rushing I'd forgotten it there. I called Anthony right away to make sure I had left it, and not lost it. "Yes, it's here I'll drop it off on my way home."

We decided to just watch TV until Anthony brought the movie. When Anthony got here Tony wanted to go to bed so he brought him up. Tony didn't want him to have to make another trip back later. We got Tony settled, and he did his exercises, and watched TV in bed. He was starting to build the muscles in his legs. It was amazing how you could actually see the muscles getting bigger. His legs had been like two, tooth picks. Now they were starting to fill out and have some definition.

After Tony's exercises, I went back downstairs to watch the movie Aida had given us, and then I went to bed.

We got to sleep in the next morning. It felt wonderful to relax and sleep without having to jump up early, and get on the roller coaster. We hadn't been able to do that in months. Just not having to rush going here or there or having all kinds of people coming in and out all day was a treat. It was a reprieve for the both of us, and it felt great.

At that time all our children; doctor, nurses, therapists, and social worker had been after me for weeks, to get a caretaker two to three times a week so I could get out to do errands, shop, whatever I wanted. Actually, they have been nagging me since the social worker was here and gave me a list of agencies. Anthony said, "It's too much on you everyday, day in and day out, for months." I guessed they could see me getting fatigued, with a shortage of patience and just plain worn out. They were afraid I would get sick if I kept up at that pace. I was very nervous about the idea of leaving Tony, and of someone else taking care of him properly. Our children kept harping on me. I kept thinking should I, shouldn't I?

I just didn't feel comfortable about the whole thing. It was really making me; a wreck, thinking about it, weighing me down, like I had an elephant on my shoulders. In addition, the daily stress of taking care of Tony, with all the problems that occurred.

Anthony said, "Are you worried about the money? You could afford it."

"It doesn't have anything to do with money. I don't have anywhere to go, nor do I want to go anywhere without your dad. When I did get out I was a nervous wreck and couldn't get back fast enough, because I was worried about him, so it wouldn't make me feel any better to have someone come here to take care of him, so I could go out!" I just wanted to be with my husband. Something didn't feel right, I couldn't decide. I was familiar with caretakers from Tony's aunt who had a stroke, and my mother-in-law.

After weeks of having to make that decision weighing on my mind, I finally put myself in Tony's shoes. Asking myself would I want a caretaker taking care of me? Or would I want my loving husband or family member taking care of me, that I felt comfortable, safe, and loved by.

That did it "Bingo" I had the answer, a light bulb went off in my mind. I made the decision and told our children. I 'Was Not' going to get someone in the house, two to three times a week, because I didn't want to! I wanted their dad taken care of by myself or by someone who loved him as I did. Someone, who genuinely cared, about his needs—, not some stranger! I convinced our children I could do it.

If they felt I needed to get out, one of them could stay with their dad a couple of hours occasionally. Then I'd consider leaving their dad, otherwise, Forget It! I don't want to hear another thing about it. When I put myself in their dad's place, I wouldn't want that done to me. I'm not going to do that to your father. I have nothing else to do, but take care of him. Period!

Once I'd made the decision that weighed on me tremendously and told our children what was decided, I felt like an elephant had been lifted off my shoulders. I had been a wreck over it for weeks. I couldn't believe the pressure that was lifted once I'd made that decision. Knowing our children meant well, but it had put more pressure on me. Pressure I didn't need!

After that our children would take their dad a few hours occasionally, so I could get out a little here, and there, doing a few errands, knowing Tony was being taken care of with love, that's when the free days started.

When I made that decision and told Tony what I had decided. Tony's response was, "I'm glad you made that decision." You could just see the anguish melt off his face, like ice melting in the sun. It must have been a burden weighing on him too. It made me feel warm and good inside to know he was also happy. I had made the right decision—!

That particular Sunday we were going by Joey for dinner, with the whole family. As soon as Tony was cleaned up, Joey needed to be called to help bring his dad downstairs. Then I made Tony some breakfast. Afterward, Joey was going to take his dad by his house so I could have a couple of hours to shop, or whatever needed to be done until dinnertime.

After Joey came and they left, I cleaned up did a few things around the house.

Then decided to go get Tony some sweatpants.

I have to admit it was a relaxed feeling to do things that needed to be done, without the constant interruptions of attending to Tony for that couple of hours. Especially knowing he was being taken care of with love and care. I could escape the stress for a while.

I thought I'd go shopping; Tony's needed sweats, so that was my chore for the day. They were the easiest to put on and off, warm, and most comfortable for him, plus the easiest to pull up and down with the elastic waist, when he needed to use the bathroom, they were much more convenient.

While driving and thinking of where to go to, Wal-Mart came to mind. I got lucky there the sweats were on sale. I bought him four pair in different colors. I was pleased as punch. I had gotten lucky at my first store, and they were on sale to boot. What more could I ask for, life was finally getting easier.

Then went to another discount store I loved to browse in, but didn't find a thing. It was fun anyway, just to look around; without the stress or fear that Tony was not being taken care of properly. I called Joey from my cell to see if everything was okay with his dad. "He's fine." I asked, "Are you ready to eat?" "Not until around six; you still have about forty-five minutes to shop."

Then I went to another discount store I liked. I wanted to see if I could find a dressier sweat outfit for Tony to go out in. One with pockets in it like Tony wanted, but had no luck there either.

Got to Joey's house just in time to eat, everyone had already started. I was starving by that time, so it worked out just perfect. They said, "Dad ate quite a bit of chips and dip, but just a little dinner. "He didn't want anymore." Then we had dessert. Tony did eat some of that. He always was a sweet eater. He seemed to be trying to eat at least, thrilled, he was trying.

I brought the movie I'd watched the night before with me. We had just started watching it when Tony wanted to go home. "My back is hurting; I want to lie flat in bed, it helps to lay flat it relieves the pain," So we left right away.

Mario followed us home to help me get his dad upstairs. Tony did his exercises then Mario, and I went downstairs to finish watching the movie we had started at Joey's house. First Mario wanted to go for cigarettes. He called while he was out to ask if I wanted anything, "No, thanks anyway." The store he went to for cigarettes was closed.

When Mario got back he had brought me a hot fudge sundaes anyway, my favorite with extra hot fudge, and nuts. That was a nice surprise. We ate our Sundae as we finished watching the movie.

Stair Lift Installation

I went to bed when the movie was over. The next day was to be a very full day. The stair lift was being installed at nine. Then the PCT for Tony's shower, then Lita would be there for Tony's leg exercises, then the OT to exercise Tony's hand. After all that, we had to be at the hospital at two for the speech therapy test, to check Tony's swallowing. We were going to be on a roll all day long.

We were up bright and early the next morning for our very busy day. Wanted to be up, ready, and organized for all the excitement that was about to follow.

The installers arrived, on the button, at nine. We were off to a good start, (I thought) so far, so good. That day we had a very tight schedule, literally one thing after the other.

The PCT was there at nine-twenty for Tony's shower. That was good he'd be done, eat, and rest before Lita came. So far, that would all work out well.

After his shower, the PCT and I got Tony downstairs without a problem, and he ate really well that morning. Thrilled Tony had eaten. Hurrah! He finished breakfast then he rested until eleven, when Lita came.

That gal was an angel that hadn't received her wings yet. The first words out of her mouth as she came through the door were. "How's he doing today?"

"Much better" since we had the attitude adjustment on Friday. He'd even been exercising at night. *(I couldn't believe it had only been three days since all that had transpired.)* "Great!" We were in the living room then, and she saw him. Saying, "Tony you look great today. A whole lot better than Friday when I saw you last. You're like a different person. "How's the back?"

"Still sore, but getting better."

"What's the pain level? "

"About five."

"Are you taking anything for pain?"

"No."

"Are you ready to do a little walking?

"Sure." He was ready, willing and able to do just about anything she asked him to do. I cannot express the joy I felt. At last we were getting somewhere. To hear Tony talk with a positive attitude was marvelous.

He did a great job exercising that day too. I was so pleased, and so was Lita. It was very exciting with, and for him he was 'at last' going the 'extra mile'.

Tony and Lita teased back and forth about her trip to Maui. She'd be leaving in about three more days. He'd see her the next few days then not for about a week and a half. He would have Jackie as his therapist during that time. Tony and I said, "Jackie's very nice but she's no Lita."

"It's just because you're used to me." We both assured her, that wasn't the reason. She has that special something some people just have. I believe it was the angelic part of her I saw, as she worked, and talked to Tony so compassionately. She truly cared.

We talked about if she thought by February Tony would be able to walk, and able to go to Maui. "Without any other object getting in the way, it's a realistic goal. If he keeps up the way he did today." Tony had done exceptionally well that day compared to Friday, when he'd felt so sick.

"I believed it was part psychosomatic when Tony was down mentally, that was part of it. When Tony was up mentally he seemed to do better, even if he wasn't feeling all that great.

At any rate, we'd take the good however and whenever it came.

I reminded her Tony was going for the swallowing test that afternoon, to find out if there was a problem. We'd be assured after the test whether something was wrong or not, and be able to rule that out if nothing showed up. Praying that everything would be okay!

Lita wished us a good day, and said, "I'll see you tomorrow."

"Can you come early, as Anthony said he'd bring his dad by his house for the day, if I could arrange the appointments earlier? He wanted me to have a free day. Whether I just lay around, and did nothing, or if I did a few things I needed to do. I'd have the whole day to myself."

"I'm all for a free day for you. She had been one of the people that were pushing me to get out. She would be there at ten-thirty, which, was going to work out well. By the time I got Tony dressed, and fed. He could rest awhile, by then Lita would be there. "Perfect, see you then."

In the meantime, the stair lift installer notified me that the company had sent him with the wrong unit. It was a keyed unit, not a remote unit. He had to go back to the shop to get the right unit. He explained that the boxes weren't marked from the manufacturer. The only way to know the difference was to open the box up and check it and they hadn't done that.

Can your helper go? "She doesn't drive a stick shift." Explaining that we had an appointment at two at the hospital, and we had to leave at one thirty, not sure how long we'd be gone. You just never know when you go for a test at the hospital. Guessed it would be at least an hour, and a half, figured we should be back by about three thirty. "I'll see if someone at the shop can bring one out to me. "I'll let you know a little later." He called the shop, but there wasn't anyone to bring one out to him. He had to go and get the unit himself. He finished up what he was doing, and said, "I'll be back as soon as I can. Don't worry, even if I have to stop so you can go to the hospital for the test. I'll come back afterwards to finish the job." He assured me it would be installed that night, for sure. They were very busy, and he had other installation jobs scheduled for the rest of the week. He was a pleasure to work with and very accommodating, confident, in what he was doing, and very knowledgeable about the equipment, which was a plus. Feeling comfortable with him, I had a lot of questions that needed answered, he explained, and answered every one of them.

The installer had been gone about an hour. When he returned he immediately went right back to work where he left off.

The OT came while the installer was working. I was watching him to make sure the lift didn't stick out too far into the foyer at the bottom of the stairs. I asked him to pitch it as much as possible, so it doesn't take up much space on the foyer floor, as I didn't want people to trip entering the living room.

Not paying much attention to the OT session that day, being too busy watching the installer, he had my full attention making sure everything was going as expected.

I did ask the OT if she could come Thursday, explaining that I could have a free day if she could. Tony was going to spend that day with Anthony. To give me some time to do whatever I wanted. She was also very accommodating. "I'll see what I can do, and let you know if it can be worked out. If not you can do the therapy yourselves that day. The one session you miss will be okay. You need the free day I think." Which I appreciated, and thought that was nice of her.

After therapy it was time for us to go to the hospital for the test. Anthony was going to help me with his dad, being unable to take Tony alone. I made arrangements with the installer to come back about three thirty or four. I gave him our phone number so he could call first if he wanted to make sure we were back by then.

It was a good thing Anthony came to help me, Tony went down off the stoop, as his knees buckled. Anthony had him by the gate belt in the front, and I had him by the belt in the back. "Push up on the walker with your arms. Don't get nervous we have you, your okay we aren't going to let you fall. Just relax your all right." I never would have been able to handle Tony alone. That could have been a catastrophe, for sure.

More Testing

After we got Tony into the car we were on our way. We made it on time for our appointment. We didn't have to wait long at the hospital at all. We went right in for the test. I was grateful for that. I was anxious to get back so the lift could be finished being installed.

They allowed me to go in with Tony to watch the test being done. I was amazed at how they had him eat and drink something, and they watched him swallow it on an X-ray screen. Tony had done super no problem there, everything worked as it should. Whew! More, great news—.

As Tony and I walked out of the test room happy as larks, Anthony had run into Ardine while he was waiting for us. She was there for a blood test. We all hugged, and kissed. She said, "Tony you look great. Maybe I'll stop over later."

After the test was over Tony didn't want to go out to eat. He just wanted to relax he was pooped, probably from being anxious about the test. Also stumbling on the stoop hadn't helped, that had frightened all of us. On the way home Tony asked Anthony if he could bring back a couple of fish sandwiches for us. I had a sandwich as soon as I got home I was starving, I couldn't wait for Tony to come back with the fish sandwiches. Then I went outside to have a cigarette. Tony was watching the movie Mario that I had watched the night before. When the phone rang; it was the doctor's office. The nurse had called to tell us all the blood tests came back normal. The cancer test came back normal, but Tony was an anemic. Otherwise his blood-looked great Tony should be doing the gig in the street. They had also already gotten the results from the hospital. The swallowing test came back prefect too. Yeah!

Once again everything seemed to be going our way. Thank You Jesus! Finally!!!!!

I told Tony the wonderful exciting news. He was very happy to hear that no cancer had shown up in the tests and he was on the road to a full recovery. I could see by the look on his face, Tony was beyond extremely happy. Tony was also ecstatically excited about the stair lift being installed.

After I ate I laid down for a while to rest, and wait for the installer to come back. I was exhausted from the full day we'd had. I was just about to fall asleep, when the doorbell rang, Ding-Dong—Ding-Dong—I got up to let him in, it was the installer, and he hadn't called first. He was alone this time. I was glad we came straight home after the test.

He went right back to work where he left off. He was working on doing the wiring part of the installation. He said, "I need a three-way plug for the outlet behind the couch."

I called Anthony on his cell to see if he could pick a three-way plug up for us. After hanging up the phone I remembered I had one outside I'd used when I had the fan and TV hooked up out there for Tony. I went outside and got that one to use for the moment, until Anthony got back.

Anthony called back saying, "A circuit breaker strip would be better."

Tony said, "We have one in the garage," I was going to get it when the installer said, "That's not a good idea, the plug you have is better for the situation you're using it for." Explaining the electric we were using in the outlet is so very little; we didn't need a circuit breaker for it.

The installation was almost done when Anthony came back with the food. Anthony took care of feeding his dad, while I was getting instructions on how to work the chair lift.

Ta! Da! Tony finally got to try the lift. The installer showed him, how it worked, and everything about it. To say that Tony was beyond elated with the lift, would be putting it mildly. The lift was very safe, strong, and easy for Tony to get in and out of with some help. He could operate it up and down himself. That gave him a feeling of independence once again. Something he hadn't felt in an extremely long time, almost a year to be exact. Even though he'd need help in and out of it, Tony didn't have to rely on our children daily or nightly anymore. He felt FREE AT LAST! I also felt relieved and made my heart happy. Not having to worry about Tony falling down the stairs was a big relief. Or having to put our children out every night was also a relief; even though they didn't mind one bit. It was a relief just not to worry about whose coming when, and Tony being able to get upstairs whenever he wanted to. The stair lift would be a pleasure for both of us, I was sure of it.

Being side tracked with the installer, filling out the papers, and learning how to work the lift. After the installer left I realized I hadn't paid attention to, how much Tony ate. By the time I realized it, Tony was already on his way back to his recliner.

I asked Anthony how much did he eat; "Not a whole lot; not even a bite of his fish sandwich."

Tony said, "I'll eat it later."

Anthony then left saying, "I won't be back but if you need me call." I told him we'd be fine. Shortly thereafter Tony said, "I want to go upstairs to bed."

"You didn't eat your fish sandwich."

He smiled and said, "I could come-down later if I want to," we both laughed. Something he hadn't been able to do for months. I'm sure that had to be a great feeling for him. A FREE AT LAST feeling, as he went up the stairs on the lift. Then I got Tony settled in bed; and he did fifteen repetitions of each exercise on each leg, that was fabulous.

I went back downstairs to relax, write, and watch TV. It had been an extremely happy eventful long day.

Tony paged me from upstairs over the intercom, a couple of hours later. He thought he had to go to the bathroom, but couldn't seem to go. I told him to try and relax; when he did, he ended up going. I asked him if he wanted his fish sandwich, banana split, fruit, Jell-O or sherbet. "I'd like some sherbet." I went downstairs to get it for him, and he ate it. Hallelujah! Tony told me how relieved he was to have the stair lift. "It's better than a new Cadillac to me," he said. I was glad he was so thrilled with it. I hoped it gave him the inspiration to do the things he needed to do to get better. I thought it would from his response thus far; it surely had given him a lift in more ways than one.

After Tony finished the sherbet, I went back downstairs. I stayed up longer writing then went to bed.

The next day Tuesday Anthony was going to take his dad by his house for the day. After he had been cleaned, had breakfast, and therapy; I was then going to be free for the day to do whatever I wanted, which was a good feeling, along with knowing Tony would be in good hands.

That morning I got-up before Tony, got my shower so I'd be ready when Tony got up. When Tony got-up I proceeded to get him ready for the day.

The home health nurse called at nine she was going to come over at ten-thirty that morning. I told her he wasn't even out of bed yet, and at ten-thirty he had a therapy session scheduled. She said, "I'll be there around eleven so I can see what the therapist is doing with Tony."

"Fine."

After I got Tony up, cleaned, and dressed. Tony got-to ride his Cadillac (that's what he called the stair lift) down the stairs. "It's a lifesaver. It was a pleasure getting down the stairs." I was so very happy for him. Going up and down the stairs had been one thing he dreaded it had been very hard for him. That morning going down the stairs had been a pleasure for him. I can't tell you how happy I was that Tony was finally getting some pleasure, out of something.

Tony even ate really well that morning. That of course made me, happy for the first time in quite awhile. We were both happy, the start of many happy days ahead. I left Tony to finish eating his breakfast as I ran upstairs to finish getting myself ready. I left the door open so if Lita came she could just walk right in.

When I heard Lita come in, I ran downstairs to help Tony finish his breakfast, and clean him up. Then he was ready to do his exercises.

I explained to Lita that Tony was having a hard time turning over in bed. She suggested that we go upstairs so; she could show him how to turn without straining so much, to make it easier until Tony got stronger.

Tony was so proud showing off his Cadillac as he rode it up the stairs; he was thrilled, like a kid at Kiddieland! Lita made a few suggestions put the footrest up on the lift until Tony got in the chair, so Tony wasn't so far from the seat when he was trying to sit, and then lower the footrest. That was a better way it seemed to work easier, and a lot safer for Tony. What a great tip!

After the ride upstairs we got Tony to the bed and had him lay down. As Lita showed Tony how to get his elbow; on his side under him, then roll onto it to dig his elbow into the mattress to help push him self up.

Then we came back downstairs, and Tony exercised extremely well. He had a great attitude and really worked hard that day. Lita was leaving for Maui so we weren't going to see her until she got back November fourteenth. She told Tony to work hard while she was gone. We bid Lita our Aloha's as she was leaving for Maui in a couple of days. Told her to have fun, a great trip, and to bring a lot of pictures back, along with a lot stories to, tell us. She said, "The PT taking her place will call you with the time she's coming."

The nurse never made it for the therapy; she was late and came just before Lita was leaving. She never did get to see what Tony and Lita had done. I told the nurse Tony had done a great job and had gotten a good work-out. The nurse and I went over his physical health. The medicine Tony was taking, and the swelling in his hands, feet, and legs. The relentless nausea Tony experienced after taking his pills in the morning. She then took his blood pressure and pulse it was good. His heart rate was up a little though, probably from all the exercise he had just done.

Anthony arrived just about then and asked how much longer the nurse would be there. She said, "About ten to fifteen minutes."

He said, "I'm going to run to the grocery store, I'll be right back." The nurse left shortly afterward, and I waited for Anthony to return.

When he got back, he put his dad's shoes on, telling him he was going take him to his house for the day. Later we'd all have dinner together. I told Tony I was going to run a few errands while he was at Anthony's house. They were leaving when Anthony said, "Dinners at six."

"I'll see you later," as I hugged and kissed Tony good-bye.

I went back in the house to do a few things before I left. I threw a load of laundry in the washer, finished putting my make-up on, and left.

I again didn't really know where I was going, except, to finally take the grab bar back, then play the rest of the day as I went along. After I returned the grab bar; I stopped to look around a couple of stores. Then I decided to stop to pick up some pizza slices at a famous pizza place, as appetizers before dinner. Then I started my way back to Anthony's house. I still needed to stop for gas, cigarettes, and then the bank. I also made a stop to get the twins a trick or treat gift. It was Halloween day, I had asked Tammy the day before to pick something up for me, but I wanted to make sure I had something for the twins. I didn't know if Tammy had done that for me, being so busy her-self.

When I got to Anthony's I handed the twins their Halloween gifts. Then I cut-up the pizza. Anthony had everything ready and we all sat down to eat.

Tony ate really well that evening. It was such a pleasure to see him eating normally, like he used to. Tony made a comment about something that had happened during the day. Anthony smiled at his dad, telling him to drop it. I of course asked what happened. It was nothing Anthony remarked. I knew by the smirks on their faces something happened. I told Anthony now that I knew something happened, you might as well tell me. Was it bad or serious, I asked. He finally said, "Dad had an accident."

I said, "Oh! No! "He said, "It had happened on the way to my house. Dad just couldn't hold it, and he wet his pants. I had to change him, and wash his clothes, but everything was okay no big deal."

Tony told me, "I don't know why I couldn't hold it, it just came out." I felt awful for him I knew he also felt embarrassed, and bad about it. I think Anthony knew it too. That's why he told his dad to drop it, so as not to have his dad, relive an embarrassing moment. The embarrassing moment I feared he might have, had happened!

By the time dinner was over Tammy had gotten there to pick up the twins. I asked Tammy if she could follow us home to help me get her dad in the house; then your brother Anthony could go to bed, "Sure no problem."

Anthony had gotten called to work on a movie the next day. They needed extras for a couple of days. He had to get up at four thirty in the morning. We had dessert right away so we could leave early. Then Anthony could go to bed, to get some rest, as we were leaving Tony asked Anthony to come help get him in the house. We didn't need Anthony to help his dad at night anymore, but we still needed assistance getting Tony into the house. Tony felt safe and secure with Anthony because he was the biggest of our son. Plus he'd been doing it for so long he knew exactly what, how, and when to do things. I told Tony Tammy and I could handle him, but he insisted he wanted Anthony, to help. "I don't mind." I think Tony was so afraid of falling again. He was secure with Anthony. I left it at that better safe than sorry. I certainly couldn't blame Tony it wasn't as though he hadn't had an accident before.

As I was driving home Tony told me what actually happened while he was with Anthony. He said, "On the way to Anthony's house we had gotten all the way to his house. When I went to get out of the car the strain of getting up, it just came out of both ends." Anthony had to clean me all up, and wash my clothes. Then later that day Anthony was in the garage. I called him, but he didn't hear me. I couldn't hold it any longer, and wet my pants again, plus I was on the couch so the couch got wet. Anthony had to wash me up, wash my clothes again, and wash the couch. I felt really bad for both of them, for Anthony to have to go through that experience. And how embarrassing it must have been for Tony to have that accident; have his son clean him up not once but twice. He said, "Anthony cleaned me real-good." I knew Anthony had a weak stomach. So I could only imagine how difficult that must have been for him, besides the feelings of seeing his dad like that. Very sad—. Poor things—.

Tammy and the twins followed us home anyway. When we got home the twins couldn't wait to get in the house to ride on Papa's "New Cadillac". They were so excited about the new toy. They couldn't wait for Tony to go upstairs, so they could try it.

I told Anthony his dad told me what happened. He just looked at me and rolled his eyes; kind of making a joke of it, by saying welcome to care-taking; we kind of chuckled to make lit of it.

We got Tony on his Cadillac, and off he went up the stairs. Smiling all the way, with that cute smirk he had. As much as to say look at me—! We got him settled in bed and he did the leg exercises while the twins counted for him.

Then it was their turn to ride the Cadillac. They got one turn-up and one-down each. They thought riding the New Cadillac was the berries. Then they had to give their dolls, a ride, then I had to take a ride, and then their mother had to try it. We all had our turn riding the New Cadillac.

The next day, Joey stopped for lunch, and he tried the New Cadillac to. Then he cut the grass for us front, and back. We were so blessed to have wonderful children that were so helpful. It was all done without even asking.

Anthony had tried the New Cadillac the day before when it was installed so we only had Mario, and Michael to go for their test ride yet. The lift surely was a blessing we should have gotten it sooner. But Tony was doing so good we thought maybe it wouldn't be necessary. I could say it immensely helped to make a change in Tony's attitude, and taken the fear, and worry of the stairs away. Tony had worried hours before he had to go upstairs. That experience was an awful one for him. It had worn him down many nights. It was worth every penny, and then some, to relieve the stress Tony felt.

After they all left, and Tony was all settled, I called Ardine to check on her. She must have been on the phone because it just rang. Otherwise her machine would have picked up, or she was on the Internet.

A while later she ended up calling me back; she was okay, but very tired. She had three shots of Neupogen, and needed three more her blood count was down. That's why she was tired all the time. Other than that she was okay. She'd be starting radiation, November eighth and she'd be getting thirty-five treatments. I hoped for her sake she didn't have a lot of side affects from it, she'd been through a lot. We were both yawning so we cut it short early. Saying we were going to bed early.

I went to bed shortly after hanging up with her.

The PCT came about nine twenty the next morning. I let her handle giving Tony his bath. I was busy in the kitchen making phone calls; taking care of business, that I had let go altogether the past month.

While Tony was getting his shower, Dee, and George called. We were supposed to do something with them that day. It was Dee's Birthday that day. I told them when Tony came down, I'd ask him what he wanted to do, and call them back.

Tony came down within a few minutes; I had his breakfast all-ready. While he was eating, I told him Dee and George had called. Tony ate a fantastic breakfast that morning. Another good day under our belts—. Thank You Jesus! I asked Tony if he'd like to take a ride, and then go eat somewhere to celebrate Dee's Birthday. It was a beautiful day outside for a change. Mid sixty's with the sun shining brightly. Tony said, "I'd like that." We had a free day all day to do whatever we wanted. No PT, or OT, or Nurse coming that day. What a great feeling. I called Dee and George back; we talked about what to do?

We decided to go to an outlet mall about an hour away. It was enclosed, and I had the wheelchair in the trunk. Dee and George said, "We'll be there in about an hour and a half." That worked for us to, we'd be ready by that time.

I made sure I had extra clothes for Tony in case of an accident. I also took the urinal just in case we should need it. Then I got myself ready real quick. By the time I'd got myself, and everything else together Dee and George was here.

Off we went. We started a very enjoyable day, and drive. When we got to the Outlet Mall and George went to help Tony get out of the car. George did not know how weak, Tony's legs could be. When Tony went to step out of the door, George wasn't ready nor use to handling Tony, his legs buckled under him like rubber, when Tony went to stand, down he went down to the doorframe of the car. Poor George hadn't given Tony the support he needed. Then when he went to lift Tony up, he hurt his and Tony's back. We finally got Tony in the wheelchair. Tony poor thing was shaking by that time, but he was okay. We were there about two hours when Tony started getting antsy. His back was hurting from sitting in the wheelchair so long, and he was getting hungry. That was a very good sign; Tony was like his old self, starting to worry about eating all the time. Yeah! That I was happy about—! We hadn't bought much, we just walked around, and browsed it was great. With Tony getting uncomfortable we started our way out of the mall.

The ride back was also enjoyable. No trouble getting Tony back in the car. Thank God! We had left early enough to beat the traffic, which was great.

We decided to go out to eat at our favorite seafood place. The dinner was very good as usual, Tony ate very well again, and we were all pleased and happy about that. His appetite was finally coming back. Tony seemed to be enjoying his food again. Another Blessing! Another Miracle!

After that we went directly home. Tony was exhausted by then, it had been a long day for him. He went right up to bed, when we got home and I got him settled, he did his exercise and I let him rest.

I went back downstairs by Dee, and George; we talked awhile reminiscing the whole day we had spent together, and then they left.

Tony called me on the intercom shortly after that. He needed his legs rubbed. I went upstairs to massage them for a while. They had been hurting him from the exercises he'd been doing the muscles were reacting to being used again. But that was a good pain if there is such a thing. At any rate I'd rub the soreness out of them, and Tony eventually would go to sleep. "With Out" a sleeping pill, and had been for the last two weeks; after taking them; for 'fifteen years', another feat beaten—.

Tony was really doing, great! His arms were clearing up since the doctor took him off the blood thinners. That was also an improvement he could see with his own eyes and couldn't be denied. Tony's hair, beard, eyebrows, and eyelashes were also starting to grow back. Another positive reinforcing thing he could see. Of course I pointed out even the smallest improvements to Tony so he would realize himself he "Was" getting better even if it was ever so slightly. We all knew his goal was to walk, that had been the 'Main Improvement' Tony was waiting to accomplish. We all were waiting anxiously for that to be accomplished to.

All in all we had a wonderful enjoyable good day. I'd take those days all day everyday. Anytime!

I had gotten up early the next morning. I had to take care of some business with Tammy. We had an appointment at nine-thirty. I had to pick her up, and. I had to be out the door by nine. The nurse was also coming that day, plus the therapists to exercise Tony.

Anthony came to take care of his dad while we were gone. I left as soon a he walked in and I was back by ten. I wanted to be back before the nurse got there, I needed to talk to her

The nurse was already at our house when I got back. Tony was still getting nauseated not as bad, but it was still happening. The nurse and I talked about the pills Tony was taking and what could be causing the nausea. Tony's appetite was getting better, and he was eating in spite of it, but we still hadn't come to any conclusion, still baffled with the cause. Then the nurse left.

The OT came shortly after the nurse left. Tony was doing very well with her to. He was really coming along great, as far as the stroke. Everyday it got a little better with Tony getting more use of his hand, but needed to keep working to strengthen it.

Michael and Lisa had asked us over for dinner that evening. We had accepted it would be something different so we would be going there. Getting out was not easy but it was good for Tony physically, and emotionally.

Lita came to work with Tony, and he did great with her too. Tony's attitude was really good that week, and he was on an upswing. He was also trying very hard to achieve his goal. Walking was his priority, his main focus. Lita worked on balance with Tony that day. I was very happy about that. I felt if his balance were better he'd be able to walk faster independently. He actually did well with the balance exercises. Lita explained, "It's a matter of re-teaching the brain how to automatically react, and how to catch your-self when going off balance instantly. Tony was on his way. That was the reason he had fallen backward in the foyer, which I didn't realize at that time. I had no idea the stroke had affected his balance until that very moment.

Later that evening we went to Michael's for dinner. It was a challenge to get Tony there. First of all Michael had to come to our house to help me get Tony into the car. I was afraid to do it myself. We didn't need any falls to set us back then or ever for that matter, so we were being very cautious. Michael has a stone driveway the least little twist of Tony's foot could cause him to fall. I backed into the driveway to avoid as much walking on stones as possible. Pulling as close to the sidewalk as I could. Then there were a few steps up, but we did it without major difficulty. It had been hard for Tony however, even with our helping him.

It was worth it though it had been a lovely dinner. However Tony for some reason hadn't eaten much. I was upset, but didn't push it. We left shortly after dinner. Tony had been eating so well. Thinking to myself, now what's wrong? I pushed it out of my mind; I didn't even want to go there again. I tried to stay focused on the positive.

I had called our priest a couple of days previous, and asked him if he could come over, and visit with Tony. He said, "I can come Friday morning at ten." I told him that would be great. I felt Tony needed some spiritual input with all he'd been going through, and to receive the holy sacrament. We both could use that.

That Friday the PCT was late, I thought wouldn't you know it.

The priest called saying he was on his way. Tony was still getting cleaned up. I explained, "The PCT had just gotten there. She was late and Tony wasn't ready yet, but he'd be down shortly. You and I could visit until then." The priest was at our house within minutes. The church is only a couple of blocks away. He and I chatted while we waited for Tony. I said, "I feel Tony needs some spiritual input. I think he's having a problem being grateful that the cancer's in remission. He's angry with God for all the problems he's been through. My feeling is Tony needs someone to help him sort out his feelings."

I also had explained, "We have experienced a tremendous amount of "Miracles" Tony has been blessed with." Which I found to be extraordinary I've mentioned throughout this book; I felt there certainly is a higher power.

When Tony came down we all talked for a while. Then I excused myself, so they could talk privately, and Tony could open up to him, which he seemed to do. The update I'd given the priest helped him key in to important things. It was good, Tony was very receptive to the priest, and liked him a lot, which helped. The one important thing the priest hit home on was. "Everyday above ground is a good day." Tony really focused on that. Afterward the priest gave us both communion and father left saying, "I'll see you next week Tony."

I had asked Tammy to bring the twins over for the day. It was good for Tony to be with the twins. The loves of our lives—the twins also sparked Tony to try harder. They liked taking care of their Papa, and he enjoyed it to. I called to remind Tammy she was to bring the twins. "I'll pick them up at school, and drop them off." I asked her to let them stay overnight, which she agreed to? It all worked out because her husband had to work, and Mario, and her were packing up the Halloween inventory. The twins staying over night had worked out good for all of us.

Lita came later that day, and they did some reflex exercises with a balloon, which Tony did very well with. His reflexes were slow and weak, but in general he did a good job. It was really fascinating to me, to see how therapy worked, what the therapist could tell from what he did and how he did it, and she knew what exercises to have him do, to improve.

She told Tony he was doing terrific. She pointed out the small positive things he conquered, which he didn't realize himself, and needed to hear. Tony's endurance had increased tremendously just in the last week. It was still a slow process though I even got frustrated that it wasn't going faster. I certainly understand his frustration. It helped me however to focus on the small improvements also. At least there were improvements we could see; he had made a total-turn around since the Friday before. Lita gave Tony a lot of reinforcement, then left saying, "I'll see you Monday. "

The twins got there around four. They kept us busy from the minute they got there. They are high maintenance, and don't stop for a minute, but their very helpful good twins, that don't do anything destructive; they just require a lot of attention. That night they helped their Papa walk to the stair lift, encouraging him as he walked. Then they did their usual routine of counting the exercises. After the exercises they watched TV with him in bed. After the work-out they fed him some sherbet. They loved helping him; and I can't emphases enough how much he adored them, relished the attention, and help he got from them. Later that evening Tony had leg cramps, and the twins were right there to rub his legs. They were a big help to me to, plus he enjoyed them being there immensely. They definitely put joy in his heart.

The next morning the cleaning lady was there at seven. I explained what I needed done, and went back to bed while she cleaned the downstairs. Then she called me she was having trouble with the toilet not flushing. We never did figure out what happened because strangely, it started working. That had been weird, and unexplainable. Once I was up again, I just stayed up, and went downstairs.

The twins came down with me, they wanted breakfast, and I gave them the cereal they asked for. Then I got prepared to give Tony a sponge bath. I had him participate by washing himself after I lathered the washcloth for him. He did very well; he seemed to be helping me more, now that he was gaining some strength. He even put his own undershirt and sweatshirt on. That probably doesn't sound like any big feat, but for him it was something he hadn't done for himself in nine months. It's the little things we take for granted that actually take more energy that we realize. Tony also lifted his legs for me somewhat, which he hadn't been able to do at all.

After I was done with Tony's bath, I had the twins take showers, and wash their hair. Then I quickly jumped in the shower. We were all clean, and dressed. We went downstairs and the twins watched TV, and played games, while I got Tony breakfast.

It was late by the time I got that all done. Tony rested a while then Lita came. I had completely forgotten she was coming that day. She didn't usually come on Saturday so I was completely thrown off schedule.

At any rate Tony was rested, and actually had been feeling good the past two days. I had stopped giving him grapefruit juice to see if that could be the problem, since all the medication he was taking were pills he'd taken before. So far that seemed to have worked, something that supposed to be healthy for you could cause nausea, but I guess with the chemicals in the pills it did. Thank God we had combated that problem. How I figured that out I don't know another "Another Miracle," was the only answer I could figure out. Somehow I had gotten the intuition to stop giving Tony the grapefruit juice, from where only God knows.

Lita had Tony doing some balance exercises. Then she walked him several times back and forth through the living room into the kitchen down the hall into the foyer to the front door, and back. Which was a lot of walking for anyone healthy let alone weak, Tony did tremendous on all the walking. Tony's improvements were unbelievable; and he actually lifted his leg about a foot off of the recliner, and had completely straightened his arm from the elbow totally, straight out. I couldn't believe my eyes, and neither could Lita we both sat there in awe. She said, "Keep that up and you'll be on your way in no time." I told her he was up to twenty repetitions of each exercise on each leg at night. Since a week ago Friday he had progressed unbelievably, Lita was totally impressed, and so was I, just as pleased as we could be—. As she was leaving she said, "I'll be seeing you Monday, Tuesday, Thursday, and Saturday of next week."

Tony's Doing Phenominal

*B*y then it was lunchtime. The twins were hungry as usual, always wanting something to eat. We had lunch, and then cleaned up the mess. Afterward, we rested until it was time for them to get picked up. They were going to their grandfather's retirement party that night.

After the twins left for dinner, Tony and I ordered pizza we just hung around, watched TV and relaxed. I fell asleep shortly after eating the pizza. Tony woke me up when the movie was over; he wanted to go to bed. I had to help him to the stair lift, and to bed. Tony was doing great, his balance and reflexes were getting better, but not perfect yet—still needed help, for fear of falling. Someone had to be with him just in case he lost his balance; he could be stabilized with the gate belt. After that few minutes I slept, I got another burst of energy, so after I got Tony settled, I did a few things around the house, and turned in.

We slept in the next morning, we were both so tired. Our children were calling, leaving messages, asking if we wanted to go out for breakfast. When we finally got up, I started calling them back to see if they still wanted to go. Joey's was the first message saying, he was on his way out for breakfast. When he got back he returned the call. He said, "I'll go with you, even thought I already ate."

"It will be at least an hour or so, before we're ready. I still have to bathe and dress dad, then myself."

"Call me when you're almost ready and I'll leave my house then."

Anthony called before we left, to see if everything was okay. To tell us to just go to his house after breakfast, instead of going back home, so we didn't have to bring his dad in, and out twice. Anthony was having the whole extended family over for dinner for my mother-in-laws, eighty-fourth birthday.

Michael had also called earlier that morning to go to breakfast but, when I tried to call him back, there was no answer.

Michael returned my call later. I told him we were going to breakfast with Joey. We'd see him later at Anthony's for the party.

Mario never answered the phone when I called, he must have been sleeping. He and Tammy had been killing themselves working at the Halloween Store the past month. It was physical, mental work, plus long grueling hours, and they were both beat to hell.

When I talked to Tammy she said, "We have to go to another party, but we'll be by Anthony's later for dinner."

After I checked in with all our children, I finally got going to get us ready. As we were getting ready we discussed how late it was already; and decided we'd only have a bowl of soup, instead of a big breakfast. When we were almost ready I called Joey and he came to get us. Tony got to the car without difficulty.

Joey pulled up in front of the restaurant. When Tony tried to get out of the car he went down on the doorframe, again! When that happens, it's very difficult to get him up because, of it being so low. Joey had to literally lift him to his feet. I explained to Joey, "He has to be at the edge of the car seat, with his feet flat and firm on the ground so he has leverage to stand." When that happened Tony got really nervous, scared, and upset, not to mention sore. However, we made it into the restaurant, and got Tony to the table.

When the waitress came to take our order, we ordered soup. I could tell Tony was still shaken from the falling incident. He knew he had to get in and out of the car several times before he was back home. Something like that gnawed at him, and he worried about it the rest of the evening, which made matters worse.

I explained to Joey how that happened, and how to avoid it from happening again. The number one thing is to take your time. His dad's feet had to be close together, and flat solid on the ground, and if he did those things it would be easier and safer in the long run. Rushing always make's it worse, plus it's dangerous. Joey's idea was to rush, to get it over with, but in essence, it took longer, and his dad could end up with broken bones as a result. If he did it slow the first time it was actually faster, and safer.

After we had our soup we went straight to Anthony's house. We didn't have any problems getting Tony back in the car. Tony felt safe at Anthony house, it was the easiest house for Tony to get into; being it's a ranch, no steps, just a couple of little ledges to go up, but no stairs to speak of. However, Tony still had to be careful not to trip. Anthony's couch was also; much higher than ours, so Tony could lie down, and get up, without a hassle.

We were there a little while when they all started to arrive. Anthony actually had a Thanksgiving Dinner spread; rigatoni, turkey, sweet potatoes, and salad, with all the trimmings. It was wonderful; everyone enjoyed it, too much food though. I said, "Why did you make so much food? What are you going to do with it all?" Tammy popped up (teasing her brother) could we wrap it up; freeze it, then all I'll have to do Thanksgiving Day is thaw it out, heat it, and it will be done." Ha! Ha! Tammy usually had Thanksgiving Dinner every year so the joke about the left-over food was funny and appropriate.

My mother-in-law was very upset to see her son walk with a walker. She hadn't seen him for a while. Plus she's really not with it all the time, and not doing that great herself. She has dementia. She comes and goes depending on what's happening, and she doesn't remember much. It was really sad; to see her like that, to live to that age like that is a shame. If you're a healthy; independent person at that age, that's another story. Actually living life! Being active and doing things you enjoy, she was just—existing. But, we don't get to make those decisions. Only God knows why these things happen. My mother-in-law has to have the caretaker, always with her. Since the accidental overdose, she had gotten progressively worse!

All in all it turned out to be a beautiful day. After the Birthday Cake and coffee, we all left. Joey came back home with me, to help his dad in, and helped him to bed. Even though we had the lift; Tony still needed guidance to the bed so, Joey helped me that night. Tony did his leg exercises; and did twenty repetitions of each exercise on each leg, super great. He'd progressed from ten to fifteen; now twenty all since he came home from the hospital, in spite of the fall and setbacks. Thinking, Tony's doing phenomenal; we praised him, for all his efforts, and told him how his muscles were building up where you could see them getting bigger by the day. In fact Joey was amazed to see how far his dad had come and that his muscles had grown so quickly, by then Tony was spent, and just wanted to sleep.

Then Joey changed the light bulb in the kitchen ceiling fan fixture, and said, "I need to go I have to work tomorrow, bye," and he left.

I stayed up a while longer, and called Ardine. I hadn't wished her

Happy Birthday, and wanted to do that before going to bed. She was on the phone and said, "I'll call you back in a few minutes." When she called back, I wished her Happy Birthday, and we talked half the night. She was intermittently having an awful time adjusting to the loss of her husband, saying even though they had their ups and downs as everyone does; she still missed the good parts of their relationship, and that it was an awful adjustment. My heart went out to her; I could only guess what it was like for her. I had only imagined; how lonely it would be the last eleven months not actually having lived it, but all the things she mentioned I had thought about. In fact, the things I feared, and shared with her, 'she was actually living.' Now I was telling her, what she had told me, to console me. She would say, "You'll be all right, you've got your kids to think about, and you're a strong person." Except Now, I was saying that to her.

The only thing I said to her that was different was, "Please hang in there because, 'I love you'. When she said, "I really just want to die, I don't care anymore."

"Please you can't do that to me, I couldn't handle it. You can't give up, and you need to have a good attitude. It's a proven fact; that people who had cancer do poorly if they give up." After the pep talk we chatted awhile longer, and then hung up. I went to bed completely drained.

The next morning when the PCT got there, it was about ten, later that usual. I told her to let Tony do as much as he can for himself. That the day before he'd put on his own undershirt, sweatshirt, and got as far as putting one leg in his sweatpants. I explained, "Help him only if he needs you to."

When he came down he was so weak he could barely walk; totally exhausted, and wiped out, from the exertion of doing his own shower and dressing himself.

The PCT said, "Tony did most of it all his self; washed his hair, showered, and dressed with little help, but while brushing his teeth he got so weak, he had to sit down. On Friday I'll have him do less, and build-up slowly." Poor guy, that was too much for him to do all at one time.

Tony was really doing fantastically. He was getting stronger and doing things he hadn't done in a long, long, time. Rebounding by leaps and bounds!

It had been an awful day from the start. The PCT was late to get Tony's shower. That started the day off on the wrong-foot. Knowing we were going to be back to back with all the people coming that day. The phone started ringing incessantly from the get-go. Our children were calling, checking on us. That was a great gesture, but not when you're trying to do five other things at the same time; it could be annoying and aggravating at times.

I called Anthony to give him the grocery list of things I needed. He told me that Tammy was going shopping for me that day. He was leaving the next day for Washington but, was however coming over later; to go-over the different vacation places we were planning on going on in December. That also made me very anxious, because, as much as I wanted to go, the truth was I was truly scared. I knew it was something Tony had wanted to do for months; however, I knew he was frightened too. I could only hope and pray everything would go well. Of course the doctor would also have to give us the go-ahead. I hoped—!

By the time the PCT was finally done with his shower, and gotten Tony down, I had Tony's breakfast ready. Then the nurse came just as he was eating; when Tony was eating, and someone came, it upset his breakfast, I was upset about it too. After finally getting Tony to eat! She was asking him a hundred questions, which seemed to be defeating the purpose. He gave up on eating; however, I managed to get him to finish eating, by feeding him. Getting more upset by the minute, the second Tony was done, the nurse immediately started taking his pulse, blood pressure, temperature, and asking another thousand questions. With most of the emphasis on the nausea, I thought we finally combated that problem. He hadn't been nauseated since stopping the grapefruit juice. She was still asking questions when the OT got there. In between all that was going on, the phone calls kept coming, therefore a lot of interruptions. Being at my wits end by the time OT came. I told the nurse, it's ridiculous—one person after the other. Something has to be done about everyone coming with no rest in between. That's too much for anyone, including me, let alone a sick person. "I realize you're all trying to help Tony, and I appreciate it, however, it's too much for both of us. I feel like I'm in a revolving door, spinning round, and round, since my feet hit the floor this morning." Running, trying to beat the clock! They could tell I was extremely frustrated. I explained to them, "By the time you leave, and I get Tony's lunch, the PT will be there with no rest in between."

I was very protective of Tony, our privacy, and the time people took from us. I almost felt like I was living the life they wanted us to live. I didn't think that was the way it should be. It was our lives we were living, not theirs, and not what fit into their schedules but, what was important to Tony's health. That was all we had right then, how our time was spent, and that's 'NOT' how it was going to be used!

In between all the ciaos; trying to wash clothes, running up and down the stairs in between all the appointments, answering phone calls, making phone calls I needed to make. Trying to figure out; if it was me or, if it really was, all that bad that day!

Tony on the other hand, had done his exercise fantastically. Thank God, that part of the day, was exciting for sure. Tony was doing great in that area, much better than expected. They kept saying he was amazing, and he truly was amazing to all of us.

Anthony came over in between the appointments while his father was resting. We went downstairs to have a cigarette, and made phone calls to airlines. Then we went over which time-sharing places were available on what dates. Trying to decide where to go, on what dates? I went upstairs to ask Tony which place he preferred to go to. He was undecided, and couldn't make-up his mind either. That was par for the course, for him. Anthony and I decided it would be better to go to the St. Petersburg, Florida area. Anthony had the newspaper with all the promotional sales the airlines were offering. When we called for the sale price on the plane tickets, the catch was that you only had specific days, you could travel. That canceled out some of the time-sharing places he'd checked into. Anthony was in a hurry; having a lot of things to get done before leaving for Washington the next morning. He asked me to call later when I got a chance, and to make whatever reservations I thought were appropriate, would be fine with him. I wasn't too keen on that idea, it was bad enough when Tony and Paul were there, and we could talk back and forth. But with them being out of town, was another story. I took the burden on my shoulders, and decided I could do it. When we asked Tony how he felt about it, he admitted he was scared, but would love to go. We told him he had a month to get stronger, and we'd get a wheelchair there. We were going to play it by ear, we'd be going mostly to get away, and just relax.

Greg called checking to see how Tony was doing, as he usually did. He also wanted to know if he and another one of Tony's friends could come over the next day. I had told him the week before; Wednesday, that was a good day, because it was a free day for Tony. But, he said, "Our other friend can't make it on Wednesday."

"Sure." Though it was against my better judgment; happy they wanted to see him. However, they had to come by ten a.m. because the other guy had something to do later that day. "That would be okay, Tony has a therapy appointment right after that."

Tammy had called earlier, asking if we wanted to see her and the twins; or did we want her husband to just drop-off the groceries on his way to work. I'd already had a very bad day, but I also loved seeing her, and the twins. Against my better judgment again, I said. "You and the twins should come." Knowing I'd be spreading myself too thin—again.

Tammy came later that evening with the twins, and groceries. I was so wound up by that time; I was like a bomb ready to explode. The twins were full of piss and vinegar as usual, going up and down the stairs, wanting this, and that. They had energy that didn't end; like the Energizer Bunny—. Now I had groceries to put-away, and already beat-up by the stress. The visit wasn't good being on edge; not able to relax to enjoy them, then felt bad about it of course, finding I spread myself too thin, but I never learned! I tried to do it all to make everybody happy; then it backfires on me. Tammy made us homemade soup; she is a very good cook, when she has the time.

Then Tammy and the twins took her dad up to bed for me. The twins did their ritual, helping Tony do his exercises by counting for him. He ate up every minute with the twins, as usual. They made sure he did each and every one of them. Tony just loved that time with them, and of course, the twins enjoyed it too. They felt they were helping with his recuperation. They were immensely! After all was said and done, they said, "Good night," gave loving hugs, and kisses, then left.

I stayed up to finish the wash and things I had to get done before turning in, knowing we both had to get to bed early to have everything done before we started getting his ten o'clock visitors.

We did get up early the next morning. Tony's friends would be there before we knew it—. I rushed getting Tony bathed, myself ready, and make him breakfast. Which took extra time; being, he had to do as much as he could for himself. He would be using his own muscles, to start gaining his own independence, to become self-reliant. Just as moving him around took extra time because, he still couldn't move fast. Plus we had to be very cautious, to prevent another accident. It all did put extra pressure on; making me less patient; always trying to beat the clock, and it made me angry at myself, for doing that. Hoping that one day, I'd learn; not to try to be super-woman. But, was like that all my life; a difficult thing to change instantly, though, I kept trying.

He finally was ready to come down, I helped him down; and he ate breakfast while I ran back-upstairs to finish getting myself ready. When his friends arrived, I shouted from upstairs for them to come in. I left the door open a bit; so they could just come right in. The coffee was made; on the table, with the cups, sugar, cream, and cookies, everything was ready so they could just help themselves when they arrived.

I stayed upstairs; finishing myself, knowing by the time they left the therapist would be there, and I wouldn't get a chance to get back-upstairs. When done, I went down to meet the other friend, which I'd never met. They stayed a bit longer then left.

Soon after they left, the OT was there, as expected. Tony said, "I'm not feeling too good, I'm nauseated again." The therapist immediately looked at me to see, what I thought about exercising. She asked, "Tony to do what he could," telling him he had to keep up his strength as best as he could; the only way he was going to do that was by exercising. He did what he could; Poor guy always really tried hard.

The doctor's office called that afternoon; asking me if I had gone through the medical bills yet, the doctor had a large balance due. They asked me to do that so, if there were any discrepancies we could take care of it right away. The nurse said, "If you need any help we'll help you any way we can." That was a nightmare job; sorting bills, you really need to have a clear head to tackle all the papers. Something I hadn't had the time to do; consequently, they piled up. But, "NOW" I had to tackle them. That was something that I wasn't looking forward to doing. More pressure! Not what I needed! The pile was insurmountable from the hospital, doctors, radiologists, laboratories, tests, technicians, chemo, radiation, and on and on. I couldn't make heads or tails out of them; that was why I hadn't done them before, it was too overwhelming. Tony had been in and out of the hospital so many times I didn't know what was from what, on what date, from whom! One had to be a CPA to figure them out, which I'm not.

When I talked to Joey that day I asked him, "Can you stop by; and bring Gyros for dinner, for all of us if he could."

"That's no problem, I'll be happy to do it." At least I wouldn't have to worry about cooking. Thank God. I'd be able to work on sorting the mounds of bills.

I firmed up our reservations for the trip. I had a few minor problems, but finally got it done. Thrilled I'd accomplished that feat—.

The other therapist Jackie came that afternoon. Lita was still in Maui. Tony had done really great with her. He exercised fantastically; and really made great strides. She was even impressed with him; "He never ceased to amaze me," she said.

Tony on the other hand, my Mr. Negative, couldn't see his accomplishments at all. I came up with the idea that if we make a progression sheet; Tony would tell me what to put on the sheet; things that he felt he had accomplished. That way when he said, "I'm not doing well," we could show him the list he himself devised. That way he couldn't feel like we were snowing him, or patronizing him. Which we hadn't been, but I think he thought that we were. The therapist also thought that was a good idea. We started the list right away that day. There were at least fifteen things on it right off the bat. Tony wasn't really impressed with the list though, we had to reinforce the things he had me write down. He kept blowing them off as not that great a progression. The therapist reinforced that those were things he had just started doing only in the last week and a half. And explained; that, that was a tremendous achievement for that amount of time. "Give your-self a break." Tony definitely was his own worst enemy. Again, I being a positive thinker had told him over and over. If you think you can—you will, if you think you can't— you won't, the mind is powerful. With that, we finished Tony's therapy for the day. That had drained me, trying to get him to see something he really couldn't or didn't want to see or believe.

Tony had a late lunch then because, he wasn't feeling good earlier, and didn't want to eat.

That evening, Joey brought the gyros for dinner, as planned. Tony didn't eat a bite of it. He did, however, come and sit at the kitchen table with us. I got him to eat some ice cream at least. I didn't push the food because of him feeling nauseated earlier. We talked for a while, and then he wanted to go to bed.

Joey took his dad up to bed for me, and then sat with him while he did the leg exercises. Tony had increased to thirty repetitions of each exercise on each leg, absolutely great strides in it self, since when he came home from the hospital he could barely do ten. He had actually tripled the strides, he made, and that was unbelievable.

I stayed up very late that evening working on the medical bills, trying desperately to concentrate. Finally I just couldn't focus, see, or, think anymore, everything was running together. I gave up, and went to bed around three in the morning.

The next morning came much earlier than I was ready for. Dead on my feet, I literally dragged myself out of bed. That day was to be a free day, except for the PCT for his shower.

Then he would have the rest of the day for himself. Tony was happy about that, he was sick of all the commotion constantly, and so was I!

That morning, after Tony's shower, he ate well. Thank God! I started on the medical bills again. I wanted to get that out of my hair, I finally figured out which doctor bills weren't paid, after hours of just sorting through the mounds.

In the interim, Dee and George called to see what we were doing. I must have sounded frustrated, which I was. She asked, "What's the matter;" I lied, saying, "Nothing."

"We'd like to stop by a little later, would that be okay?"

"Yes." Again trying to spread myself too thin; being really involved in the medical mess, but thrilled they wanted to see Tony. I didn't have the heart to say, now isn't a good time, as I'm buried in paperwork!

I was trying to get through that medical mess before they arrived. I got Tony his lunch so he'd be done with that, and would be able to visit with them, but I didn't make it. They came while Tony was eating, and I still had to call the doctor's office with the information I'd found.

I excused myself for a moment, explaining that I had to call the doctor's office while all the information was still fresh in my mind. I couldn't hear with all the talk around me, so I excused myself, and went upstairs so I could concentrate, and hear better. The nurse said, "You have to call Medicare, to find out why they haven't paid some of the bills"

I immediately called Medicare, and went over everything with them. They told me why the bills hadn't been paid. It was a matter, of not having the right paperwork, and documentation for the bills that were submitted.

I called the doctors office back right away, but they were out to lunch, and was told to call back in fifteen minutes.

I went back downstairs to visit with Dee and George in the meantime. They had just bought a new truck, and were all excited. I was happy for them; they needed the truck for their move to Florida, and to pull the trailer with all their belongings. I apologized for having to make those phone calls, but I had to rectify the mess while it was fresh in my mind, and that I had to call the doctor back in fifteen minutes, to finalize everything so I could be done with it, and put it out of my mind

They decided to leave; they wanted to get home before the traffic started. I went to the door with them to look at their new truck, and wished them the best of luck. It was a beautiful truck, and they were very excited, I told them to enjoy and drive safely. It was too cold to go out to see it up close, and I couldn't leave Tony alone in the house. I told them maybe that weekend we could get-together, and it was left at that, we'd talk later on through the week.

Mario stopped by that evening that was a surprise. He'd been working hard, with long hours like Tammy was due, to the Halloween season. It had been difficult for either of them to spend much time with us the past month but, kept in close contact by phone. It was great to have Mario come and spend some time with us. He was going to meet Tammy there, and then they were going by her house to finalize the Halloween paperwork.

Tammy was also coming to bring us dinner. Which was so thoughtful of her; with her busy schedule, and the dinner was very much appreciated. Finalizing all the medical bills to completion; had been a bear, but made me feel like I had accomplished something Huge!

Mario stayed after Tammy brought dinner, and he helped his dad exercise and chatted for a while, then left.

After Mario left I heated the dinner Tammy brought; Mario didn't want to stay. He was going to have dinner with Tammy and the twins. She had made veal roast, roasted potatoes, and green bean casserole, and it was delicious. After dinner I asked Tony if he wanted to play cards.

"Okay." The therapist had reminded us that playing cards was good therapy. I was thrilled that he agreed to play. Playing cards was something we had done many years ago to pass time when we first got married, which had brought back many happy memories of our younger days.

On the other hand it made me very sad, to watch Tony struggle with the cards. He was having such a difficult time holding, and separating them. Shuffling them was out of the question, period. I didn't make a big deal of it; I just helped him straighten his cards out, and continued to play. He was sharp as a tack though as far as the playing part. Making sets, and going out on me, like in the old days, and that pleased me. He complained about not being able to hold the cards properly, I told him he would, in time when his hand got stronger. We played for a while, until he got tired of sitting, and decided to finish the game the following night.

Tony went to bed, did his exercises and then watched television for a while.

I went back downstairs to do the few things I wasn't able to get done through out the day.

After finishing a few things, I called Ardine to check on her. She'd been on my mind all day. When we were through talking, I found out she was alone. I thought her daughter was still there, but she had gone back to Colorado; to get her car, and wrap-up a few loose ends. I was glad I called her; she was down and very lonely. We talked until the wee hours.

We were both exhausted; finally deciding we should go to bed to get some much needed rest.

When Tony got up the next day; after he bathed, dressed, and brushed his teeth by himself, I helped him down the stairs. That being a big achievement for him! To have done those things himself, was remarkable. Then I got Tony set-up, for breakfast. He was eating well, when the OT came, just as he started to eat. I noticed Tony got nervous when people were there watching him eat. I didn't blame him; I wouldn't want people gawking at me eating either. I explained, "This is a bad time; could you come at eleven fifteen that would be perfect? Tony would be finished with breakfast by then."

"I could watch him eat." Dumb founded by that statement, that made absolutely no sense to me!

"What is he going to benefit or gain from you watching him eat?" When she couldn't answer; I suggested we cancel the therapy for that day, frustrated by her comment!

"Maybe you should get someone in the afternoon, I don't work after twelve."

"I really don't want to change therapists, but that time just isn't working out. It's too hard on Tony." I was getting angry, and immediately decided that I was going to take control of our lives, not what was good for all the medical staff. We had enough going on without my worrying about their schedules, and the therapist left. They were supposed to make things better, not worse.

Later, Jackie (the therapist taking Lita's place) came, Tony was weak that day. Why? Not steady on his feet, Why? *Those questions without answers drove me absolutely crazy.*

Tony was also complaining about his arm that he had the stroke in.

"It's tingly and sore." *What did that mean?* I asked the therapist, but she didn't know either? I did say to her, "I remembered that when his aunt had a stroke. She complained that she had pain in her arm too. When I asked the nurse at the nursing home, she had explained that the nerves fire off to the brain, kind of like electric wires connecting, and disconnecting. I attributed the pain Tony's experiencing to be somewhat the same."

To top everything off, it was a crummy, cold, rainy, damp, gloomy, and depressing day to add to the unpleasantness, neither one of us needed.

Tony wanted to go to bed early that evening. However, did all his exercises really well that night. The stroke he had was weighing heavy on his mind and he was worried about having another one. If he got any kind of unusual sensation, he got scared, and thought he may be having another stroke. I felt so helpless when it came to that. I didn't exactly know how to comfort Tony, except to say, "I'll watch you closely, and if I become suspicious of anything wrong. I'll call the doctor immediately. DO NOT worry because worrying isn't good for you, it could only cause you to have more problems." It was hard for him though, when he was having pain in that same arm. *Like a constant nagging, reminder—*

I actually went to bed early that night too; beat, and emotionally exhausted. Plus the weather hadn't helped—.

The next morning the PCT was there early, and got Tony out of bed. Actually, she had called saying, "I was there at nine, and no one answered the door."

"Hmm, I didn't hear you at all?" hard to believe but, a possibility. I had the alarm set for nine that morning because I was expecting her between nine, and nine-thirty. However, she hadn't been getting there until nine-fifty, so I never expected her there at nine sharp. I was sure I would have heard the doorbell ring, especially since I was already awake from the alarm buzzing. Nevertheless, she came right back to give Tony his shower, and brought him down.

Tony again, ate really well that morning, which always pleased me tremendously. This time the nurse came just as Tony was eating, which irritated the hell out of me. But I had been concerned about the swelling in his feet; the pain he'd been having in his arm, and hand. We told her about his fear of having another stroke, and asked her how we would know. She really didn't tell me anything I didn't already know. Assuring me, "You'll know by the symptoms he's having." *Really!*

"What would happen if we give him an extra diuretic, for the fluid?"

"If we do that, he'll need to take another potassium pill." My concern was congestive heart failure, and the swelling in his feet, which made it harder to walk and exercise. She suggested we call the doctor, to ask her what she thought. She called, the doctor's office but she wasn't there; she was at a convention the nurse told her. However, she would be calling in, and she would ask her what she wanted us to do.

The home health nurse then reiterated what the doctor's nurse told her, saying. "They'll either call you or me. If they call me I'll call and let you know what the doctor decided."

Tony also seemed to be exceptionally weak that day. I was Not able to come up with an explanation; or excuse for the weakness, other than the swelling. That really had me frightened, because I didn't know what was going on! The questions in my mind started again. *Was Tony, going to have another stroke? Was that the start of one? Was he just having a bad day?* Of course, I didn't have answers to those questions. Just a lot of unanswered questions to taunt me that drove me crazy, and a nervous wreck, never letting Tony know I was a basket case. Always trying to keep a smile; on my face, and a positive attitude. My being upset wasn't something he needed to deal with. That certainly would have thrown him over the edge, so I tried to keep my fears to myself, as much as possible.

I also had a lot of errands I needed to get done. I'd been putting them off for a few days; waiting to see if any of our children would come by. If so, I would have asked them if they could do them. But, no one came; so I never mentioned anything to them about it.

Finally, on Friday I called Joey at work, and asked if he could come over after work, so I could get them done, and maybe get out a couple of hours.

"I could do that; I'll be over right after work." I was happy about that; I'd been in the house all week and really needed to get away from the intense anxiety.

When Anthony was home, we had at least gotten out having dinner by his house, but he was out of town, and I hadn't been out of the house at all. I was ready to flip out. The pressure was at a boiling point. *(Whatever was going on with Tony had me down!)*

The nurse called from the doctor's office saying, the doctor said, "Increase the diuretic, and increase the potassium pill to an extra one every other day." I was going to pick-up prescriptions when Joey came, so getting another wasn't a problem.

About five fifteen I called Ardine. I told her, "I'm going to get out for a couple of hours, would you like to go for coffee? I also have a few errands to run." She had been taking a nap, which I think was part depression. She jumped at the offer, I was glad. It would be good for both of us. I told her, "I'll be there within thirty minutes. I have to go to the bank and pick-up some prescriptions."

Joey called me a few minutes later to tell me he was in a conference, and would be a little late. "Okay thanks for calling, I would have wondered where you were."

I called Ardine back right away, so she didn't think I'd forgotten her. I apologized to her for the delay.

"Don't be silly, it's no problem."

"I'll be there as soon as Joey gets here."

It was getting later and later, I was worried that the bank would close before Joey got there. Tony finally said," Why don't you go to the bank, and come right back." It got later; I finally agreed to go before they closed.

"I'll be right back, I have my cell if you need me, and I'll only be a minute away." It was close to seven and the bank would be closing, so I left.

I called Ardine back again from my cell and told her Joey still hadn't come yet.

"It's okay, don't worry."

"I'll be there as soon as I can, it shouldn't be much longer."

When I got to the bank, a couple minutes from the house, having just gotten off the phone with Ardine, Joey called to let me know he was on his way.

"Continue doing what you planned, I'll be with dad in a minute. I already called dad to let him know I was on my way."

"Are you sure? I continued talking to him until he got to the house. "I have dinner for you and dad all ready; make sure your father eats."

"I'll take care of it, don't worry. What time will you be home?"

"Would ten be okay, since it's already after seven?"

"Not a problem, but no later because I want to go when you get back;" I thanked him and explained, "I need the time away for a while."

"It's not a problem, I'm glad I can help, don't worry, and enjoy yourself."

I went straight to Ardine's house to pick her up. She was ready, waiting, and came right out. I had already gone to the bank, so I only had to pick-up the prescriptions. That only took a few minutes, and then I asked her if she'd like to shop for a while, and then get something to eat. She was easy, saying, "Whatever you want to do." I was so glad to be out away from all the problems if only for just a little while. It felt good, and I knew she needed to get out too. She explained how much she missed Mikey, and how lonely it was. I could only imagine how awful it was for her. I told her we weren't going to talk about anything sad, just have a few hours of fun and shopping. *(I'm sorry, now that I didn't let her talk about how she was feeling. I didn't know the importance of it then.)* She agreed to shop, and then go get something to eat. It was a great release for both of us. I felt like a kid with a curfew. In fact, we told the waiter we were in a hurry; we had a curfew and had to be home by ten. He looked at us like we were nuts. We rushed eating, so we would be home on time. We make it, I dropped her off and told her it was fun; we had to do it again soon.

"If you get out again call me, I'd like to go." I waited for her to get in the house and left.

I made it back by ten. When I got in the house, I told Joey I felt like I was in the Indy Five Hundred race. "I picked Ardine up, and we went out to eat. She needed to get out."

"I'm glad you both enjoyed yourselves. You didn't need to be home at exactly ten, I'm sorry you rushed. I wasn't thinking when I came."

"You should have called me, and told me that."

"I was just glad to get out, and ten was good enough. I just wished you had called so I didn't rush to get back exactly by ten. Ten minutes would have made it more relaxing but, no big deal."

"I changed my mind; I'm not going to go out after all." He started to tell me about his conference he had with the owner of the company. He was talking to him about a raise, since he's one of the main employee's at the company, and that he felt stifled, had no security, and on, and on. Anyway, we talked from ten until one in the morning. By that time we were both falling asleep. We finally decided to call it a night, and get some sleep as we wrapped up the conversation.

"I'll call you when we get-up. Maybe we could go out for breakfast if you want."

"That sounds good, call me."

"The PT is coming tomorrow, but I don't know what time yet. I'll have to call you after she calls me to let you know what time." I thanked him again. "No problem" we hugged and kissed, said "Good night," and he left.

I don't think he was out the door, or even off the driveway, before I was in bed. I was really tired by then, and I had to be up early.

When I got up the next morning, I jumped into the shower right away so I could get Tony sponge bathed, and dressed. So when the PT called, and I knew when she was coming, we could go for breakfast before she came, if we were ready and had time. Then the therapist called saying, "I'll be there about one or two." I called Joey right away, "We'll be ready in about a half-hour."

"That will be good. I still have to get ready too."

When Joey came; we decided to go to the restaurant around the corner from our house that Tony would go to daily for coffee, and read the paper before he got sick. The people there always asked about him. When we got there, they were happy to see Tony. Each came to say hello, and asked him how he was doing. Which happened to be better, Tony was getting stronger with every day that passed. I filled them in about him having a stroke, and about the fall that set him back, and that Tony's attitude was great. He's a fighter!

Tony didn't eat much, only half of the egg sandwich he ordered. That upset me immensely, made me even more nervous. "I feel nauseated." I didn't know what was making him feel that way, I thought, *here we go again. Now what?* We visited awhile, and then went home. Joey wanted to leave right away, but first inquired if he could do anything, or if we needed anything before he left.

Tony seemed to be very strong that day even though feeling nauseated.

When Jackie arrived Tony was still nauseated, and didn't want to exercise at all. He refused to do anything. We both explained that if he didn't exercise he'd get weak again. He said, "I'm just too sick to my stomach." I gave him a pill for nausea.

The therapist said, "I don't mind waiting to see if the pill helps. Maybe we could get some exercise in if you feel better." She seemed concerned about how he was feeling, because he kept talking about a stroke and the pain in his arm. She suggested that maybe we should call the doctor. I explained, "I'm really not concerned because the pain has been going on for a couple of days; I think the pain is symptoms from the stroke, Tony's aunt had the same symptoms when she had her stroke. I really think it's side effects of the stroke, not another stroke coming on." We sat for a while, and talked. She told us some about herself and her family, just making small talk. She told Tony she really didn't want to end her therapy that way. That was her last visit with us; Lita would be back from Maui next week.

After a while, I asked Tony how he was feeling. "I'm feeling better" it had been about a half-hour. The therapist and I were thrilled the pill had worked. I asked him if he could do some exercises. "Sure." What a trooper he was. Now the therapist and I were ecstatic, he must have really felt terrible, for totally refusing to exercise at all. Usually, he at least tried, but was willing to do them then, and that's what was important. He did the exercises; did them very well, and felt a sense of accomplishment. Then went over his list of things he had successfully achieved, in a short period of only one, and half weeks. Reminding Tony the list was what he had compiled himself.

Anthony called later that day from work. They were back from Washington. He asked what we were doing. I explained that his dad was feeling punk. However, he expressed that he wanted to go out for fish dinner.

"I'll call you when I'm done at work. That sounds okay to me, I'll check with Paul to see if he wants to go."

I then asked Tony if he wanted to eat lunch. Much to my surprise he said, "I do want something." That was, music to my ears, whipping him up a light snack, just enough to hold him, until we went out for dinner that evening.

The rest of that day we relaxed, Tony took a short nap, and then we watched a movie.

Anthony called after work, about four-thirty. I explained, "I just gave dad a little something because, I didn't know when you'd be getting off work. I didn't want him to wait that long to eat."

"Is seven-thirty okay with you?"

"That sounds fine with me."

"I'll be there around six forty-five."

"Great, see you then."

I had fallen asleep while we were watching the movie. When the phone rang, it woke me up, it was Anthony calling.

"We'll be there in a few minutes." I jumped up, and rushed to get ready.

They were there within minutes just like they said. They helped Tony to the car, and we left.

We got to the restaurant, and inside without a problem. Tony didn't eat much though; he only had a bowl of soup. He just couldn't eat anymore. We ordered ice cream for him but he ate very little of that. Anthony had ordered a pecan waffle. When it came Tony said, "The smell of that waffle is making me sick," so, Anthony and I switched places, but Tony still couldn't eat. I guess I should have been satisfied that he ate at all, but I wasn't. We finished our dinners, and left.

We stopped for gas, and cigarettes, to save me from making another trip. When we got home Anthony helped his dad upstairs for me. Tony didn't want to do his exercises so we gave him a break. He just wanted to go to sleep, and rest. Then Anthony and Paul left saying, "We'll see you tomorrow for dinner."

As usual, I stayed up later doing a few things, and then went to bed.

The next day was Sunday, our only day to sleep in. We stayed in bed quite late the next morning. We didn't get up until twelve to be exact. We were both just so tired from all the anxiety, and the busy week we'd had, we had crashed.

We finally rose from the dead and started the ritual of getting ready. Michael had called, and wanted to go out to breakfast with us, but Tony didn't want to go. He didn't seem to enjoy eating breakfast out anymore, and when we did, he didn't eat that much. It seemed he ate breakfast better at home. We called Michael back and told him dad reneged on the invite, and thanked him for offering. I went on to explain to Michael that his dad seemed to eat better at home lately. I didn't understand why but, he did not need to feel bad.

After we got dressed, Tony ate breakfast, not all that great, but he did eat. Then we just lazed around until it was time to go by Anthony for dinner.

Joey called to let us know he was coming around five thirty to help his dad to the car. We'd been going places; ourselves up until the time that Tony had the fall; that petrified me to take him out alone. I certainly didn't want to take a chance of him falling again. Not when he was doing so well, that would have been devastating for him, and me to have a set-back like that, again. That would surely throw him into depression, since it had been one thing after the other happening. We went through all sorts of extra precautions, and didn't take any chances of anything happening.

We continued watching a movie until it was time for me to finish getting ready. Joey came in, just as I went upstairs to comb my hair and finish freshening up. I hurried, and we left.

We had a real nice time by Anthony; the dinner was good, as usual. We had watched a movie together, with our whole family, which was really nice for Tony and me.

We also discussed a surprise party for Anthony I hadn't realized that his fortieth birthday was the following week, until just the other day. I asked Paul if he was going to do anything for him.

"Anthony doesn't want a party."

Paul stated that, Anthony had said, "Whatever you'd spend on a party just buy me something for that amount. We also don't know how my fathers going to feel."

"With all he does for everyone, we've got to have a party for him of some sort." I suggested just having family, cousins, aunts, grandmother, us. At least it was something; just serve, beef sandwiches, and potato salad, at your house. That way we are keeping his wishes. "Kind Of" if his dad should get sick at least you wouldn't have a big deposit at a restaurant to lose, should you have to cancel it; and going to your house isn't that big a deal if dad isn't feeling all that great." We all agreed, so Paul was going to take care of calling everyone, as it was too late to send invitations.

That was our plan for Anthony's fortieth Birthday; my job was to call Anthony on Sunday morning; to get him over to our house, so Paul could get everything ready at their house. And I was going to tell Anthony he had to come over so I could go by Ardine because, she needed me right away.

Mario came home with us that night after the movie was over. I had a few things that needed; to get done before winter set in; cover the patio furniture and Mario was going to help me. He decided to spend the night so we could get them done the next day, agreeing that was a great idea.

We stayed up late, I writing this book; while Mario read what I had already written. We were extremely tired by three in the morning, and decided to call it a night. The PCT would be there at nine; needing to be up to let her in, and start my day, so, we went directly to bed.

The next morning I got up at eight-thirty to take my shower before the PCT got there. When I got up I opened the door so if I wasn't done she could come right in. Which worked out good, because, I wasn't quite done when she arrived.

She got Tony up, and showered, while I finished getting myself ready; then went downstairs to start breakfast for him. He wanted oatmeal, toast, and coffee. Plus I gave him prunes every morning to keep his bowels moving smoothly, and pineapple with Jell-O. I figure if I couldn't get Tony to eat one thing, I have a multiple of other flavors to tempt him with. He ate pretty well; but he was having a lot of hand tremors that morning, which made him quite frustrated while trying to eat. Feeling so bad for him; wishing there was something I could do to make the tremors stop. We were told Tony's hand would come back, after a time. I couldn't wait for that to happen for Tony's sake. 'A time' seemed too long to wait, and I'm positive Tony felt the same.

After breakfast Tony went to lie down. "I didn't sleep too good last night. My legs hurt, and woke me up with muscle cramps." That seemed to be happening quite often. They told us it was because of all the exercise he was doing. On the other hand you could actually see the muscles' building in his legs. Right before my very eyes in the last two weeks, I had actually seen the muscles getting larger in his calves and thighs. It was amazing to witness! WOW!

While Tony was resting, the home health nurse came to check him. "He's supposed to get a blood test today."

"I don't have an order for one."

"The nurse from the doctor's office told me on Friday when she called back with the orders to increase the diuretic, and potassium."

"We should call the doctor, if that's the case, I could take it while I'm still here."

She called the doctor's office to ask about the blood test; telling the nurse, "I'll be here for at least another thirty minutes. If the doctor wants a blood test today, call me back, and I'll take it." She continued with checking Tony, looking at his feet, and hand. She commented that the swelling had gone down quite a bit with the extra diuretic, it must have worked. Tony's blood pressure was also good, and had no fever. He was feeling good, but tired because of his restless night.

The doctor's office called back within a few minutes, she did want a blood test. I was glad to hear that. I felt better when they kept a close watch on Tony, hoping that would keep anything else from going wrong with him.

"We should find out; the results tomorrow, if there's any problems. Hopefully, everything would be okay; since Tony really wasn't sick per se'. I asked her if she knew anything about why no one had called me about an appointment for another OT to come out.

"I don't know but, I'll look into it. They usually try to get that taken care of right away. They don't like to let appointments get passed up." I let her know I was concerned because Tony had already missed two therapy appointments. The nurse left saying, "If I hear anything about Tony's blood today, I'll call you; I'll see you again, on Friday."

I then woke Mario up so we could get the few things done that, needed to be done. Mario finally came strolling down the stairs still groggy.

By then, I was busy getting his dad lunch. Again, Tony didn't eat a whole lot, but he did eat something, with no complaints of nausea. Thank God! Tony and I had also walked into the kitchen without the walker that morning. Of course, I asked Tony if he felt strong enough to try it before hand. He definitely was getting stronger, and more confident.

"Yes," so we went for it. I was scared to death in one way, and confident in another; mixed feelings, but I could tell it certainly lifted Tony's spirits that he had achieved that feat. I made a big deal about it too. It was a great stride for him to have made. My husband was truly unbelievable, and a fantastic fighter. He finally saw light at the end of his tunnel. Thank God! Tony surely deserved to make those strides, and to see a little light; it was way over due.

After Tony had lunch, and was resting, Mario and I got the things outside done. We then all decided to watch a movie. I suggested that after the movie maybe we could go to an inside mall, so Tony could walk pushing the wheelchair to build his endurance in walking. Tony said, "I'd like that." Then suggested we could get something to eat afterward.

They both said, "That sounds great." I was glad they agreed, because that wasn't something I could do myself, and I didn't always have someone there to go with me to help with walking him. I personally thought it was very good therapy to help build Tony's endurance in walking. Because if he was walking through a mall looking in windows talking, he wouldn't really pay that much attention to the distance he was walking, how long or, how far. So, I was excited to try that new adventure.

It was brutally cold out that night, and we were expecting snow. Not, one of my favorite days to be out. Hating the cold or even going out in it for that matter, but the cause was worth it.

Tony, Mario, and I watched a comedy movie, and all laughed a lot. That was something we needed and hadn't done in our house for a long, long, time. It felt good just to laugh again, and it was great Mario was there to share it. We got several phone calls during the movie so we had to stop it several times. When it was over, we left for the mall. It was colder than hell, and snowing just as the weatherman had predicted. They're usually never right, but that day of all days they were 'right on.'

When we arrived at the mall the wind was blowing like crazy, and so hard. I thought we were going to get blown over. It also was the first really cold day we'd gotten, so it seemed colder than it really was. The wind was damp and biting; we couldn't get into the mall fast enough. When we finally did; Tony was freezing and couldn't get warm. He kept his coat on and his scarf up around his ears, he was that chilled. "Do you want to get out of the wheelchair, and push it?"

"No, I'm too cold!" So, we walked around for a while looking in the windows aimlessly, waiting for him to warm up. I explained, "The purpose of going to go to the mall was for you to walk around, to build up your strength."

"I'm ready to push the wheelchair now." Words can't even express what a wonderful feeling that was to hear, him ask, to take the challenge. Mario and I were both excited for him. We took his coat off so it didn't weigh him down. Then locked the wheelchair wheels; so we could get him positioned behind it, and then loosened them, so he could push it. "Don't get nervous; when you're tired you can sit-down, take your time."

Tony Succeeds

Tony started pushing the wheelchair; Mario and I both hung onto him for dear life, by the gait belt. Should he lose his balance, we could prevent him from falling. However, Tony seemed solid on his feet, strong, and steady. I slowed down the wheelchair by locking the wheels to some extent, so if he should lose his balance it wouldn't go flying away. We talked as we walked, looking in windows when Tony finally said, "I'm tired." We got him in front of the wheelchair and sat him down, told him to look behind him to see how far he had walked. He even was amazed at the distance he'd walked. So, were we! He had walked at least two-hundred feet; that was a long way for the first time. We were excited for him and he was excited for himself. We told Tony he was on his way to SUCCESS! His goal was to walk—and he had walked—.

"Next time we'll walk a little farther; little by little you'll get stronger, and stronger."

It was a wonderful exuberant feeling seeing him achieve the beginning of his goal; feeling it was an excellent, exciting start.

Mario stopped to get his ear pierced, and bought a set of CZ earrings. He was happy about his purchase. I was happy for him too. It was good to see him happy. It was a fun exciting evening for all of us.

We then discussed where to eat, since the mall only had fast food. We decided to go to the Outback Steak House. It was on the way home, and we all loved it there. It was a great place to finish off a fantastic evening.

After dinner we came right back home. Tony wanted to go to bed right away, he was tired. It had been a full day for him. We shared a dinner; he didn't eat much, but neither did I. By the time we ate the appetizer and the salad we were both full, taking the balance of the dinner home. Mario ordered a full dinner, but he's a growing boy. He couldn't finish his dinner either though; we all ending up with doggie bags.

Tony went right up to bed, and even did his leg exercises, reluctantly, but he did do them like a trooper, and then went to sleep.

Mario and I stayed up to watch a movie, but I fell asleep shortly after it started, being beat. Mario woke me after it was over. I heard him moaning to himself about the pain he was having all day from hemorrhoids. He had been saying he had a weird pain, and tried to explain it to his dad, and me. I told him, that he needed to go to the doctor the next day to have it checked. When I heard him mumbling, "Are you still in pain?"

"Yes"

"Worse or the same?"

"I feel it going down my legs it's a numbing feeling, do you think I should go to the emergency room?"

"If I was that worried, I'd already be at the emergency room, why wait? Go have it checked out." He decided to call the emergency room, they said, "It could be an infection, do you have a fever."

"I don't think so," but after he hung up. He took his temperature; and he did have a low fever.

"Get to the emergency room, don't fool around. Find out what's wrong, and get medicine, why wait until morning if you're in pain." That's what he did.

At three in the morning I called the hospital, as I hadn't heard from Mario. He informed me that they didn't know what was wrong with him yet. They had given him a shot for the pain, and they were waiting for a urine specimen.

"They said, something about my spinal cord, and that scares me." As it did me and of course made me very upset and a nervous wreck. "They said, something about the prostate, and slight hernia too."

"Call me as soon as you find out what's wrong," asking him about driving with the pain shot.

"I'll call you back as soon as I know anything more, you should go to sleep."

He called me back at around four a.m., saying, "I really don't know what's wrong they gave me a prescription for pain medicine, and told me to call my infectious disease doctor at eight-thirty in the morning to make an appointment to see him today."

When he got back, he let me know he was back, and we both went to sleep.

The next morning I had the alarm set for nine. When I got up I told Mario, "It's nine you should call the doctor right away." He was really knocked out from all the pain medication he had just gotten a few hours earlier, but he did get-up, and called the doctor. He had to leave a message with the answering service, for the doctor to call him back.

Anthony called around nine-thirty a.m... He had told me the night before; he would come and get his dad cleaned up and dressed to give me a break. "It's not necessary," but he insisted. I told him, "Were not up yet."

"I'll come a little later."

"That will be good I'm exhausted, from being up half the night with Mario. He went to the hospital; we'll talk about it when you get here, and hung up."

When Anthony came about ten-thirty, we were all still in bed. He came right up, and started taking care of his dad. "I'm going to stay in bed a few more minutes." I could hear him helping his dad it was so cute the way they were talking. Anthony was telling his dad to try, and help himself. I listened, and laughed to myself; realizing I wasn't able to sleep anymore, wide-awake, so I got out of bed.

I freshened up, and continued on with my day. We had two therapists coming that day. The new OT and Lita was back from her vacation. She would be doing Tony's physical therapy, and telling us all about her trip to Maui, so we had a busy day.

By the time I came down Anthony had gotten his dad breakfast and Tony was already eating.

I went back-up to ask Mario about the doctor, he hadn't called back yet; suggesting he call-back again. Mario was still drugged up from the pills, and shot from the night before. He was very angry he had left the hospital without actually knowing what was wrong. I was very happy he had gotten home safely, with all the pain medication; he could have had a bad car accident. I couldn't believe the hospital had let him drive like that.

He finally got up, and called the doctor back. He got the answering service again. He left another message for the doctor. Mario also had an appointment with the psychologist at two that afternoon. "Are you going?"

"No, I'm too whacked out on medicine and couldn't drive if I wanted to." Suggesting he should call and cancel that appointment so, the doctor isn't waiting for you, and he did.

The phone finally rang, and it was the doctor. I only heard Mario say, "I'm not blaming you, I'm just letting you know." Then the phone rang again, I had no idea who it was, and when Mario hung up. I asked, "What's going on? I heard you on the phone with the doctor."

"I have an appointment with his associate at two."

"Go ahead, and sleep I'll wake you up later."

When I went back downstairs Tony was done with his breakfast. I helped him to his recliner so he could relax a few minutes. The OT would be there soon.

I cleaned up the kitchen, and by the time I was done the new therapist was there. She introduced herself and explained what she was going to be doing, and why. She also explained about strokes; and that the first sixty days was the most important time for therapy. I told her: about the tremors that Tony was having along with a difficult time eating. How he often got frustrated, and wouldn't eat. She explained that sometime heavier silverware did the trick, or that putting a weight on that hand helped. "There are many items to help with that." We were both very happy to hear that something could be done. Being a firm believer, that out of bad comes good. Sometimes we can't see the good or what possibly could come from it, but it does eventually. When the other therapist couldn't come later; feeling maybe I'd made a mistake, since Tony knew her, and felt comfortable with her, but, now knew it was for the better. The new therapist meant business, had a lot of experience, and would be much better for Tony. She was also a mature woman, who seemed to have a lot of knowledge about stroke victims; she knew her stuff. We were both more than very pleased with her. She also cared about scheduling us, and our feelings about having time in between for him to rest, that alone was a big help. She'd try to schedule Tony; so we could get used to her coming at that time every time, which also would make life less stressful, instead of pressure of who's coming when, and on what day at what time. With so many people coming, it made it hard to keep track, especially when they gave you an hour lead way so, we couldn't schedule other people if need be. That schedule would work much better all the way around, and we were thrilled. Maybe we could get some normalcy in our lives. Hallelujah!

The OT no sooner left, and Lita came. I knew I booked them back-to-back but I was anxious to get Tony going, with the OT again. He had already missed a few sessions. While Lita was working with Tony, I again tried to get Mario up for his appointment. He told me, "I'm not going. There must not be anything wrong with me or they wouldn't have let me leave the hospital, and the pain is getting better." I had no time to argue with him, so I let him sleep.

I went back to Lita, and Tony; we talked about her Maui trip, as Tony and I reminisced about our Paradise! She really had a great time, and just loved Maui as much as we did, thinking every one does that goes there. They finished his exercises; set-up the schedule for the rest of the week, then left.

I could hardly believe that next week was already Thanksgiving. A year almost had passed since we started the horrible nightmare experience. It was three months since Tony had been in remission with NO CHEMO, a "Miracle" in itself, and he was finally getting stronger, each and every day. That week had really been the best week in an extremely long time. A positive attitude and perseverance had paid off. A week we needed, and one he had really earned, to say the least.

Right after Lita left the phone rang. It was the doctor Mario was supposed to see at the hospital at two-thirty. He asked for Mario, and I went up to give him the phone. Mario shared his being upset over the whole situation. The doctor asked him to come in to see him; he'd wait for him. I told Mario we'd get him there somehow.

Tony wanted shrimp for lunch anyway, so we'd be out in the car. I told Mario it wouldn't be any big deal to bring him to the hospital. Mario told the doctor he'd be there. Anthony called just then, and I told him what was going on. I asked him to either take Mario to the hospital or come there and take his dad, and I would take Mario. He opted to take his dad.

"Come over right away I have to get Mario to the hospital."

"I'll be right there."

When he got there he took his dad, and I left with Mario right away. When we got to the hospital, the nurse paged the doctor, and he came right down to see Mario. He asked a lot of questions, and said, "I think its neuropathy." "Mario and I looked at each other asking, what's that?"

"Its side affects from the medication your taking."

"How do I get rid of it?"

"We first have to find out what medicine is causing it, and you'll need to go off all your medicine to see which one was causing it. I'd like a MRI taken just to make sure, nothing else is going on."

We explained, the circumstances about his dad being sick, and with Mario on the pain pills; wouldn't be able to drive. We need to get as much done as fast as we can.

"I'm not free to drive Mario around."

"I'll go check to see when the MRI can be done." He came back quickly, saying,

"I have an appointment for six forty five, tonight is that okay?"

"That's super!"

"I'm shocked, to get an appointment, right away." So were we!

"Usually you have to wait two to three weeks." Everything, was working in our favor.

"Call me tomorrow for the results."

We had about an hour to kill before going for the MRI that was just down the street. I hadn't eaten a thing all day, and was starving. "We'll stop, and get something light to eat because, Anthony is making us dinner." We ate, and still had plenty of time to get to the medical center. We didn't have to wait at the medical center either; we practically went right in. After Mario filled out all the papers, the girl at the counter took us right back to the MRI department. We did have to wait back there for about forty-five minutes though. Then the technician came to get Mario. Stating, "It will take about thirty minutes." I watched television while I waited for him. He was back before I knew it, and we were finally on our way to Anthony's house late for dinner.

Once there, we pretty much ate dinner, and came right back home. It was late, and Tony wanted to go to bed he was tired.

Mario and I stayed up, to watch a movie. I fell asleep pretty quickly on the couch. I woke up about one in the morning, and went to bed, Mario stayed up a tad longer.

The next morning I got up really early. I somehow had the alarm set for eight. I went downstairs to have a cigarette, and set-up Tony's breakfast. When I looked at the clock it was only eight am not nine as, I thought. I finished what I was doing and went upstairs to take a shower. Then I threw a load of laundry in, and by that time the PCT was at the door.

She got Tony showered, and dressed. Then she brought him down; I asked her how he did. She said, "Pretty good, he seemed to be much stronger." That verified what I thought too. He really was doing much better. Thank God!

Tony ate really well that morning, which thrilled me to no end. I thought, but afraid to think, he's finally on the road to getting back to himself. Thank God! I knew there was a higher power, because we had gone through some very rough times. Without God's help we couldn't have done it. That's when God must have carried us. I just love that prayer "Footsteps". Because I believe it's true. At least I found it to be true in my life many times at very difficult times.

Tony had not been nauseated the last few days. I believe it was due to not taking all the pills at one time. I had been separating the vitamins from the rest of the pills, and that seemed to have worked.

After breakfast Tony did the usual, and went to rest before Lita came.

Mario had slept on the floor in the living room that night. I asked him to go upstairs, and lay in bed, but he preferred to stay on the floor.

Lita came at one, and I had just woken Tony telling him Lita would be there shortly. He did very well, she had commented, "Remarkably Well!" He was making great strides. We were both very happy, I loved that positive reinforcement. She had given Tony some difficult exercises to strengthen his balance and was pleasantly surprised he had no trouble doing them. Then had Tony stand on one foot, and take his hands off the walker. That exercise he had trouble with, he told her that one was hard.

"I need to keep challenging you, for you to get strong. If we keep doing the same exercises you won't get stronger."

"Will I be doing that one again,"

"Yes, tomorrow as a matter of fact."

"Oh! No, tomorrow?"

"Yes."

"You don't come on Saturday do you?"

"Laughing, I could, "I'm not doing anything." They both laughed. It was good to see him laughing, and joking. She left then saying; "I'll see you on Monday again."

We didn't do much that Sunday. I was really tired from the trauma with Mario the past couple of days, and being up half the night. With the emergency room episode and the stress of not being able to go with him, I felt awful about that, and they let him drive having all those drugs, aboard! Thank God nothing happened. Never feeling like I caught up with sleep, so when I laid down to watch the movie with Tony and Mario, I fell asleep.

I woke up a little later, when I heard Tony and Mario talking about what to eat for dinner. Mario was going to the store for us to get a few groceries. I told him, "You get the groceries, and I'll get up and cook. By the time you get back I'll have dinner ready.

It worked out perfect dinner was ready, just as Mario walked in. We put the groceries away real quick, and had dinner. Mario stayed awhile then said, "I have to get home because I have an appointment tomorrow with a sales representative." He left, and then Tony wanted to go up to bed. The stair lift was a blessing; being able to get Tony upstairs and in bed myself, relieving the boys from the nightly chore. That alone was a great feeling for us both. We stayed up, a bit longer then, turned in.

We both slept in that next morning and it felt good, we were exhausted. I guess from all the humdrum all the time never a dull moment. But we couldn't stay in bed too late; I had to get Tony up, and ready for his therapy.

By the time Tony was ready and fed he only had a little while to rest.

The OT came and gave Tony a real work-out. She was really good. She left; Tony had lunch, and then rested before Lita came.

Lita came and started right in with him. Doing some new exercises, explaining that what he was doing was more difficult then he'd been doing. He was getting much better, and stronger. She did one exercise that Tony had a hard time with. It was standing on one foot with his hands at his side. He couldn't do it, but kept trying. Finally, he did conquer it for a bit, but not for long. "That's a really hard exercise. It takes a lot of endurance, and balance; you really did well today and should to be proud of your accomplishments. You're really doing very well. Keep up the good work. I'll see you tomorrow."

"We're going to go to the mall again tonight to walk."

"Just be very careful." I assured her we would, as she left.

We both rested until Joey came after work. Mario was going to the mall too. I didn't,

Dare take Tony by myself—.When Joey came we decided to wait until the traffic died down before leaving. But by the time we were ready to leave; it had gotten brutally cold, windy, and had started to snow. That wind went right through us. As we all scurried to the car; not getting there fast enough to stay warm, frozen by the time we got into the cold car.

It didn't take us long to get to the mall. I pulled up to the front of the mall so Joey could go get the wheelchair. I had called the night before to see if they had them, they did and I reserved one. When Joey came back he brought his dad in the mall while I parked the car.

Tony walked pretty far that night too. He was gaining strength with every day that passed, and becoming confident with each exercise he conquered.

Joey wanted to look at jeans while we were there. We had planned on eating at the mall, but the wheelchair had to be back by eight-thirty. We decided that we'd look for Anthony's birthday gift then go somewhere else to eat. It's a good thing we did because we looked for Anthony's Birthday gift for over an hour. Then Joey decided to have it wrapped, which took more time. By the time we were finished, Tony had to use the bathroom. I told them I'd go get the car, so when they were done, Joey could just bring him to the car. Then take the wheelchair back, so we could get it back in time.

Then we went to eat at a restaurant close by. After eating, we came back home and brought Tony up to bed to relax. Joey took the garbage out for me, and then left.

It seemed that, as of lately, I had to stay up to unwind from the day, before I could sleep.

At about four that morning, Tony woke me, by calling my name. He had to use the urinal. I was so tired, I just handed it to him, 'against my better judgment.' A few seconds later I asked if he was okay, he said, "No, I feel pee going up my arm."

I said, "You've got to be kidding." I felt him and he wasn't kidding. I was livid; I jumped up out of bed grabbing a towel to soak up the urine, and said," You can't just lie there, and hope you're peeing in the urinal, you've got to be sure." I cleaned Tony up, and went to bed angry with him that he hadn't made sure he was using the urinal right, before peeing. And angry with myself, it really was my fault; because I was so tired, I had let him try to do it himself.

The next morning we had to be up early. As usual, the PCT would be there at nine! We had a full day ahead of us; we'd be on a roll all day. Right after breakfast the nurse would be there. Tony would get to rest awhile then the OT, he'd get to rest, and Lita would be there.

We were waiting for Lita to come when I realized she had made a mistake with the dates, because she wasn't there, she had meant to mark the following Friday at two. Which meant she wouldn't be there until three; so I had Tony eat lunch otherwise, it would have been too late for him to eat.

We had made plans to go out to dinner that night with Greg and Loraine. We were going for Mexican food, one of Tony's many favorite meals.

Lita came, just as Tony was finishing his lunch, so she waited a few minutes for him to finish. Then they started right in. His attitude was great; he was ready to work like hell again. He did a super great job of it too.

"Tony you did even better than yesterday," she was amazed at his progress. As she was leaving, she said to me, "He did exceptionally well today." He had mastered holding one leg up, not holding onto the walker, and that's a difficult exercise to master, he should be extremely proud of that feat!

After I finished the wash, I told Tony, "I'm going up to get ready to go out for dinner."

While upstairs Loraine called to verify our plans. "We'll be there at six thirty to pick you up."

"We'll be ready by then." After I was done with myself, I went back downstairs to freshen up Tony.

My sister called in the interim, and I talked to her awhile. Getting her up to date about what had transpired. By the time I hung up, Greg and Loraine were at the door, right on time. Tony had done great walking, with only our help to the car, and into the restaurant. Tony was most definitely stronger than he was the last time we'd gone to dinner with them.

We had a lovely evening talking, laughing, and eating. Just having; a great time, like we did before Tony got sick. It was such an exuberant evening; along with celebrating Loraine's birthday that evening. It turned out great; the food exceptional, margaritas super delicious, and Loraine had a wonderful time also.

When we came home, Greg and Loraine helped me get Tony in the house, and then they left. Tony went right up to bed. I went to bed shortly thereafter, I was still exhausted.

We slept in later than usual, and then got up to have a day of just relaxing. I told Tony we needed a lazy day to just lie around, relax, and watch television, nap, and do absolutely nothing. That's exactly what we did. We got up to eat, then back to just lying around all day. It did us both a world of good.

A whole week had gone by, and the next day was Sunday, the day of Anthony's surprise party. We were going to have our hands full getting Anthony over to our house and trying to keep him busy for 'three hours. While Paul arranged for Anthony's surprise Birthday Party it would be fun, and I hoped Anthony would enjoy it, and be as surprised, as we had planned.

We went to bed early so we'd be ready for the challenge of keeping Anthony out, and away from the house those three hours.

Anthony's Surprise Party

Sunday morning when we got up, I gave Tony a shower, and got him dressed. Then got myself ready, to go out for breakfast with Anthony; we had it all planned the day before, how we were going to detain Anthony so, Paul could get everything done for the party. Our job was to keep Anthony busy for three hours. That feat was, almost impossibility, since he always wanted to be home, on his couch, relaxing, when not working. Tony knew we had to keep his son busy, so I told him to go through some of his tactics; he sometimes put us through, when we were ready to leave. Like he had to go to the bathroom—or we have to wait because he might have to go to the bathroom—or he wanted to see the end of a movie, to name a few—.

Ardine was also in on it. I had called her, to ask if she'd help. She said, "Anything I can do."

"You're supposed to have called me while I was waiting for Anthony to come, and I invited you to go for breakfast with us. I won't tell Anthony until we're on our way to your house, and he's in my car. Otherwise he'd want to take his own car, and say, "I'll meet you at the restaurant.""

Ardine was all for it, "I'll pick you up." She wasn't supposed to be ready, so we could waste more time. "I need to go to the drug store to pick up prescriptions."

"I have to pick one up also," Great, that will waste more time.

"Then we'll waste time ordering our food at the restaurant; pretending we can't decide what we want to eat." Anything to waste more time; every minute counts, trying to keep him busy and away from home for those three hours.

When Anthony got there, Tony started his tricks of stalling. First, he had to go to the bathroom. Then he wanted to finish seeing the end of the movie, it was almost over, "That will take too long." Anthony suggested he'd go with us in our car so; he could help with his dad when we got home from Tammy's house after dinner. That's where he thought we were going later that evening. I was thrilled he made that suggestion. As I was worried about how I was going to convince him to go in my car. That was a lucky break for us. As we were preparing to leave Tony blew it. "Don't say anything about us going to Florida."

"Why, what are you talking about?" I could have just died and wanted to strangle him at that moment; trying to change gears saying, "Why?" Tony continued with, "I have my reasons."

"What are you talking about?"

"I have my reasons."

"Why?"

"I don't want to talk about it in front of my sister." Oops!" Anthony pops up saying, "She already knows we're going to Florida."

I quickly said, "What are you talking about your sister, isn't going to be at Tammy's house." I could have just died at that moment. Tony had blown it—Big Time! Anthony instantly said, "Oh!" I thought, *he's getting suspicious!* "What's going on is that where Paul is?"

Immediately saying, "No, your father doesn't know what he's talking about. It's just going to be our family, that's all and I dropped it right away." We finally got Tony in the car.

While we were driving I softly said, "We have to pick Ardine up, she called while we were waiting for you, and I invited her to go eat with us. She's alone, and depressed so I thought you wouldn't mind." He likes Ardine, and thought it was great she was going with us. When we got to her house, she pretended she was on the phone, so we had to wait a few minutes for her. She got in the car apologizing all over the place for detaining us.

I had also told him, the truth that we had to pick up prescriptions, right away. Your father needs to take the pills as soon as possible; he really should have had the pills that morning. I tried to get someone to pick the prescriptions up the night before, but it was a project, Mario was sick, Joey hadn't gotten dressed all day, Tammy was at a party, Michael was busy working, and you had just gotten home from work; when I noticed he needed the prescriptions so, I just decided it would be all right to wait until the next morning if we got the pills right away.

At the drug store, Ardine, and I stalled some more inside. Then we were on our way to the restaurant when we got there, I pulled in front of the door, so Tony didn't have so far to walk. Anthony and Tony got out of the car, while Ardine and I went to park. We took our time going into the restaurant. So far success, everything was going as planned. I had also told Tony to stall, at the restaurant; by saying he had to go to the bathroom, again.

We finally were all in the restaurant and we ordered coffee, and took our time ordering, as planned. We finally decided, and ordered. When we were done eating, Tony told his son he had to go to the bathroom, 'again'? Ardine and I also went to the bathroom to have a cigarette. We still had about an hour to kill before we could bring Anthony home.

I got the brainstorm to go look at a condo that was being built in town. By then Anthony was getting real antsy, and fidgety. He wanted to get home and relax before going by Tammy for dinner; he was in a bad mood.

"It'll only take a minute; it's just a little out of the way from taking Ardine back home anyway." I was glad; I had him in my car. He was kidnapped as he would say, and had no choice but to go. We found the condos and I said, "I want to go in and get brochures so I could see there floor plans." But, first we had to locate the door to go in. When I finally found the door, Ardine and I got out of the car and went in. As we were leaving Anthony said, "Don't be gone to long, I want to go home." Ardine, and I were giggling as we went in, saying he's really getting fidgety. We looked at the floor plans asked the prices and a few other questions. When suddenly Anthony came in and said, "Your time's up; we have to go now."

"We'll be right out." Explaining; to the sales women, that we had to go, the warden had spoke. Ardine and I giggled again, as we walked back to the car. When I got in the car I told Anthony, "I'm going to kill you, for embarrassing me."

Ardine said, "You're acting like a baby. I've never seen you act like that."

"I don't like to get kidnapped." On the way to Ardine's house, I told Anthony. "You have two hours to relax before going by Tammy's house, cool your jets." We dropped Ardine off said, our "Good-byes" and were on our way to his house finally. Anthony told me to jump on the highway because it's faster. I had to quickly come up with another excuse to stall; we still had twenty minutes to kill. I quickly said, "Oh! I forgot your father's pills for later; I have to go back home and get them." Of course that was a fib, I had them in my purse but I had to tell him something. When we got back to our house, I ran into the house, and called Paul right away, and told them, "I hope you're ready. I can't stall him one more minute!" We're on our way.

"We're ready." Thank God! It had been one hell of a day. Anthony really gave us a hard time all day, which had me shaking. It was three hours of torture.

As I drove to his house I tried to drive slow to stall a few more minutes, talking small talk with him to keep his mind off the time. As we pulled down his block he said, "What are all those cars doing in my driveway."

"What are you talking about?"

"I'm going to kill you I told you I didn't want a party."

"Be grateful, and enjoy it."

"I didn't act like that when he had my Surprise Party." He did however, want to kill me, I could tell.

Of course when he got into the house and everyone shouted "Surprise," he got into the party mode, finally! I told everybody how brutal he had been to keep out three hours and how I had to keep stalling, and how it was driving him crazy. Whew! I was happy that part was over.

All in all it was a great party Paul had done a super job. The food was great, decorations were super, and everything was perfect. Anthony did end up enjoying the party, and appreciated it after all. Everyone there seemed to enjoy it too. I was glad it was over, and behind us. It had really been a chore keeping him out of the house he had me; a nervous wreck, knowing he was antsy.

The party ended about nine that evening and we were all getting ready to leave. When Mario told us he wasn't feeling very good, and was having a hard time urinating.

"Call the doctor that's very dangerous." He finally called and we waited for the doctor to call back. He called back pretty quickly, stating, "You should get to the hospital, and get catheterized, that could be very dangerous." Just like I had said, so Anthony said, "You should go with Mario to the hospital."

"Someone has to go with Mario." Either he should or I would but someone had to stay with dad.

"I'll stay with dad for you; while you go with Mario to the hospital."

Mario's Hospitalized

That's how we worked it out, we brought Mario's car to our house, and I went to the hospital with Mario in my car. It was about eleven by that time. I told Mario what torture it was for me to be going back to that hospital. I actually hated going there; I had been there so much with so many horrible memories. I really wasn't looking forward to that at all. Of course, he knew I would never have let him go alone. Once we got there they took him back to the emergency room right away. They weren't to busy that evening as a matter of fact I'd never seen the hospital that slow. It did take awhile for the doctor to come though, because of the shift change. We got there; just at the right time for that to be happening. They did finally give Mario something for pain, and decided to catheterize him. Mario was scared to death it would hurt horribly, so the male nurse told him he'd give him something to numb the area which Mario was grateful for. When they finally got him catheterized he expelled six hundred CCU's of urine. Quite a lot; since you usually only expels about one hundred and fifty CCU's every time you urinate. Mario was also running a low grade, fever and the doctor decided to keep him in the hospital. He wanted a private room, but there wasn't one to be had. He wasn't happy about that, but had no choice. They finally got him into a room about three thirty in the morning. I waited until he was comfortable and resting before I left. It was about four thirty by that time. I was exhausted, and had to be up at eight-thirty for the PCT, and the rest of the crew that was coming that day.

Tony had a full day on Monday's, so I knew I wouldn't get any rest until later that afternoon. When I got home, I woke up Anthony, he had fallen asleep on the couch; he got up half dazed, and left. I got right into bed. I couldn't get in bed fast enough. I don't even remember my head hitting the pillow before I was out.

The next day was actually Anthony's Birthday November 20, 2000. We got an early to start that morning, with the PCT there at nine-thirty, then the nurse, the OT, and then Lita would be there.

It was a brutally cold; horrible, rainy, windy, gloomy day, very depressing outside, and a good day to stay in bed all day, I would have loved to do just that.

I talked to Mario several times through out that day he said, "I had a spinal tap." I wasn't happy to hear that, and I was a nervous wreck. I had asked him to call me to let me know what was going on through the day. I had also told him to ask questions about what was going on, what for, and why, and to keep a handle on everything. I felt just awful that I couldn't be there to handle it for him; Mario was in so much pain. However I had no choice I had to be home with Tony. I tried to do what I could from home, over the phone by asking questions.

I also made the call about the oxygen should Tony need it while we were in Florida, and about renting a wheelchair. I had called several places, but the first one I called was the most helpful, and professional. I could have saved myself a lot of time had I just taken the one the resort referred. Between appointments Tony had, and balancing my checkbook, paying bills, and all the fun stuff I needed to do, that was a necessary. I thought I'd lose my mind.

Anthony was going to take his dad for a while, but I told him I wasn't going anywhere in that brutal weather. It was just to cold for me to go out in, I hate the cold weather. We ate breakfast, lunch, and dinner, and rested the rest of the evening, then went to bed early.

The next morning we slept in until we felt like getting up. Anthony was going to take his dad for the day so I could get out. He was also going to do my hair, as it was, icky and needed to be done for the holiday.

Anthony called saying, "I'll take dad so you could get out for awhile." Since the weather wasn't so bad that day, I looked forward to getting out for a while. Anthony came right after Tony and Lita were done with the therapy. I had a couple of errands to get accomplished, and wanted to go see Mario at the hospital. When Anthony came I left, to do my errands right away. I went to the bank, went to get cigarettes, and then I called Mario from my cell to see if he needed anything.

"I really don't want anything." Then changed his mind saying, "Maybe a hamburger for later would be good." I stopped and got the hamburger for him. When I got to the hospital, I stopped at the gift shop to get Mario and Lisa candy. Then I went up to Mario's room he was drugged but, had no pain. Thank God! Joey was there too when I got there he had gone right from work. We all talked for a while about what had been done to and for Mario. Joey then asked me what I was going to do for dinner. I told him, I was going by Anthony when I left, but first I had to go see Lisa.

Lisa was also in the hospital, on the third floor. Her lung had collapsed again; that was the second time in a month. They had done a procedure on her last time to see if that would help it from happening again, but it hadn't. I then went down to see Lisa, to bring her the candy. While I was in the room I saw a business card a surgeon had left, he had done several surgeries on Tony. I asked her why that doctors card was on her hospital stand. "I'm having surgery tomorrow the other procedure didn't work. He's the doctor that's going to do a different kind of surgery this time." I told her she had an excellent surgeon, and I wished her well. She had other company with her, so I left shortly after that. I told her I'd check on her the next day; and try not to be too nervous you're in good hands.

Then I raced by Anthony thinking I was holding them up for dinner, but I hadn't it was pot-luck; fine with me; except I wouldn't have had to rush, it wasn't a big deal. Anthony was having a lazy day, and said, "I'll do your hair tomorrow I just don't feel like doing it now." He was probably exhausted from taking care of his dad it wasn't an easy task. Waiting to get my hair done the next day was fine with me I didn't really care either. Tony, and I ate dinner; and Tony wanted to go home pretty much right after. We stayed a little while longer then got ready, and left.

"I can probably get dad in the house myself, you don't have to follow me home in the cold weather." He had been relaxing, I hated to see him have to get up, and go out in the cold, then follow us home just to bring his dad in, as we had the stair lift, and I could get Tony upstairs with no problem. However, he insisted being afraid that he might slip and fall, on some ice or something. We did it Anthony's way; he had a good point, after we got Tony in the house. "I could take care of the rest, I appreciate everything you've done, go home we'll be fine now," and he did. I got Tony in bed then went downstairs, and watched some television, and kicked back for a while.

Then I went to bed. All Tony's appointments would start all over again, early the next morning.

The next day started out to be a nightmare of a day; I was up at eight-thirty. Waiting for the PCT to come she was usually there by nine, or nine-thirty. At ten-thirty, I called the Home Health Service to see where she was. They told me they'd have to check, and have her call me. I couldn't wait any longer I had to feed Tony, if I didn't; he wouldn't have had time to eat breakfast, before the nurse got there. The nurse was to be there at eleven or eleven-thirty. I brought Tony down, and gave him breakfast right away. The PCT finally called, and said, "I had a flat tire, I'll be there in a few minutes." She came while Tony was eating his breakfast, he finished right away, and she took him back-up for his shower. A few minutes after Tony went up for his shower the nurse came. She waited for Tony to finish.

She naturally asked Tony the thousand questions about how he was feeling; and checked his hands, and feet, for swelling. Then checked his blood pressure, temperature, and told him he was doing great. Tony was doing absolutely; positively, super. She asked Tony a few more questions, and left. She had cut herself down to once a week instead of twice, which worked out a lot better all the way around, and one less appointment to cope with.

Then the OT came, then Lita. Tony did really well with all his exercises. He had a good attitude, and had worked hard. After they all left we just had a lazy day the rest of the day. I was just beat up, and drained, I think everything was just catching up to me once again.

Anthony called later to tell me he'd be there around five to do my hair for Thanksgiving. I was in such a funk I really didn't care if it got done or not; I had laid down, and fell asleep while watching television. The next thing I knew Anthony was there to do my hair. I washed it right away, and he blew dry and styled it for me. I have to say it did feel good, and it gave me the lift, I needed desperately.

I called Mario to see how he was feeling, he was complaining about his medicine running out, and was in a lot of pain. I asked why that had happened, he said, "They have to wait for it to come up from pharmacy."

He explained, "When I have to wait for the medicine, by the time they get it I'm in excruciating pain. I can get the medicine every three to four hours. By one, and half-hours I'm already in pain, and by the time the three hours are up I'm in so much pain I can't tolerate it." He had asked them to please have the medicine ready when he's due for the shot, so he didn't have to wait the extra forty minutes until they got it, which made perfect sense to me. I called the nurse's station to ask her what was going on. She explained, "I'm waiting for the medication to come from pharmacy and when I get it I'll give it to him." Not being there myself I was given the run-around.

By the time, I got off the phone with her, and called Mario right back she was in the room giving him the medicine. Therefore, I thought it was taken care of, and there would be no more problems, I was relieved.

I then went upstairs to lay our clothes out for the next day. We were going by Aida's house for dinner. It was Thanksgiving Day; the entire family was going there.

We had dinner later that evening, and then watched some TV. After that Tony wanted to go to bed he was tired of sitting in his recliner. I got him up to bed and settled; then went back down stairs, and made a few phone calls to friends to wish them Happy Thanksgiving, afterward turned in.

I got up late the next morning; I had slept in, I was either depressed or just plain out of it. I didn't know which, or both; we were going out for breakfast with Anthony that morning he was going to come, and dress his dad for me, so I didn't have to, that was great, and considerate of him. Anthony sure had been a great help to us. He also lived the closest, which made it a little easier.

When I called the hospital to check on Mario that morning, there was no answer. I didn't understand why he wasn't answering so; I called the nurse's station to find out what was going on. I asked if the doctor was in, "No." I asked them to have the doctor call me when he got in.

"We will, Mario's resting," which I thought was good.

I called another friend in the meantime to wish her Happy Thanksgiving, when the other line rang. I asked her to hold on; when I clicked over, it was the doctor calling. I asked the doctor if he could hold on a second, so I could hang-up with the other party. He said, "Yes." What I heard next I didn't expect!

The doctor informed me that Mario had a tantrum the night before. "He had a visitor there who said, she was his sister, she was a large woman, and she swore at me."

"She was not Mario's sister!" That he already knew, because he knew all of us.

The doctor continued, "Mario fired me as his doctor, and called security on me to have me removed from his room." I was appalled, and embarrassed, and actually wanted to just die, speechless, for a moment. The doctor continued, "I had to go to the hospital at eleven-thirty last night because Mario had a tantrum. He was swearing at the nurse, and had her in tears." Mario was being difficult. He had to have some patients; they were working to find out what was wrong with him, as fast as they could. Mario wasn't cooperating, and it wasn't in his best interest to have the medical staff crying, and upset. Mario has a urinary infection, and some kind of herpes virus. They did a spinal tap but I don't have the results yet. My job is to make him well; I'll stay on the case until you find another doctor."

"I'll talk to Mario, I'm so terribly sorry," apologizing for Mario's attitude. Needless to say I was furious with Mario for starting such a ruckus.

The hospital called a little later asking me to come to the hospital. "Mario's a little agitated; maybe you could calm him down."

"I'm working on getting there. I'll be there as fast as I can." I called Tammy to see if she could get there any faster than I could?

"I'm getting ready to go there. I called Joey, and he's going there too." I then called Anthony to ask him to come and stay with his father sooner so; I could get to the hospital faster. By the time Anthony got there I was almost ready to leave, I had just finished giving Tony a shower. Anthony took over taking care of his dad; getting him dressed, and fed. I finished getting myself ready; "I'll meet you by Aida later for Thanksgiving dinner, and ran out the door."

"Drive carefully," he could tell I was extremely upset.

When I got to the hospital Joey, Tammy, her husband Mike, Adriana and Carissa were already there with Mario. He was quite agitated all right and acting way out of character. He was very demanding, and wanted to be in control of his care. He felt; he could tell the medical professionals, how to treat his condition. We still really didn't know exactly what it was. It was his attitude getting him in trouble, very arrogant, and controlling. I was trying to figure out why he was having so much pain; also scared for his well-being, and dealing with the unknown. Again—if the pain were really that bad, why would they let Mario suffer? It didn't make any sense to me at all. I was totally baffled and with Mario being so demanding that wasn't helping at all. He was turning everyone off with his attitude instead of getting to the issue of getting the medicine before the pain escalated.

I tried to explain that to Mario, but he was out of control. There was no talking to him. You couldn't talk to him logically, at all. He was either going to get the pain medicine the way he wanted or he'd have a tantrum. We were getting nowhere fast. He was talking brutally to all of us around him. I couldn't figure out if it was the pain or a control thing, and I was sure the hospital staff didn't know either. I couldn't imagine him making up that pain, but he seemed to be obsessed with the pain medicine. That gave the hospital staff, the wrong message; aggravated them and the rest of us. I felt really bad but he was so out of control there was no calming him. I had enough, and decided to leave before matters got worse, I couldn't handle it. Joey and Tammy were still there with him they could figure it out; I couldn't take anymore at that point. The stress was too much for me to bear at that point. I was ready to have a break-down. It had been one thing after the other, Nonstop!

Thanksgiving Day

I went to Aida's house for Thanksgiving Dinner, but it wasn't a happy day by any means. I was thankful however for Tony being in remission, and doing so well. Thank You Jesus! The rest of the day all I did was think about Mario, and what was going on with him, and how was I going to handle that situation. I was however completely burned out by all this stress all the way around. I was on overload again.

Dinner was great, and everyone seemed to have a good time, I personally couldn't wait to get back home; wanting to sleep, feeling exhausted, and totally beat up. We got home about nine thirty and Tony went right to bed. I stayed up for awhile to relax, and went to bed shortly thereafter.

The PCT was there at nine the next morning, off to an early start. The OT would be there at twelve-thirty, and Lita would be there at two. It would be a full day, all day. Again!

Shed Installation

*M*ichael, his friend Ryan, Joey, and our son-in-law Mike came to put the shed up for Tony. Michael said, "It won't be a mess." Not!

I was already, ready for a breakdown; and didn't need extra stress at that time. However I knew our children meant well. I'd just have to tolerate it.

When I opened the blinds in the kitchen that morning, I immediately closed them. It looked like a rags a line out-there in the yard. Everything that was in the shed was at that point all over the yard. Of course that had to be done, for them to tear-down the old shed so; they could put up the new one. I personally didn't give a damn about a new shed. It was a nice thought for their father but, wasn't necessary. I just didn't have the patients to cope; or worry about what they were going to eat, or deal with the mess, or what they were doing, or throwing out. I couldn't be out there watching them. They'd be there for at least two days, and that wasn't on my priority list. Of course, I had no choice but, go with all of it. It would be good next year when summer came but, that was a long way off. Maybe I was not being appreciative, but I really couldn't get excited about being stressed.

I did however make them a hot lunch, it was cold outside, and I felt awful about them being outside working their, 'Asses Off'; that was the least I could do.

On top of all the people coming, and going all day, maybe the stress of the past months was catching up to me, I really didn't know. I do know the stress from Mario was getting to me. It had been too much to fast and hadn't stopped for months. Our family just seemed to go from one thing to another. I felt I really couldn't take much more.

As far as Tony, he was doing great, but I felt like I was falling apart. I couldn't figure out why, I felt like everything had gotten easier. I should be doing better myself, but it seemed that I did what had to be done, when it had to be done. Just when everything was going good I wasn't holding up. I was good in a crisis, after it was over was when I fell apart.

Anyway, Tony had eaten real well that day, which always made me happy.

I was going to try, and run to the store while the boys were there. But, by the time all the therapists left it was too late, and I really didn't feel like going anywhere anymore. I was exhausted.

Later that evening Tammy called to talk to her husband; she wanted to see how long he was going to be there. She said, "I have a gift to buy, do you want to go with me."

"I really don't want to; I haven't even combed my hair all day."

"I'm not looking all that good either."

"We just ordered pizza for dinner come here, and have some pizza, and I'll go with you." I had wanted to run to K-Mart, to get a card table, and chairs set they had on sale for a Christmas gift. My son-in-law Mike said, "I'll stay with dad until you get back don't worry." That was very nice of him, and that's what we ended up doing. When Tammy came, we ate right away and left to shop.

Then Tammy had to go pick-up her daughters by their cousin's house. They had spent the day there.

When we got back from shopping, Tammy left right away to go get the twins. It had been a productive couple of hours. I had gotten a few Christmas gifts bought, and felt great about that!

Tony was already in bed when I got home, and my son-in-law Mike left right away too. Shortly thereafter the boys called it a day, wrapping it up for the evening; they'd be back early the next morning, they assured me, to finish the job.

I stayed up doing a few things. Watched a movie, and then went to bed.

The next morning the boys weren't there when we got up, which was already late.

I called Michael on his cell to find out what they were doing. "I'm at the hardware store getting the stones, and other things I need to finish the job; then we're going to eat breakfast." I had heard on the news it was going to rain that afternoon. I told Michael, what the news had said, about rain coming, again he told me not to worry. I was very nervous by then, with all the stuff from the shed all over the lawn, and the potential of rain coming. That would be a total disaster and mess!

The boys got there a little later, and started right in to finish up. I told them, "I'm going to run to the store, after your dads done eating breakfast. "No problem;" I just had to give them the monitor so they could hear Tony from outside, in case he had to go to the bathroom or he needed something.

Christmas Time

I got Tony all fed, and settled. Then I left. It was getting close to Christmas, and I felt like everything was closing in on me. We were going to Florida December ninth through the sixteenth. Which was our choice, a vacation well needed, and something Tony had wanted to do for months. However the timing was going to make it tough for me to get everything done for the holiday. To be honest Mario being in the hospital didn't help. I was worried about leaving him in the condition he was in. Mario's situation wasn't in the scenario when we booked the trip to Florida. Tammy was starting her new job that Monday too. I was worried about the party store, and who was going to over-see it. There was too much pressure on me, and I felt it.

Anyway I left to go get another Christmas gift; I wanted to get out of the way. That day was the last day of the sale so, I had to go or miss the sale. Feeling if I only got that one gift that would make me happy. Again the boys said, "Don't worry take your time". They would look after their dad while I was gone. I did get that gift out of the way, and then I was going to see if I could accomplish getting a few more out of the way. But, when I got in my car, there was a message on my cell. When I called to retrieve it, it was Tammy. She said, "Mario's very sick throwing up, and has diarrhea. He's asking for his mom, don't hurry but go to the hospital when you can."

I had planned on stopping at the hospital before I went home, anyway. But, never expected a call like that—summonsing me there—.

Naturally I immediately went straight to the hospital, being very concerned, as to what was causing him to be so ill, so much for shopping!

Mario was very sick, when I arrived at the hospital; uncomfortable, nasty, demanding, and very controlling. He was again complaining about pain. My not being able to be there; on a daily basis, only getting bits, and pieces. Made the not knowing how much of what Mario said, I could count on, was almost impossible to deal with. He was having an obsessive, manipulative episode, and he had tried to manipulate every doctor, pain doctor, nurse, and charge nurse that would listen to his explanation of what should be done for him. It was his way, and how he wanted it done. Period! I didn't need and found it difficult to handle that extra pressure, being on overload as it was, my nerves were shot to hell!

Trying to juggle Tony; all the daily scheduling, the shed dilemma, trip to Florida, packing, Christmas shopping, wrapping, decorating, then there was the baking, and Christmas Eve dinner. I was ready to jump off a bridge. The pressure was that intense.

Tammy and I stayed at the hospital until Mario was finally comfortable. Then we left to get a soda so we could talk. Then we went back to see if Mario was still comfortable, and resting. He was, so we explained to him that we were leaving, it was nine thirty in the evening, and we left.

When I did get back home Michael, and his friend Ryan were waiting for me. Working in the rain all day they were sopping, and soaking wet. Just as I'd been worried 'they'd be,' and they needed to get home to get the wet clothes off and dry ones on. Poor guys!

The instant I walked through the door Tony told me to tape a movie. I just about jumped down his throat. I couldn't believe I reacted that way. But, excusing myself; as I had just gone through a traumatic episode with our son Mario, and he wanted me to immediately tape a movie. I could give a damn about taping a movie. I was stressed to the max! I thanked Michael and told them to go home and get dry. They could leave, I was home, and tomorrow was another day. I'd had it, and I didn't want to deal with anyone about anything. Plus I was worried they'd both get sick from working in the cold, damp rain in wet clothes.

Tony finished watching the movie, and went to bed. Poor thing he caught the flack, when it was Mario that had me so upset.

As for me I stayed up for awhile, washing clothes, and doing little things that needed to be done. Then I turned in; I really hadn't slept a full night's sleep for quite awhile, Since everything, and everyone was on my mind.

Tony and I slept late, I never really felt like getting up. It seemed I never got a good night sleep because, there was always something. I think that was the reason, and part of all the anxiety, but, not getting a good night sleep was really wearing me thin.

The next morning when I went down to the kitchen, Tony had requested biscuits the day before. However, I wasn't able to make them so; I decided to make them that morning. While I prepared breakfast, I called Mario. That was a BIG mistake! He had me half nuts over the pain again. Stating, they weren't helping him, no one cared how much pain he was in. Again I tried to rationalize with him, telling him to stay calm, take some deep breaths, instead of focusing on the pain medicine. I told Mario to explain the pain to the nurses, and doctors; and how the pain escalated without the medicine. But, the pain got worse; you don't know why, or how. That's how you get help. Not by demanding what you want and how you want it done. He followed exactly as I suggested, and they did figure out that the pain pump had malfunctioned. That's why the pain had spiked, I happened to be on the phone when all that happened, so I knew that to be fact, and he did act rational. Mario got the results he should have gotten. I was relieved that had worked, and thought he'd continue with that procedure. Especially since he got results, but I guess later that evening Mario was still obsessed with that damn pump again.

Tony and I were home for most of that day. I finished the wash, then folded, and put it away. Michael had stopped over to pick up some things, and I gave him the leftover biscuits.

Anthony was coming to help me get Tony in the car. We were going to go by his house for dinner about four-thirty. Anthony had taken the twins to see the movie 'Grench,' that day.

After the movie Anthony came to pick us up, and we left right away to go by his house. Tammy had a big party to decorate that day too. That's the reason Anthony had the twins. He told her, "I'll take them to the show, so you can work." That was very sweet of him with all he was doing, he's really is a super son and brother.

Tammy had gone to the hospital to see how Mario was doing. He was still obsessed with the pain pump. I was frustrated when, Mario wanted her to stay there all night to press the pump, so he could sleep. The pump had to be pressed manually, as the pain spiked. However, if it was pushed every three hours, he could sleep painlessly. Tammy told him, "I need to go home, the twins have homework. I'm sorry, I can't stay, and I also have to pick-up the twins from Anthony's house." And of course I wasn't able to go there. I had his dad to take care of. The fact that my hands were tied was probably part of the reason that I was stressed, and added to it. I felt that I was between heaven and hell! Heaven with Tony—. Hell with Mario—.

The dinner by Anthony was fantastic. That Anthony can cook! Tammy was so tired she could hardly eat, and so were the twins. They left right away so she could get them in bed. We left shortly after them also, with Anthony following us to help his dad in the house. As soon as we got in I told Anthony he could go home, he was tired too. He had a long day with taking care of the twins, cooking etc. He needed to relax. Actually the entire family had been on overload! Between, Tony, Mario and worrying about me, plus all that they were doing. They had to be stressed beyond also.

We got Tony to bed, and told him to exercise his legs like he suppose to do every night. He started to give me some flack, and I flew off the handle. I told him I was tired of waiting, and counting, and coaxing him every night. That it was his responsibility to exercise if he wanted to walk. That's what he had to do, and I really didn't give a damn if he did them or not. That was totally out of character for me to act like that. I knew by the way I acted I was stressed to the max. Naturally, later I beat myself up for flying off the handle and I felt just awful about it. I had been an 'Absolute Witch, started with a 'B!'

That was not like me, blowing up like that! I had been very loving, concerned, and encouraging. That's how I knew I was on overload. I just wasn't able to handle everyone's problems, plus my own, and stay calm to keep my patients. I just didn't have any thing left in me anymore; totally burnt out to the max.

I keep praying, please dear God give me the patients I need. I tried to please everyone, but it took a toll on me. I never learned either, because I still kept pushing myself to the breaking point.

I went downstairs, and called Ardine to see how she was doing. There I went again, worrying about everyone but myself; guessing it's just my nature, I couldn't help it. We talked until it was late, again. She was having a problem with her daughter. A little misunderstanding no big deal just a mother daughter thing; she was also having terrible problems with her medical insurance, which we discussed. We both finally decided it was very late, and we'd better get some sleep. "Good-bye," and hung up. I immediately went to bed; knowing eight-thirty was going to come mighty fast.

Up at eight-thirty getting ready for the PCT; so when Tony was done with his shower he could have breakfast, as he had a doctor's appointment that day.

The PCT still wasn't there yet, so, I decided to take my shower so I'd be ready to go to the doctor. Even though his appointment wasn't until eleven-thirty; I wanted her to check him to make sure he was in good health to travel to Florida.

When the PCT still wasn't there; I got nervous because Tony wasn't going to have the time to eat breakfast.

Mario called or I called Mario. I really don't remember which. Mario said, "That doctor's really a nut." Telling me that the doctor told him, "You were supposed to call another doctor."

When Mario had said, earlier that week that the doctor said, he would talk to another doctor on Monday. However, the doctor that Mario wanted wasn't going to be there until Monday. Mario told me, "The doctor said, he never said that." That it was Mario's responsibility to call another doctor. Mario then got irate on the phone. I told him, "I have to go to the doctor with your dad and I'll call you when I get back." Mario wanted to go to our family Dr. but they had a falling-out a few years earlier. I told him, "I really don't want to talk to the doctor about you; while seeing her during your father's appointment." Mario wasn't happy about that at all. I suggested he call her to work it out. I'd see what I could do when I was there.

Mario told me that his Dr. was on sick leave, and wasn't at the hospital anymore at all. That's how that whole situation with Tony's doctor got into the picture. We all liked Mario's doctor, he actually was a personal friend of our doctor, but had been ill for quite awhile. We didn't know what the story was with him, not practicing suddenly, other than he was sick.

The PCT didn't get there until ten after ten that morning. I was on the phone trying to find out where she was; when she got there.

Then I had to make sure the home health center got a hold of the OT because she hadn't given me a time on Friday before leaving. If she intended on coming at the usual time we wouldn't be home, and I asked the home health center to notify the OT that three that afternoon would be good because, we had Lita coming at two.

From the gecko it was another very stressful day—.

Anthony came after eleven as planned, to help with his dad. I called the doctor's office to make sure she was running on time. She was, so we had to leave right away. They had asked me to hold on, someone in the office wanted to talk to me. When the nurse got back on the phone she asked me to bring the papers I had talked to the nurse about, with me. "You've got to be kidding."

"If you don't have time just bring them another time." I was really angry, and frustrated about that. Had they called me earlier I could have gotten the papers together, but not at the last minute, not when I was ready to walk out the door.

We left, and got there just in time for Tony's appointment. However, we ended up waiting in the waiting room, and then waited some more in the exam room. I went to take care of the bill part, while waiting for the Dr... But, the accountant was just running to the bank; we had to wait until she got back. By the time she got back the doctor was about to come in any minute.

When she finally came; I didn't feel she was herself. I felt a rat in the pack; maybe I just surmised that, because of Mario. At any rate she examined Tony, and she had nothing but good to things to say about him. His heart was great, lungs sounded good; and he looked like a new person; she was more than pleased with his progress.

Everyone at the doctor's office stated, "Tony you look great," which he did. The doctor said, "Keep Tony on the same medicine he's taking. He seems to be doing fine on them." We asked about going on the Florida trip. She replied, "He'll be fine they have hospitals; good doctors almost everywhere these days. Plus there are faxes, phones and computers, "If God forbid there's a problem!"

Florida Trip

I was a little nervous about our Florida trip; as Mario was being released from the hospital, he'd be alone, and worrying about how he was going to get along, being all by him self?

I'd stopped writing this book the end of November, When I had to reference something about the cancer. I read that people with the type of cancer Tony had rarely lived a year. I didn't want to read that, deal with it, or believe it. I had to stay positive, Tony was doing great, and I didn't want to dwell on that scenario at all; Tony wasn't one of those statistics. He was going to make it, and be in medical books for all to read about. After all he was the "Miracle Man!"

Tony was actually doing very well, in most areas. He was trying very hard, and he was eating much better. Certainly not the appetite he'd had before he got sick, but at least he was eating. He was doing more challenging exercises, and trying to feed himself. I'd still help when he got frustrated but he was doing better.

However, it was Mario I was now worried about that poor kid had gone to hell, and back. He had always been there for me whenever I needed him. Now that he needed me my hands were tied. I couldn't be in two places at the same time. The guilt gnawed at me. I suggested to Mario to stay at our house when he got out of the hospital, but he wanted to be in his own house. I couldn't blame him, and that was his decision, knowing my circumstances. I guessed I'd have to live with his decision. Mario had a lot to deal with, that was just one more thing to add to the list.

On top of the clinical depression, Mario had contacted the HIV virus the previous year, that's another book in itself! Therefore Mario had gotten nerve damage due to all the medicines he was taking. I talked to Mario later that day to find out about the tests. Another blessing they came back negative. He only had the nerve damage, and that would get better in time we prayed.

The doctors were talking about releasing him but, they had to wean him off the morphine drip first. Then he would be put-on pain pills so that could be taken at home.

That child is very strong willed. He got off the morphine, and came home within a few days. Just before we were to leave for Florida; he was also going to have a home health nurse, and therapy. Lita was going to be his therapist that was a wonderful blessing. I knew she'd get him back on his feet as quickly as possible. If anyone could do it she was the one. I was elated, and relieved knowing she'd be seeing Mario while I was gone. Feeling she was almost like family, so I knew he'd be in good hands

It was December already, and with all that was going on it was quite overwhelming. The holidays, Tony, Mario, and the trip to Florida, was a lot to handle. However, Tony was doing well, and that was my survival link. I tried to stay focused on that; and take the rest on a day-by-day basis.

As for our life's I tried to keep it as normal as possible. In between all the people in, and out of the house OT, PT, PCT, nurse, and priest; became a hectic schedule, but it had been like that for months that we had hassle; only before it we were going back and forth to the hospital daily, many times twice a day. Between the two I'd take the latter. At least they were coming to our house; and I didn't have to struggle with getting Tony in and out.

However, just before we left for Florida I had a run-in with the nurse. She had said, "I have to be the last one to see Tony so I can close his file. No one can come after the file is closed. I'll come the morning before you leave." That meant Tony wouldn't have gotten his therapy that day. We hadn't seen eye to eye on a couple of other occasions before that day. I explained to the nurse, "That was unacceptable." Tony needed his therapy that day. She'd have to come after his sessions to close his file. Besides Lita, offered to close the file, if needed. I didn't know if she had a big head over her job or what. But she insisted that it had to be her that closed the file. We both had our say, and I stuck to mine. She suggested that when we returned from Florida, maybe I should consider getting another nurse, sometime there's a personality conflict.

I thought to myself whatever. I really didn't need that in my life right then. Just close the file after his therapy, and I'd deal with the rest when I get back. Tony did however get his therapy that day, and the nurse did close the file herself.

Tony and I had been going out to dinner as often as we could, when Tony felt up to it with Greg, and Loraine. We'd also go out for breakfast; lunch, dinner with our children, or by their houses as often as we could. That helped to break up the monotony, and keep our life as active, and as normal as possible.

We were all packed for our Florida trip. I had gone to get my hair done, and was now totally ready for the trip. Nerves were on edge though; as to how it would all go. We had waited for that trip for along time, and now, it was actually going to transpire. One of my original prayers was being answered.

I had ordered the wheelchair; it was going to be at the resort when we arrived. The oxygen would be available twenty-four hours a day should Tony need it. Tony has been off the oxygen for about a month or so and off the morphine completely since summer. Which helped with his breathing, because morphine slows the breathing, and lowers your blood pressure, therefore less oxygen gets in the blood. That had been a great feat. "Another Miracle "being Tony had "lung cancer." Everything was all covered; in order, extra prescriptions, and a prescription for oxygen should it be needed. No stone was left unturned, I hoped! We were as ready as we'd ever be. Excited, and scared at the same time we'd be leaving for Florida in the morning.

The next morning was hectic rushing to get both of us ready on time and getting the luggage downstairs last minute. Making sure the toiletries were packed, and luggage locked, before the limousine got there. I felt like, I was on the program, "Beat the Clock," but won. Plus our nerves were on edge with worry that everything would go okay. Being that far away from the hospital and doctor's was scary.

A wheelchair was already scheduled to be at the airport, so it would be waiting when we got there. That way we could get Tony to the gate without having to wait for a skycap to either get one, or find one. Tony never would have been able to walk that distance; that was entirely out of the question. He never would have accomplished that distance even though he was tremendously better.

When Tony and Paul arrived with the limousine we loaded the luggage in the limo and we were off. Hurrah!

Tammy had assured me that she was going to look in on Mario, so that should all work-out.

When we got to the airport we unloaded the luggage, and the wheelchair was there waiting. One fear down—!

The next challenge was getting Tony on the airplane and to his seat with the walker. That to, worked out wonderfully. The attendants take the handicap people on board first. They also had an elevator to bring the wheelchair up on, and then they take him to the door of the plane. There they transferred him to a tiny wheelchair that fits through the isles, and they helped him into his seat. Another fear down!

I was amazed at how all that was done. I had never seen that before, nor did I know it even existed. It was wonderful that the airlines had it all down to a science. I was extremely impressed.

The only other clinker, left was, if Tony should have to go to the bathroom while we were in flight. Tony had an isle seat, and he could hold on the seats for guidance, with Anthony behind him holding him by the gate belt but it still would be hectic. We were hoping with it being a short flight Anthony wouldn't have to deal with that difficult ordeal to many times and he didn't.

After we arrived in Florida and since the flight and everything had gone perfect that far. We were all excited, and couldn't be happier. Again the wheelchair was there when we got off the plane. Paul stayed with Tony, and got the luggage, all lined it up while Anthony and I went to get the rental car. We had rented a big Lincoln to fit all the luggage; walker, and so Tony would be comfortable, with plenty of room. Plus we needed the extra room for the wheelchair, which would be waiting at the resort for us. We had planned on using the wheelchair for site seeing so we needed a big trunk. We were afraid if we got a smaller car the wheelchair wouldn't fit.

We had reservations at a Marriott resort in Orlando, one we had stayed at before, that we were familiar with. So far every single thing worked out perfect.

When we arrived at the resort, it was just beautiful. We were lucky it was also a beautiful day. The wheelchair was in the office waiting as expected. We got Tony out of the car and in the wheelchair then to the lobby, while Anthony went to the desk to get our room, as Paul parked the car.

Anthony and I had a little difficulty getting a room close to the recreation, and pool area, on a ground floor, but they finally shifted things around to accommodate us. We were very pleased and thankful for that. The girl at the counter couldn't have been sweeter once we explained our circumstances, to her. That had also worked out perfect. All ours fears seemed to dwindle away.

We were there at last—we made it—to Florida at a beautiful resort—. Tony was tickled to death, he couldn't have been happier. All of us were for that matter, just as elated as we could be. The resort was just gorgeous and couldn't have been prettier. The picture window in the condo over-looked a lake that had boat rides you could take across the lake to the other side, where the recreation room, pool tables, ping-pong, and card games were. And you could rent paddleboats in animal shapes; it was pleasant view to look at. You could also see the pools, walkways, hot tubs, and bridges from the window. The flowers and shrubs looked gorgeous, in vibrant colors, the landscaping was impeccable, and something too feast your eyes on. The trip was turning out to be better than our wildest dreams.

We gave Anthony and Paul the larger bedroom. Tony and I took the room with the twin beds pushed together. The bathroom was right outside the door, and had less walking for Tony to get to, and it worked out wonderfully.

We started to make plans; as to what we were going to do, but decided to go out for something to eat, and discuss it. It was a little hectic getting Tony in, and out of the car. He wanted to use the wheelchair but we discouraged him by telling him he couldn't depend on it. He needed to use his own strength to keep his muscles strong. Tony reluctantly used the walker into the restaurant.

We had planned to go to an amusement park one of the days, when Tony and I realized that we had been there on our last trip, which was just before he'd gotten sick. That was out for us, we told Anthony and Paul to go their selves, but they decided not to go either. Then we decided to play the days by ear, so we could do whatever we wanted, whenever, and not have plans at all. Mainly we wanted to enjoy the sun, pool, relax, and enjoy the moment. That's exactly what we did, and loved every minute of it?

We went to the grocery store; got the things we needed for breakfast, lunch, liquor for cocktails and snacks to pick on. Paul made great Pina~ Coladas, also a ritual when we arrived at our destination; we'd make a toast to a great vacation as we started it off.

The next day we drove around Orlando to see what we wanted to do the rest of the week. Then went out for breakfast and picked up a few brochures, literature, and we found a new outlet mall to shop at. We stopped there, to check it out. It turned out to be great we found a lot of bargains and bought quite a few Christmas gifts. It was great fun to shop in the sun for Christmas it was enjoyable. It was definitely different from the Chicago winter weather, Christmas shopping. It was fun, warm, and enjoyable.

After the shopping spree we went back to the condo, then to the pool, to relax. We decided we'd go back to the mall later, after we freshened up, and had dinner.

While at the pool we just lay around; talked, and even got Tony in the pool for a while. It was a challenge, but he seemed to enjoy it, and he did some exercises in the water. After we came back from the pool we started getting ready. While I was in the bedroom getting dressed, I hadn't noticed, but when I came out of the bedroom out of my peripheral vision I saw Tony going back to the couch, "What are you doing?"

"I went to the bathroom." I couldn't believe my eyes; Tony had gone to the bathroom without the walker, by himself— As he sat down on the couch, he gave me the biggest cutest grin as if to say, 'I did it all by myself'. The excitement I felt in my heart for him was unexplainable. The thrill was that intense, but told him, "Don't do that again without the walker. Because, if you lose your balance; fall, hurt yourself, we'd really be in a pickle." On the other hand seeing Tony so happy and proud was an exuberant feeling.

After we readied ourselves were all dressed. We went out for dinner. After dinner we just drove around for a while taking in the sights, then went back to the outlet mall.

Tony and I had taken in a Mystery Dinner the last time we were in Florida. And we were telling Anthony and Paul about it, and decided to go again. They said, they thought they would enjoy it. It would be something Tony could do without getting too fatigued. We made reservations to go there a couple of days before we were to leave

Most of the days we spent by the pool in the sun, relaxing. Anthony loves the sun, and it was good for his dad to get in the pool, and move around to exercise. It was less fatiguing to exercise that way because it was less strenuous and he was weightless.

Late afternoons we'd freshen up; sight see, and shop. Then out to dinner later in the evening. We were having a wonderful time.

Our friends, Benny, and Josephine live in Florida about two hours away from Orlando in St. Petersburg Florida, If I called them they'd want to come up to see Tony, and I didn't want to inconvenience them, especially since I'd already waited several days. But Anthony kept saying, "You should call them. They're going to be angry with you when they find out we were there." I relented, and called to let them know we were in Florida. As expected they wanted to drive up to see us. The problem was by the time I had finally called them we only had a couple of days left. Benny and Josephine decided to come up the next day. They were upset we hadn't called earlier in the week, but they definitely wanted to make the trip. It was also two days before we were to leave, and that evening had the Mystery Dinner reserved, so we couldn't spend a long day together. I could have kicked myself, I felt just terrible that I hadn't called them sooner.

The resort was going to have entertainment by the pool, later that evening. And we were looking forward to going. It was a Hawaiian Luau with music, dancers, and Hawaiian cocktails. What a great show it was, we got a taste of Hawaii, while being in Florida. We had enjoyed the nice touch put-on by the resort, even though it was a cool evening and we had to put a blanket over Tony's shoulders and legs.

Afterward we went back to the room and went to bed. Benny and Josephine would be there early the next morning. Tony was on pins, and needles, anxiously awaiting their arrival. We had told them we'd be by the pool. We planned to spend the day swimming, lying in the sun, having a few cocktails, lunch, and just hang around, and talk. Then we'd take them inside for dessert and coffee afterward, so they could see the condo inside, and the rest of the grounds.

That next morning we had breakfast, and went to the pool to wait for their arrival. Tony was getting very anxious; he was such a worrywart. Worrying that they'd get lost and wouldn't be able to find us by the pool. Just as Anthony was going to check to see if he saw them roaming around, they showed up by the pool. They hadn't had a problem at all and it was great to see them again. We had seen them in August when they were in Chicago visiting, and we had gone out to dinner. Tony had been in really bad shape. Then they couldn't have been more pleased to see the progress he'd made. How good he looked, and what he had accomplished since they last saw him. Thrilled to see he was doing so well.

The day went as planned we all got in the water a while, talked, and then had lunch. We had decided to have pizza by the pool. Anthony offered to pick the pizza up for us, so we could continue visiting, and enjoying each other's company. After lunch we took them back to the condo for coffee, and dessert as planned. We all had enjoyed the day together. After coffee, and dessert, they decided to get on the road. They had another two-hour drive. We embraced each other, and thanked them for making the extensive trip to see us. We were very happy to have seen them. I was glad I had called them after all.

After they left we started to get ready for the Mystery Dinner.

It was difficult to give Tony a shower. We had to go into the boy's room, because they had a shower stall. The problem was it had glass doors, and we had to be, super cautious, that Tony didn't lose his balance. It put my nerves on edge, one false move or slip could have been potentially disastrous. I put the plastic lawn chair from the lanai inside the shower for Tony to sit on like we did at home. I also put a towel down inside the shower floor, to prevent him from slipping. Once he was in the shower, it was no big deal to shower him I was used to it. It was more the worrying that something would or could happen. It also was a long way to get Tony there with the walker. He was fatigued by then and lost his strength. But all the worry was in vain, it worked out. He was really drained by the time it was all over though. It had been very exerting for him to complete that task. I had planned it so he could lie down afterwards before he got dressed. That seemed to be a good idea, and helped Tony revitalize, and gain some strength. I got Tony dressed last, so he could rest while the rest of us finished primping. I was glad I had planned it that way it helped a lot.

We used the wheelchair so we didn't have a problem getting Tony into the playhouse. Making it easier on him; so, he could enjoy the play, without being spent before it began. We all enjoyed the play it was cute the way they involved the audience, in figuring out the murderer. The people were enjoyable at our table and the dinner was good also. It made for an enjoyable evening.

I asked Tony how he liked it, he said, "It was just okay." He wasn't all that thrilled about it, but it could have been just the way he was feeling. He had been cold through the whole play, which could have absolutely put a damper on his evening.

We went right back to the condo. It had been a lot of sitting for Tony, and could also have contributed to the reason he hadn't enjoyed it as much. When we got back we put him on the couch, so he could lay flat, stretch out to watch TV for a while before bed.

We had only one more; full day before leaving, on the journey home. We spent that day by the pool, shopping, and trying to fit all the things we'd bought for Christmas in the suitcases. That was a feat in itself, but we managed. I had a couple of fold up totes that came in handy on many trips. I pulled those out, my little lifesavers, opened them up, and WALLA, they hold a lot and that solved our problem.

We were happy once that was done, and out of the way. We made it all fit. All we had left to pack were the toiletries; we'd need in the morning. After all that work we felt we deserved a nice dinner.

That was our plan for our last night there. We went to a very nice restaurant for Lobster Dinner. Tony ordered the largest lobster they had, but hardly ate it. He hadn't been eating well, which upset me. What he did eat though he enjoyed tremendously. His eyes had always been bigger than his stomach; always thought he was getting cheated, so for him to order the Largest Lobster Tail was no surprise!

We weren't as anxious to go home, as we had been to get there. Everything had worked out so well and we really had enjoyed the whole trip. Plus we weren't looking forward to going back to the cold winter, and snow.

Our last morning we got up early, and got the car loaded with all our goodies, and luggage. Our flight was later, and we had asked for a late check-out, so we didn't have to rush. I made breakfast for Tony, got myself ready, then him, ready. We got him in the car, returned the wheelchair, checked out, and were on our way.

Everything worked out well on the way home. No problems at all. It couldn't have been better. We had done it,—one dream fulfilled—we'd had a wonderful time—!

We were back to the real world. With Christmas only nine days away, I had a lot to get done, in a short amount of time. Then all the normal Christmas preparation of wrapping gifts, last minute gifts to purchases, make cookies, and on, and on; first and foremost; had to get Tony all set up again, with his schedule for the PCT, PT, OT, Nurse, and Priest.

I called the home health center right away Monday morning to get the ball rolling for Tony's rescheduling. It pretty much would work the same, except for the nurse. Tony had gotten a new one, and that worked out good to. We started up, like we'd never left. Tony had done his exercises while we were gone pretty regularly, and used the wheelchair minimally, so he hadn't lost any muscle or strength. On the contrary he had strengthened his muscles.

The new nurse was scheduled to come on Wednesday. Lita would be back on again on Thursday. We'd be back in the swing of things in no time.

We were all very busy getting ready for the holidays. Our children helping as much as they could with their dad, so I could do all the things I needed to do to get done. It was getting very hectic the list of things to be done was endless.

Anthony, and Paul were having us for dinner almost every night that helped a lot and got us out of the house with different scenery, and company, plus I didn't have to worry about cooking.

We were all extremely happy; putting it mildly, Tony was doing so good, and getting better every day. Tony seemed to be in high spirits, and it felt good to see him that way. However, I had noticed slushiness, a kind of gurgle in Tony's throat when he talked. He had to keep clearing his throat to stop the gurgle when he talked. I had a bad feeling about that. He had done the same thing before he was diagnosed with the cancer. I immediately dismissed the thought by saying to myself, you're jumping to conclusions again; your brain is playing tricks on you. I didn't want to focus or dwell on the negative. Thinking to myself he's doing great and getting stronger with each passing day. Fighting with myself; back and fourth mentally; 'after all' the tests had come-back negative—! So I tried to put it out of my mind, but that really didn't work. Somehow I felt there was something, not quite right!

Tony had really never stopped having pain in his back, legs, or arms. I attributed that pain to all the exercises he was doing, by using the muscles and building them.

We had another appointment with Dr. Bane just before Christmas. She said, "Tony's doing great, but I want another set of chest X-rays and a CT scan done to stay on top of things."

Tony had been complaining about soreness in his stomach for quite sometime. I attributed that pain, and upset due to all the pills he was taking.

Tony's appetite was also sporadic; sometimes he'd eat a lot sometimes he ate very little, I couldn't put my finger on the reason, as to what or why that would happen.

The tests were set-up for the week of Christmas. That was the fourth year in a row—. That we'd be going through at the same exact thing. I was frightened to death. It hadn't been good news the last three years. I could only pray, and hope that everything would be all right. I had to keep a positive attitude. It was the only way I could cope.

I continued to get ready for Christmas. Trying desperately to stay focused. Tony was doing his exercises, along with the therapy as usual. Some days he'd do great, other days not so great—. Though continuously trying to give his all—!

For Christmas our granddaughters wanted bigger two-wheelers with hand brakes for Christmas that year. I couldn't get them myself nor would they fit in my car, so Tammy and Mike agreed to pick them up with the van. Then Joey put them together in the garage. We put them in the basement in the furnace room and I covered them with a sheet so the twins wouldn't see them, should they go down there. We had always gotten them what they wanted the most, and that year was there choice 'bikes.' Buying their bikes was a tradition; and Tony and I wanted to keep that tradition up. We had bought them every bike they have ever owned. I assume that's why they asked us for them that year. That was to be their big gift from us, plus some other little things.

It was very hard for me to get ready for Christmas with the worry about Tony, hanging over my head. *What was going on with Tony? Silently, my thoughts ran away with me. I had thought would that be his last Christmas with us. Ridding that thought as soon as it entered my head. It scared the shit out of me to have those thoughts. Thinking was God trying to warn me? Was it a premonition? Trying desperately to force the thoughts out of my mind, I couldn't help but be frightened to death.*

I'd say to our children occasionally have you noticed the cough dad has, and the phlegm in his throat. Testing them; to see if they'd also had noticed, and wasn't saying anything to me? They said, "Kind of," but they didn't elaborate on it. On the other hand they weren't with Tony as much as I was. Still trying not to focus on that; trying desperately to stay focused with what was going on with the holidays but, it was a very difficult task to stay focused. My mind was all over the place, at times. My gut was in turmoil, I just felt something was wrong—my gut told me so—.

I was having Christmas Eve as I usually did, with all the trimmings, and traditional fish. Tammy had offered to have it, because she thought it was too much for me to handle but, I insisted, even though it was hard trying to take care of Tony's needs, shop, cook, bake, and all. I didn't want to change a thing, and our granddaughters cried when my daughter offered. They wanted to come by Nane's house for Christmas Eve, saying to her, "It's tradition." I had gotten a kick out of that, they had been using that word a lot, and they were right it was tradition for me to have Christmas Eve. I wouldn't have disappointed them for the world. After all what was Christmas all about if not for your children and grandchildren?

Since Tony had gotten better the last couple of months our children had slacked off helping, a little. When I asked; Joey to pick up the clams, and open them at his house, he gave me flack but, he reluctantly agreed to do it. It was a lot of work and a big mess, one I did not think I could cope with that year. I was going to make the breading for them, and bake them here. I just didn't want to deal with the opening of the clams or mess. Plus Tony, and the boys had always done that together for years; I didn't want him to feel he was missing out on that bonding with the boys either. If Joey opened the clams at his house it would alleviate that problem.

I did all the baking I usually did even thought I couldn't have cared less, about it. I knew if I didn't keep everything as normal as possible Tony would read something into it. I tried very hard to be my normal self. After I'd get him all tucked in at night I'd go downstairs and cry my eyes out, in fear of what I may be facing. It was very hard to keep up a front, trying to be as normal as I could, with my heart breaking into little pieces day after day, and the worry was horrendous.

A few days before Christmas, our son-in-law Mike came to put our new tree up. I had bought a new one at the end of the season the year before. Tammy and I both had gotten one, so Mike knew exactly how it went together since he had just put there's up. The new tree had all the lights on it, and it was way too heavy for me to lift. I was very grateful that he had done that for us. Then Anthony came to decorate it, Mario usually decorated the tree for us, but he still wasn't up to par.

We went for the tests the doctor had ordered two days before Christmas. My heart was in my mouth; I would be on baited breath until we got the results. Anthony had gone with to help with his dad. The chest X-ray was a breeze, Tony had a hard time standing there but the technician said, "He did great." Then on to the CT scan department. The nurse gave Tony barium to drink, and he wasn't happy about that one bit. She said, "You have to drink as much as possible." Then they wanted to give him an enema that was the last straw; Tony wasn't about to do that at all. The technician said, "It will be all right, don't push it." So Tony got out of having to take the enema, I was happy about that for his sake. After drinking as much barium as he could get down; they finally they took him in for the test. I knew the technician that was taking the test. I had smoked with her in the smoking shed; at the hospital on numerous, occasions over the year, when Tony was hospitalized. She had also done tests on Tony before. Anthony and I impatiently waited for the test to be over. After it was over, and as she was helping Tony back, while Anthony helped his dad with his coat. I looked straight into the technician's eyes, and mouthed how did it look?

She looked at me with saddened eyes, and said, "You know I can't tell you that." She then continued, "Look in my eyes, as she whispered, Not good!" That was all she had to say. I could have, and wanted to die right there on the spot. I kept saying to myself over, and over in my mind I knew it—I knew it—. Then I thought, *what did she mean, not good? What exactly did that mean? Was he going to die? Was the cancer back? Where? How bad? Telling myself maybe she didn't know what she was talking about. After all she's not a doctor!* My mind was just whirling out of control; at that moment I fought desperately to stay in control of my emotions. Finally, I tried to appease myself, by saying don't go jumping to conclusions. Wait until you hear from the doctor to see what she had to say. Then saying to myself maybe that girl wanted to ruin my Christmas. On the other hand saying to myself, why would she want to do that? I had myself up, and down and all around I was really letting it get the best of me. Then I decided I wasn't going to drive myself crazy, I had a lot to get done for the holiday. I had to have a positive attitude to get through it. Trying desperately to convenience myself to not jump to conclusions and wait for the doctor's report.

Every night after I'd get Tony settled in bed, I'd go back downstairs, and cry my eyes out, which, I had done many nights for months before. I was so scared. Then the thinking would start. *What was I going to do without Tony—? How could I go on alone—? Tony can't leave me! He's my whole life—!*

I called Ardine, and told her what the technician had said. She said, "Don't go jumping to conclusions wait, until you hear from the doctor, maybe she's wrong." That's what I said, to myself too.

I had no one else to talk to. I didn't want to tell our children, and ruin their holidays, so I suffered silently, and tortured myself endlessly; suffering turmoil, excruciating, emotional, pain secretly. My mind was like a broken film repeating endlessly the same thing over and over, in my mind.

I was watching Tony even more closely, if that was possible. He seemed to be doing okay; except for the aches and pains he'd had all along. The only thing different was that slushiness in his throat when he talked. Tony at that point still wasn't; on oxygen, morphine, or having a hard time breathing. I just couldn't understand it. Part of me really didn't want to know anything before the holidays. Knowing I'd never make it through them; for sure, ignorance was bliss, at that point, 'anyway'!

Christmas Eve finally came, and we were ready. I had beaten the clock again! All the gifts were bought, wrapped, baking was done, and all the cooking for that evening was ready. Anthony had made the squid with Joey, and Paul's help, and they had that ready. Everything was on schedule. Our children started arriving one at a time. Bringing in their gifts with the living room closing in with gifts as each one arrived. By the time they were all there half the living room was taken up with gifts. Literally! There barely was enough room for all of us to sit. With some of us barricaded in our seats by gifts. If you decided to move you actually had to crawl through, and over the gifts to get out. Christmas Eve was a big holiday for us. I had always loved Christmas, and loved buying gifts for our kids.

Our granddaughter's were just as tickled as they could be. Looking at all the gifts, trying to figure out which ones were for them; the biggest ones, had to be for them from Nane, and Papa whether they were or not. In their little imagination the biggest gifts were theirs. They couldn't wait to start opening them. The thrill to see their eyes just sparkling, and light up with joy, was worth it all.

Our evening usually started with having a couple of cocktails, appetizers, and chatting. Then we pick someone to pass out the gifts, taking turns from year to year. We open the gifts one at a time each taking a turn from our stack, so that we all could see, and appreciate what we got from whom. I felt a lot of work, shopping, wrapping, and planning went into that part. I didn't think ripping open a bunch of gifts all at once was fun or enjoyable, so all our children went along with my wishes. We open gifts for a couple of hours then we stop to eat dinner, after dinner we'd continue where we left off with the gifts.

I have to say that the twins were very good about waiting, because they didn't always get their big gift from us, until we'd go back the second time to open gifts. That night I think my son-in-law Mike was more excited than they were. He kept saying to me, "Now ma?" I had said, "No, a couple of times because; I didn't want them to be side-tracked by the bikes, and not pay attention to appreciate the rest of the gifts. Finally by the third time asked, I said, "Okay." But, first we have to get dad at the kitchen table so he could sit and see their faces. They're just wasn't any room to bring two, two-wheeler bikes into the living room. We got Tony all settled at the kitchen table told the twins to cover their eyes, as we readied our cameras, while Mike (their dad) went downstairs, and brought the bikes up, once they were both there. We told the twins "Open your eyes." They were screaming, and jumping with glee, they were so happy, hugging, kissing, and thanking their Papa, and I. They were just so thrilled, after all the, picture taking was over; we went back to the living room to finish opening the rest of the gifts.

The twins had gotten their Papa a T-shirt that said, "Papa is my name spoiling was my game". He was delighted, and got a kick out of it. My heart was breaking at every passing moment, a little at a time.

We were all flourished with gifts beyond belief. After all the gift opening, we went back to the dining room for dessert, and coffee, as we all sat around as usual, and talked. What was unusual was Tony usually went to bed right away after dessert, and had for years? That year he stayed with us, and talked never mentioning bed at all. I found that very unusual, and I keyed in on it immediately with my mind going 'absolutely, berserk, crazy' again. *Was he staying up with us because he knew it was going to be his last Christmas? Trying to take control of my mind once again, saying to myself there you go again letting your mind run-off with you. He's just simply enjoying himself. Telling myself don't start going off the deep end again.*

Tony finally did say he was getting tired, after Tammy said, "We need to clean up. I have to get home. I still have a lot to get done before Santa comes during the night for Christmas morning." Christmas morning was when the twins opened their gifts that Santa had brought them at home.

After we got Tony settled in bed; our children helped me clean-up the mess. Most everything was done for me, so I could just concentrate on getting Tony and I ready the next morning. We were going by Anthony's house for Christmas dinner; with the entire extended family.

They had started loading their cars up with all their gifts, finally leaving about one in the morning. I straightened out our gifts under the tree. Did some last minute straightening; and made a cookie tray for Anthony's house. Then I got Tony's and my clothes ready for the next day. Then literally fell into bed.

Christmas day Anthony and Paul had the whole family over; there were thirty of us altogether for a sit-down dinner. They had a lot to prepare for, and did a fabulous job. The decorations were breathtaking; the tables set gorgeously, and gifts wrapped beautifully, the whole house looked like a winter wonderland.

The holidays were lovely all the way around, but there was a damper in them for me, dreading the results of the tests. Hoping beyond hope I'd be able to breathe lightly again; I kept praying very hard for more "Miracles" to transpire.

The holidays were behind us; and that was a relief, for the hustle and bustle of that was over; on with the, regular schedule of; therapists, nurses, PCT, and the results of the 'TESTS'! Those, damn tests kept taunting me. I told Lita when she came what the technician had said, at the hospital. She expressed I should wait for the doctor's report before jumping to conclusions to. It was absolute torture watching Tony exercise that day, struggling and trying so hard to increase the exercises, he'd been doing. As Lita was leaving that day, I had tears in my eyes, and said, "All that for what?"

"It's important to Tony; don't let him see you upset. Saying as she left, I'll see you tomorrow,"

Anthony called saying, "Come over for dinner tonight." We had accepted the invite, and looked forward to it. At dinner we talked a little about Maui. That usually was the time of year; we were anxiously waiting to leave. Tony said, "I'd love to be going to Maui," I couldn't speak at that moment to make a comment, one-way or the other. My heart was in my throat. That conversation ended abruptly—.

We still had New Years Eve to get through, Anthony and Paul said, "We'll get-together for dinner that night. Anthony said, "I'll call the rest of my siblings to see if they have plans. If not whoever wants to come is welcome."

"That sounds great to me."

The doctor never called with the results after Christmas. Anthony kept asking me if I'd gotten the report. "No, I haven't heard from the doctor yet." Anthony finally took things in his own hands, and called the doctor's office himself, I was too scared to call; terrified of the results! I didn't want to hear the results, for fear it wasn't, going to be good. I also found it peculiar that the doctor hadn't called yet. When Anthony called the office the nurse said, "I haven't received the results, and the doctor is out of town until after New Year." I was secretly glad. I didn't want to deal with it now, or ever for that matter. I really believed that the doctor had gotten the results but, didn't want to ruin the holidays for our family. She wanted to wait until the holidays were over. I was relieved to hear that she actually was, out of town, not just holding out on us. Thinking maybe that was a good sign, I hoped. Anthony continued, "You jumped the gun. The nurse re-checked saying, 'I do have the results they're negative."

"The results from both tests? Yes, and were going to Maui. I'm going to make the reservations, right away."

When Anthony came back later that day, and told me everything was booked I was flabbergasted! I couldn't believe my ears. He had accomplished it all within two to three hours. He had everything all booked. That was unheard of! It normally took us about two to three months in advance minimum to book everything. Anthony had gotten the condo that we loved for the whole month, which was totally unheard of. We usually had to make a move; from one condo, to our favorite one after a week, in order to get, that particular unit, we loved. Or, we didn't know for sure if we'd even get that unit until we got there, so that alone was a "Miracle" in disguise 'For Sure'! To call, and get that unit, two weeks before, for four weeks, a whole month without moving was totally unheard of. That wouldn't happen again in a million years. Plus Anthony had gotten the airfare at a reasonable rate. "Another Miracle!" He actually had booked the, condo, airfare, cars, with the dates we wanted, and all. We'd be leaving for Maui January 14, and staying until February 11. That was totally unbelievable, I was speechless!

Tony was beyond excited when Anthony told him the tests were negative, and we were going to Maui. I on the other hand was totally befuddled, and scared, but excited and happy at the same time. My emotions were all over the place. I wanted to believe the nurse at the doctor's office but my gut told me different!

I decided to call the doctor's office myself to talk to the nurse. I went upstairs so Tony couldn't hear me, and made the dreaded call. I asked the nurse about the tests, explaining that I knew Anthony had called already. I just wanted to confirm what she had told him? I asked her if both tests came back, negative? She said, "All I have is the X-ray report, and it's negative." I told her what the technician had told me at the hospital. I went on to tell her that when the doctor came back if there was anything bad about the tests that I didn't want Tony to know. I asked her to have the doctor call, and talk to only me —! I also told her about the trip we had booked to Maui. Then I had to call Anthony and tell him, that it was only the chest X-ray not the CT scans that was negative. The results on the CT scan weren't in yet. I told him what I had told the nurse, to tell the doctor. Anthony was shaken when I then told him what the technician had said, at the hospital. He said, "When did she say that to you? I was right there

I didn't hear that." I explained that he was busy getting his dad's coat on, when I asked her. He was shocked also saying, "Wait for the doctor to call." We'd have to wait until after New Year to get all the facts. *Was that God's way of helping me absorb the situation a little at a time?*

We continued with our plans of going by Anthony, and Paul's for New Years Eve dinner. It was as nice as it could be with the circumstances being what they were. Trying to focus on the trip to Maui, and how wonderful it was going be to be there in the sun. Out of the cold and nasty winter weather, we were having. That part would be a blessing for us.

Lita came the day after New Years for Tony's therapy. We talked about New Year's Eve, what we each had done, while she had Tony going up, and down the first step in the foyer, as part of his therapy. This was really difficult, for Tony to do. Some he'd do on his own, some he needed help with. The more he did the harder it got for him, but he was trying hard, and doing pretty good. Lita also had Tony doing balancing exercises with a balloon. She had me participate with that one. We bounced a balloon back and forth between us, while Tony was in a standing position, to help with his balance. When doing that exercise he had to shift his weight to accomplish it, and he did well. She commented that we were a cute couple. She loved to come there, that we worked together as a team. I loved seeing Tony doing so well. Telling him he had to work hard, he only had two weeks to get stronger for the trip.

*I kept thinking how could the tests not be good? He was doing so well, wasn't he? Maybe it's not cancer at all? Maybe it's something else that's not good? How could he possibly do all those exercises if there was anything really wrong? Question after question they never stopped they kept taunting me, over and over again—.*The phone rang, Tony answered—. It was the doctor's nurse on the other end of the line. I had Tony answering the phone, with the nine million calls that had been coming in, it gave him something he could do, and it relieved me, so I could do things I had to do. That helped me immensely, and took the stress off of, running for the phone all the time. The nurse asked Tony how he was doing, and then asked to talk to me. The call I had been dreading for over a week had come—. Was that news going to be gloom, and doom? Oh God! I need your help here to control myself. I picked up the extension; and told Tony I had it he could hang-up. As I watched him from the kitchen to make sure he had hung up, so he didn't hear the conversation of what was said. She proceeded to say, "The Doctor Wants to See You!" My heart fell all the way down to the floor of the basement, and pounding like it was going to pop right out of my chest, my body was trembling, my head spinning, and my legs like jelly. I had to use every ounce of control I could muster to continue, as I made the appointment for the next day.

When I got off the phone I contained myself, how I don't know. I told Tony I had to go to the doctor's office to get all the written prescriptions for the trip to Maui. 'I Lied.' That we had to have enough medicine for a month before we left; we needed to have back-up prescriptions should we need them. Tony didn't question me. Thank God!

I called Anthony right away to tell him about the appointment with the doctor. He said, "I want to go with you.' I was glad I didn't know what I was going to have to face. I don't even remember who stayed with Tony that day while Anthony and I were gone. I was a nervous wreck, distraught beyond belief. I really didn't need to see her; I guess I knew in my heart all along, for quite awhile now that it was not good. To what extent I didn't know, nor did I really want to. But if someone had to be told better me than, Tony! I had kept trying to fool myself into believing that everything was okay, but to no avail.

I cried, and cried uncontrollably that night. How was I ever going to get through the horrible nightmare? Trying to be quite while crying so Tony wouldn't hear me; not knowing what to do or how I was going to do it! Finally went to bed that night filled with anguish. Tony was sleeping as I quietly cried to myself. I didn't sleep a wink that night, rolling all those frightful thoughts over and over in my mind, I was in agony.

The next morning after Tony was all taken care of; I got ready to go to the doctor. I had Anthony meet me on the driveway. I didn't want Tony to see him or, for sure he would have known something wasn't right.

When I walked out the front door Anthony was in the driveway waiting, I got in his car fighting back the tears. Saying over and over that I knew it, in my mind; like a broken record. I told Anthony we didn't even need to go to see the doctor that I already knew what the doctor was going to say. I was trying to control myself so as not to freak Anthony out. We were both like time bombs ready to explode. I cried silently the whole time we waited in the office. I was so anxious I didn't know what to do with myself, rocking back and forth, trying to comfort myself, moaning and just trembling all over.

The nurse finally called us into the inner office. I was trying to calm myself so I could comprehend, and remember exactly what the doctor had to say. If I wasn't in control of myself; I couldn't make logical decisions, or hear what I needed to hear to make those decisions.

Now our usual bubbly, funny, doctor entered with saddened eyes, and her head hanging. That did it—and she started; this saddens me, and every one of us in the office. We're all very fond of Tony. The CT scan report was positive. My mind went blank for a moment, and then I said, to myself, did I hear her correctly?

She continued, "He's loaded with cancer," naturally I lost it, stating I knew it, I knew it. "I just got off the phone with Dr. Even stating, 'The trip to Maui is out of the question.'" Dr. Bane had the same opinion regarding the Maui trip. She went on to explain, "It could get very rough. He's loaded with cancer in the lymph nodes, liver, lungs, bones, it's everywhere." I couldn't believe what I was hearing, someone Pinch Me!

"But he's doing so well now. Doing all his exercises, he's doing better than ever." I just couldn't understand how that could be?

She proceeded, "Tony has a right to know." I explained that we had talked about, if the cancer should ever come-back, would he want to know, and he had said, "No!" If I went home, and told him the results, I might as well go home with a shotgun, and blow his brains out. It would have the same effect. Anthony asked, "How bad is bad?"

"He'd be vomiting constantly, plus not eating, and losing weight. It could get really rough. We were hell-bent to get Tony to Maui if it killed us. I asked her about getting another chemo treatment before we left.

"I don't know if he could handle one right now, and it could make him very sick while you're gone, and he wouldn't be able to enjoy himself."

"He's doing great right now, and I don't want him to know." As far as it getting rough,

"Anthony and Paul are going to be with us. We'd be all right they're both big guys."

She finally relented, "You know your husband better than I do. You've been with him a long time. Go on your trip take a lot of pictures, have a lot of cocktails, enjoy him, and have a good time." I was happy about that, and scared shitless at the same time. To tell you the truth, I don't know what I thought, at that time except, scared to death. Anthony said, to the doctor, "She'll make this decision, and then she'll beat herself up about it later."

"You've made the decision, and you've got to stick to it. You've made the decisions for good reasons, and that's what you've got to remember." She wished us luck, and a good trip; if we needed anything at all, call her.

They had been just wonderful all of them at that office; including offering to help me sort out all the bills that kept rolling in, on their own time. Inviting me over to their houses to get away from the situation; for a short time; feeling it was important; in order for me, to continue giving Tony my all. They had also said, "Call anytime for anything you need including giving me their home phone numbers. How often does that happen?

Now I was faced with the prognosis of what I feared, and cried over for almost a year. *Tony was going to heaven! When? How long? Only God knew!*

My feeling's were Tony had pulled through before, and he could do it again. They didn't call Tony "Miracle Man" for nothing! And they don't know "God's Power"! Tony's going to beat the cancer, he's doing great.

I certainly had my work cut-out for me though. I had to go home; pretend everything was routine, and be happy or Tony would read into it immediately. When I got home I was cheery, and happy on the outside, dying on the inside. Telling Tony I had all the prescriptions under control. All the medications ordered for the month, so that it would work-out wonderfully with no problems. I had the prescription for oxygen should he need it, I was trying to be as bubbly as possible. Whether he bought it or not I don't know,—but he never questioned me.

When Tony was resting, I called all our children, and told them the devastating awful news. They of course were all as shaken, and as upset as I was. They controlled themselves for my benefit; I'm sure, as I did for them. We discussed the trip to Maui, they were concerned about it, and how their father was going to handle it. I assured them that he would be fine; Anthony and Paul would be there with me. Of course I never would have ever attempted the trip alone! That was an impossibility for sure; there was no way, I could handle Tony alone, nor would I have tried. I told all our children what the doctor had said, about getting very rough, which concerned them even more, and scared them, I'm sure. But I felt it was necessary to be as up front with them as I could, as I always had.

Maui

I explained, once we get to Maui. The sun and warm weather would be wonderful for their dad. It would be more pleasant; fewer clothes and a beautiful ocean view to look at through, the floor-to-ceiling, wall-to-wall windows, not, to mention the fact, that we both love it there.

Anthony said, "We'll rent a recliner and toilet riser for dad, so it will be as comfortable for him as possible." We had the walker and wheelchair with us, so it would be just like being home away from home.

I was a basket case however, I cried and cried, I was anxious, and scared beyond belief. My heart was being ripped up in tiny pieces. I was trying to be optimistic I still had faith, and prayed like crazy. I was incredibly nervous that we'd even be able to make the trip at all; not knowing what, very rough meant, my mind still whirling out of control. How bad would Tony get? How fast? Oh God! Please help Tony, and I, let him make the trip he's so looking forward too. Help me to act as normal as possible, so Tony does not sense anything is wrong.

When I talked to Michael a couple of days later; he told me he decided he'd like to come to Maui too, for a week. We were going to be there four weeks, so one week wasn't a problem. We would still have three weeks alone. Anthony was upset at first, because he wanted to get away alone, but realized under the circumstances, and not thinking too clear about the other siblings feelings. I told Tony that Michael had decided to join us. I acted perturbed about it, saying jokingly, "We can't even take a vacation without our children horning in on it."

Tony said, "It's only a week, it will work-out." Tony's famous last words—he would always say, "It will work-out" about different situations throughout our lives, and he was always right, it had always worked out.

When Lita came; a couple of days later, I whispered what the doctor said, as I opened the door to let her in. She acknowledged what I had said, with tears in her eyes, without speaking a word, so as not to let Tony hear. Tony was not feeling too good that day at all. His stomach was bothering him, and he was quiet. Bubbly Lita said, "Tony what's wrong?" He was kind of sick to his stomach and depressed.

She said, her famous last words, "WHAT'S GOING ON WITH YOU TONY?"

"I was just thinking where we would put a hospital bed in the living room?" It took every bit of stamina I could muster to keep myself composed. I wanted to burst out in tears! Instead I said, "Tony—what in the world are you thinking about that for; what made you think about that? You're doing great: if we should ever have to put a hospital bed in the living room, we'll worry about it then." Don't worry, speaking as adamantly, and convincing, as I could be, with the biggest lump in my throat, I could barely speak. I told Tony what he needed to worry about was himself, to let me worry about a hospital bed if that day ever came. That wasn't a concern for us "now." Thinking, *was he testing me, to see my reaction? Was he fishing for information, did he sense something? Oh God please help me to say the right things to him. Or did he actually intuitively know something wasn't right, and that he wasn't doing all that well medically?*

Tony had extraordinarily been accomplishing all the exercises. Lita challenged him by working him very hard to get him strong for the trip to Maui. It just killed me to see him work that way, knowing it had to be so difficult for him. Seeing him struggle with the stair exercises, trying desperately hard, was ripping at my heart and almost more than I could handle. At the same time encouraging him, and telling him how well he was doing. Focusing on the positive, at the same time asking myself, how could he be so sick, and do so well at the same time? It was mind boggling, just driving me crazy.

I talked to Lita regarding getting us a wheelchair for our trip. She was very responsive to our needs. She relieved us by saying, "I can do that for you." That was a load off.

When Lita left that day, as I was walking her to the door, I started crying. I just couldn't hold-back the emotions or tears one more second. I was bursting at the seams. I whispered to her, "All that for what?"

"He needs to do it for himself—it's important—don't let him see you crying."

She left saying, "I'll see you in two days, and keep your chin up."

I immediately went into the bathroom to throw cold water on my face, wipe my tearful eyes, and put my cheery face, back on. That was very difficult for me; I'd been doing a lot of crying the last couple of days. I was just terrified most of the time, tearful, sad, and scared.

When I returned to the living room, I told Tony how great he had done, and how proud I was of him. That he shouldn't worry about hospital beds; we are nowhere near, needing a hospital bed. Worry wasn't good for him, and if we were ever at that point, God forbid, I'd do all the worrying; to put that thought out of you're mind. Period!

Also so worried; that Tony would fail as quickly; as the doctor mentioned, he wouldn't be able to handle a trip of that length. We still had a week and a half before we'd be leaving for Maui. I worried constantly about if we'd even make it. Tony was in fact doing pretty well, but the fear was still haunting me. As I tried to keep myself as busy as I could, so as not to dwell on the negative.

To keep my mind on other things, I started washing clothes we'd need, packing, planning, and preparing for the trip. Making lists so I wouldn't over-look anything important. Anthony and I talked frequently going-over every last detail. So if I'd forgotten something or he remembered something he could remind me or suggest something, and vise versa.

I had planned to buy a plastic lawn chair for Tony, once we got to Maui, to put inside the tub for his showers. We had everything covered that we could think of we'd need. We decided if something else should come up, we'd figure out a solution then.

After Michael had decided to definitely go with us, within a day or so, when Joey found out. He said, "I'd like to go to."

Michael then said, "I'd like to take Lisa, we could all get a room, and stay together." That would work-out better for them also; having their own room. However, worrying was about them getting; reservations at the same condo, airfare at the same rates, at the same time we were leaving, same dates we were to leave, with such short notice!

I then had to explain to Tony that now, Joey wanted to go, and Michael wanted to bring Lisa I had to act up set and adamant about it, so as not to let on that, it was actually being planned. Saying to Tony, "What the hell, we can't even get-away without our children."

Tony replied, "It would only be for a week". We'd still have three weeks alone. Anthony had to act upset also, which he really was, but under the circumstances understood.

We had all gone to Maui together before. That had been a nightmare, trying to keep everyone happy, who wanted to go where, when, with whom, really had been a trying, difficult situation. We were only there for seven days. And they wanted to see it all, which made it difficult trying to get all minds on the same track, at the same time, and have them see it all in that amount of time was definitely, a challenge.

As I told Tony and Anthony they had all been there before, they could do whatever they wanted. We didn't necessarily need to be doing what they were doing, and they had seen all the sights already, so it shouldn't be as confusing as the last time.

Whenever we went on vacations with others in the past; we had a rule that we would do what we wanted to do, and the others would do what they wanted. If we all wanted to do the same thing we'd do it together. Otherwise there could be hard feelings. That had worked in the past, and we'd implement that same rule for the trip. Now that they'd be in their own room, it would actually work-out better.

Of course talking; to all our children, on a daily basis, it didn't take any time at all for Mario and Tammy to find out, that Michael, Lisa, and Joey, were going. Then Mario expressed, he'd like to go to.

When the OT came that day, to work Tony's arm, and hand, Tony expressed his concern about the flight to Maui. It was a long grueling trip for a healthy person, so for him it was going to be extremely, fatiguing. We'd always flown, where we'd have a lay-over, so we could get off the plane to stretch our legs, and a change of scenery for about an hour, after flying four hours. We had found that to be helpful, and then we'd get back on the same plane for the next five-hour stretch to Maui. However, that wasn't Tony's fear at all. He was worried he wouldn't be able to get to the bathroom in time, and would wet his pants. Since the stroke he didn't seem to be able to hold his urine for any length of time, lately. If Tony didn't get to the bathroom quick enough, it would automatically start to seep out. He didn't want to be embarrassed by that happening, a legitimate concern for him. The therapist had a great solution. She said, "Why don't you get panty liners just for the flight." You could put them inside your underwear, and they're not noticeable, buy liners as soon as you can. If that should happen by mistake you could just change it. No one would be the wiser. Tony was so relieved, that problem was solved. I immediately, went to buy the liners; to ease Tony's mind, and he could put that, thought at rest. So he didn't worry about a thing. They say worry weakens your resistance; I didn't want anything to compromise his resistance.

It was getting closer to the day we were to leave, it was about a week before we'd be on our way, and we were counting the days. We were excited, and scared at the same time. Tony was still having pain in his stomach, legs and arms. Nothing had changed there; he'd been having that all along. Only now I didn't know if it was the same pain or the cancer? I preferred to believe it was the same pain. He still wasn't on any pain medication of any kind, even though I had it for him. He didn't seem to need it or ask for it.

The rest of our children were expressing their wanting to go on the trip to Maui, one at a time. I said, "How will I ever explain that to your dad without him getting suspicious. At the same time I was thrilled that they wanted to go to that extent, to be with their dad as much as possible. It was an extremely emotional time for all of us. My emotions were at a peak; up, and down, between heaven, and hell. Sad one minute—; optimistic the next—, bouncing like a ball—, Tony had rallied so many times in the past. I finally convinced myself that he would rally again; fool all the doctors, with God's help, he was going to make it! God can do anything; he's going to help Tony get better! I just knew it. Looking back at what Tony had accomplished with God's help thus far.

Mario made plans to also join us for a week, and he even made his plane reservations. He also had gotten the same rate, dates, flight and time. I couldn't believe it. Mario was going to stay in our condo with us for the week.

Tammy then expressed that she'd like to go, but couldn't afford it, with having a family of four the expenses were much greater

I then called Tammy, to tell her Mario was now going for sure. I thought she should also go or she may regret it the rest of her life. I told her to take the money out of the business. She also owned a week of time-sharing in Maui. She said, "I'm going to call there, to see if I can get a condo for that week with this short notice." Then she'd need flight reservations for four of them. By that time, it was late afternoon. Tammy called me back saying, "I got a condo," "Another Miracle!" Again I couldn't believe it— I was baffled by it all— Unheard of! She got the same flight, and held four seats, but the airfare was going to be higher because it was by then less than a week before we'd be leaving. Now all our children changed their minds and they were going to stay ten days instead of a week. They felt if they were going to travel that far, they should take advantage of the trip and be with their dad as long as they could.

Mario then got on the phone with the airlines, and told them about our circumstances. Not only did he get his ticket changed for the ten days, but he also got Tammy's family the same rate as the rest of them. I was dumbfounded; that it worked out, on one week notice, it was more-then unbelievable, it was incredible! We were all on the same flight; same days, same condo only doors apart, all together, "Another Miracle!" All twelve of us were going to Maui with their dad. I was more than impressed. I felt very blessed—.

Now I had to tell Tony all our children were going, every one of them! I also had to express how upset; I was that they had all gotten on the bandwagon. That it had snow-balled once one found out the other was going. None of them wanted to be left out. Tony said, "It will only be for a week, I kind of chuckled, and said, "Nooooooo, it's now grown to ten days."

He said, "It will all work-out," and we laughed. (His famous last words.)

I was so happy; our children were going to spend, all day, every day, for ten days, with their dad in Maui.

I was still flabbergasted that they all were able to get off work at the last minute, with no trouble, condos at the same resort, and air reservations on the same flight, at the same time all got cars with the same dates. I just couldn't get over it. It truly was a "Miracle." the whole trip would never have taken place if it weren't for that explanation. As for Tony he continued with his therapy, some days good, some not so good, but always giving his all. He tried his hardest to get stronger, for Maui!

All of us encouraged Tony; cheering him on daily, he really for the most part was doing pretty well, in spite of his condition. I still couldn't understand how he could be so loaded with cancer, and do all of that, or even want to try for that matter. The doctors had to be wrong!

Our days were still very busy with the group; coming and going, in, and out all day, along with the phone insistently ringing, off the wall.

At that time; trying to stay extra busy, I decided to make an agenda for the ten days our children would be there. I made a list of all the places to go, and see. Then I called each of our children to see who was interested in doing what and when so that when we got to Maui. There wouldn't be mass confusion, with twelve ideas, all trying to decide what to do when, and with whom. Thinking it would be less stressful, and confusing all the way around. I knew I was going to have my hands full, and I didn't want Tony getting nervous either. Or have any of our children having hard feelings with each other. I worked on the schedule then typed it in the computer after finding out who wanted to do what. I made each of us a copy, and it seemed to simplify things. Everyone would know when we were doing what, when, with whom. They agreed it was a great idea.

Everyone was rushing around doing last minute things; packing, getting ready for the trip. We were leaving on a Monday, which helped our children, they had all of Saturday, and Sunday to get, and do whatever else had to be done before we left.

The Limo's were ordered; Anthony, Paul, Tony, and I were going in one Limo. Tammy's family went in another Limo. Then Michael, Lisa, Mario, and Joey, were going in the other Limo. We were all to meet at the airport.

Our granddaughters were just as thrilled as they could be. They were going to Maui with their Papa, and the whole family.

Sunday morning the day before we were to leave, I noticed Tony's appetite had already started to fail, and he seemed to not be feeling all that great. I also noticed that he hadn't moved his bowels for a few days, and he was bloated. He'd try, but he just couldn't go; getting very frustrated, and upset. All his life he that problem; he had tried suppositories, and that did absolutely nothing. When Tony tried to go, and I wiped him, I could feel the stool was right there; it just wouldn't or couldn't come out. Tony said, "Call Anthony; have him pick-up a Fleet enema, and bring it here." Which Anthony immediately did! As soon as he brought the Fleet, I immediately gave it to Tony. Tony had been saying, "Do something."

I responded helplessly, "What do you want me to do, I'm not a doctor." I was getting so nervous; frustrated, feeling totally incompetent, and losing my patience but, I didn't know what to do either! Poor Tony! He couldn't help that he was in such agony.

We were all upstairs in the bedroom, Tony, Anthony, and I. Tony lying across the end of the bed on a towel, in absolute torture, with me trying to console him, telling him to relax, and let the fleet work. It was noon by then or there about. I had been going back and forth to the bathroom with Tony all morning since he'd gotten up. All along thinking I've got to do, something! Praying for answers; to a nerve racking situation, and what could be done? We were leaving for Maui in the morning. OR WERE WE? Tony was back and forth to the bathroom with the enema, but the fleet didn't break-up the stool either. Tony was saying, "Take me to the hospital to have it dug out." Petrified that if I did take him to the hospital he'd never leave! I finally got the bedpan, plastic bed pad, and a plastic spoon, sterilized it with hot water, and put rubber gloves on. Put Tony on his side at the edge of the bed, and started digging the stool out myself. Being very cautious not to hurt him; all the while Anthony was watching in horror, retching the whole time. He couldn't believe what was happening, "What are you doing? How could you do that, I could never do that!"

"You just do what you have to do, when you need to do it". He insisted he'd never do that; "I would have taken him to the hospital before I'd do that."

"I'm not exactly thrilled about it myself." I have to admit; I was scared to death I would hurt Tony, I could plainly see, and feel the stool, was too large, and hard he would never have passed it without help! Shaking, sweating with fear, all the while Anthony still retching, but, it worked!

Once the passage was cleared, and that rock was out of the way. My poor husband was relieved, and Anthony helped him to the bathroom. Tony was totally drained, and relieved by that time, and so was I. After Tony rested awhile, I continued with getting him showered, and all cleaned up for the next morning. He'd be showered all I had to do; was to freshen, and dress him. We'd be up very early, and I didn't want to take him out in the cold just after a shower.

After we were done with the shower, we went downstairs, and I made him something to eat. Tony did eat better after that. I thought, Ah! Huh! That's why he wasn't eating, that good. Tony had been blocked up and it was nothing other than that.

I checked with all our children, they were all finishing up getting ready. Everything; and everyone was on schedule. We'd be seeing them at the airport, bright and early the next morning.

We went by Anthony and Paul later that night for dinner. We decided to just order pizza so Anthony didn't have to cook either. He was tired, and had a stressful day, that day too. We ate the pizza then came right back home. We all had to be up early the next morning about four-thirty. I wanted Tony to get a good night sleep before we left for the long, grueling trip.

I finished checking all my notes to make sure I hadn't forgotten anything. All the pills, extra prescriptions, extra panty liners, walker, urinal, tote bag, wheelchair, everything was in order, and ready. I brought the suitcases down, and then took my shower. All our clothes were laid out for the next morning. All we had to do was get dressed with warm clothes, which could be easily removed, so we could put shorts on when we were on our lay-over in Arizona. When you land in Maui it's really hot. I had everything all ready to go. Then I set the clock, and turned in. I was extremely exhausted by then. However, I wasn't able to sleep really. I was worried that I'd forgotten something important, as I rolled the list over and over in my mind.

The next morning was hectic as I expected it to be, trying to get both of us ready. I had to be sure Tony ate something, so when he took his pills, it wasn't on an empty stomach. That way he wouldn't get an upset stomach. Feat accomplished, allowed plenty of time in case some sort of problem occurred, but it didn't. Thank God!

Tony actually had time to sit, and relax before Anthony and Paul got there with the Limo. That worked out wonderfully; he didn't get anxious over rushing.

When Anthony and Paul arrived, they helped get the luggage and wheelchair, all in the Limo. Then they helped Tony with his coat; and helped him to the Limo with the walker.

So far so good! We were on our way to, MAUI———. Ya Hoo!

"Our Paradise"

*A*ll our children were already at the airport. When we got there, they came to greet us. We put Tony in the wheelchair, and hooked the walker on the back of it, which worked out perfect; we didn't have to carry it. We were all excited, and saddened at the same time, but all of us had our smiley faces on. The twins still half asleep, not really knowing what was going on, were so excited. I thought they'd just bust with enthusiasm.

My insides were twirling I was still a nervous wreck, and scared to death. My patients were 'Nil,' by then. All the stress was finally catching up to me, and taking a toll, but I was also thrilled, and excited that Tony was going to make it to Maui. After that long haul, and working so hard for that day, Tony was absolutely, thrilled, beyond, imagination!

The flight went smoothly with our children and granddaughters taking turns sitting with their (Dad, Papa), making their trip more an enjoyable trip for all. Of course, the boys helped Tony to the bathroom when needed. We had gotten bulk head seats, so Tony would have plenty of room to stretch his legs, and that helped immensely. Michael was taking pictures and movies on the plane of everyone. After the take off Michael came up to us and asked, where are we were going? "To paradise!"

"Where?"

"Heaven," to me it was the closest place to heaven.

I think our children sensed that; I was burned out, and frazzled. So they relieved me as much as possible, taking care of their dad.

The lay-over in Arizona worked out too, Anthony took his dad to the bathroom to take his sweatpants off, and put shorts on him, while there. Then they came back to the bar, and Tony ordered a cocktail. Then we were all off again. Next stop "MAUI."

We arrived in Maui about two in the afternoon Hawaii Time, which was about seven p.m. our time back home. It had already been a long day for Tony. We had been up since three thirty that morning, and going on sixteen hours by then. Anthony, Tammy, Michael and I went for the cars, while the rest got the luggage lined up. God knows we had enough. The mound was unbelievable for twelve of us. We usually had one get the luggage, while the other went for the car when we traveled, to save time, instead of waiting for the luggage, then lugging the luggage on the shuttle to get the rental car. We've found that way to be much easier and faster, plus—no lugging involved.

After we got the cars, everyone loaded their cars with their luggage. We'd made it to 'MAUI!' YIPPEE! Finally at last; and were on our way to our condos. We made a stop at K-Mart to pick up a lawn chair for Tony's shower, but they were all too big to fit in the tub. "We'll check at the other stores later. It's not an emergency right at this moment," and we left.

The drive is just breath-taking on the way to the condo. I said to Tony, "Did you ever think you'd get back here."

"No", he was happy to be back once again. I asked him if he was okay.

"Yes, just tired". He had been in a sitting position all those hours, and I could see he was fatigued and wanted to lie down.

I was following Anthony and Paul, as we drove directly to the condo. We decided to shop later Tony needed to lie down, and rest. The sooner the better! Tony had been a good sport, and hadn't complained 'once'!

When we arrived at the condo; Anthony went to get the key, as I drove around to get Tony inside. Anthony and Paul helped me get him inside so he could lie on the couch. Anthony and Paul then unloaded our luggage. Tony was happy to stretch out flat, while we organized the luggage and got settled in.

The rest of the tribe hadn't arrived yet; I couldn't imagine where they were. I started to get worried when they finally pulled up. They had stopped to look at the ocean at the look-out point, and had gotten to see some whales. They were all so excited to have seen whales in the ocean, with their own eyes. A Hawaiian lady was there, and she had made the twins an insect made from palm. They were thrilled beyond belief. Then they all dispersed to their own rooms, to get them-selves settled, and organized.

There's was a great fresh fish restaurant right next door to the condo, and that's where we were going for dinner that night. That's where we usually went when we got in. It was so convenient. Just a jaunt across the grass, and we'd be there. We were so pooped when we finally arrived, after getting settled it couldn't be more convenient. There's no pressure of where to go for dinner, and we love it there. We'd even become friends with the proprietor; and looked forward to seeing her every year. We'd planned to meet about seven for an early dinner.

When Anthony, Paul, Tony and I were ready we went right over to the restaurant to wait for everybody else to arrive. We ordered drinks, and they started to arrive shortly after us. It was a memories moment, and lots of pictures were taken. Our dinner was scrumptious as expected, and our vacation was off to a marvelous start. We were all exhausted. Especially after eating, we decided to call it a night, and turn-in. We were planning on getting up early the next morning to see and do all that we had planned.

I was watching Tony like a hawk; as far as going to the bathroom, not wanting him to get bound up ever, AGAIN!

Anthony solved the problem for Tony's bath. He bought a baby pool; put the Lanai lawn chair in the center, sat Tony on it, bathed, and rinsed him off. Just as if he was in the shower. It actually worked out better; Tony didn't have to step over the tub ledge. Where there's a will, there's a way.

Even though our intentions were to get up early, we slept in the next morning. Later than expected, we were just pooped. Once I opened the blinds, our children started strolling in. They had been up early; some as early as five that morning, wanting to see the sun rise. Michael and Lisa had decided they were going to make breakfast for the whole clan. They had already gone to the store and had everything set-to go. We on the other hand, didn't have a thing yet, so that worked out to be wonderful. I thought that was a very thoughtful gesture to go to all that work for us.

I freshened Tony; then myself, and went to their condo two doors down for breakfast. It was awesome, they had coffee, juice, eggs, bacon, sausage, toast, pancakes, fresh fruit and fried potatoes. It was quite the feast if you couldn't find anything you liked there, you just didn't want to eat or weren't hungry. I was quite impressed that they had done all that work, and planned it on their own, and had done a great job to boot. We all had breakfast then went to Lahaina to show the twins the banyan tree that was a block square—as planned for that first full day—.

When we got to Lahaina, we parked in the parking lot that was across from the ice cream parlor. The first thing they all did was get some homemade ice-cream cones, which were delicious. Then we continued our walk across the street to the banyan tree. The twins were amazed seeing the tree that is a block square, and they had a ball climbing all over it like monkeys. Then we walked around the town of Lahaina, and on to the pier. Where we saw the biggest huge sailfish that someone had caught, we took pictures of it with the twins standing next to it. Then we continued on to some historical sites; went in and out of the unique shops as we strolled along Front St. We had taken the wheelchair for Tony; it would have been too much walking for him, and we took turns pushing him. It was a joyful start. Before going back to the car we took the twins to see the baby pot belly pigs, and exotic birds at a garden shop; which also happened to be right across the street from where we parked. The twins both wanted to take a baby pig home; that was until they each got to hold a baby pig, and they squealed incessantly the entire time they had them in their arms. They didn't hold them for long, and that changed their minds, and cured them real quick. They wanted no part of squealing pigs after that—.

We were all tired after all the walking, and went back to the condo. It had gotten hotter, and the twins wanted to swim, the rest of us wanted to relax, we were still exhausted.

At the pool, we tried to convince Tony to get in the pool, but he didn't want to. I told him he could play with the twins, but he insisted it just wasn't the same. I felt so bad for him, wondering; 'what' was going through his mind? For lunch we bought everybody hamburgers from Mc Donald's. We were trying to save our children as much money as possible. They had spent a large amount of money just getting there; to spend time with their dad. I greatly appreciated their thoughtfulness; generosity, and loss of work.

Our children; never ceased to amaze me, with all their help, support, and now the trip. That meant loads to us, showing their dad just how much he meant to them. THE WORLD! To each of them in a different way—; I'm so proud, and honored to have them as our children. We must have done something right, somewhere, raising them.

The next day we had planned to go on a whale watch tour. We saw more whales on that tour than we'd ever seen before. There had been two pods, which had several whales in each with their babies. Our children were all excited, and they were taking pictures like crazy. A day, I'm sure, they'll never forget. It truly was exciting, and a beautiful, sunny day to boot. With the ocean just glistening and gleaming, in the most vibrant turquoise blue you've ever seen. It couldn't have been better. Tony got tired and hot, so we had to bring him inside the boat for a while, but he enjoyed seeing the twins excited and enjoying themselves.

Then we went back to the condo to rest, and got cleaned up for the evening. We were going back to Lahaina for dinner.

When we were rested and ready, we all met by our cars and followed each other to Lahaina. Before dinner we walked around, going in and out of the little shops. On the famous Front St., Tony and the twins took pictures with the exotic colorful parrots, all around them. We could buy the pictures the next day, if we liked the way they came out. The twins got a kick out of that; they'd never seen or done anything like that before. Afterward we went to have dinner.

The next day we had planed to go to Whalers Village Shopping Center, and then to have lunch on the beach. But first, we stopped at the airport up the hill from the condo. That was the airport up in the side of the mountain that Tony and I had flown into back when we bought our first week of time-sharing. The time-share company had flown us in to view the unit from Oahu. The view up there is just spectacular. You actually feel like your standing on the edge of a pie. As you stand there and look from left to right all you see is ocean all the way around you. It's the most wonderful, free feeling; breath-taking sight you could ever imagine. I wanted our children to see that site, because unless someone took you up there you'd never know what you were missing. Then we went to the Westin to see that hotel. It's a beautiful hotel, and the grounds have all the tropical ambiance of Hawaii. Tropical birds in the open air, Chinese fish, and swans' swimming in the ponds—it's just gorgeous. The pool has waterfalls, slides, and coves; it's a beautiful hotel to see. All the hotels are spectacular in Hawaii, one prettier than the other. We sat by the pool; so the twins could swim for a while, but they shagged us. We continued on our way, to the little restaurant just off the beach that we intended to eat at. We could see the ocean while we were eating. We watched people frolic in the ocean, and children playing in the sand. Tony was not eating a lot, and I was getting very nervous about that. I coaxed Tony to eat as much as I could get down him. His strength was holding up though, Thank God! We had let Tony walk when it wasn't a long distance, to help keep his strength up.

We had planned a big dinner for the next evening at another of our favorite restaurants. We eat there every time we go to Maui. It's on a bay, and the view is absolutely spectacular. The food was delicious too; in fact, I don't think you could get a bad meal in Hawaii. Our whole family was going for dinner that night. We had made reservations for seven that evening. We all got gussied up for that special dinner. Everyone; looked so nice, they'd all put in an extra effort to look their best. We all ordered drinks, kiddy cocktails for the twins, and then made toasts. My favorite toast, that I always use, is health, wealth, and happiness. Others toasted to a great vacation, as we clanged our glasses with each other. I got up to have a cigarette out on the deck. As I stood by the railing smoking, I started crying, when the boys came to join me to have a cigarette. They were at a loss for words, and just didn't know what to say to me. What was there to say? No words could make the position we were all in any better, None! I went through all the memories I held in my mind; that Tony and I had shared there at that restaurant. I didn't know if we'd have any more after that year? I felt the agonizing, emotional pain, and sadness building like a volcano, and I knew I had to compose myself and go back to the table as cheerful and bubbly as I could. I wiped my tears, put-on my cheery smile, and returned to the table with an aching heart.

Tony, on the other hand, was delighted beyond. He was so happy seeming without a care in the world. He was out to dinner with his whole family, and he was as proud as a peacock. I said, to him, "Look around you we are responsible for all of this." And we both chuckled; as we looked around the table, at all our children. Just then; a Hawaiian girl came around selling flower leis; Tony bought one for all the girls, Lisa, Tammy, I, and the twins. We each chose the one we liked the most, and Tony placed them on our necks. It was the most touching moment. One we'll never forget! Mario then bought his father; a Lei and placed it on his neck. Pictures were flashing like crazy. There were so many pictures being taken, Tony said, "I feel like a movie star."

"You are a movie star, you're my movie star." He looked great all dressed up! Happy—he really looked totally healthy. No one would have ever guessed how sick he was, I wasn't even convinced. I again wondered if the doctors knew what they were talking about. Hoping against hope and praying the doctors were wrong. I prayed silently and secretly. Constantly! It was a memorable; wonderful evening that everyone thoroughly enjoyed, that whole evening.

The next day was a lazy day; we just went across the street to the beach to watch all our children play in the ocean and sand. As they splashed each other, and buried each other in the sand, they were having an absolute ball, enjoying the beautiful Maui weather and gorgeous view.

The next day we planned to go for breakfast across the street to yet another favorite restaurant. Tony had gone there many times for coffee; to read the Maui paper on lazy mornings. We ordered our breakfast as we chatted about what we had done, and what our children were planning to do next. When breakfast came, Tony again ate very little; so our granddaughters tried to coax him, by feeding him, a little at a time. It was a precious sight; to see them feeding their Papa. Wiping his mouth as they fed him; telling him, "Come on Papa, you've got to eat. "Try to eat just a tiny bit more," Taking good care of him; like two little nurses. He did eat a bit more for them; but not much.

I had planned a barbecue for dinner that evening by the pool. I had brought Italian Sausage from home, and Tammy and I went to the grocery store to by the rest of the trimmings.

The guys were going deep sea fishing the next morning. Tony had always wanted to go deep-sea fishing, and never had. At one point we couldn't afford it; then he didn't want to go alone. I told him, "This is a chance of a lifetime to going deep-sea fishing with all his boys. Your dream, come true!"

"I don't want to go unless Anthony goes." Anthony was no more interested in deep-sea fishing than the man on the moon. But, because his dad wanted him to go, he went. They had to be up and at the boat by four in the morning. I was worried about Tony; but Anthony was going to be there, knowing he'd watch out for him, I tried not to worry, and hoped they'd have a great time.

While the guys were fishing, us girls and the twins were going to spend our day going out for breakfast, and then shopping. We planned to be back by the time the guys got back, so if they wanted to do anything afterward, we'd be back. I took them to a quaint favorite place of Tony and I, that we'd enjoyed many times, called the Gazebo. Another hidden place you'd never find, unless someone took you there. It's a hidden treasure, and they loved it. The food is exceptional, and again, the view is fabulous. I don't think there's a place in Maui where the view isn't beautiful no matter where you are. After breakfast, we went to Whalers Village shopping. I took the twins to the Whale Museum in the mall, and they loved it. They learned all about the whales they had seen on the whale watching tour. There was a gigantic sand sculpture in the middle of the outside mall. The twins were mesmerized watching the sculptor work on his masterpiece. They thought he was 'awesome' were the twins, words. He was building a sculpture of the deep sea, making it look very realistic. He was extremely talented, and the twins were in awe. We had a fun day, but I couldn't wait to get back to the condo. Tony was on my mind constantly, and I couldn't relax. When we got back to the condo; I immediately noticed that the guys were back already. I couldn't believe they were back. I got concerned and upset as I pulled into the parking lot, wondering what happened. Something must have happened! I couldn't get in the condo fast enough to see if Tony was all right. He was in one piece, but had gotten sick on the boat. The water was rough way out, in the middle of the ocean. He couldn't tolerate all the bouncing around, plus he had bumped his head coming out of the bathroom, due to all the turbulence. Tony had spent most of that trip in the cabin, lying down. He was really sick and sore from all the bouncing. I felt bad about pushing him to go. The turbulence of the ocean had never even entered my mind. Naturally they never caught a thing; the whole trip was a bust and a horribly bad idea. That boat trip had really wrecked Tony; he rested most of the rest of that day.

The high-light for the next night was going to a Luau, Michael, Lisa, Mario, Tammy, Mike, Tony, the twins and I we're going. Anthony and Paul weren't interested in going. Tony had been in bed most of the day. He'd really gotten banged up on the boat, and ached all over. By evening, he said, "I don't want to go to the Luau."

"The twins are looking forward to you going,"

"Go without me."

"I'd never do that."

He finally said, after much coaxing, "I'll go," but, I could see from the look on his face he wasn't himself. He was going to be congenial!

Before we left for the Luau, Michael insisted he had to take pictures, since we were all dressed up. We were already running late and I was nervous. Tony wasn't feeling that good and I didn't want him to get upset or have to rush once we got there. But Michael wanted that family picture, and had us moving this way and that way, until he had the perfect family picture he was satisfied with.

Once we arrived at the Luau; the twins really enjoyed themselves, seeing Hawaiian's that were selling hand crafted Hawaiian gifts, the twins bought their Papa what they were told was a sacred bracelet. Tony was touched by the twin's thoughtfulness; and wore the bracelet proudly, from that day on. Everyone seemed to enjoy seeing the roasted pig; and the ceremony of removing the pig from the ground, after it was cooked. Then the Hawaiian's cut it up and served it on the buffet; along with all the traditional Hawaiian trimmings. After dinner; we enjoyed the Luau, with all the gracious traditional dances and the colorful gorgeous costumes. It was absolutely beautiful under the moonlight by the ocean. The twins were all over their Papa, hanging on him like glue, and he loved every minute of it. But, I could see by his eyes he wasn't feeling well; 'At All'! Afterward, we went straight back to the condo and I got Tony in bed as fast as I could, so he could relax.

The next day we went to another hotel for the day. First, we stopped for lunch on the beach again. Then we continued our way to the hotel to lie around by the pool, and just relaxed, most of the day. We stayed there until they did the horn blowing, and torch lighting presentation that they did at dusk nightly. Afterward they had a Hula show; which the twins participated in; once again, pictures flashed like crazy, Tony was really enjoying seeing, the twins so happy, and having so much fun. We all were enjoying seeing them, just having a ball. We went back to the condo after the shows; I was making dinner for all of us that night

The menu was linguine and clams for dinner that evening. That's one of the twin's favorite meals. Our children only had one more, full day; before they'd be leaving. The time had just flown by. They wanted me to cook in Tammy and Mike's condo; it was bigger than the rest of ours. Tony had sent the boys to get beer for that night's dinner. We hadn't been up there before, so that was going to be fun. We'd have a lot more room up there. Anthony took care of Tony while I went up, to cook. Everyone started arriving just as I finished. They seemed to really enjoy the home cooked meal, and they all ate well. Tony even ate fairly well that night; even though his appetite had really decreased, the last few days. I'd make or buy whatever he had a taste for; to get him to eat, Popsicle, Jell-O, pudding, fresh fruit, ice cream, insure, anything to temp his taste buds. He walked to Tammy's condo; upstairs from ours; first taking the elevator to her floor, then walked the rest of the way with the walker, and Anthony's guidance. It was quite a distance; Tony was proud of his accomplishment, and we were thrilled for him. After dinner we all disbursed to our condos, and got ready for bed.

As I was getting Tony ready for bed, he was telling me how much he had enjoyed the dinner, and being with our children. As we were talking, I told him where I was putting his change and the receipt for the beer he had bought. "I don't need the receipt I trust you with my heart." Tony said. I thought to *myself, what did he mean by that?* At that moment, I had mixed emotions, from being flattered, to loved, and trusted. On the other hand, I felt like I was deceiving him, by not being honest with him about the cancer. *Wondering if he knew. Was he testing me? What made him say that?* Not knowing what to think; nor was he telling me he knew, understood I had his best interest at heart? I felt good and bad at the same time. I was also feeling depressed, over our children leaving. I didn't know what I was going to be facing after that, and I was panicky.

The next day our children were packing, getting ready to leave, and trying to fit all their goodies they had bought in their suitcases. We were going to a casual, great hamburger place that we all loved, for their last night. We went to Lahaina and walked around before going to dinner. We had the wheelchair for Tony, so it was pleasant and comfortable for him. After we shopped around we went to get the hamburgers. As we ate, we talked about the next morning, discussing what time they should leave to get to the airport on time. I told them, I was going to make breakfast for them in the morning so they didn't need to worry about stopping to eat. When we were done eating, we left and looked in the windows, and shopped some as we walked back to our cars. When we got back to our condos, I told our children we'd see them in the morning.

The next morning I made biscuits, coffee, fresh fruit, juice, and soft-boiled eggs. The twins love biscuits; knowing they would eat a good breakfast before leaving, on their long journey home. I knew emotions were going to be at their peak; tense—and unhappy— leaving their father behind—. I told them, I'd have breakfast ready after they packed up their cars and checked out, so after breakfast they could just leave right away, and be on their way. I was trying to make it as easy as I could for them. I knew it was going to be hard, leaving us there.

That morning breakfast went as planned. The tension was as high as I as I thought it would be. Everyone was getting on each other's nerves. The stress was extremely at its peak for every one of us. They did, nonetheless, enjoy the breakfast. They all ate well, but you could just feel the tension in the air; it was as thick as tar. It was also very difficult and heart wrenching for me. I tried to hide my feelings as much as possible for our children's sake. I didn't want Tony to get the feeling of how serious and hard it was for the rest of us

When it was time for us to say our, "Good-byes," we wished them a safe trip home; and to be careful driving to the airport, take your time. It was a dreadful site to see each of them saying good-bye to their dad. They didn't like leaving him one bit! They pulled themselves away one by one, each with hidden tears in their eyes—as they left. It took every morsel of courage and oomph I had to hold back my tears. As they were leaving I said, "We'll see you in a couple of weeks, call us when you get home so we know you got back safely."

I had decided to make a scrapbook of Maui, with all the places we had gone to through the years. Restaurants we'd eaten at, things we had done, while there. When we shopped I looked for a Tapas (a Hawaiian craft) Scrap Book I kept looking every time we went out until I found one at the right price. After I finally found one, I started my project right away.

Knowing I was going to be in the condo more now that our children were gone, which was fine. I just wanted something to keep me busy in between taking care of Tony, and I enjoyed doing things like that. I started looking through brochures, magazines, and anything I could find pertaining to Maui, that I thought would be appropriate, cutting articles out, and putting them in the album. I kept busy with that during the day after Anthony and Paul left. I was content just being in Maui with Tony doing little things. I didn't even mind being in the room; I kept busy playing solitaire, or working word search puzzles, while Tony watched TV.

Our children called when they got back home. They had a lay-over in Oahu for a couple of hours, so it had been a long haul for them. They were very tired by the time they eventually got home. I told them I hoped that we didn't have any problems getting home. That was all we'd need.

Anthony stayed with his dad one day for awhile, and I ran to see my Hawaiian friends I'd made over the years. I asked them to pray for Tony. They had prayed for him the last time we were there. That was after his second lung surgery; two years prior. We needed all the prayers we could get, so we prayed together. She prayed that God do what was best for Tony, since we were only here on borrowed time anyway. She preyed to let God's will be done. I was a little upset by that prayer, because I wanted her to pray for Tony to get better, and be healed. However, I thought a prayer was a prayer and appreciated their kindness.

Anthony and Paul were interested in purchasing another week of time-sharing at the condo complex we already owned at. I thought if we got a good deal, Tony and I would buy another week too. We had looked at the new condos across the street, and the prices were astronomical, we loved where we stayed so we were investigating our options. Tony said, "If I was well; it would be a good idea but, I don't think it's a good time for us to be buying, at this time." Anthony, and Paul did find a time-share resale where we owned, and we each decided to put in a low bid. If we got it good, if not, nothing was lost except our time. We had the agent come to the condo to fill out the contracts. When he saw Tony, I explained that he was very ill. "I'm a minister, and I'll pray for him Sunday at mass," he said.

We had done something of some sort each and everyday, since our children left. Whether it was going out to breakfast, lunch, dinner, or shopping just to get Tony out of the condo. Anthony had rented an electric recliner lift chair for his dad. Tony seemed weaker; and having a hard time getting up from the chair in the condo. Anthony felt he'd be more comfortable in that recliner, and he was. Plus, it was easier for him to get in and out of it. Tony wasn't doing well at all. He was eating less; and I was getting more nervous and anxious by the minute. It seemed ever since the boat trip he wasn't the same. He seemed to be getting weaker and weaker! I noticed one day; when Anthony was helping his dad to the couch after coming back from the bathroom that he was getting frail. I said to Tony, "Look at you, you're getting too skinny, you've got to eat."

"That's how people look when they have cancer Mar," Tony replied. I was speechless; I didn't know what to say to him without lying. I wanted to just scream and cry, but I ignored the comment, and didn't say a word. He'd been taking pain pills every now and then since the boat trip; driving myself nuts trying to figure out if it was soreness from bouncing around the boat, or the cancer giving him the pain? Hoping it was the boat trip; 'Not Cancer'! Preferring to believe it was the boat trip.

I called Dr. Bane from Maui to tell her how Tony was doing; and explain that he was only taking a half a Vicodin, but he was sleeping a lot. The nurse explained that the liver purifies everything, and when it's working slowly it doesn't process as fast and the effects of pills last longer. That explained a lot, because Tony was on a lot of other pills. Ahha! That's why he was so groggy.

About a week after our children left, we decided to take a ride around the head of the island for something to do. It's a beautiful drive with breathtaking views, and it was a gorgeous, sunny day to do that. We put Tony in the convertible, and set pillows all around him, so he'd be comfy for the ride. And off we went. We had just gotten to the first look-out when, Tony said, "Take me back."

"We just left, what's wrong,"

"I'm in pain. Take me back I want to lay down," so we turned around, and went back. *My mind was going haywire again, what was happening? Was Tony in that much pain? Or was he just scared to be too far from the condo? Or was he afraid to be in the car for that long ride.* Finally I asked, "Are you afraid to take the long ride?"

"Yes, because I'm already getting uncomfortable." When we got back, he laid on the couch, and he felt better. I told Anthony and Paul to go for the ride them selves; we'll be fine, dad's just going to rest, I'll keep busy with my scrap-book. I was stressed, and terrified over what was happening to Tony. And I was worrying about how we were going to get Tony back home, with the long flight.

Our children called everyday so they could talk to their dad, and I'd give them the update on how he was doing. He seemed to have gotten worse since they left. He was very weak, he couldn't even walk with the walker himself anymore, he was that weak. We now had to use the wheelchair to move him around. When I talked to Tammy about the middle of that week, I asked her to call the American Cancer Society to find out about getting a hospital bed because; by the time we got home he was definitely going to need one. He had gotten that bad, that fast! He would never make it back and forth upstairs anymore, even with the stair lift. It was absolutely killing me to have to consider doing that. I knew that was his biggest fear, but I couldn't see any other way around it. I had been racking my brain trying to figure another way, but there just wasn't one. I had to have a hospital bed there for when we got home. Tammy was going to take care of checking, get the information, and call me back.

Later that day, she called back saying, "The lady at the Cancer Society said, "You can get hospice in Maui, you should look into it." I got terrified when she said that. Did she think we needed hospice? What made her think that? He still wasn't taking very much pain medicine only half a Vicodin every three to four hours, if that. I did have all kinds of pain medicine if he needed it, even liquid morphine if the pain should get severe. But he wasn't having severe pain, why would she even suggest hospice, he was just weak that's all.

However, Tony had in fact gone from walking with the walker independently, to walking with the walker with help, to barely walking, to the wheelchair in a matter of days. Just that quick!

Anthony had told Tony, anytime you want to go home dad just say the word, and well leave, but Tony wanted to stay.

Tony was hardly eating, and had said to me when I'd nag him about not eating. "Why don't you take me to the hospital, what are you waiting for. They'll force-feed me, like the doctor said."

"I don't want to do that, because they'll put you through all kinds of tests, and I don't want you to go through that turmoil," I said. However, the real reason was, that I was petrified they'd tell him the cancer was back or worse yet; I'd never get him back out of the hospital—. Knowing they'd drug him up, because of the cancer, and that would be that. I'd never bring Tony home again. That would have been awful. However under normal circumstances, I would have had Tony at the hospital before you could say scat. I would have taken him immediately; he wouldn't have had to ask. Which I'm sure he figured out. He knew me like a book after forty-three years of marriage.

I was protecting him, and he was protecting me! "I'm dying." he said, on another occasion. I ignored that comment too. Thinking *is he trying to feel me out.* I didn't know how to respond. I was at a loss for words, so I said, "Nothing." Under normal circumstances, I would have corrected him and been Adamant about that comment.

After our children went home, we asked Tony if he'd like to see the Hawaiian Play Ulahlena. "Sure." So we made reservations to see it. I made sure they knew we had a wheelchair and they told us it wouldn't be a problem, they would help us bring Tony to his seat. We were going to see the play that evening. Later in the day, I asked Tony if he still wanted to go, "Yes." Even though he was getting weaker; we still took him out to do things every day, at least one thing a day, whether it was breakfast, lunch, dinner, or just to walk around a mall. Of course, we used the wheelchair; we'd used the wheelchair all along, so that was no different. The difference was he couldn't walk anymore.

We went to the theatre that afternoon for the matinee. There had been a big field fire, which had closed the only highway into Lahaina. Unfortunately; some of the actors couldn't get to the playhouse, so the play was cancelled for the matinee. We were asked if we'd like to attend the evening play. We discussed the option, and decided we would. We went to have dinner to kill some time. Then we'd go back for the evening show, instead of going back to the condo, only to return in the traffic. We had; a difficult time getting there in the first place, what normally, took ten minutes, took forever. But now, knew why the traffic was backed up both ways, and made the decision to stay. We wouldn't have been able to get back to the condo anyway. We walked across the street to Ruth Chis Steak House for dinner. Tony loved it there; steaks are great, that being his favorite meat, the decision was easy. We ordered some appetizers; while we were waiting for them to come, I excused myself.

Earlier that day, Tony and I had discussed getting Anthony a Maui Monkey. You could get the Maui Monkey dressed up like different characters. Naturally, we had one made like a hairdresser for Anthony. He had been so wonderful to both of us; we wanted to give him a memorable souvenir to put on his station at work. The Maui Monkey is supposed to be a Lucky Monkey; and we thought it was appropriate, and a cute idea. He'd always have the Maui Monkey to remind him how much we loved and appreciated him. I had called and ordered the monkey for him that day, and the owner was going to deliver it to the condo for me. She knew Tony was sick, as I'd been there a few days earlier with the twins. We had also ordered each of the twins one dressed as surfers, to give them when we got back. Anthony thought they were cute, which made the decision to get him one easy. I ran to the store; it was just around the corner, to pick it up, and rushed back as soon as I could, hoping Anthony didn't get suspicious about where, I disappeared too. The monkey was ready when I got there. It ended up working out for both of us, she didn't have to deliver it, and I could give it to Tony at dinner. When I got back to the restaurant they were starting to eat appetizers. I handed Anthony the bag.

"What's this?"

"Open it."

He liked the monkey, and thought it was cute, I asked him what he preferred pants or shorts.

"I prefer shorts." so I ran right back, and she changed the pants, to shorts right away. When I brought it back to Anthony, he was pleased. It was so cute; it had on a Hawaiian shirt, shorts, and a little scissors hanging around its neck, with sunglasses. By the time I got back our dinner came. Tony, and I shared a steak, but he didn't eat much. Anthony said, "He ate some bread, and butter, and some appetizers, while you were gone," so I didn't push him. After dinner, we walked back across the street for the play. We went right in the lobby, but had to wait until the theatre doors opened, so we walked around the gift shop and took a couple of pictures as we waited. When the doors opened, we pushed Tony in and the staff literally carried Tony up in the wheelchair to our seats and held the wheelchair until Tony was in his seat. Then they took the wheelchair back down, and placed it in the hall. We all enjoyed the play; it was very unusual, about the beginning of Hawaii. I could see Tony was getting very tired. After the play was over; the staff again, helped Tony back in the Wheelchair, and down the stairs. We went right home; it had been a trying day for him.

The next morning after breakfast, we helped Tony to the recliner, so he could watch TV, and rest. He was sleeping on and off until that noon. It was Saturday, and the cleaning people were there. They cleaned around him, trying to be as quiet as they could, looking at him, then me, with saddened eyes, and turning their heads back and fourth in a saddened "no" motion. I was sitting on the couch all curled up with my legs pulled up to my chest with my arms holding them up. Just looking at Tony with tears running down my face, I whispered to them as they looked at me for answers. He's dying! He has cancer! I don't know where those words came from, or even what made me say them? I was shocked at myself. *What had made me say that? Was he dying? Why did I say that? Where did that come from? Me?*

Anthony and Paul came back around lunchtime; they had been at the beach across the street. They had taken the Walkie Talkies, in case I needed them. They asked us if we wanted to go across the street for lunch, then to the beach. I asked Tony if he wanted to go, and he said, "Yes". He'd been in the recliner sleeping for quite awhile, and needed a change of scenery.

I freshened; Tony, helped him to the wheelchair, and walked across the street to the restaurant. When the waitress came over to take our order, Tony only wanted lemonade. Anthony and Paul ordered a sandwich; Anthony and I shared his. Tony was sitting in the wheelchair, with his eyes closed, when Anthony saw him like that. He got upset and said, "I'm not going to sit here and eat with dad like that we'll; take the sandwiches back to the room. With that, Tony opened his eyes and said, "No, I'm okay". After lunch, we went to the beach, which was directly in front of the restaurant. We set Tony all up under the tree so he could see the ocean, watch the swimmers, look for whales, and enjoy the scenery. In the distance, as I saw whales breach, I'd point them out to him. You could see them from shore every once in awhile when they surfaced, and blew water through their blowholes. It was an exciting experience to behold.

As Anthony and Paul ran back to the condo for something they forgot, they shouted, "We'll be right back."

Tony and I were enjoying watching the people playing in the ocean; when all of a sudden, from nowhere, a cold wind came whipping through, blowing everything all over like crazy. All the papers and magazines we'd brought to read went every which way. And it started to downpour. There I was with all that stuff blowing around as I chased it trying to catch it, with Tony in the wheelchair—by myself—. And all the parfinalia, magazines, books, cooler, towels, tote bags, things you take with for a day at the beach. I didn't know what to do first; I started throwing things together as quickly as I could. First I threw a towel over Tony, so he didn't get a chill or wet. I threw everything on top of Tony and frantically pushed the wheelchair as fast as I could, then running with Tony to get him back inside of the condo where he'd be dry. As I was running across the street, Anthony and Paul were coming to help me. By the time we got across the street the rain stopped, as quickly as it started. Which sometimes happened in Maui; but I couldn't take the risk of that happening again. I didn't want Tony to get wet, chilled, or sick; he didn't need that, so we continued back to the condo. I'd had it by then and I was exhausted.

There was no way I was going back to the beach. Tony and I took the safe way out and went to sit out on the Lanai in the sun, to look at the ocean where we'd stay dry. We sat there until I saw Tony was getting tired of being in the wheelchair, and he wanted to go back inside. I brought him back in, and put him in the recliner to rest. He could still see the ocean from the recliner; we had rearranged the furniture that way. The one wall in the condo has all mirror, wall-to-wall, floor to ceiling. The other wall has wall-to-wall, floor to ceiling sliding doors that face the ocean. Either way Tony looked, he could see the ocean.

The next morning, I asked Tony what he wanted for breakfast, he said, "Soft boiled eggs," I was more than delighted to make them for him. Saying, I was delighted is an understatement! I was so happy—he wanted to eat. I made him toast, eggs, coffee, and Jell-O with fresh fruit. Tony amazed me with how much he ate that morning. He ate the most he'd eaten in days, and .I was thrilled! I just couldn't get over that he had eaten that well.

Everyone was calling from home to see how he was doing. His sister, Aida, called just after he finished breakfast, and I told her how great he'd eaten. I was ecstatic about him eating so well, his sister was also very pleased to hear he had eaten so well. That was very encouraging to everyone back home.

When our children called, I told them how much their dad had eaten. Everyone was so happy to hear that—he was at last eating good. Everyone was as happy as I was. That was a good sign; I just knew it, even though he was still very tired, and weak. Thinking that *if he ate well, he'd gain his strength back.*

I got everything out to work on the album, while Tony rested, and watched TV. Anthony and Paul had gone back to the beach; so Anthony could lie in the sun, he's such a sun worshiper. Tony had been sleeping a lot that day, I thought. It made me very fidgety, but he had eaten well, so I just let him rest.

I busied myself looking through magazines; books, and brochures, planning what I was going to do with the scrapbook, and how. Looking over at Tony every few minutes, to check on him—even though he'd eaten well that morning somehow, I had a very uneasy feeling I couldn't explain—.

Anthony and Paul came back a little later, Tony was still resting, when Anthony said, "I'll stay with dad a while. Why don't you get out for a while?"

"No, I'm fine, and I'm keeping busy, I don't need to go anywhere." He insisted I should take a ride to the craft fair. Ordinarily I loved to go to the craft fair.

"Just to get out for an hour, you love to walk around there. Just go for awhile," he paused, "Dad's sleeping anyway. You've been in the condo a lot, and I feel bad, so just go you don't have to stay long, just go to breakup your day."

I took his advice, and went for just about an hour. I did find some beautiful rings, and I bought them very reasonable. I had enjoyed the break, and I was delighted with my bargains.

When I got back, Anthony said, "Dad's still sleeping on and off." Something wasn't right I just felt it—. Something; was different than the days before—. I couldn't figure out; what though. I pulled up a kitchen chair next to Tony. I sat there, rubbing his arm, holding it, trying to comfort him. My heart was pounding with pain, what more could I do for him, but that? I felt so helpless, that it stirred emotions deep in my soul, even though he seemed to be comfortable, and relaxed. I told Tony about my bargains, he seemed half interested in them. I kept asking him if he had any pain.

"No."

"There's no reason for you to suffer with pain, I have medicine for that if you need it."

Tears streaming down my face, coming and going, I couldn't control them anymore. I cried silently as I sat at his side comforting him.

Tony had gone from standing up, and peeing in the bathroom independently, and peeing in the urinal at night next to the bed independently, to peeing in the panty liner within a couple of days. There are no words to express the extreme pain I felt at that moment! My emotions were in frenzy, and I was trembling all over. My whole body was just shaking; every nerve was reacting to the stress I was feeling.

When Anthony and Paul came back, I was still sitting next to Tony holding his arm, and just rubbing it. Anthony asked his dad what he wanted for dinner. Giving him a choice of; pork chops, or lamb chops, he chose lamb chops. Anthony started preparing things for dinner; I got up to, set the table, and helped him with the rest of the preparation. When it was just about ready to put on the table; I asked Tony what he wanted to drink, he said, "A beer". We put everything on the table, and brought Tony to the table in the wheelchair, to eat. He took a few big gulps of beer to start, but he seemed to be only half awake, and, not eating that much. I was feeding him, but he was hardly chewing, he was just pushing the food around his mouth. "Come on Hon; chew your food, what's wrong with you?" Then as I was feeding him he started turning his head back and forth, in a "No" gesture.

"You don't want anymore?"

"No." I insisted you've got to eat 'Something'. I gave him his pills, and water to swallow them with. Then I asked him if he wanted a Popsicle?

"Yes." After I went to get the Popsicle, as I went to give it to him, I noticed he still had the pills in his mouth.

"The pills are still in your mouth swallow them." I gave him a piece of the Popsicle I had bitten off for him. Then he started to chew the pills. He sat there with a frail face, unexplainable expression, chewing the pills. *I said, to myself he doesn't even look like Tony.* At that moment, he looked like a stranger for some reason. I said, "Tony, why are you chewing your pills? Swallow them," he didn't answer me. I quickly gave him some more Popsicle to swallow the pills with, saying to him frantically, "You've got to swallow the pills," biting off pieces of Popsicle, and putting them in his mouth, until ultimately, he swallowed the pills. I couldn't for the life of me, figure out what had made him chew the pills. He'd never done that before? I thought to myself *at least I got the pills down him.* Then Anthony helped me get his dad back in the recliner; he was dead weight, hardly helping us like he had been. I asked myself, *what's happening to him? Maybe it's just the medicine all building up in his system?* I was racking my brain trying to figure out what was going on. Tony was going to watch TV for a while, we thought—

Anthony, Paul, and I cleaned up the dinner mess, and then sat around for a while, Anthony and Paul was watching TV. I worked on my project. When Anthony said, about nine-thirty, "Lets get dad in bed, he's sleeping anyway."

"Okay, come on Hon. we're going to get you in bed, so you can rest better". We took him to bed in the wheelchair; got him settled, checked his panty liner changed it, and cleaned him up. After he was all settled I heard him calling his sister—, his aunt Sophie—, and his mom.

"Tony why are you calling them, you know were in Maui, and there not here. We'll be seeing them again in about a week or so." Then he was saying, "Ma? Ma?" As in a question I thought, *why would he ask for his mom with a question, like he was confused?* It didn't make sense. I'd heard when people are going to die they see people that have died, but his mother was alive. Saying to myself; *"Oh you're crazy, jumping to conclusions again. "* He's just so tired; plus he took his pills, he doesn't know what he's saying. When I leaned down to kiss him; I noticed he was having little trouble breathing. A thought *came into my mind, he's going to die tonight, and I immediately threw that thought out thinking, why did you think that?* It was hot; and I attributed the trouble Tony was having breathing, to the heat. I asked him, "Are you having trouble breathing?

"Yes."

"I'll put the fan on so it will blow the air around in your face, and it will give you more air.

"Okay" I turned the fan on and asked him if that helped.

"Yes"

"I'll be coming to bed shortly myself."

I went back to the dining room to clean up the I mess had all over; from cutting pictures out for the scrapbook. When Anthony and Paul said, "We're going to bed too."

After I finished cleaning the mess, I went back into the bedroom. As I was straightening up, I said to Tony "Do you love me?" I don't know why I asked that question? I didn't really have a reason; I guess I just wanted to hear it. That must have been what I needed at that moment was the only reason I could figure out. He said, "Of course," in the most normal, loudest, strongest voice, I'd heard from him in a long time. Maybe it was to convince myself, that the thought I'd had earlier was a crazy one. I couldn't believe how coherent; and alert he had been when he said, "Of Course," so strongly—. When I got into bed I hugged and held him saying, "Don't be afraid, I'm right here next to you." I fell asleep immediately. Like someone hit me in the head with a sludge hammer.

Passing

At exactly four-ten I woke up, out of a sound sleep, wide-awake. I immediately looked at Tony, he wasn't breathing I laid my ear to his chest, no sound or movement. I felt him; he was still warm all over. I was frantic! I wanted to run into the living room SCREAMING—on the top of my lungs. "YOUR FATHER DIED"—but I didn't. I'd heard somewhere, that the hearing was the last to go, plus I didn't want to shock the hell out of Anthony. I collected myself within seconds. I immediately ran into the hall and called Anthony, saying, "I think your father has expired." Poor kid, he jumped up, leaping off the bed, and came running, still half asleep, into the bedroom. He put his head on his dad's chest as I had just done, gently calling Dad,—Dad,—nothing! Paul was in the other room; up by then, asking if he should call 911. "Yes." He asked what should he say, Anthony said, "Tell them what's happened." Now Anthony and I are both hysterical, not knowing exactly what to do with ourselves, trying our dam-nest to stay calm. I was crying uncontrollably, babbling Oh My God, Oh My God, what am I going to do—what am I going to do—I was babbling like an idiot. Paul called back to us asking, "They want to know, do you want him resuscitated. Anthony looked at me, and I said, "No." Where I got the guts to say that, I don't know, other than I knew if they resuscitated Tony; and he hadn't had oxygen for any length of time, he'd have brain damage. And when Tony and I had talked about a living will, I said, "I don't want you to sign one. I'll make that decision when I'm faced with the situation." I just knew from our conversations, Tony wouldn't have wanted to be resuscitated at that point. Then I fell apart, completely.

The ambulance got there within a couple of minutes. They put all the monitors on Tony; as I paced back and forth, not able to stay still. I looked into the bedroom to see what they had to say, I looked at the paramedic and he shook his head back and forth, in a, "NO" gesture. I immediately said, "I have to clean him up."

"We'll take care of that, don't worry," I had also heard that when you die, you lose all control of your bodily functions, and I wanted to make sure he was cleaned up. I was hugging Tony, and kissing him, telling him I didn't mean it was okay to die on me—when I said, "It's okay I'm right here next to you, don't be afraid." I felt Tony thought I'd given him permission to leave me, but I hadn't— that's not what I meant at all— I was just comforting him, letting him know I was there for him. I'd also heard that a person waits for permission sometimes, before they leave this earth, and I associated that with the horror I was facing—repeating it over and over, like a broken record. 'THAT'S not what I meant at all.' I went totally ballistic, then completely out of control. I was like a caged animal, pacing back and forth through the hall; to say I was beside myself is an understatement. I was absolutely; totally out of my mind not knowing where to go, or what to do. I was totally out of control. By then; a Sergeant from the Police came, and he was consoling me, holding me, talking calmly to me. Telling me; "It will be all right, just take it easy; take deep breaths, calm down." I don't even remember all he said; but I do remember him comforting me, and I did calm down, somewhat. However; I kept repeating to Tony, like he could hear me, "I didn't mean it was okay, for you to leave me," when I said, "It's okay don't be afraid I'm right here with you," as I was hugging him——. I couldn't get over the thought that Tony thought I'd given him permission to "LEAVE ME", I hadn't—!

There had to be four or five paramedics in the bedroom; and more policemen arriving. There was, I'd say, a total of seven or eight, plus the minister was on his way. I kept saying to the paramedics, No Body Bag! I didn't want Tony taken out in a body bag. They said, "We won't." I was still pacing like a caged animal back and forth, up and back. Totally out of control; the men were consoling me, holding and rocking me, patting my head, in my hysteria. I just didn't know where to go, or what to do with myself. I just plainly couldn't believe what was happening. I kept saying this can't be happening—this can't be happening—. I was stomping my feet, pounding on the chair with my hands, I just didn't know what to do with myself. I was having a tantrum. I wanted to go with Tony; I didn't want to be there. I kept saying, Oh God, Oh God, pleaseeeeeeeeeee give me the strength. Pleaseeeeeee. Dear God in heaven——. The officer said, "The Chaplain will be here shortly. When the Chaplain arrived, I asked him to please give Tony the last blessing.

I asked Anthony to call all our children; to tell them, so they could say good-bye to their dad, before they took Tony away. Anthony had his cell, so he was able to put it up to Tony's ear, as he lay lifeless in the bed. Anthony called each; and every one of our children—and they each got to say good-bye to their dad—! I kept saying, this can't be happening—. It's a nightmare—. Wake me up—. What made me wake up at four-ten, all of a sudden, wide-awake? Tony must have just expired, being he was still warm all over, when I woke up. Did God do it that way, so I wouldn't have to make the decision about life support?

It must have been, "God", he put me to sleep instantly, and woke me up at just the right time. "Another Miracle!" What were the chances of me waking up like that? Wide awake, I felt it had to be a "Miracle"

We had never gone to bed that early in Maui before, "Never", in all the years we'd gone there. Why did we all go to bed that early that night? Nor have I ever gone to sleep just like that. I always had to read, watch TV or something to fall asleep. That was very mysterious. 'Another Miracle,' In my eyes.

What had made me say what I said to Tony? It was as if someone or something took over the words I spoke. Mysteriously—

I had heard that dying people wait for permission to leave; 'Now' I had given it, without even realizing it or meaning—it wasn't okay to leave me. This couldn't be happening, I didn't mean for him to die, that it was okay why,—why,—had I said that. What made me say that?

I had thought to myself that night; that he's dying, and as quick as that thought came, that was how quick I pushed it out of my mind. I said, to myself at the time, there you go again, off the deep end. Had that been a message from God, warning me, preparing me?

I can't explain it—. It was as if something took over me—. Was that God putting words in my mouth—? How else could it be explained—?

I can only say the whole direction that was taken, was as if God was preparing me for the devastating—. Horrible—! Excruciating situation I had to deal with!

I had asked God from the beginning of Tony's illness: Not to let Tony expire in our bed at home. I knew I'd never be able to sleep in the bed again. That memory would haunt me forever—. That prayer was answered!

I didn't want Tony to expire in the hospital either; that would have been too hard to bear, hooked up to all the machines and needles, he despised, with such a cold atmosphere—. That prayer was answered!

I had prayed to God to let me get Tony to Florida—.That, prayer was answered!

I had prayed that it be as easy on him as possible, without suffering—. That prayer was answered!

I had prayed to God to let me get Tony back to Maui—that prayer was answered!

Everything I had prayed for—. Had been fulfilled! "ALL MIRACLES"

Everything seemed to be in slow motion, or I was so out of control, I really wasn't there in full body, and mind.

When the Chaplain arrived; he was consoling me, trying to calm me down. I kept repeating over and over, I didn't mean it was okay for him, to leave me I was like a crazed person.

The Sergeant of the police then said to me, "Try and calm down, I'll need some information." I explained the whole evening to him, starting with the night before, getting hysterical every once in awhile. I told him, "I don't want an autopsy done, I do not want Tony cut-up, there's no reason for it." He was a cancer patient and that's what he died from!" Explaining what our doctor had said, before we left. I explained, "She didn't even want Tony to come there, and that she said it could get rough."

At that point I got hysterical again, saying, I didn't expect him to die there though. Explaining to the sergeant that I was making plans with hospice and the cancer society for a hospital bed to be delivered at home, and now he's gone. I couldn't get very much information out without bursting into tears and getting hysterical again.

Trying desperately to stay in control; so I made the right decisions, and did the right things for Tony, and asked the right questions, I didn't know what was going to happen, or how? We weren't home, and I was frightened about all that was involved. I was asking, what we should do? What would transpire, and how?

The Sergeant said, "If you don't want an autopsy, the only way we can do that, is if your doctor agrees to sign the death certificate. "I'm sure she will."

"Would it be okay if we called her?"

"Yes, we can call right now; with the time change she'll be in the office". So he called, I was out of control again. I don't even know what she said to him, or he to her. It was just too much for me to handle.

When he got off the phone, he said, "Your doctor will sign the death certificate," there would be no problem there. He continued with, "She said, she sends her deepest condolences to the family."

He then asked for a list of the medication Tony was taking; and explained that the coroner was on a different island, and wouldn't be back until the next day. I said, "I have no idea of what to do, or how."

"The Chaplain will take you to the funeral home and help you with all the things that have to be set-up." Every one of them; had all been so sweet, kind, and consoling, I'm very grateful to them for that.

The other officer and paramedics came from the bedroom and said, "We're going to take Tony; would you like to say good-bye to him, before we take him away?"

They had Tony on the stretcher, in the hall, by the door, all cleaned with the sheet on him up to his chin. (No-body bag) He looked as if he was sleeping and at peace. I hugged him and kissed him. The paramedics said, "We're going to put the sheet over him, because it has started to rain and we want to keep the rain off of him, would that be okay?"

"Of course, Yes."

The paramedics said, "We're going to take Tony to the hospital to wait for the coroner to get there" They told me what hospital he'd be at and that they'd take good care of him.

As the Sergeant was leaving he said, "The officer will make your flight changes for you, don't worry about that either. Just let him know when you plan to return home." He then gave us his name and phone number, and told us to call him when we decided to leave, when we were ready to handle that end.

The officers left all their names and phone numbers, should we need them for anything. I thanked them all for being so helpful and kind.

Then the Chaplain called me back into the dining room to talk to us about what was to happen next. The Chaplain said, "I'll take you to the funeral home to make all the arrangements." He'd leave for about an hour, so we could get freshened up and dressed. Asking if that would be all right? Or did we think we'd need more time that would be okay too, it wasn't a problem. We said, "An hour is enough time, and will be okay."

The Chaplain said, "Bring clothes for Tony to go home in, with you to the funeral home. The funeral director will make all the arrangements. Don't worry at all, and I'll be here for you, anytime if you need me for any reason."

The Chaplain went on to explain that we could go to one of two places; it didn't make a difference to him. They both did a great job; but if it were his family member, he preferred the one that had been there the longest, that he didn't gain anything, one way or the other. We took his suggestion and went to the one that was there the longest the one he'd take his family to. He also explained the funeral director was fair, it was a family business for years, and that the prices were comparable to Chicago. He had dealt with him more than the other funeral director.

He explained that we could either send Tony home in a shipping box, or pick out a casket there. It was entirely up to us. I asked in shock, "What kind of box?"

"It would be like a wooden box with padding," he said.

Naturally, I said, "I have no intentions of sending Tony home in a box"; it was tearing me apart just talking about it.

Then the Chaplain left saying, "I'll be back in an hour to pick you up"

After he left; I was in such a dither, I didn't know what I was doing. Basically, walking around in circles, it was about six in the morning by that time

Anthony said, "We have to hurry if we were all to be ready in an hour, when the Chaplain comes back. Go get showered and dressed, then decide what to bring dad home in."

After I was showered and dressed, I asked Anthony, "What clothes should we bring to the funeral home."

"You pick them out". I didn't have a suit with us, so I picked out clothes I liked Tony in. I showed Anthony my choice.

"That will be fine. We'll have to have him changed in Chicago anyway, when he gets back home."

We were all dressed and ready when the Chaplain came back; we'd made it just in time.

We all got in the Chaplain's van. I was still crying, and very distraught. The Chaplain was very comforting and consoling; saying we had done the right thing for Tony. Most people would have just laid there and waited to die. That he had lived his life until the last minute with our help and he commended us for that.

He added that Tony had been in a beautiful place; and had died, a peaceful death! He knew how hard it was on us not being at home and all, but we had done the right thing.

I kept saying to him that I didn't mean to give him permission. That's not what I meant at all. And why had I said that, I couldn't figure it out for the life of me. My mind was reeling; the whole thing over, and over, in my mind. He suggested I ask God for help with that.

He also said, "Tony had gone from paradise to heaven". The traffic was horrendously crazy. Everyone was rushing to work that Monday morning. He then went on to explain what was going to happen next.

"I'll go past the hospital so you can actually see where Tony's being held." Which I thought was very nice and accommodating.

He then asked us if we'd like to go out to breakfast before we went to the funeral home, but we weren't hungry. Food was the last thing on my mind.

I was worried about how I would pay for the fees. I didn't have that much money with me or in my checking account, would I have to transfer funds. I didn't know how it was all going to work out; and I was frantic.

When we got to the funeral home, Anthony and I stayed outside to have a cigarette, I was practically chewing my nails by the time we got there. We were both dying to have a cigarette, but we didn't want to smoke in the Chaplain's van. With the stress we were under that had been more torment for us.

The Chaplain said, "I'll go in and let the funeral director know your here, while you smoke your cigarette."

I dreaded entering the two doors that lead into the funeral home. I was having a very hard time processing the trauma I'd been through—. Let alone further continue with it—. Not having a choice, I continued going through the motions—.

As Anthony, Paul, and I entered the funeral home, the funeral director greeted us. The very first words he spoke were to express his sympathy to us. That he understood how difficult it was for us, and he'd make the next steps as painless as he could. He had a very warm, consoling face, which helped put me; at ease, somewhat. He introduced himself to us and the Chaplain introduced us to him.

They guided us into a room that was very brightly lit by the sunlight coming through the windows that were all the way around the two walls. They offered us a cup of coffee, and we all accepted graciously. We hadn't had a morsel of anything yet; that gesture seemed to hit the spot; at that time of morning.

I was still trembling, and my mind was in a whirlwind of thoughts and fears.

The funeral director gently guided us through the procedures and options that needed to be attended to. We were still very fragile and discombobulated with the whole horror. I kept asking God for his assistance and help to get me through what I had to deal with.

The funeral director explained the procedure. After the coroner had seen Tony, and he was released, they would pick him up and bring him there, and he would prepare Tony for the journey home. That would take a couple of days, since the coroner wasn't on the island yet, and the funeral director would need a day for the preparation. He asked if we'd brought Tony's clothes, "Yes," and gave them to him.

He went on to explain that Tony wouldn't leave until Wednesday night, and he'd return home that Friday by the time everything transpired. He said, "You can come-back and view him before he leaves the funeral home Wednesday night."

He went on to explain the wooden box verses the actual coffin. I interrupted him, telling him the Chaplain had gone through that with us already. I didn't want to hear about that box again! He continued, the casket prices were the same as back home, I didn't care about that I told him adamantly, "Tony is not going home in a box."

He then gently guided us to a room full of caskets to choose from. That was a torturous awakening. As we entered the room, I got hysterical again, and so did Anthony. The director said, "Take as much time as you need, there's no hurry. I'll leave you for a few minutes. I'll just be in the other room if you have any questions." I kept chanting over and over, I don't believe this—I don't believe this—. It takes a while to over come shock. I was in fact, doing all of that in a haze. My brain was all fogged up, I was going through the motions, but I wasn't fully there.

After we somewhat composed ourselves, trying to accept what we had to do, we narrowed it down to a black casket with silver trim. It reminded me of our bedroom set at home, that Tony loved. The design on the trim reminded me of Hawaiian flowers. I thought it was very appropriate; Anthony and Paul liked it too. That was the one we chose.

The funeral director then carefully guided us through all the other procedures telling us when Tony would be ready to view. What time he'd be back at the funeral home, the flight Tony would be on, and what time he'd arrive back home.

He asked, what funeral home; back home I wanted to use, he would contact them and they would pick Tony up, and he'd arrange all those details, not to worry ourselves with that. When we got home we'd go to the funeral home and make the rest of the arrangements there.

When we were done the funeral director gave us the charges that would be incurred for all that had to be one. "You can charge the expenses," which I did, being I didn't have that much money on me.

We thanked him for his help and kindness, and left saying, "We'll see you on Wednesday afternoon." We left with the Chaplain, for our journey back to the condo. I was still babbling about my disbelief of what had transpired, and was still totally numb.

The Chaplain kept focusing on how Tony had lived life to the last minute, and that most people would choose that, if they could.

"Yes, great for him, but a nightmare for us left on earth."

He pointed out the positive again, that we had done a great deed. What a wonderful way he had transcended to the other side. In my arms; in his sleep, he went gently; I have to agree it was beautiful for Tony, if there even was such a thing.

But a trauma for us, one I didn't think I'd get through. He assured me that I would, that it would take some time.

I told Anthony, "I didn't want to leave until his dad left." I wasn't leaving Tony there in Maui alone.

We had the officer make our flight back home for Thursday. We'd all arrive around the same time that way.

The Chaplain again asked if we wanted to stop to eat something on the way back, again we declined. When we got back to the condo, we thanked the Chaplain immensely for his help and kindness. We told the Chaplain we didn't know how we would have gotten through all that, if it hadn't been for him. Which was the absolute truth; the whole group had pretty much taken us by the hand and guided us through the whole trauma. The Chaplain left saying, "If you need me, don't hesitate to call," and he gave us his card.

Now we had the dilemma of what we were going to do with ourselves, until Thursday. We'd be leaving about two that afternoon.

My son had the rental equipment picked up. I didn't want to look at it. I couldn't bare to see it there in the condo.

Anthony called house keeping to have; the sheets changed on the bed. "We'll sleep in the bedroom," Anthony said. I couldn't bare to go in there either. I kept seeing Tony lying there lifeless. It was to heart wrenching for me too deal with. It was very difficult to stay in the condo—. Period!

Then we went through the, woulda, shoulda, coulda's! Hindsight after the fact, with guilt! Talking and reliving the whole trauma of what transpired, and how, and over and over—.

I had talked to the Chaplain; about how I really felt there were, "Miracles" that had transpired throughout the past year and that evening."

I was sure of it, and how I had asked God not to have me make the decision of resuscitating off a machine. He had even answered that prayer for me. I couldn't be mad at God; he had answered every one of my prayers, including that.

We packed up all the medical things I'd had for Tony, and left them for the minister to donate to someone in need.

The phone in the condo started ringing off the wall, with all our friends giving their condolences. With me repeating insistently, that I couldn't believe it.

We called each sibling, to see how they were all doing. They were pretty much in the same place emotionally as we were. "All In Shock!" Our children couldn't wait for me to get home. We explained the procedure that would take place, the plans that were made, and when we'd be home.

We talked about the funeral plans and I asked Tammy to go to the cemetery to see what was available there. We made the luncheon reservation; and discussed all the details that needed to be done over the phone with each other, to accomplish as much as possible before I got home, since I was going to be in Maui two more days. We ordered Hawaiian flower arrangements, we felt they were appropriate. With everything we did, a part of me died, a little each time. I didn't want to be doing this or deal with it, I was falling apart.

I asked the boys to please get all the medical equipment out of the house and have the oxygen paraphernalia picked up before I got home. I didn't want to see it.

Anthony, Paul and I rode around aimlessly staying out of the condo with all the memories.

Talking about how the Hawaiian people had made a devastating situation as kind and loving as they could, under the circumstances.

I felt that if Tony had died at home; in Chicago, it would have been cold, cut, and dried. Not a loving, kind, genuine, spiritual, experience, like it was in Hawaii. I felt blessed and I was more than grateful for that.

Anthony and Paul were trying their dam nest to keep me busy, and out of the condo. To keep my mind off of reliving every detail over and over and over; it was as if my mind was stuck like a broken record that went haywire. I thought I was going crazy.

I slept on the couch that night, but didn't get much sleep. I kept going-over and over, and over, the whole scenario. Somewhere along the way, I realized that when Tony was calling Ma? Ma? He must have been calling 'my mother'. She must have been the one that came for him that would explain his talking, as if a question. Because he hadn't seen her in over twenty years; when she expired, surely, she would have been the one to come for him, she adored him.

The mind is a powerful thing—I would think why I had done this—or why hadn't I done that— or I should have done this—. Almost as if the end result would change—it was wishful thinking.

At last, it was Wednesday; we were going to get to see my husband, that afternoon. We were packing up all our things, getting ready to leave the next day.

Then we were off to the funeral home.

Viewing in Maui

$\mathcal{W}$ e stopped at a store to get roses so I could place them in the casket for Tony's journey home. I was apprehensive about entering the funeral home once we got there. I didn't know what to expect or how I'd react. The funeral home director didn't know Tony; nor did he have a picture of him to go by, so I was afraid of what I'd see, when I went in.

Anthony and Paul each held my arms as we entered the chapel, hesitantly. There was a gorgeous stained glass window of Hawaiian flowers above the casket, and the sun was brightly shining through, which seemed to make the flowers glow with life. We continued shoulder-to-shoulder step by silent step, we walked slowly up to the casket.

As I stood there looking at Tony, I was more than pleased, Tony looked healthy, actually fantastic! He looked exactly like he did before he got sick, healthy, and at peace, as if he was just sleeping—. I was in awe, and amazed that the undertaker had made him look just like his old self. "Another Miracle" had just transpired. How could the funeral director have possibly known how Tony used to look? Tony's face was full, his coloring perfect, his hair combed just the way he combed it. He couldn't have looked better. When the director asked if everything was okay, I told him, "He looks great and couldn't look more perfect." I was beyond pleased. Actually, I was amazed—. It made me feel good to see Tony look so healthy, at peace, and I felt relieved for him.

The funeral director advised us that the roses couldn't be shipped with Tony, because of agriculture regulations. He explained that if we left them with Tony, and they should check, it could cause a problem. I wasn't too happy about that, but there wasn't a thing I could do about it. I thanked the director for the wonderful job he'd done. "If you need anything at all, or have any questions, call, me."

I took off a rose bud and slipped it in Tony's jacket pocket anyway. One rose means I love you, and I was willing to take that chance. I wanted Tony to always know just how much I loved him, and wanted my love to go with him.

There was a bible and a grief book on top of the casket. When the realtor minister called us regarding the time-sharing contract; I told him, "Tony had expired," he offered his condolences, and asked me if I'd like a bible, and grief book to help, console me.

"I would love that; how thoughtful of you."

"I'll have my wife pick them up, and place them on the casket, for you. You can pick them up at the funeral home; when you go back." At that moment; I felt so blessed, and fortunate to have had all those loving people around me. He suggested; I read them on the long flight home, to help, comfort me. I thanked him; and told him how grateful I was, and that I would read them on the plane.

The next day when we were on our way to the airport, Anthony drove with me, so I wouldn't be alone, and Paul drove the other car. I was frantic about getting on the plane without Tony. How was I ever going to do that? I knew it was going to be awful and very difficult for all of us. As we drove to the airport, I mulled that around in my mind, worrying.

After we arrived at the airport, we returned the cars, checked the luggage and went to the gate. As we waited to board, I was getting fidgety and scared. I went up to the attendent and asked if we could board early. I explained that I had lost my husband in Maui, and that it was going to be difficult for us. She was very accommodating, and let us board early. It was devastating going on that plane without my best friend, and partner—. I felt like part of my body was missing—. It was Tony"—! My heart was broken and I didn't know if it could ever be repaired. Ever—!

We weren't to arrive back in Chicago until early Friday morning with the time change.

We had made plans that Anthony and I would go to the cemetery to pick out the plot, after he picked up his car.

Funeral Arrangements

Then we'd go to the funeral parlor to make the rest of the arrangements and finalize them. Then we'd view Tony again, he'd be at the funeral home by then. Our children were going to meet us at the funeral home, so they could see their dad. I had asked them to wait until I was done with all the arrangements, so we could all go in together.

By the time we got back to Chicago, we were totally exhausted, mentally, physically, and emotionally. We still had a full day ahead of us, making all the arrangements after picking out the plot. It was just horrible out, cold, damp, and raining outside that day. A gloomy, sullen, day added to the dreadfulness we had to face. The anguish was awful.

When we got to my house, Tammy and Michael were waiting for us, as we expected. Anthony and Paul went to their house, so Anthony could pick-up his car and come back to pick us up. We were all going to the cemetery, but first we had to pick out Tony's suit, shirt, tie, shoes, sox, and new underwear to bring to the funeral home, so the director could change him.

I kind of knew in my mind what I wanted Tony to wear; I'd had several days to think about it, so I gathered his clothes, numb to any feelings. I had cried non stop for days, and now that I was home, I seemed to be functioning on automatic, since I'd always picked Tony's clothes out for him.

Tammy and Michael had checked out the plots that were available, to save time and narrow the decision down. They wanted me to make the final choice. It was raining and muddy at the cemetery, making it very difficult to walk around. And being that it was so cold, with us just coming from Maui, Anthony and I were freezing. I had certain things in mind that I wanted for Tony's plot. I had a hard time deciding, plus the twins had begged Tammy to not let me put their Papa in a wall. In addition, Tony had always said he wanted to be on high ground, so the water could run-off. The plot I picked was on high ground and had a tree near by. Tony loved nature, it was perfect.

The plots I chose were in a section that was just across from, our first baby we lost forty-two years earlier. The way the plots were set up, the baby's grave faced the two plots I chose. Tony's plot would face our house; I felt that way he could look over me. That was very important to me. Across the street, in the other section, were Tony's younger brother and his uncle. I felt very comfortable, with my decision. After I'd made the decision, our children said, "That's the area we chose too." 'Another Miracle,' what were the chances; forty-two years later, finding plots, in the area right by our first baby?

After that fiasco, we went straight to the funeral home, to make all the other arrangements. There was much more than I realized that had to be done; verses, songs, speakers, Mass cards with verse and prayers, it seemed endless, I was totally incapacitated by that time. Everything was becoming a blur; I was so tired, I couldn't see straight anymore. I'd been up for almost twenty-four hours, plus I really hadn't slept much in Maui the last couple of days either.

The arrangements were all set. Tony was to be waked Sunday night with the mass and funeral on Monday. Everything was taken care of, how I got through all that I really don't know. You just do—!

After finishing the arrangements, our family went to see Tony, all together. All our children had been waiting. It was very hard on all of us. But they were also pleased that their dad looked so nice. They couldn't believe how healthy and peaceful he looked either. However, I found out later, that our children had gone in to see him earlier, while I was making the arrangements. They couldn't wait. Which worked out for the better; they were more able to control themselves when we all went in. Plus they got to spend time alone with their dad, which was extremely important to them.

All our children came back to my house afterwards. When we got back, there was a house full of people. Family, friends, and neighbors were there expressing their condolences. The food was endless with all kinds of cakes, beverages, and the works. By then, I was <u>numb</u> and <u>delirious</u> beyond my limits. My body was there; but my mind was miles away in another orbit, all by itself. I was astonished that I could be with all those people, and at the same time <u>feel</u> so alone—and separated—.

Tammy spent that night with me I slept until mid morning. When I got up; I was still very tired, I really hadn't slept well, and I had jet lag from the time difference. My mind was still whirling out of control; replaying the whole episode over, and over. I told Tammy that I wanted to go to the funeral home to see her dad, so she took me. It made me feel good; to be close to Tony; he looked so good and at peace. But I couldn't accept the fact that he was gone; he looked so good, just as though he was just sleeping. I expected him; to wake up at any moment, and take us out on the town. He looked like he was just taking a nap. (Something he often did). That's how good and healthy he looked—.

I had to get my clothes ready that I was going to wear. I had plenty of clothes, so that wasn't a problem. The problem was I really didn't give a damn about clothes—as I pulled everything out, asking Tammy if it was okay.

Wake

The next day our family met at our house, and we all went to the funeral home together. It got so crowed, so fast that I never got to leave the spot I was standing in. The funeral director was very attentive bringing me water, hard candy, collecting the cards, and he put them by my purse, he was just wonderful. The floral pieces were beautiful; one just as beautiful as the other, they were spectacular. The arrangements went all the way around the room; Tony would have just loved them. He would have been as pleased as I, and his buttons would have been popping with pride.

During the wake Mario was having trouble with his eye, all that day. By evening, he couldn't see out of it, keep it open, and was in pain. It was driving him crazy. When Mario couldn't stand the pain any longer, my son-in-law Mike took him to the emergency room. When he returned, he told us he had another eye ulcer, which is caused from stress. God knows he was under tremendous stress. What could possibly have more stress; than losing your father? They gave him medication to numb and heal it. He'd had an eye ulcer before so I knew the medicine would help. But he was so frustrated and angry that he had to leave his father's wake, which really upset him even more.

People kept coming till the last minute, it was non-stop. I couldn't believe all the people that came. At the end of the evening; before the priest said the prayer, the twins had written a speech they wanted to give about their Papa. It was the most; heart wrenching speech, there wasn't a dry eye, in the funeral home.

Afterward, a lot of family came back, to the house. They prepared the food that was brought. Again, I was in orbit—all alone—with a house full of people—. During that night, I got a premonition to play the song, 'My Way' by Frank Sinatra (Tony's favorite song and singer) as the guests passed Tony for the last time. I told our children about my thoughts, and asked them what they thought. They agreed it was a perfect closing for their dad. Where that thought came from I couldn't tell you, except I felt Tony had done it his way—. I felt he would have liked it, and it couldn't have been more appropriate. After we ate, the family didn't stay too late. We all had to be back at the funeral home early the next morning for the mass. Tammy spent the night with me again.

Funeral

*E*veryone was touched by the song, and thought it added something special. Everyone seemed to agree it was appropriate, and was Tony all the way.

After the mass and ceremony at the cemetery; we went to lunch, everyone enjoyed the food, and afterward some family came back to the house, I was totally wiped out, and drained by then. As we sat around talking; I couldn't help repeating what happened. Going over every detail as it had happened, over, and over and over. And that I couldn't believe it all really happened. Tony in fact was gone—, and I wouldn't see him anymore—. Ever—! It was too much to bear; but that was just the beginning—.

Mario decided he was going to stay with me; Tammy had to get back to her family. The twins had to get back to school, and back on track. Everyone had to get back to the real world. Except me!

We were all grieving tremendously—my heart was broken—but I also hurt even more, because I knew how sad our children were and there was not a thing I could do to make it better.

Our granddaughters were sad and just crushed beyond words. To see them hurt made it even worse, for me. It was just awful to see all that pain—all around me—and I was helpless—.

I couldn't deal with my own grief, let alone theirs. In the days that followed, I was despondent, sad, suicidal, miserable, angry, frightened and lonely. I didn't know where to go, or what to do with myself. I was totally "lost".

What does one do in this situation? How do you get through it? Would it ever get better? Would I make it? How? When? Feelings of I don't really want to live like this (without him). My life is over. Half of me had died with Tony. I just wanted to run. Where would I go?

I'm very lucky I have five great children, and wonderful, compassionate friends and family.

I had always said," I don't know why God gave, me five children. I never really had a lot of patience for five children." But now, I knew the answer. It took all five of them to help me keep my head on straight.

We reversed roles, they were now saying to me, what I had said to them all their lives, when things got tough. Like, "Things are never that bad, that they can't get worse—. "You'll be okay, it will just take time—, keep a positive attitude—stay busy—, and on and on." Somehow, I couldn't take my own advice. This was different, half of me was gone.

I had called Wellness House to let the counselor that had taught connections know I had lost Tony. She expressed her condolences, and told me that they had a grief group there; I should consider getting involved with. She gave me the time and day that it was being conducted. It was a drop in group, so I could attend if I wanted to; but wouldn't be committed.

Our children kept harping on me; to check the grief group out. "It sure couldn't hurt; if you don't like it, you don't have to go back."

I just didn't want to do anything. I tried to go shopping for things to change the decorations in the bedroom. I did buy new sheets and accessories, but that didn't make me happy—I shopped for clothes that didn't make me happy either. Nothing did—!

Since Mario was staying there with me, at least I wasn't all alone.

Our friends Dee and George and Benny and Josephine had asked me to go to their houses in Florida for a while. They each said, "They would love to have me." But, I couldn't decide where I wanted to be, or what I wanted to do. I was just so confused I wanted to die myself.

I finally agreed to go to Wellness House and attend the grief group to check it out, to see if it helped. I wasn't sleeping; eating, and I was truly in a tailspin. I knew I definitely needed help. Wellness House was a place where I could express my feelings; and receive some kind of guidance, feed-back, and support. I didn't want to talk to our children, for fear of making them sadder than they already were. I felt that I was between a rock and hard place.

"I was definitely stuck"

After attending a few grief groups, bouncing my feelings and thoughts around with the other widows and widowers, we all shared our sadness. I made the decision to go see Dee and George's new house in Florida. Our children were all for it, they said, "It will be good for you, something to do to get away for a while." I thought maybe I could help them in some way. They wanted me to see their new home. They wanted to show all their planning and efforts they put in the past year. I was excited for them, and couldn't wait to see their house.

I chose not to go by Benny and Josephine because; Tony and I had visited there together many times. I felt there would be too many memories for me to deal with there. That it would have been too difficult, at that time.

I loved and appreciated them immensely for offering. But I also knew I'd see them when I went to Florida in April with Tammy and the twins. A trip we had planned way before Tony expired. Tony had wanted the twins to go with us, and there was no way I could handle the twins and him alone, so Tammy was going to come with us.

Dee and George picked me up from the airport. Then we had to go to the furniture store to pick up a mattress and bedding. They hadn't been in the new house for very long and weren't finished furnishing it. I felt awful about the expense, but they assured me that they just hadn't had a chance to get one yet. As we arrived at their house; I saw it was just beautiful; everything I had expected, and more. They treated me like gold and couldn't have been better to me. They had even planted a tree in the yard dedicated to Tony, with a little placard hanging on it. That touched me deep down in my soul, they were as kind and gentle as they could be. And kept me busy by showing me around the area; It did help that I went there, however, even being, there I still had a hard time accepting that Tony was gone and I'd never see him again. I stayed there a week; but when I got home, I was right back where I started. LOST!

While I was in Florida, the twins had told me they had a surprise for me when I got home. I couldn't even imagine what it could possibly be.

When I got back home, they were waiting for me at the house. They had bought me the most beautiful, precious pastel colored "Love Bird" you've ever seen. Cage, food, toys, and everything I'd need to take care of it. They even had it trained for me, so I could hold it to talk to it. The twins told me, "Now you'll have someone to keep you company and talk to in the morning, you won't be alone."

The bird is beautifully colored and has a bright yellow-head, so when they asked me what I was going to name it. I said, "Sunshine", because she was going to be my sunshine and her head was the color of sunshine.

The bird helped with the healing of grief. She was my salvation. I'd talk to her, cry with her, and she sang to me in the morning, to cheer me up. She definitely has helped. My focus was on the bird, reading about birds, buying her toys, and playing with her. She kept me busy and amused when I needed it most. She listened intently to all my woes, without judging.

After the trip by Dee and George, I went back to Wellness house and grief group. It was a place to go where I felt safe to express my feelings.

They also have a library there; and I started reading books by the dozens, on grief, to help me understand what I was going through. And what I could do about the situation to help myself.

What I've learned is there's no going under, over or around grief. You simply have to go through it, one day at a time. Sometimes it's minute, by minute, but I highly recommend some sort of support.

It's now a year and a half since I lost Tony. I still miss Tony immensely, every second of every day. There isn't a day that goes by that I don't think of Tony several times throughout the day. The loss I feel is excruciating. You just don't ever get over forty-three years of togetherness over night, and all the memories from over the years. However, I'm trying to find my way in the world, one day at a time, and I try to keep myself busy.

What I have realized is, all the "Miracles" that had transpired through the journey? That God had provided, and all the prayers that had been fulfilled—. How fortunate we were to have had Tony as long as we did, and leave us the way he did so peacefully. With the diagnosis of stage four cancer and eleven weeks to live—, Tony had lived over a year.

There is a super being, super power, and mystical happenings that can and has happened through out this book and all through my life to this very day.

I know that if Tony and I had all those "Miracles" with God's help. He is in fact also watching over me, and will continue to show me the way. I need to keep going until my time comes to cross over to the other side and once again, see the love of my life. I'm confident of that, and I will continue to live life one day at a time, with each a little better than the last.

End